FALASTIN

A COOKBOOK

FALASTIN

Foreword by Yotam Ottolenghi

SAMI TAMIMI TARA WIGLEY

Photographs by Jenny Zarins

TEN SPEED PRESS
California | New York

عقبة
ASCENT

Contents

Foreword

I love Palestinian food. I probably love it more than any other cuisine. That's a tricky thing to say, I know, since I am not a Palestinian. As a Jewish boy from the Jerusalem of the 1970s and '80s, though, I probably had enough kubbeh, bamia, and ma'amoul for these magnificent foods to insert themselves deep in my young psyche. Not to mention those dishes that were also becoming part of the nascent Israeli cuisine—like falafel, hummus, and tabbouleh—either as a direct result of Palestinian influence on our food or through Jewish emigrants from the Arab world settling in the city.

I had been living outside Jerusalem for more than twenty years when I got to revisit all these pleasurable memories while writing *Jerusalem* with Sami Tamimi in 2012. That book was an unashamed celebration of a rather eclectic set of dishes that Sami and I liked to eat growing up, or that we felt were instrumental to understanding the soul of our city. The job was complicated, politically, since we had to put aside the harsh reality of the occupation of the West Bank. But it was a labor of love: love of ingredients, love of our city, love of our families and childhood memories. Through our friendship, helped by a "healthy" distance of 3,600 kilometers separating London from Jerusalem, we told a story that was pure deliciousness and joy.

Once Sami and I put our proverbial pens down, though, we both knew that there was another story to tell, and that is the wider story of Palestinian cuisine: a tale of a formidable food nation that gave the region and the rest of the world some of its most beloved foods.

In *Falastin*, Tara and Sami have picked up the baton where it was left after *Jerusalem*. Once again, this is a purely delicious affair (you can take my word for it; I was lucky enough to be there when they tested the recipes). It is based on Sami's childhood in Palestine and Tara's journey into the universe of tahini, za'atar, and precarious savory rice cakes (e.g., maqlubeh). Being the two formidable culinary forces that they are, Tara and Sami are the best guides I can possibly think of to take you into this world, to learn, like me, to enjoy it and absolutely love it.

Yotam Ottolenghi

Introduction

This is a book about Palestine—its food, its produce, its history, its future, its people and their voices. It is a book about the common themes that all these elements share, and how Palestine weaves narrative and cooking into the fabric of its identity. The two go hand in hand. Recipes are like stories: events brought to life and shared in the making and telling. They are passed from one person to the next, and in that movement, some details change, others come to the fore, while others will be left by the wayside. And stories are like recipes: a series of individual experiences blended together to create a whole. Where stories and recipes intersect is the nexus, the point, of this book. Rather than telling "a" story or "the" story of Palestine, then, we're telling lots of stories. These come in the form of both our recipes and the profiles of some of the people and places we've met along the way.

First, however, an outline of what is at the heart of this book: the story of Falastin, the place and its people; the story of *Falastin*, our book; and the story of Sami, your host, and Tara, your guide.

Falastin: the place and people

There is no letter "P" in the Arabic language so "Falastin" is, on the one hand, simply the way "Falastinians" refer to themselves. On the other hand, though—and in the Middle East there is always an "on the other hand"—the word is a big one, going far beyond a straightforward label. It is about geography, history, language, land, identity, and culture. Ask a Palestinian what the word "Falastin" means to them: the answer will rarely be short and will often end with the word "home."

For us, for the purposes of our book, "Falastin" is about all of these things. Geographically, it refers to a small piece of land at the easternmost corner of the Mediterranean Sea where Palestinians have been living for many centuries. This statement is complicated by the fact that this land is also home to other peoples, Israelis; something of which we are very mindful. Our aim with *Falastin* is to tread the fine line between paying heed to the situation on one hand and remembering, at the same time, that our book is first and foremost a celebration of the food and people of Palestine.

As well as being a geographical label, "Falastin" is also about identity. For us, it embraces all those who identify as Palestinian, wherever in the world they're now living. The Palestinian story, post 1948 and with the creation of Israel, could be seen as one of relocation. There are as many different stories as to why a Palestinian is now living where they are living as there are Palestinians. And with more than 12 million Palestinians worldwide, that's a lot.

There are those who've chosen to live abroad and those who have had no choice but to live abroad. There are those who have been displaced closer to home and those who are still living where their parents and grandparents lived before them. Some have known nothing but life in a refugee camp and have never seen the nearby coast, and others have traveled the world freely and have now chosen to return. And then there are those who've never actually been to the country itself but who still strongly identify as Palestinian, through the stories and memories passed down from their Palestinian family.

The people of Palestine go by several different names, depending on whom you ask. Some favor "Palestinian," others prefer "the people of the north," "Arabs of the Negev," "Arab refugees," or "48ers." "Arab-Israeli," "Israeli-Arab," and "Palestinian-Israeli" are also used. For us, the words "Falastin" and "Falastinian" are inclusive, managing to incorporate all these various words at the same time as somehow transcending their often loaded meanings.

Falastin: our book

Falastin is a new kind of Palestinian cookbook: a contemporary collection of more than 110 recipes we hope you'll cook, eat, love, and make your own. It's the culmination of Sami's lifetime obsession with Middle Eastern food and cooking—born and raised in East Jerusalem, relocated to London in his late twenties, and a founding member of Ottolenghi—and Tara's decade-long obsession with Middle Eastern food and home cooking—raised in London and adopted into the Ottolenghi family.

The recipes come, therefore, from all sorts of places. Some are those Sami grew up with and which will always remind him of home. His father's easy za'atar eggs, for example, or his mother's buttermilk fattoush. Others are those most Palestinians grew up on: classics such as chicken musakhan or the upside-down rice cake, maqlubeh. One recipe—that for hummus—remains untouched from when Sami first published it in his second cookbook, *Jerusalem*. After all, there are some things that can't be played around with or improved upon.

We haven't felt bound by a set list of "traditional Palestinian dishes," though. We'd rather shine a new light on an old classic than re-create it verbatim. Doing this—"playing around"—is a risk, we know, because loyalty to the way a dish is cooked is not, of course, just about the dish. It's about tradition and identity and being able to own these things through food. The process has not always been easy for Sami. Like a lot of Palestinian chefs working today, he keenly feels this tension—between a sense of loyalty to the way a dish is traditionally cooked and the desire to move it forward so as to keep it fresh and relevant.

If *Jerusalem* was Sami and Yotam's joint effort to celebrate the food of their hometown and bring it to a wider audience, then *Falastin* is Sami and Tara's focus on the food of Palestine. Speaking in general terms about "Middle Eastern food" is rather like saying "European food," or "Italian food": it does not pay heed to all the distinct people, produce, and dishes that distinguish one country from another within a region. It doesn't allow for the importance of sumac in a dish such as chicken musakhan to shine, for example, or reveal how many Gazan dishes have the trio of dill, garlic, and chile shaping them. It doesn't tell us anything about the red tahini of Gaza or the white salty cheese of Nablus or Akka. Keeping our focus exclusively on Palestine allows us to explore not only the food of this land and people but the regional differences within.

At the same time that it explores the regions of Palestine, the purpose of *Falastin* is to be full of recipes that work for and delight the home cook today. We really want you to cook from the recipes in our book—to find them practical and doable as well as delicious. This means you'll find fewer recipes for stuffed vegetables in *Falastin* than you would in a "traditional" Palestinian cookbook, fewer recipes for celebratory dishes that take half a day to prepare, less call for hard-to-find kishek or jameed, the fermented discs of yogurt and wheat in which to bake a leg of lamb. Loyalty to the Palestinian pantry, though—and a reliance on the ground allspice and cumin, olive oil, pulses, grains, za'atar, sumac, lemons, yogurt, dill, garlic, and green chiles that fill it—is unwavering. Our recipes feel distinctly Palestinian, even when they are presented in a slightly new light. Luckily, for those living outside the Middle East, the Palestinian pantry is also one that can be easily sourced and put together from mainstream stores and websites.

As well as our recipes, another way to get to know the country is through its people. When talking about Palestine in general terms, conversation can quickly become political and difficult. The day-to-day frustrations for a Palestinian trying to go about their business, when heard by those who don't need to carry an ID card with them or require a permit to travel around their country, are easy not to comprehend. For most Palestinians in the West Bank, the reality of checkpoints, a separation wall, and the complicated systems and differing rules surrounding Areas A, B, and C (see page 130 for more on this) makes, frankly, for a pretty grim picture.

Focus, though—travel around the country meeting and eating with people—and the picture painted is a different one. The link between the land and the produce and the people who grow, farm, and make it is strong. Meet someone who explains how they make their labneh or yogurt from the milk of their own sheep or goat, for example, or smell the fresh za'atar leaves on a small farm holding on a sunny spring afternoon, and the outlook is clearly brighter. How things are seen depends on who is looking and through what lens. For all the differing points of view, the reality of someone's story—the story they live with day in, day out—cannot be denied. This is why we want to tell the story of *Falastin* through profiles as well as recipes. These are not our stories. They're not even always our views. They are, however, stories we've been moved to tell from people whom we've met.

Writing these stories—indeed writing a Palestinian cookbook—feels like a big responsibility. All the food and hospitality that a recipe book celebrates must be served, in the case of Palestine, against a very sobering backdrop. We want this backdrop to be properly painted—things cannot be changed until they are fully seen—but, also, our hope is that everyone will come around the table to cook, eat, and talk. When *Jerusalem* was published, Sami was asked many times, with varying degrees of irony to seriousness, about the role hummus could play in the Middle Eastern peace process. On the one hand, as Sami used to say, it's only food. It's chickpeas, it's lemons, it's tahini. At the same time, though, food can mean more. Sharing food is not just about sharing food. It's about sharing time, space, ideas, and stories.

Sami Tamimi: your host

Palestinian home cooks tend to be women. Palestinian cookbooks tend to be written by women sharing the recipes they have, in turn, learned from the women in their lives. Stories of wise *ums* and *tetas*—mothers and grandmothers—and aunties pepper the pages of the traditional Palestinian cookbook. This Palestinian home cook and chef, though, lost his mother when he was young—Sami's mother died when he was just seven—and he spent much of his childhood being shooed away from the kitchen by aunties and sisters.

How did this little Palestinian boy from East Jerusalem—whose place was certainly *not* meant to be in the kitchen—then end up spending the best part of his life at the stove?

Sami left home and the cobbled streets of East Jerusalem when he was seventeen. Home was full and busy while he was growing up. On top of the seven kids, Sami's dad, Hassan, had with Na'ama, Sami's mother, five more were born after he remarried. Twelve kids calls for a lot of pita and a really big pot. Hungry for life farther afield, Sami moved to Tel Aviv. He spent twelve years there, learning his trade, the last five spent at Lilith, which was the restaurant to be at then. Setting sail next for London, Sami firmly found his feet at Baker & Spice, where he met Yotam Ottolenghi and, soon after, they set up Ottolenghi together.

Life then happened and, before Sami knew it, the gap between leaving home and returning to see his family was seventeen years. Seventeen years is a long time and a lot had changed. At the same time as Sami was becoming a big name in cooking, more than thirty nieces and nephews had been born, siblings had divorced and remarried, and Sami's father had died. A long time for everything to change but, at the same time, for nothing to change when Sami, after nearly twenty years, went home to reunite with his family.

Sinking into one of the enormous sofas lining the walls of his sister Sawsan's sitting room, Sami knew exactly what would follow. A cold sweet juice first appears, innocently suggesting that, this time, he might be let off the onslaught of food, gossip, and teasing to come. Wishful thinking, of course. Next, little bowls of nuts and pickles, saucers of olive oil and za'atar, chopped salad, Arabic salad, monk's salad, and tabbouleh salad are shared. Then the magnificent "upside down" maqlubeh appears, in all its glory, flipped over onto a large platter, ready to be tucked into and served with thick yogurt.

And finally, of course—this is a family, after all—the teasing. For all the big, probing questions that could follow so much time apart, Sami and his siblings just tease each other instead. About growing old and growing tummies and joking about things they used to do as kids. Everyone thinks everyone else is just a little bit bonkers—everyone is a bit bonkers!—no one really listens but, at the same time, the love in the air is thick enough to bottle. In the absence of words that can do justice to a family's longing to connect, it falls on the food they are sharing to do the job. Bread is torn apart and handed around.

Maybe this scene contains some clues to the question of what got Sami into the kitchen and kept him there for so long. Maybe it was the memory of his mother's food—which played such a big and important part in the first six years of Sami's life—and his desire never to let this connection disappear. Maybe it was his memory of the food of Palestine more generally—carried with him every time he drizzles tahini on his toast or sprinkles a pinch of za'atar on his morning eggs or white cheese. Maybe it was the sheer *lack* of questions being asked when you are in the kitchen, on your feet, working hard and working fast. Sometimes it's enough just to be getting food that makes you happy on the table for people who are hungry in the hope that it, too, will make them happy. Maybe he's just really, really good at grilling wedges of eggplants. Maybe it's all these things combined.

Falastin is the book that brings things full circle for Sami. It's his love letter to his country and also to his mother. It's also for his Falastinian family more generally, whom he traveled away from all those years ago but for whom, really, he still cooks every day.

Tara Wigley: your guide

Tara has been part of the Ottolenghi family since 2010. She turned up on her bike, fresh out of cooking school in Ireland, where she'd been for three months. She'd gone there with her eighteen-month-old twins and a great big Bosnian dog named Andie. Tara was leaving a decade in publishing. The plan—the answer to the question of why she was trading in words and writing for food and cooking—was not yet clear.

Luckily, though, Tara didn't need to see the light. In the Ottolenghi family, it quickly became clear, you can actually have your cake and eat it; you could learn to cook and still work with words. After a few years collaborating with Yotam on both the writing and cooking of his recipes in the test kitchen, Tara focused exclusively on the writing side of things. She remains a passionate home cook and knows very well how to fill a table with a feast.

For all that Tara is, then—food writer, feast maker, home cook, mom—she is not, clearly, Palestinian. She has traveled the country many times over several years, inadvertently run the Palestine marathon (the plan was to do just the half!), and fully immersed herself in the food but, still, the point needs addressing. When it comes to all things Palestinian, questions about legitimacy, ownership, and who gets to tell the story are very close to the surface. It's one of the reasons why we wanted to tell lots of stories—through the profiles—rather than "a" story or "the" story (or even "Sami's" story).

Tara's story, indeed, is more one of growing up in south London, eating lots of pork tenderloins, smashed thin, dipped in breadcrumbs, and pan-fried. When it came to inheriting recipes from grannies, the heights of exoticism came from the package of Angel Delight tipped out into a bowl and whisked up with milk. With a choice of five flavors and with a sponge finger sticking out of the side, the pinnacle of 1980s sophistication had clearly been reached.

It's all a far cry, indeed, from the world of tahini and olive oil that Tara is dripping in today. Pomegranates and za'atar were things she wasn't going to hear of, let alone taste, for another thirty years. The first thing Tara remembers saying to Sami, in fact, was that she thought preserved lemons tasted like soap! Little did she know that, far from tasting of soap, these little bursts of flavor would be the beginning of her culinary epiphany. That her love of food was not going to come in five flavors with a sponge finger sticking out the side; that her home was soon going to be filled with the smell of eggplants charring on the stove and that her fruit bowl was going to be taken over by lemons. Barely a meal now gets made without the chopped skin and flesh of a preserved lemon being added. Tahini sauce is included in every supper, every egg gets sprinkled with za'atar and drizzled in olive oil, and shatta is such an addiction that she and Sami now think of it as "shat*tara*." Tara is stuck knee-deep in tahini and, as anyone who has ever been stuck knee-deep in tahini knows, it's wonderfully impossible to get out. This is not Tara's story to tell, but it is her adventure. If any of our readers become half as obsessed with tahini or shatta as Tara has become since discovering them, then we'll know that the adventure has been a shared one.

Sahtein! Welcome to *Falastin*: a book of recipes and stories. Sami, wooden spoon in hand is your host, and Tara, pen in hand, is your guide. Our hope with the recipes is that they will bring you lots of great meals, good times, and a strong connection with Palestinian cooking. Our hope with the stories is that they make you want to find out more, talk more, question more, ask more. The story of Palestine—its past, present, and, crucially, its future—needs to keep being told, heard, and celebrated.

BREAKFAST

Breakfast in Palestine is a proper meal. This is no quick bowl of cereal or piece of fruit eaten on the go: it's a spread of dishes, often savory, served with sweet mint tea or a short black coffee, to really fuel you up for the day. "Go to work on an egg," indeed. And then some! We have included some quick one-bowl options—fruit and yogurt with sesame crumble, for example, and easy eggs with za'atar and lemon—but if you want to make a feast of it, then breakfast is a great place to start.

Breakfast, in fact, is where it all started for Sami, whose first job at age sixteen was working as a kitchen porter in a large hotel in West Jerusalem. Seeing Sami pay more attention to what the chefs were doing than to the dirty dishes at hand, head chef Hans saw his potential and soon moved him up to breakfast service. Cracking about 300 eggs every morning to make scrambled eggs for 150 hungry people allowed Sami to perfect the art of cracking eggs—with conviction, in short—to learn how to make scrambled eggs in a pot wider than his sixteen-year-old skinny self, and to know that he'd found the place he was meant to be.

If either the thought of 300 eggs or, indeed, some of what is included on the breakfast table in Palestine all sounds like a bit too much for the early morning, that's totally fine. One of the many great things about the dishes in this chapter is that they all work as well for lunch and supper (or even dessert, in the case of the yogurt and fruit bowl) as they do first thing.

On the table there can be bowls of thick, creamy, warm hummus. All sorts of pickles and olives sit alongside, with a bowl of plain yogurt and a freshly chopped salad. Cubes of white cheese might also be there, sprinkled with za'atar, sumac, or little black nigella seeds and drizzled generously with olive oil. Or a thick spread of labneh, hard-boiled eggs, and sliced cucumber. Little cubes of halva, maybe, if something sweet is wanted to go with a short black coffee. Whatever the combination of dishes, the holy trinity that is lemon juice, olive oil, and za'atar should always be within arm's reach in order to make everything sing. And bread, always bread: warm, fluffy, and freshly baked. If you want to bake for the breakfast table, there are a few recipes in the Bread and Pastries chapter that work particularly well. See page 282 for Jerusalem Sesame Bread, for example, or page 287 for Sweet Tahini Rolls.

For those with more time on the weekend, things such as falafel, fritters, labneh, and pickles really come into play. These are as good for snacks before supper as they are for breakfast, so have a look through the Snacks, Spreads, and Sauces chapter as well.

Hassan's easy eggs with za'atar and lemon

These eggs will always remind Sami of his father, Hassan, who used to make them on the weekend for Sami and his siblings. It's proof, if ever proof were needed, that few things are not improved by the addition of some good-quality olive oil, a squeeze of lemon, and a sprinkle of za'atar. Serve with some warm bread or pita to mop up the oil.

Playing around: Eggs pair well with all sorts of chile flakes, so use what you have. Urfa chile flakes, if you have some, look particularly great and bring a smoky flavor. Sumac can replace the za'atar, and cubes of creamy avocado are also a lovely addition.

Serves four

- 6 eggs
- 1½ tbsp lemon juice
- 3 tbsp olive oil
- 1 tbsp za'atar
- Salt and black pepper
- 2 green onions, finely sliced (¼ cup/20g)
- ⅛ tsp Aleppo (or any other) chile flakes

Bring a medium saucepan of water to a boil and carefully lower in the eggs. Boil for 5–6 minutes, then rinse at once under plenty of cold running water.

Meanwhile, whisk together the lemon juice, olive oil, and za'atar and set aside.

Peel and roughly quarter the eggs, by hand so that they're not too neat, and arrange on a serving plate, yolk side up. Sprinkle with ¼ tsp of salt and a generous grind of black pepper and drizzle the lemon juice–olive oil mix over the top. Sprinkle with the green onions and chile flakes and serve at once.

Fresh herb omelette with caramelized onions
Ijeh

Palestinian omelettes have a little bit of flour and baking powder added to the mix. This (along with the fact that they are fried in a generous amount of olive oil) makes them something between an omelette, a pancake, and a frittata. They're crisp around the edges, puffed up in the middle, and comforting through and through. The fresh herbs and white cheese are traditional, the caramelized onions less so.

Ijeh can be eaten either warm and fresh from the pan, for breakfast or a light supper, or at room temperature later if taken to work or on a picnic. Serve with a chopped or leafy salad (see pages 92 and 93, respectively) and some bread, if you like.

Playing around: Use whatever soft herbs you have and like—dill, chives, tarragon, basil, cilantro—in any combination; they all work well. Just keep the total amount about the same.

Getting ahead: You can double or triple the quantities for the caramelized onions; they keep well in the fridge for up to five days and are lovely to have around, to make more omelettes with or to spoon on top of cheese and bread.

Serves four

7½ tbsp/110ml olive oil
2 tbsp unsalted butter
3 onions, thinly sliced (3¾ cups/450g)
8 eggs, beaten
2½ tbsp all-purpose flour
6 green onions, trimmed and finely sliced (¾ cup/60g)
1 green chile, seeded and finely chopped
1 cup/20g parsley leaves, half roughly chopped and the remainder left whole
1 cup/20g mint leaves, half roughly chopped and the remainder left whole
¾ tsp dried mint
4½ oz/125g feta, roughly crumbled
Salt and black pepper
½ tsp baking powder
2½ tsp za'atar

Put 2 tbsp of oil and all the butter into a medium frying pan and place over medium-high heat. Add the onions and cook for about 20 minutes, stirring from time to time, until deep brown and caramelized. Set aside for about 10 minutes, to cool.

Put the eggs and flour into a mixing bowl and whisk well to combine, then add the green onions, chile, chopped parsley, chopped mint, dried mint, 1¾ oz/50g of feta, ¾ tsp of salt, and a good grind of black pepper. Mix well to combine. Add the baking powder, mix again to combine, and set aside.

Combine the caramelized onions with the whole herbs, remaining 2¾ oz/75g of feta, and 1½ tsp of za'atar and set aside.

Put about 2 tsp of oil into a medium frying pan and place over medium-high heat. Add 4–5 tbsp of the egg mixture—about 1¼ oz/35g, if you're weighing it out—and cook for about 1½ minutes, until the bottom is golden. Using a spatula, carefully flip the omelette and cook for another 30 seconds or so, until golden brown on both sides. Carefully slide the omelette onto a plate and return the pan to the heat. Repeat the process with the remaining oil and egg mixture, to make eight omelettes in total.

Divide the omelettes among four plates, two per person. Top with the caramelized onions, sprinkle with the remaining 1 tsp of za'atar, and serve.

Fruit and yogurt with sesame oat crumble and tahini-date syrup

For those who like fruit and yogurt in the morning, rather than a more hearty chickpea-based breakfasts, this is a great (though not strictly traditional) choice. The crumble is unusually *unsweet*, by a lot of granola standards, which we love, allowing for the tahini-date syrup to really stand out.

Getting ahead: Double or triple the recipe for the crumble, if you like, so that you're all set for the next breakfast (or snack). It keeps well in a sealed container for up to two weeks.

Serves four

Sesame oat crumble

⅓ cup/50g white sesame seeds
3 tbsp black sesame seeds (or just increase total of white sesame seeds to ½ cup/75g)
1⅔ cups/150g rolled oats
½ cup/50g sliced almonds
¼ tsp flaky sea salt
1½ tsp cardamom pods (about 14), outer shells crushed, removed, and discarded; seeds crushed in a mortar and pestle (or ¼ tsp ground cardamom)
3 tbsp smooth unsweetened peanut butter
5 tbsp/100g honey
1 egg white
1 tbsp rose water
2 tbsp olive oil

Tahini-date syrup

3 tbsp date syrup
3 tbsp tahini
2 tsp orange blossom water
3 tbsp water

2½ cups/600g Greek yogurt
⅔ cup/80g strawberries, quartered
¼ cup/40g pomegranate seeds (from ½ pomegranate)
½ cup/60g pistachios, roughly chopped
2 tsp dried rose petals (optional)

Preheat the oven to 350°F. Line a baking sheet with parchment paper.

To make the crumble, stir together all the sesame seeds, the oats, almonds, salt, and cardamom in a large mixing bowl. Put the peanut butter, honey, egg white, rose water, and oil into a separate bowl and whisk until well combined. Add the wet mixture to the dry ingredients and, using a rubber spatula or your hands, mix until everything is well coated. Spread out on the prepared baking sheet and bake for 18–20 minutes, stirring once or twice during baking, until golden brown. Remove from the oven and set aside to cool completely, then transfer to a food processor. Blitz as far as you want to take it: for just a few seconds if you want to keep the crumble rough and granola-like, or for longer if you prefer the texture sandy.

To make the tahini-date syrup, place all the ingredients in a bowl. Whisk well to combine and then set aside.

Divide the yogurt among four bowls and drizzle on the tahini-date syrup. Follow this with a generous helping of the crumble—and top with the fruit, pistachios, and rose petals (if using) and serve.

Pictured on page 27

Scrambled red shakshuka

Shakshuka: the signature breakfast of the Middle East. It's a wonderfully informal dish, brought to the table in the pan it's cooked in and served straight from there. There are so many versions of shakshuka, all variations on the same theme of eggs cooked in a nice thick sauce. The eggs are usually braised, which is what we've done with the green shakshuka on the facing page. Here they've been gently scrambled.

Playing around: The shakshuka base can go in all sorts of directions and colors—red here with the tomatoes and red bell pepper, or green with any leaves and herbs in need of using up. Either way, it's a really versatile and robust dish, so feel free to play around with the spices and toppings. Spice-wise, for example, smoked paprika and roughly crushed caraway seeds work in the red shakshuka instead of the regular paprika and cumin seeds. Toppings-wise, for either of the shakshukas, chunks of tangy feta, black olives, or finely chopped preserved lemon peel work well dotted on top. A drizzle of tahini or a spoonful of yogurt is also great when serving, along with some crusty fresh bread and a crisp green salad.

Getting ahead: The base sauce can be made a day or two ahead, up to the point before the eggs are added. The feta can also be marinated up to three days in advance. Make more of the feta than you need here, if you like; it's a lovely thing to dot over roasted wedges of sweet potato, or all sorts of salads.

Serves two generously

1½ oz/45g feta, roughly crumbled
¼ cup/5g parsley leaves, roughly chopped
¾ tsp Aleppo chile flakes (or ½ tsp regular chile flakes)
5 tbsp/75ml olive oil
1½ tsp coriander seeds, lightly toasted and roughly crushed in a mortar and pestle
1 onion, thinly sliced (1⅔ cups/150g)
1 red bell pepper, seeded and cut into long slices, ½ inch/1cm thick (5 oz/140g)
3 garlic cloves, crushed
½ tsp cumin seeds, lightly toasted and roughly crushed in a mortar and pestle
1 tsp tomato paste
¼ tsp paprika
5–6 tomatoes, roughly chopped (1 lb 2 oz/500g)
2½ oz/75g cherry tomatoes
2 tsp red shatta (see page 73) or rose harissa
⅓ cup/80ml water
Salt and black pepper
4 eggs, lightly beaten

Place the feta in a bowl with the parsley, ½ tsp of chile flakes, 3 tbsp of oil, and ½ tsp of coriander seeds. Mix well and set aside (in the fridge if making in advance) until needed.

Put the remaining 2 tbsp of oil into a large sauté pan with a lid and place over medium-high heat. Add the onion and cook for 5 minutes, until softened and lightly browned. Add the bell pepper, cook for another 5 minutes, then add the garlic, cumin seeds, tomato paste, paprika, and remaining 1 tsp of coriander seeds. Cook for another 1 minute, until fragrant, and then add all the tomatoes, the shatta, water, 1 tsp of salt, and a generous grind of black pepper. Cook over medium heat for about 15 minutes, stirring occasionally, until the tomatoes have broken down and the sauce has thickened.

Add a pinch of salt and a good grind of black pepper to the eggs and mix well. Slowly pour this into the tomato mixture, swirling the pan and giving it a couple of gentle folds—you don't want the eggs to be too mixed in. Decrease the heat to medium-low, cover the pan, and let cook for 4 minutes.

Remove the pan from the heat, spoon the marinated feta over the top, sprinkle with the remaining ¼ tsp of chile flakes, and serve at once.

Pictured on page 30

Green shakshuka

Serves two

2½ tbsp olive oil
1 tsp green shatta (see page 73) or green harissa
1 tbsp unsalted butter
1 large leek, halved lengthwise and the white parts sliced ¾ inch/2cm thick (1⅔ cups/180g)
14 oz/400g Swiss chard, leaves pulled off the stems and chopped into roughly ¾-inch/2cm pieces; stems cut into roughly ¾-inch/2cm dice
6 green onions, thinly sliced (¾ cup/60g)
½ green chile, finely chopped (1½ tsp/5g)
1 garlic clove, crushed
¾ tsp ground cumin
¾ tsp ground coriander
1 cup/20g parsley leaves, roughly chopped
½ cup/10g dill, roughly chopped
Salt
7 tbsp/100ml water
1 tbsp lemon juice
4 eggs
Black pepper
Greek yogurt, to serve (optional)

Playing around: Chunks of feta dotted on top are a lovely addition here; instead of, or as well as, the yogurt. A final sprinkle of za'atar also works really well.

Getting ahead: As with the red shakshuka opposite, the base can be prepared a day or two in advance if you want to get ahead. If you do this, just hold back on adding the lemon juice (as well as the eggs) until you are ready to eat. Adding the lemon juice too early to the leaves will cause them to discolor.

Mix 1½ tsp of olive oil with the shatta and set aside.

Put the remaining 2 tbsp of oil and all the butter into a large sauté pan with a lid and place over medium heat. Once hot, add the leek, then decrease the heat to medium-low and cook for 6 minutes, covered, stirring a few times, until the leek has softened but has not taken on any color.

Add the chard stems—in batches, if you need to—and green onions and cook for another 6 minutes, covered, stirring occasionally, until completely softened. Add the chile, garlic, and ground spices and cook, uncovered, for 1 minute before adding the chard leaves, parsley, dill, and ¾ tsp of salt. Stir to wilt slightly, then add the water and cook for 10 minutes, covered, until the leaves cook down and completely wilt. Add the lemon juice, then use a spoon to make four wells in the mix. Crack an egg into each well and sprinkle each one lightly with salt and pepper. Cover the pan and cook for a final 4 minutes or so, until the egg whites are set but the yolks are still runny. Dot the shatta-oil mix over the eggs and serve at once, with a spoonful of yogurt alongside, if desired.

Pictured on page 31

Ful medames

Ful medames is best known as an Egyptian staple. It's just as popular in Palestine, though, particularly during Ramadan where it's often served for suhur, the pre-fast Ramadan meal. As with all pulses, the dish either sets you up for the day, if eaten in the morning, or provides comfort at the end of it, if eaten for a simple supper. Warm pita, as ever, is a must.

Playing around: We've given the directions for some sumac onions, a simple sauce, and a soft-boiled egg but, really, you can go in all sorts of directions; fried eggs, a simple sprinkle of parsley, some chopped green onions, coarsely grated hard-boiled eggs—they all work well.

Dried vs. canned fava beans: We choose to start with canned beans here because they are easier to find than dried and, also, they cook with much more consistency. Dried beans also require peeling, which takes the edge off the quick morning option (see "Pulses," on page 340).

Serves two generously, or four if bulked up with eggs and pita

3 x 14-oz/400g cans cooked fava beans, drained and rinsed (2¾ cups/470g)
3 lemons: squeeze 2 to get 4 tbsp/60ml juice and cut 1 into wedges
4 garlic cloves, crushed
½ green chile, finely chopped (1½ tsp/5g)
1½ tsp ground cumin
Salt
½ small red onion, thinly sliced (½ cup/60g)
¾ tsp sumac
¼ cup/5g parsley leaves
1 large avocado, cut into ¼-inch/6mm dice
1 tomato, cut into ¼-inch/6mm dice (⅓ cup/70g)
2 tbsp olive oil
4 soft-boiled eggs (optional)
Warm pita bread (see page 278), to serve

Pour 1 qt/1L of water into a medium saucepan and bring to a boil. Add the beans and simmer over medium heat for 5 minutes, just to warm through and soften up. Drain, reserving about 3 tbsp of the water, and return the beans to the pan. Add the reserved cooking water to the beans, along with 2 tbsp of lemon juice, the garlic, chile, cumin, and ¾ tsp of salt. Using a fork, crush the beans to form a rough mash. Set aside (or keep warm, if eating soon) until needed.

Place the onion in a bowl with ¼ tsp of salt. Use your hands to rub the salt in a bit, then set aside for 10 minutes, for the onion to soften. Mix in the sumac and parsley and set aside until needed.

Put the avocado and tomato in a bowl with the remaining 2 tbsp lemon juice and ¼ tsp of salt. Mix to combine and set this salsa aside.

Heat up the fava bean mixture, if needed, then transfer it to a large serving platter. Smooth out the surface and make a little well in the center. Top with the salsa, followed by the onion mixture and drizzle on the oil. Serve as is, with a wedge of lemon to squeeze over, or with soft-boiled eggs on top, if desired, and some warm pita alongside.

Warm hummus with toasted bread and pine nuts
Fattet hummus

Fatteh roughly translates as "crushed" or "crumbled." It refers to a group of dishes where chunks of flatbread (either stale bread in need of using up, or fresh) are layered in a dish with various toppings. Fattet hummus, where the layers are chickpea, tahini, and yogurt, feels like a sort of savory chickpea "bread pudding." It's warm, comforting, hearty, and rich and can be eaten for breakfast, lunch, or supper.

Dried vs. canned chickpeas: Instructions are given for dried chickpeas. If starting with canned, drain and rinse the chickpeas and put them into a pan with 2½ cups/600ml of water, 1 tsp of ground cumin, and the 4 whole garlic cloves. Simmer for 8–10 minutes, then transfer to a blender or food processor, as per the recipe instructions, along with the yogurt, tahini, lemon juice, and remaining garlic.

Serves six for breakfast or as a side for lunch or supper

3 pitas (see page 278), torn into roughly 1-inch/2cm pieces (7 oz/200g)
6 tbsp/90ml olive oil
1½ tsp ground cumin
Salt
½ cup/10g parsley leaves, finely chopped
2 lemons: finely grate the zest of 1 to get 1 tsp, then squeeze both to get ¼ cup/60ml juice
1⅓ cups/250g dried chickpeas, soaked overnight in double their volume of water and 1 tsp baking soda (or 3¾ cups/600g cooked chickpeas—from about 3 cans)
¼ tsp baking soda (you don't need this if you are starting with canned chickpeas)
5 garlic cloves: 4 peeled and left whole, 1 crushed
⅔ cup/200g Greek yogurt
Rounded ½ cup/150g tahini
½ cup/60g pine nuts, lightly toasted (see "Nuts," page 339)
½ tsp sumac
¼ tsp paprika

Preheat the oven to 350°F. Line a baking sheet with parchment paper.

Put the pita pieces into a bowl with 2 tbsp of olive oil, ½ tsp of cumin, and ¼ tsp of salt. Mix well until coated, then tip out onto the prepared baking sheet. Bake for 20–25 minutes, until the pita is golden and crispy. Transfer two-thirds of the pita to a 9 x 13-inch/23 x 33cm dish with sides that rise up about 3 inches/8cm (or individual plates with a lip, if making individual portions) and set the remaining third aside.

Combine the parsley, lemon zest, remaining 4 tbsp/60ml of olive oil, and ⅛ tsp of salt in a small bowl and set aside.

Drain the chickpeas and put them into a large saucepan with a lid, along with the ¼ tsp of baking soda, 4 whole garlic cloves, and remaining 1 tsp of ground cumin. Pour in 1 qt/1L of water and bring to a boil over high heat. Decrease the heat to medium-low, cover loosely with the lid, and simmer for 30–40 minutes, stirring a few times, removing any foam as you go. Add a bit more water, if you need to, to keep the chickpeas submerged, until they are completely soft and cooked through. Stir in ½ tsp of salt, then (without draining the chickpeas, as you need the cooking water later on) transfer about 1¼ cups/200g of cooked chickpeas to a blender or food processor along with the yogurt, tahini, lemon juice, crushed garlic clove, ¾ tsp of salt, and 7 tbsp/100ml of the hot cooking liquid. Blitz until smooth and set aside. Keep this and the remaining chickpeas in the pan warm.

Top the pita in the baking dish (or individual plates) with half the pine nuts, two-thirds of the whole chickpeas, and 7 tbsp/100ml of their cooking liquid. Pour in all of the chickpea-tahini sauce and stir together. Top with the remaining pita, the remaining chickpeas (but without any extra cooking liquid), and the remaining pine nuts. Spoon in the parsley oil, sprinkle with the sumac and paprika, and serve at once.

Hummus: two ways

If anything is going to keep you going until lunch, it's a dish of hummus to start the day. It's filling and hearty and pairs with all sorts of things. If meatballs seem a bit too epic for breakfast (though they're no more epic than the bacon or sausage we might not think twice about), try the version with fried eggplant. Cubes of eggplant have a "meaty" quality that makes them a great substitute for meat, if you're looking for one.

We like to double the quantity for the hummus and make both versions at the same time so that there is something for everyone (and both things for some!). Either way, serve the hummus with warm pita (see page 278) for scooping, along with a chopped salad (see page 92) to lighten things up. And if this still all sounds like a bit too much for breakfast, that's fine; it works just as well for lunch or supper instead.

Getting ahead: Hummus should, ideally, be served freshly made and still warm. For anyone who's grown up on little tubs of hummus bought from the refrigerated section of a supermarket aisle, eating it while still warm, smooth, creamy, and "loose" will be a revelation. If you do want to make it in advance, though, that's fine; just store it in an air-tight container and keep it in the fridge for up to four days. If the hummus develops a bit of a "skin" just give it a stir before serving. The most important thing if storing in the fridge, is to bring it back to room temperature before serving, to warm and loosen up.

The meatballs can be made, rolled, and kept in an airtight container in the fridge for up to three days; but don't pack them too tightly, you want them to keep their round shape. They also freeze well, for up to one month. If you fry them from frozen, they will need a couple minutes more in the oven to warm through.

Serves six

Hummus

1⅓ cups/250g dried chickpeas, soaked overnight in double their volume of water
1 tsp baking soda
Scant 1 cup/270g tahini
¼ cup/60ml lemon juice
4 garlic cloves, crushed
1½ tsp salt
7 tbsp/100ml ice-cold water

Kofta version

Meatballs

1 lb 2 oz/500g ground beef or veal (or a mixture of both)
1 small onion, coarsely grated (¾ cup/120g)
1 large tomato, coarsely grated and skin discarded (⅓ cup/65g)
1 cup/20g parsley, finely chopped
1 red chile, seeded and finely chopped
Salt and black pepper

About ¼ cup/60ml olive oil, plus more for drizzling
¼ cup/25g pine nuts
¼ cup/5g parsley, roughly chopped
½ tsp Aleppo chile flakes (or ¼ tsp regular chile flakes)
A few small mint leaves (optional)

Eggplant version

2 large eggplants, cut into roughly ¾-inch/2cm cubes (6 cups/500g)
½ tsp salt
About 1¼ cups/300ml sunflower oil
1½ cups/160g walnut halves, roughly chopped
½ cup/10g parsley leaves, roughly chopped
½ cup/10g mint leaves, roughly chopped
2 tbsp lemon juice
2 tbsp olive oil
½ tsp Aleppo chile flakes

To make the hummus, drain the chickpeas and place them in a medium saucepan over high heat. Add the baking soda and cook for about 3 minutes, stirring constantly. Add 6⅓ cups/1.5L of water and bring to a boil. Cook for about 30 minutes—timing can vary from 20 to 40 minutes depending on the freshness of the chickpeas—skimming off any foam that appears. The chickpeas are ready when they collapse easily when pressed between your thumb and finger—almost but not quite mushy.

Drain the chickpeas and transfer them to a food processor. Process to form a stiff paste and then, with the machine still running, add the tahini, lemon juice, garlic, and salt. Slowly drizzle in the ice water and continue to process for another 5 minutes; this will feel like a long time but it is what is needed to get a very smooth and creamy paste. Transfer to a bowl and set aside at room temperature, until needed. If you are making it in advance, then transfer to an airtight container and keep in the fridge. Remove it half an hour before serving, to bring back to room temperature, and give it a good stir if a "skin" has formed.

Continued

If making the kofta version: Place all the ingredients for the meatballs in a medium bowl with 1 tsp of salt and a good grind of black pepper. Using your hands, mix well to combine. With wet hands, roll the mixture into roughly 1¼-inch/3cm balls (weighing about ½ oz/15g each); you should make about 45 balls.

Put 1 tbsp of oil into a large frying pan and place over medium heat. Add the pine nuts and cook for 1 minute, stirring constantly, until they are golden brown. Spoon the nuts, along with the oil from the pan, into a little bowl and set aside.

Add 1 tbsp of oil to the same pan and keep over medium heat. Add a third of the meatballs—or as many as you can fit into the pan without crowding—and cook for about 3 minutes, turning throughout so that all sides take on color and the balls are just cooked through. Transfer to a plate and keep warm while you continue with the remaining meatballs, adding another 1 tbsp of oil with each batch.

Spoon the hummus into individual shallow bowls, creating a slight hollow in the center of each. Divide the meatballs among the bowls, placing them in the middle of the hummus. Spoon the pine nuts and their cooking oil over the meatballs and sprinkle with the parsley, chile flakes, and mint, if desired. Serve with a final drizzle of olive oil.

If making the eggplant version: Line two baking sheets with paper towels. Place the eggplants in a colander placed over a bowl or in the sink and sprinkle with the salt. Use your hands to mix well, then set aside for about 45 minutes; this is so that the bitter juices can be released (see page 336 for more). Transfer the eggplants to a prepared baking sheet and pat dry as best you can.

Put the sunflower oil into a medium frying pan and place over medium-high heat. Once hot, add the eggplants—in two or three batches so as to not crowd the pan—and fry for about 8 minutes, until completely softened and golden brown. Using a slotted spoon, transfer the eggplants to the second prepared baking sheet and set aside, for the excess oil to be absorbed, while you continue with the remaining batches. Transfer the eggplants to a bowl; add the walnuts, parsley, mint, lemon juice, olive oil, and chile flakes; and mix well to combine.

Spoon the hummus into individual shallow bowls, creating a slight hollow in the center of each. Spoon in the eggplant and serve at once.

Warm chickpeas with green chile sauce and toasted pita
Musabaha

The word *musabaha* means "swimming" or "floating," here describing the chickpeas floating around in the tahini sauce. It's essentially hummus a step or two before it gets blitzed. The dish should be warm and creamy enough to eat with a spoon or a strip of pita. This is lovely for breakfast, lunch, or supper.

Getting ahead: The toasted pita can be made up to a day ahead and kept in a sealed container at room temperature. The green chile sauce can be made a few hours in advance, but hold back on the parsley until just before serving; it will discolor if it sits around. The chickpeas can be made a few hours in advance and just warmed through to serve. Once assembled, the dish needs to be eaten fresh and warm.

Serves four

1⅓ cups/250g dried chickpeas, soaked overnight in twice their volume of water and 1 tsp baking soda (or 2 x 14-oz/400g cans cooked chickpeas)
Salt

Toasted pita
2 small pitas (see page 278; about 5¼ oz/150g)
1 tbsp olive oil

Green chile sauce
1 green chile, seeded and finely chopped
3 tbsp lemon juice
1½ tbsp white wine vinegar
1 large garlic clove, crushed
⅛ tsp salt
¼ cup/5g parsley, finely chopped

3½ tbsp olive oil
4 large garlic cloves, crushed
1 green chile, finely chopped
1 tbsp ground cumin
⅓ cup/100g tahini, plus about ¼ cup/60g
6 tbsp/100g Greek yogurt
2 tbsp lemon juice
½ tsp paprika

If starting with dried chickpeas, drain and put them in a large saucepan. Cover with plenty of cold water and place over high heat. Bring to a boil, skim any foam from the surface, then decrease the heat to medium-low and simmer for 45–60 minutes, adding 1 tsp of salt toward the end of the cooking time, until the chickpeas are very soft but still retain their shape. Drain the chickpeas, reserving 7 tbsp/100ml of the cooking liquid, and set aside.

If starting with canned chickpeas, drain and put them in a medium saucepan. Cover with plenty of cold water and place over medium heat. Bring to a simmer and cook for about 8 minutes, just to soften them up a bit more. Add 1 tsp of salt toward the end of the cooking time. Drain the chickpeas, reserving 7 tbsp/100ml of the cooking liquid, and set aside.

While the chickpeas are cooking, preheat the broiler.

Continued

To toast the pitas, pull open the pitas and tear each half in two. Brush the insides of the pitas lightly with the oil and place under the broiler for about 2 minutes, until crisp and golden brown. Keep a close eye on them while they are under the broiler so that they don't burn. Remove from the oven and, once cool enough to handle, break the pitas apart into roughly 1½-inch/4cm pieces. Set aside until ready to use.

To make the green chile sauce, mix together all the ingredients in a small bowl. If you are making this in advance, hold back on the parsley and just mix this in before serving. It will discolor if it sits around for too long.

Once the chickpeas are cooked and drained, put 2 tbsp of oil in a medium saucepan and place over medium heat. Add the garlic and cook for 2 minutes, stirring often, until the garlic is starting to color. Add the chile, cook for another 1 minute, then add the chickpeas, reserved cooking liquid, cumin, tahini, yogurt, lemon juice, and ½ tsp of salt. Bring to a boil, then decrease the heat to low and simmer for 2–3 minutes, stirring from time to time.

Transfer the warm chickpeas to a large serving platter with a lip or to a wide shallow bowl. Spoon in the green chile sauce and drizzle with the ¼ cup/60g tahini. Sprinkle with the paprika and finish with the remaining 1½ tbsp of oil. Serve with the toasted pita.

SNACKS, SPREADS, AND SAUCES

The Palestinian table is only really happy when it's covered with food. Once empty breakfast dishes get cleared away, the table is ready and waiting for the next array of snacks, spreads, and sauces. These are themselves just a prelude to the main meal later on. It's not, however, all about the food. A table constantly covered with all these dishes says a number of things.

The first thing it says is "Welcome!" Welcome to the table, everyone's invited and please tuck in! Please be hungry and try all sorts of things. It's a way to convey bounty, hospitality, and generosity. There will always be more than enough food on the table. If someone turns up unannounced, it's simply a case of pulling up an extra chair or making room on one of the great, big sofas.

The secret behind these "instantly appearing" spreads is, often, the freezer. This way of cooking—of preparing things ahead and freezing for whenever they are needed—is a big part of the heart and hospitality behind Palestinian cooking. *Hawader*, the name of the practice, translates roughly as "ready-to-eat." Open most freezers across the West Bank and they will be full of things such as kubbeh (see page 71), fritters (see pages 66 and 67), and breads and pastries, like fatayer (see page 296) or the open-topped flatbread sfiha (see page 226). Groups of women often get together for these big-batch cooking sessions, chatting as kubbeh is rolled and packed, fatayer is stuffed and shaped. Freezers and friends: that winning combination behind so much feasting.

The second thing it says is "Let's share." Maza or mezzeh are the small dishes, sharing plates or appetizers to have with a drink at the beginning of a meal. With a large number of small plates filling the table, no one dish steals the show or acts as centerpiece. Similarly, no one person sits and works their way through a whole plate of m'tabbal (see page 82) or a bowl of labneh (see page 48). These are, by their very nature, informal "family style" dishes that need to be shared and passed around the table. It's a way to say "Let's eat this together and let's chat while we do."

These dishes can also be a way of both cooking with the season and being able to still eat something when it is no longer in season. Preserving, pickling, drying, and fermenting all play a key part in supplying the Palestinian pantry. It's called mooneh. If *hawader* translates as "filling up the freezer," then *mooneh* translates as "filling up the pantry shelves" with things that last in glass jars for months. They're often little flavor bombs—makdous (see page 56), labneh balls (see page 49), or shatta (see page 73)—there to reach for as a condiment to any meal. A table covered with spreads and dips says so much about the Palestinian way of preparing, cooking, and eating food. Welcome, tuck in, and pass around. Sahtein! May your health be redoubled!

Sweet and spicy seeds and nuts

These are everything you want from a pre-supper snack: spicy, sweet, crunchy, and very, very craveable.

Playing around: The combination of cashews and seeds works really well here; the nuts remain crunchy while the seeds become chewy. A combination of other nuts works just as well, though; macadamias, Brazil nuts, and almonds, for example. Use what you have, just keep the total amount of all the nuts and seeds combined the same.

Keeping notes: Double or triple the batch, if you like; they keep well in a sealed container for up to two weeks. If you do this, increase the sugar by only 50 percent—the batch will become too syrupy otherwise. If you are doubling the recipe, for example, you'll only need to increase to 3 tbsp of brown sugar. All the other ingredients are fine to double.

Serves four as a snack

2 tbsp light brown sugar
2 tsp flaky sea salt
1 tbsp olive oil
1 tsp mild curry powder
¼ tsp ground turmeric
½ tsp Aleppo chile flakes (or ¼ tsp regular chile flakes)
2 tbsp water
1¼ cups/180g raw unsalted cashews
2 tbsp sunflower seeds
2 tbsp pumpkin seeds

Preheat the oven to 350°F. Line a baking sheet with parchment paper.

Put everything except the cashews and seeds into a small saucepan. Bring to a boil over medium heat, stirring often, then add the nuts and seeds. Cook for 3 minutes or so, stirring constantly, until the nuts and seeds are coated in a sticky glaze.

Transfer the mixture to the prepared baking sheet, then, using a spatula, spread the nuts out so that they're not stuck together. Bake for 14 minutes, stirring once halfway through, until golden. Remove from the oven and set aside to cool completely, then transfer to a serving bowl or to an airtight container, if making in advance.

Labneh

Labneh is an Arabic cheese made by draining yogurt so that it loses most of its liquid; the longer it's left to drain, the drier and firmer it becomes. You can either have it as it is, to cook with or just to spread on toast drizzled with olive oil and za'atar, or you can shape it into balls, for a pre-dinner snack.

Making labneh is one of those things that can feel like a step too far until you actually get around to doing it and realize how simple it is. It honestly takes more effort to hang out your laundry than it does to hang up your yogurt.

Playing around: Use either a combination of goat-milk (or sheep-milk or ewe-milk) yogurt and Greek yogurt, or just stick to Greek yogurt. The combination option has a bit more of a tang, which we like, but they both work very well.

Keeping notes: Once covered with (and therefore preserved by) oil, labneh keeps in the fridge for up to two months. Without the oil it keeps for up to two weeks.

Makes about 2 cups plus 2 tbsp/500g

3¾ cups/900g Greek yogurt (or a combination of 1¾ cups plus 2 tbsp/450g goat-milk yogurt and 1¾ cups plus 2 tbsp/450g Greek yogurt)
Salt
Olive oil, to seal

Line a deep bowl with cheesecloth or muslin and set aside.

In a separate bowl, mix the yogurt with 1 tsp of salt. Pour into the prepared bowl, then bring the edges of the cloth together and wrap tightly to form a bundle. Tie firmly with a piece of twine. Hang the bundle over a bowl (or attach to the handle of a tall jug so that the bundle can hang free—and drip—inside the jug).

Another method is to put the bundle into a sieve placed over a bowl, with the weight of a plate, or a couple of cans, sitting on top. This weight speeds up the draining process.

Let rest in the fridge for 24–36 hours, until much of the liquid is lost and the yogurt is thick and fairly dry.

Transfer the labneh to an airtight sterilized container or jar (see page 341); top with just enough olive oil so that the labneh is covered and sealed.

Pictured on page 51

Labneh balls
Labneh tabat

Makes about 20 balls; serves ten as part of a larger spread

3¾ cups/900g Greek yogurt (or a combination of 1¾ cups plus 2 tbsp/450g goat-milk yogurt and 1¾ cups plus 2 tbsp/450g Greek yogurt)
About 2 cups/500ml olive oil
3 sprigs thyme or oregano, or a mixture of both
About 1½ tbsp chile flakes (enough to coat 10 balls)
About 2½ tbsp za'atar (enough to coat 10 balls)
Salt

Playing around: Play around with coatings and combinations here; a clash of colors and flavors works really well as part of a larger mezzeh spread. We've given instructions for a combination of chile flakes and za'atar, but all sorts of coatings work—Nigella seeds, sesame seeds, other chile flakes (smoky Urfa or sweet Aleppo look great), sumac, chopped pistachios, or a combination of crushed garlic, chopped walnuts, and finely diced red chile. Play around with the size of the balls as well—large balls work well as a snack or as part of a mezzeh spread; smaller balls work well for nibbles with drinks.

Keeping notes: The balls keep for up to two months in the fridge. The oil will set in the fridge, so you'll have to bring it back to room temperature before being able to remove the balls and coat them. Save the oil; it can be used again to preserve future batches of labneh.

Line a baking sheet with a clean, damp piece of cheesecloth.

Follow the instructions in the recipe on the facing page up to the point before the labneh gets transferred to an airtight sterilized container. Then, with lightly oiled hands, spoon a small amount—about ¾ oz/20g—of the labneh into the palm of one hand. Roll it around to shape it into a 1¼-inch/3cm ball, and transfer it to the prepared baking sheet. Continue with the remaining labneh until all the balls are rolled. Transfer to the fridge for a couple of hours (or overnight) to firm up.

Half fill a jar (large enough to fit all the rolled labneh; about 4 inches/10cm wide and 5 inches/12cm tall) or other airtight container with the olive oil and add the balls. Top with more oil, if necessary—you want the balls to be completely covered with oil—and add the thyme or oregano. Seal the jar and transfer to the fridge.

When ready to coat—you can do this up to a day before serving—remove the jar from the fridge and bring to room temperature, so that the oil becomes unset. Lift the balls out of the oil and roll them in the chile flakes or za'atar: an easy way to do this is to spread your chosen coating on a plate, place a few balls at a time on top, and shake the plate—the balls will be coated in seconds. If not eating at once, return them to the fridge on a plate (but not in the oil). Bring back to room temperature before serving, you don't want them to be fridge-cold.

Pictured on page 50

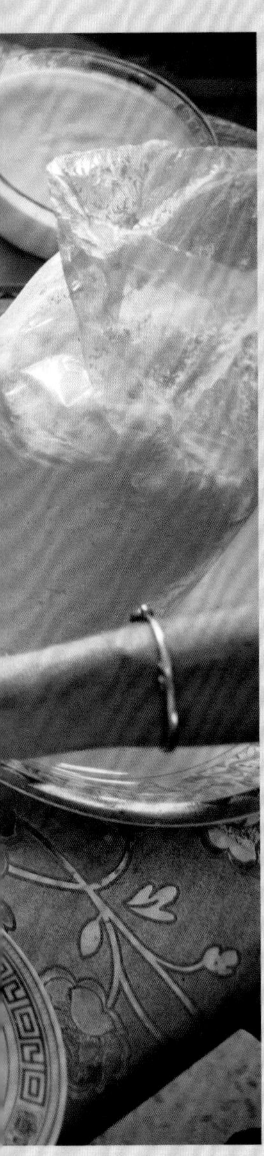

The yogurt-making ladies of Bethlehem

Meeting up with "the yogurt-making ladies of Bethlehem" felt a bit like doing a deal. Our friend Vivien Sansour (see page 106), who was in London when we were in Bethlehem, WhatsApped the number of her friend Siham Kalibieh to our friend Raya Manaa, who was driving us around. Siham, we were told, would point us in the right direction. We met Siham by what felt like chance. We were meant to meet on a street corner on the outskirts of Bethlehem, but relying on Waze—our navigational tool of choice—was not always, we quickly found, entirely reliable. Satellite navigation, it turns out, can get just as confused as the next person trying to get their head around the geography of the area. We might be in what we thought of as Palestine as we drove around Bethlehem. Waze, on the other hand, rather than focusing in on any useful directions, just informed us that we were *entering an area of high risk.* The evidence, looking around us, bore no relation to the warning.

Happenstance *was* on our side. After a few left turns, a few right turns, and a few going-around-in-circles turns, we spotted the shop we'd been told to keep an eye out for, and Siham was standing outside. Happily, she hopped in and, happily, sat nav was turned off in favor of our local in tow and in-the-know! Up a winding hill we went—more lefts and rights and bends—what a view!—before we were "handed over," package-like, to another lady, Majida Shaalan. She, in turn, led us through the main entrance to a block of apartments, up several flights of stairs, and into her small home. It's here, finally, that we met the local crew to see and sample the goods: "the yogurt-making ladies of Bethlehem" and their range of white (and yellowy-white) offerings.

From where it was spread out on the easy-wipe plastic tablecloth in her immaculate kitchen, Majida scooped up a tablespoon of butter for us to try straight away. It was incredibly rich and intense; delicious but full-on. Easier to snack on were the balls of labneh, made from yogurt that has been salted, hung, and drained of much of its liquid (see page 48). The yogurt left behind, after twenty-four hours or so, is then thick enough to shape into balls. Stored in jars and preserved by being covered in oil, these balls can be rolled in all sorts of things—za'atar, sumac, shatta, chile flakes, or nigella seeds (see page 49)—before being eaten. They're also delicious as they are, without any coating; rich, as with the butter, but with a tartness and saltiness that cuts through to allow for continued snacking.

Much of the tartness of these products comes from the fact that it's generally sheep or goats that are being milked locally, rather than cows with their creamier milk. Kishek (also known as jameed) was also on display for us and offered up for tasting. Kishek are hard discs of sun-dried fermented yogurt and cracked bulgur wheat. Before refrigeration was available, these discs were a way to conserve and use milk throughout the year. Nowadays, though, they are still widely used: crumbled into stews or savory pastries or sprinkled over pulses, grains, and salads. In Gaza, kishek is flavored with dill seeds and chile flakes. The version we try, on the outskirts of Bethlehem, is plain, allowing the full force of its sharp, sour nature to punch through.

Sitting down on one of the three large velvet sofas that line the otherwise bare walls, little glasses of *laban*, a thick, drinking sheep yogurt, appear to continue the dairy theme. It's rich and refreshing at once, smooth and sharp. Slightly yellow versions of all the products sit alongside their white counterparts; they are the same product, just with turmeric or safflower, a spice that is used instead of (but which is not nearly as good as) saffron. Ramallah prefers the white yogurt, Majida says, Bethlehem prefers the yellow.

We sipped our laban, Majida told us about the network of women—the cooperatives—who get together to make the yogurt, the labneh, the butter, and the kishek. The milking is either done by the husband (who then hands the milk over to his wife to carry on the next stages) or the woman does the milking as well and is in control at every stage: the milking, drying, hanging, and shaking. Someone seriously in control of her game is grandma Noura Shaalan, who does it all. Noura has ten sons, five daughters, twenty-five sheep, and sixty-five grandchildren, half of whom (the grandchildren, not the sheep) appear at the door as we are sitting around and chatting. Conversation flows as quickly as our plates are replenished when they come close to being emptied. "Force of nature" is an understatement. "I've had enough, thank you" is an ignored statement.

Typically, ladies such as Noura and Majida sell their produce locally; they have around twenty local customers who buy from them regularly or they sell to one or two shops in Bethlehem, Beit Sahour, or Ramallah. The operations are small scale, but their importance to the community is large. These are women who look out for each other, girls sitting on the laps of their mothers and grandmothers, young women bonding with their mothers-in-law, aunties, cousins, sisters. When they're not making dairy products, some of the ladies lead women's empowerment groups, who might do a craft activity such as embroidery to sell cards, bags, shawls, cushions, or tapestries to local tourists. We are all given a little embroidered card to take away with us: an olive tree with the word "Palestine" sewn below it. Offers of payment are waved away, little glasses of yogurt are topped up, someone says something to someone else, in Arabic, which makes everyone laugh. Tara misses the meaning of the words but recalls her own "stitch and bitch" group back in London, smiling to think of the power of women, of connection, of sewing and chatting and making and doing and how much all these things truly mean. We might have lost our way with Waze but sitting there, for that moment, it all feels very much like home.

Preserved stuffed eggplants
Makdous

Preserves and pickles are a big part of the Palestinian table, adding a real hit of flavor to any meal. They also allow for seasonal vegetables to be eaten year-round. The name *makdous* comes from the Arabic verb *kadasa*, meaning "to stack." Stacking the stuffed eggplants on their sides and letting them sit for nearly two weeks before eating them makes their taste intense. The result is hot, strong, nutty, sharp, and garlicky in all the right ways. Start with eggplants as small as you can find; it's nice to be able to eat a whole eggplant at a time, so you don't want to be working your way through a large one.

Keeping notes: Once stuffed and covered in oil, these need to rest for twelve days, to ferment. They keep for up to six months.

Equipment note: You'll need a tall sterilized jar—about 8 inches/20cm tall and 4 inches/10cm wide—to store the eggplants in. For notes on how to sterilize your jar, see page 341.

Serves eight as part of a larger spread

1¾ lb/800g baby eggplants (between 12 and 22, depending on size!), long stems trimmed, leaving the green base
1 tbsp sugar

Stuffing

⅔ cup/70g walnut halves, roughly chopped
2 green chiles, finely chopped (3 tbsp/30g)
5 garlic cloves, crushed (about 3 tbsp/25g)
2 tbsp Aleppo chile flakes (or 1 tbsp regular chile flakes)
¾ cup/15g parsley, finely chopped
½ tsp salt

Salt
1⅓ cups/320ml olive oil

Pour about 3 qt/3L of water into a large pot (about 12 inches/30cm wide and 7 inches/18cm deep) and add the eggplants and sugar. Place a heatproof plate on top of the eggplants and place a bowl on top of this, so that the eggplants are completely submerged. Bring to a boil, then cook over medium-high heat for 30 minutes, until the eggplants are soft and have started to pale. Using a slotted spoon, lift the eggplants out of the water and place them in a colander. (You don't need to keep the water, but don't be tempted to pour them through a sieve; the eggplants are soft, so they will lose their shape if you do this.) Set aside for about 15 minutes, to cool slightly.

To make the stuffing, while the eggplants are cooking, place all the ingredients in a medium bowl. Mix well to combine, then place in the fridge, covered, until needed.

With a small sharp knife, make one slit down the side of each eggplant, about 1 inch/2.5cm long. Spoon between ⅛ and ¼ tsp of salt into each eggplant, depending on the size, and spread it inside each cavity. Once the eggplants are all salted, return them to the colander, cut side down, and set the colander over a large bowl. Place the plate on top of the eggplants and place a heavy object on top of that. Let rest in the fridge for 12 hours for the eggplants to release water; the amount of water released will depend on the eggplants—it can be anywhere between 3 tbsp/50ml and 10 tbsp/150ml.

Stuff each eggplant with 1–2 tsp of the stuffing, depending on size, then arrange them, stacked up sideways, in a sterilized jar. Pour in the oil—the eggplants need to be completely covered, otherwise they will become moldy—then seal the jar. Sit the jar upside down in a deep saucepan or tray, to catch any oil that might seep out, and set aside for 1 hour. Turn the jar right side up and store in a cool, dark place; such as a kitchen cupboard or pantry. Let ferment for 12 days before using.

Battir: how a little village made a big mark on the map

Battir is a Palestinian farming village in the West Bank. Just over 6 kilometers west of Bethlehem, with a population of around 4,500, it's located on one of the steep sides of the Refaim Valley, just above the modern route of the Jaffa–Jerusalem railway. Farming in Battir is made possible by its stone terraces, which stretch for more than 800 acres/325 hectares. The village itself is tiny, but it's well known for three reasons: (1) its ancient irrigation system and terraces (and the UNESCO World Heritage Site status gained as a result); (2) its long, thin, sweet Battiri eggplants; and (3) politically, for its bringing together of Palestinian and Israeli activists to successfully resist the building of the separation wall.

First: irrigation. In a region where access to water is often a matter of politics and who has control, Battir shows how much can be achieved on land that has a natural and reliable water source. Supplying the land with all the fresh water it needs is a Roman-era network fed by seven springs. It's been doing its job for over 2,000 years, and Battir, verdant and fertile, is evidence of its success. Responsibility for making sure that all the terraces are getting all the water they need is shared between the eight main families of the village. These eight clans rotate their roles from one day to the next. The discrepancy between the number of families—eight—and the number of days in the week—seven—is simply worked around: the local saying in the village is that a Battiri week "lasts eight days, not seven!"

The methods employed to water and farm the land are traditional—timeless, even. The amount the main spring goes down each day is measured by a simple white stick. It's literally just stuck into the water each morning and night to check the difference in depth. In doing so, the amount of water that has been used the previous day can be gleaned. For years, these traditional practices have delivered a resulting bounty of tomatoes, spinach, oranges, figs, apples, peaches, grapes, lemons, olives, and, of course, the famous Battiri eggplant.

A Battiri eggplant is smaller, longer, and sweeter than a regular eggplant. Its sweetness is attributed to the quality of the spring water that supplies it and helps it grow. Locals use eggplants in all sorts of ways in their cooking, from their maqlubeh (see page 264) to their m'tabbal (see page 82). The eggplants' small size and distinct shape, though, make them particularly well suited to being stuffed in dishes such as makdous (see page 56), where garlic, crushed walnuts, and chiles are piled into them before they are pickled and preserved.

Battir is also on the map for political reasons: for its successful resistance to the building of the separation wall through the village. Had this not been successful, the wall would have cut villagers off from their land and effectively decimated the traditional farming practices. Back in 1949, the railway track that the village looks over served as the armistice line along which the Green Line was drawn up between Israel and Jordan before Israel's decisive victory in the Six-Day War of 1967. Now, the Green Line is the boundary that Israel professes to follow in the building of the separation wall, a massive project that began during the second intifada in 2000, separating Israel on the one side from the West Bank on the other.

The purpose of the wall from the Israeli point of view is to protect its people from Palestinian attacks. The purpose of the wall from the Palestinian point of view is to impede its people's freedom of movement and to destroy the land on which their olive trees grow and their houses and farms are built. Perspective on this depends, of course, very much on what side of the line (or wall) you are standing.

For the villagers of Battir, had the wall followed the Green Line, as planned, the terraces and unique farming system of their village would have been destroyed. Both Palestinian and Israeli activists, therefore, came together in 2007 to sue the Israeli Ministry of Defense to try to change the planned route. The Israel Nature and Parks Authority, who'd previously agreed to the wall's original route in 2005, was persuaded to change its mind. It was a landmark case and, in 2012, the barrier's route had to be reconfigured. It was the first time that an Israeli government agency permitted a change to the planned construction of a segment of the fence.

The atmosphere in the village today is communal and positive, but the day-to-day is still hard. For the villagers, selling their produce requires trips to Bethlehem and beyond, and the village's location, still so close to the Green Line, prevents them from becoming complacent about what the future might hold. Still, it's a real David-and-Goliath story, a testament to the power of the present to preserve the past, about how enough attention, energy, and action can move mountains; or, in this case, walls.

Falafel with sumac onion

In Palestine, falafel are more often than not picked up on street corners (rather than made at home), freshly fried and piled into pita bread or paper cones. It's rare to find this street vendor setup outside the Middle East, though, so for anything resembling the real deal, these need to be made freshly at home. The success of precooked, fridge-cold supermarket falafel is, for Sami—and anyone who grew up eating them in the Middle East—one of life's great mysteries.

A three-part manifesto, therefore, for those who want to eat falafel as they should be eaten:

1. Don't fry them until you want to eat them. They need to be eaten fresh from the fryer.

2. The chickpeas get soaked overnight, but they do not get cooked. This instruction will not make sense until you have made and eaten your first batch.

3. Pair them with a chopped salad (see page 92), some (warm) hummus (see page 34), or (creamy) tahini sauce (see page 87). Eat them as they are, or forget about the plate and just pile them into a pita.

Forgive the lesson, but falafel are pretty much part of the DNA of every Palestinian kid walking to or from school. Lines form around the corner where street vendors set up, shaping their falafel mixture with a large falafel scoop (see page 336). Sami used to take his place in line nearly every day, ready to fill up his pita or paper cone so as to fill up his tummy.

Getting ahead: The falafel can be made a day in advance, taken right up to the stage where they are sprinkled with sesame seeds. At this point they can be kept in the fridge for a day or in the freezer for up to a month. If freezing them, freeze initially on the baking sheet and then, when they are solid, transfer them to a sealable bag. If you are frying them from frozen, just fry as per the recipe, then finish them off in a 400°F oven for about 5 minutes, until cooked through.

Shortcut: The sumac onion is an untraditional addition. It adds a nice bite of tart surprise to the falafel but you can skip this stage, if you like, and just make the falafel without the filling.

Makes 16 falafel; serves four to six

1⅓ cups/250g dried chickpeas
2 garlic cloves, crushed
1¼ cups/25g parsley leaves, roughly chopped
1¼ cups/25g cilantro leaves, roughly chopped
¾ cup/15g mint leaves, roughly chopped
2 medium onions, finely chopped (2 cups/300g)
¾ tsp Aleppo chile flakes (or ½ tsp regular chile flakes)
1¼ tsp ground cumin
1¼ tsp coriander seeds, finely crushed in a mortar and pestle
Salt
¾ tsp baking soda
1 tbsp sumac
About 1 tbsp sesame seeds
About 3⅓ cups/800ml sunflower oil

Place the chickpeas in a large bowl and cover with at least twice their volume of cold water. Set aside overnight to soak.

The next day, drain the chickpeas (they should weigh 1 lb 1oz/480g now), then combine them with the garlic, parsley, cilantro, mint, and three-fourths of the chopped onions. Put half the mix into a food processor and blitz for about 2 minutes, scraping down the sides a couple of times if you need to, until the paste is damp and slightly mushy. Transfer to a large bowl and repeat with the remaining half of the mix. Add this to the bowl as well, along with the chile flakes, cumin, coriander, and 1½ tsp of salt. Using your hands, mix well to combine. Add the baking soda and give everything another good mix.

Place the remaining onions in a bowl with the sumac and ¼ tsp of salt. Mix well and set aside.

When shaping the falafel, have a small bowl of water nearby so that you can keep your hands wet. This makes it easier to work with the mixture. Line a baking sheet with parchment paper and a colander with paper towels.

Spoon 2 tbsp of the mixture—about 1¾ oz/50g—into the palm of your hand and form a ball. Don't press too hard, as this will make the falafel dense. Dip your finger into the bowl of water and then make a large hollow in the middle of each ball. Spoon 1 tsp of the sumac onion mixture into the hollow and shape it again, so that most of the filling is covered. Flatten into a patty—about 2½ inches/6cm wide and ¾ inch/2cm thick—then, using your little finger, make a small indentation; this will ensure that the inside gets evenly cooked. Place on the prepared baking sheet and continue with the remaining mixture; you should have enough to shape 16 falafel. Sprinkle the tops lightly with the sesame seeds, pressing them in slightly so that they don't fall off when the falafel are fried. At this stage the falafel can be frozen, if you like (see Getting ahead).

Fill a deep, heavy-bottomed medium saucepan—about 8 inches/20cm wide—with enough of the oil so that it rises about 3 inches/7cm up the side of the pan. Place over medium-high heat and bring the oil to a temperature of 355°F, if you have a thermometer. If you don't have a thermometer, just add a little bit of the falafel mixture to the pan: if it sizzles at once, you'll know the oil is hot enough.

Carefully lower the falafel, in batches, into the oil—you should be able to fit four in the pan at once—and cook for 5–6 minutes, or until well browned and cooked through. They need to spend this long in the oil to really dry out the inside, so don't be tempted to take them out too soon. Use a slotted spoon to transfer them to the prepared colander while you continue with the remaining batches. Serve at once.

פירות ברעם

Pea, spinach, za'atar, and preserved lemon fritters

These work well as either a starter or a snack, or as a meal in themselves, if bulked out with some smoked salmon or trout or some poached or fried eggs. They can be eaten straight from the oven, all hot and crispy, or at room temperature later on if taken to work or on a picnic. They'll lose their crunch, but their flavor will increase.

Getting ahead: Both the sauce and the batter can be made up to a day ahead and kept in the fridge, if you like, ready to fry and serve.

Makes 14–15 fritters; serves six

Sauce

1¼ cups/300g sour cream
1 tbsp sumac
1 lemon: finely grate the zest to get 1 tsp, then juice to get 1 tbsp
1 tbsp olive oil
¼ tsp salt

7½ cups/150g baby spinach
2½ cups/300g frozen peas, defrosted
2 preserved lemons, flesh and seeds discarded, peel finely chopped (2 tbsp/20g)
1 green chile, seeded and finely chopped
3 eggs, beaten
6 tbsp/100g ricotta
⅓ cup/45g cornstarch
3 tbsp za'atar
½ tsp Aleppo chile flakes (or ¼ tsp regular chile flakes)
¼ tsp baharat (see page 335)
⅓ tsp ground cardamom
¼ tsp ground aniseed
¾ cup/15g mint leaves, finely shredded
¾ cup/15g parsley, roughly chopped
¾ cup/15g dill, roughly chopped
Salt and black pepper
7 tbsp/100ml sunflower oil
1 lemon, cut into wedges

To make the sauce, place all the ingredients for the sauce in a bowl. Whisk well to combine and keep in the fridge until ready to serve.

Line a baking sheet with paper towels.

Bring a medium saucepan of salted water to a boil and add the spinach. Stir, just to wilt, then drain through a sieve. Rinse under cold running water, to stop the spinach from overcooking, and drain well. Transfer to the prepared baking sheet, well spread out, and set aside for 5 minutes to dry. Finely chop the spinach, then place in a large mixing bowl and set aside.

Place the peas in a food processor, pulse a few times until roughly crushed, then add them to the spinach along with the preserved lemon, chile, eggs, ricotta, cornstarch, za'atar, chile flakes, baharat, cardamom, aniseed, mint, parsley, dill, 1 tsp of salt, and a good grind of black pepper. Mix until just combined.

Preheat the oven to 400°F. Line a plate with paper towels, and a baking sheet with parchment paper.

Pour the oil into a large, flat frying pan and place over medium-high heat. Once very hot, use two small spoons to scoop up the mixture; don't worry about making them uniform in shape, but they should be about 3¼ inches/8cm wide and ¾ inch/2cm thick. Carefully lower into the oil—you should be able to do three or four fritters at a time—and fry for 3–4 minutes, turning once, until they are golden brown. If they are cooking too quickly and taking on too much color, just decrease the temperature.

Using a slotted spoon, transfer the fritters to the prepared plate while you continue with the remaining fritters. Once they are all fried, lay the fritters out on the prepared baking sheet and bake for 4–5 minutes, or until cooked through. Serve warm or at room temperature, with the sauce and a wedge of lemon alongside.

Pictured on page 68

Cauliflower and cumin fritters with mint yogurt

A version of these fritters featured in Sami's first book, *Ottolenghi: The Cookbook*. We tried to play around with them—adding broccoli to the mix, for example—but kept returning to the classic as something too hard to move far from.

The fritters were something Sami's mother used to make, packing them up for her kids to take to school. They're still a Tamimi favorite, eaten either fresh out of the pan or at room temperature later on. Leftovers are also fine the next day, eaten at room temperature or reheated in the oven for a few minutes. As ever, piling them into flatbread makes for the best kind of quick lunch, but they're also great as they are, to snack on before supper. If you're serving them as a snack, make them half the size so that they can be eaten in a few bites.

Getting ahead: The batter keeps for a day in the fridge, if you want to get ahead, ready and waiting to fry.

Shortcut: The mint yogurt is a lovely addition, but there's enough going on, flavor-wise, for the fritters to be eaten as they are, if you like, with just a squeeze of lemon.

Makes about 10 fritters; serves four to six

Mint yogurt (optional)
1 cup/250g Greek yogurt
½ tsp dried mint
2 tbsp lemon juice
1 tbsp olive oil
½ tsp salt

1 small cauliflower, cut into 1½-inch/4cm florets (3 cups/300g)
1 cup/120g all-purpose flour
1 cup/20g parsley, finely chopped
1 small onion, finely chopped (¾ cup/100g)
2 eggs
1½ tsp ground cumin
¾ tsp ground cinnamon
½ tsp ground turmeric
½ tsp Aleppo chile flakes (or ¼ tsp regular chile flakes)
½ tsp baking powder
Salt and black pepper
1 cup/240ml sunflower oil

To make the yogurt, place all the ingredients for the mint yogurt in a bowl. Mix to combine and keep in the fridge until ready to serve.

Bring a medium saucepan of salted water to a boil and add the cauliflower. Simmer for 4 minutes, then (making sure to reserve 3–4 tbsp of the cooking water) drain it into a colander. Using a fork or potato masher, slightly crush the cauliflower, then transfer it to a large bowl along with the flour, parsley, onion, eggs, cumin, cinnamon, turmeric, chile flakes, baking powder, 1¼ tsp of salt, and a good grind of black pepper. Add 3 tbsp of the cooking water and mix well, until the mix has the consistency of a slightly runny batter.

Line a plate with paper towels.

Heat the oil in a large sauté pan—about 9 inches/23cm wide—and, once very hot, carefully spoon 2–3 tbsp of batter per fritter into the oil. You'll need to do this in batches—four or five fritters at a time—so as not to crowd the pan, and use a spatula to keep them apart. Fry for about 5 minutes, flipping them over halfway through, until both sides are golden brown. Using a slotted spoon, transfer to the prepared plate and set aside while you continue with the remaining batches. Serve warm or at room temperature, with the mint yogurt on the side.

Pictured on page 69

Kubbeh

On every table full of mezzeh, in every kitchen across the Levant, there will be kubbeh. These tightly packed balls of bulgur and ground meat are the king of all snacks, eaten with your hands and dipped in tahini sauce or served as part of a large mezzeh spread, with a freshly chopped salad.

Getting ahead: Kubbeh can be made up to a day ahead and kept in the fridge before frying. They can also be frozen once shaped and cooked straight from the freezer. To freeze, lay them out on a baking sheet (one that fits into your freezer). Once they are frozen, transfer them to a sealable bag or airtight container so that they don't take up all the freezer space. For more on the practice of hawader—getting things into the freezer for whenever they are needed—see page 337.

Makes about 32 kubbeh; serves twelve as a snack, or six as a main

Filling
2½ tbsp olive oil
⅓ cup/45g pine nuts
3 onions, finely chopped (3¼ cups/450g)
7 oz/200g ground beef (at least 15% fat)
1 tsp ground cinnamon
1 tsp ground allspice
4 tsp pomegranate molasses
¼ cup/5g parsley leaves, roughly chopped
Salt and black pepper

Shell
1 onion, roughly chopped (1 cup/140g)
1 lb 2 oz/500g ground beef (at least 15% fat)
2 tsp ground cinnamon
1½ tsp ground allspice
Salt and black pepper
1⅔ cups/270g fine bulgur

Tahini sauce
¼ cup/75g tahini
5 tbsp/75ml water
1½ tbsp lemon juice
¼ tsp salt

About 2 cups/500ml sunflower oil
1 tsp sumac

To make the filling, put 1½ tbsp of olive oil into a large sauté pan and place over medium-high heat. Add the pine nuts and cook for about 3 minutes, stirring continuously, until evenly golden. Drain in a sieve placed over a bowl, to collect the oil, then return the oil to the pan. Add the remaining 1 tbsp of oil, along with the onions, and cook for about 10 minutes, stirring from time to time, until soft and lightly golden. Add the beef, cinnamon, and allspice and cook for another 2 minutes, using a spoon to break up the beef, until the meat is no longer pink. Remove from the heat and stir in the pine nuts, molasses, parsley, 1¼ tsp of salt, and a good grind of black pepper. Set aside to cool.

To make the shell, put the onion into a food processor and pulse until very finely minced but not liquidized. Add the beef, cinnamon, allspice, 1 tbsp of salt (a lot, we know, but it needs it), and a good grind of black pepper. Pulse a few times, about 15 seconds in total, to form a paste. Transfer to a separate large bowl and set aside.

Put the bulgur into a sieve and place under running water for about 2 minutes, or until the water runs clear. Set aside to drain for a couple of minutes, then add to the raw beef mixture. Knead for about 3 minutes, or until you have a sticky mass that holds together well when pinched.

Continued

Line a baking sheet with parchment paper and have a bowl of water nearby; you'll need to dip your hands into the water as you shape the kubbeh, to help seal.

Begin by rolling out Ping-Pong-size balls of the kubbeh shell—they should weigh about 1¼ oz/35g each. You should make about 32 balls. Working one at a time, hold a ball in your left hand and use the index finger of your right hand to make an indentation in the center of the ball. (Hands are reversed if you are left-handed.) Gently swivel your finger around, while pushing upward with your left hand, to form a cavity with sides about ⅛ inch/3mm thick. Fill the cavity with 1½ tsp of the filling and gently seal the shell around it, so no filling is exposed. Using both hands, form the kubbeh into an oval that is somewhat pointed at one end, making sure no cracks appear and that the kubbeh is completely sealed on all sides. Transfer to the prepared baking sheet and continue with the remaining filling and shell mixture.

To make the tahini sauce, put all the ingredients into a bowl. Whisk well to combine and set aside.

When ready to fry, line a plate with paper towels. Put the oil into a medium saucepan and place over medium-high heat. When the oil is hot (355°F, if you have a thermometer), add the kubbeh in batches of six or seven, and fry for about 4 minutes, until deeply browned and crispy on all sides. Transfer to the prepared plate and keep warm while you continue with the remaining kubbeh. Transfer to a serving platter, sprinkle with the sumac, and serve warm, with the tahini sauce to dip into or pour over.

Spicy olives and roasted red pepper
Zaytoun bil shatta

This is somewhere between a condiment and a salsa, as happy to be spooned alongside some pan-fried fish or meat as it is to be stirred into a simple bowl of rice.

Keeping notes: This keeps for about four days in the fridge; make more than you need so that you have it on hand.

Serves four as a condiment or as part of a mezzeh spread

1 large red bell pepper (5¼ oz/150g)
4 tsp olive oil
½ tsp red shatta (recipe follows) or rose harissa
1 cup/170g pitted green olives
2 small preserved lemons, flesh and pith discarded, peel finely sliced (2 tbsp/25g)
½ cup/10g parsley, finely chopped
2 green onions, finely sliced (¼ cup/20g)
½ green chile, seeded and finely sliced
1½ tbsp lemon juice

Preheat the oven to 450°F. Line a baking sheet with parchment paper.

Place the bell pepper on the prepared baking sheet, toss with 1 tsp of oil, and bake for 35–40 minutes, until soft and charred. Transfer the pepper to a bowl, cover, and set aside for 10 minutes or so. Once cool enough to handle, remove the skin, stem, and seeds and place the flesh—you should have about 3 oz/80g—in the small bowl of a food processor. Blitz until smooth, then transfer to a bowl with the shatta or harissa and the remaining 1 tbsp of oil. Mix well to combine, then add all the remaining ingredients and stir again.

Pictured on page 74

Shatta (red or green)

Sami knew that he had a true partner in culinary crime in Tara when he spotted a jar of this in her bike basket one day. "I don't go anywhere without some," Tara said, as casually as if talking about her house keys. This fiery condiment is as easy to make as it is easy to become addicted to. Shatta(ra!) is on every Palestinian table, cutting through rich foods or pepping up others. Eggs, fish, meat, vegetables—they all love it. Our recommendation is to keep a jar in your fridge at all times. Or your bike basket, if so inclined.

Equipment note: As with anything being left to ferment, the jar you put your chiles into needs to be properly sterilized (see page 341 for instructions).

Makes 1 medium jar

9 oz/250g red or green chiles (with seeds), stems trimmed, very thinly sliced
1 tbsp salt
3 tbsp cider vinegar
1 tbsp lemon juice
Olive oil, to cover

Place the chiles and salt in a medium sterilized jar and mix well. Seal the jar and store in the fridge for 3 days. On the third day, drain the chiles, transfer them to a food processor, and blitz; you can either blitz well to form a fine paste or roughly blitz so that some texture remains. Add the vinegar and lemon juice, mix to combine, then return the mixture to the same jar. Pour enough olive oil on top to cover, and keep in the fridge for up to 6 months. The oil will firm up and separate from the chiles once it's in the fridge, so just give it a good stir, for everything to combine, before using.

Pictured on page 75

Beet and sweet potato dip with pistachio bulgur sauce

Serves four as part of a mezzeh spread

1 lb 2 oz/500g raw beets (about 4 medium), unpeeled
1 medium sweet potato (8½ oz/240g)
½ cup/70g bulgur
5 tbsp/75ml water
Salt
½ cup plus 1 tbsp/75g pistachios, lightly toasted (see "Nuts," page 339) and finely chopped
¾ cup/15g parsley, finely chopped
¾ cup/15g mint, roughly chopped, plus a few leaves to serve
1½ tbsp lemon juice
7 tbsp/100ml olive oil
Black pepper
4 garlic cloves, crushed
½ tsp ground cinnamon
¼ tsp ground allspice
1 Medjool date (¾ oz/20g), pitted and soaked in 3 tbsp of boiling water for about 20 minutes
2 tbsp cider vinegar
6 tbsp/100g labneh (see page 48) or Greek yogurt
1¼ oz/35g feta, roughly crumbled

Beet was not something Sami grew up eating. This dish, therefore, shows how the ingredients that bookend Sami's palate—the ground cinnamon and allspice, the labneh and tangy feta, the bulgur and olive oil—can be used in a fresh way. The dip is lovely as it is, as part of a spread, or can be served as a side to an oily fish, like salmon or mackerel.

Getting ahead: If you are making your own labneh, you'll need to get this going at least 24 hours before serving. The dip keeps well in the fridge for up to three days. The sauce can be made up to a day before serving and kept in the fridge. As always, bring both elements back to room temperature before serving.

Shortcut: The dip works well alone without the bulgur sauce, if you are keeping things simple. If you do this, just increase the pistachios to ¾ cup/100g. If you want the sauce to be gluten-free, use cooked quinoa instead of the bulgur.

Preheat the oven to 450°F.

Tightly wrap the beets and sweet potato individually in aluminum foil and bake for about 1 hour, or until a knife inserted into the middle of each beet and the potato goes in easily. Timing will vary, depending on the size of the beets. Remove from the oven and, once cool enough to handle, peel and discard the skins of both vegetables. You should end up with about 7 oz/200g of cooked sweet potato flesh and about 14 oz/400g of beet. Roughly chop the beets into large chunks and set aside. The sweet potato can stay as it is. Keep the two separate, until needed.

Put the bulgur into a small saucepan with a lid, along with the water and ⅛ tsp of salt. Bring to a boil over high heat, then remove from the heat. Set aside, covered, for about 20 minutes, then fluff the bulgur up with a fork. Tip into a bowl and set aside for about 20 minutes, to cool. Stir in the pistachios, parsley, mint, lemon juice, 3 tbsp of oil, ½ tsp of salt, and a grind of black pepper. Set aside until needed.

Put 3 tbsp of oil into a small sauté pan and place over medium-high heat. Once hot, add the garlic and cook for about 2 minutes, or until lightly browned. Add the spices, cook for another couple of seconds, stirring frequently, then remove from the heat. Set aside to cool slightly and then put into the bowl of a food processor. Add the beets, 1 tsp of salt, and a good grind of black pepper. Remove the date from its water, add to the food processor, and blitz the mixture for about 1 minute, or until smooth. Add the sweet potato and pulse for another 20 seconds, until just incorporated.

Transfer the mixture to a bowl and add the cider vinegar and 3 tbsp/50g of labneh. Fold to combine—you still want to see some streaks of the labneh—then spread out on a large platter or in a shallow bowl. With the back of a spoon, smooth out the surface and make a well in the center. Top with the remaining 3 tbsp/50g of labneh, swirling it gently into the mix without incorporating it too much. Spoon on the bulgur sauce, top with the feta and additional mint leaves, drizzle with the remaining 1 tbsp of oil, and serve.

Nablus

Say "Nablus" to someone who hasn't traveled around Israel, the West Bank, or the Galilee and, chances are, they won't have heard of it. Destination-wise, other places are clearly on the map. Bethlehem, Nazareth, Jerusalem: these are the cities firmly rooted in the minds of those who want to bear witness to various sites of huge religious importance. The Church of the Nativity, Manger Square, the Basilica of the Annunciation, Temple Mount, the Church of the Holy Sepulchre, the Mount of Olives, the Garden of Gethsemane; this is to name just a few of the landmarks that mean so much to those who want to stand where the birth, life, and death of Jesus are said to have taken place. The buses getting everyone from Bethlehem to Nazareth and Jerusalem are big, full, and constantly on the move, as are the hotels housing and feeding everyone along the way. The well-trodden path is as smooth as the olive-wood carvings being bought as souvenirs to take back from the Holy Land.

There's something about all the wood, though—to invert the forest-for-the-trees saying—that can hide the reality of being able to see the everyday "trees": the day-to-day stuff of life going on in a busy, bustling, functioning city. The selling and buying of fresh food and household goods, for example, the everyday business of moving about, commuting, navigating honking cars and yellow taxis, chatting over coffee and slices of cake: the highs and lows, the bitter and sweet, the norms of city life.

For all this—and for the sweet things in particular—Nablus is the place to be. Slightly off the tourist track (65 kilometers north of Jerusalem, located between Mount Ebal and Mount Gerizim), the city has always been a key trading point for olive oil, soap, and cotton across the Levant. With a population of just under 130,000, it's one of Palestine's largest cities. It's had a tough and troubled past, though, suffering badly during the height of the second intifada in 2002, and continues to be challenged by the Israeli military occupation. The reality of multiple checkpoints interrupting the flow of goods in and out of the city, for example, is a huge problem. Despite all this, the city has a strong sense of resilience about it; defiance, even.

If the sense of resilience is palpable, then so too is the smell. The smell of warm sugar being poured over mild white cheese in a baking sheet that looks like a giant lily pad turning around, day in and day out, inside one of the many bakeries in town. Nablus is, for those whose pilgrimages are shaped more by their appetites than by their faith, the city for pastries and sweets. If you want the best knafeh around—the warm, soft, sugar-syrup-drenched, melt-in-the-mouth cheesy pastry

(see page 302) so popular in the region—Nablus is where the compass needs to be pointing. Walking around the cobbled streets of the bustling market, the smell of melted ghee, baked semolina pastry, and sweet white cheese wafts around each corner, pulling people from the piles of seeds and nuts they've stopped to try or buy. If it's not nuts and seeds, it'll be mountains of fresh soft herbs, enormous eggplants, tiny eggplants, plastic buckets full of hallucinogenically colored pickles, Jenga-like displays of peaches stacked up into a pyramid, live chickens, not-so-live fish and meat, Adidas sneakers, shiny high heels, and vast arrays of variously colored pants.

The market, in short, is a welcome assault on the senses: the colors, the smells, the sounds, the clash of offerings on display. But step into Majdi Abu Hamidi's Al-Aqsa bakery on Al-Naser street, a well-known institution in the city, and time stands still for a moment. Plastic stools are pulled up at Formica tables, and portions of knafeh are transferred from meter-wide round trays to the plates they are being served on. Portions are either large or *really* large, and strong, black coffee appears in small cups on big trays. Abu Hamidi, who has been making and serving knafeh from this spot for over forty-five years, hands out the coffee. Coffee is fine—necessary, even, to take the edge off the sweetness—but customers are encouraged (only half-jokingly) not to drink water for half an hour after eating his knafeh, to allow the taste to linger. Memories last for a lot longer than this, though; the sight of groups of friends or family huddled around a table, sharing a sweet moment, or—just as common and as meaningful—locals pulling up a bench by themselves, taking five or ten minutes out from their day to sit and delight in the sheer comfort, simple sweetness, and incomparable pleasure that is knafeh Nabulseyeh.

المركز الوطني للخدمات
09 2371579
City Coffee Shop
شركة الحنبلي
المحاميان
علاء عنبتاوي
حركة التحرير الوطني الفلسطيني فتح
اقليم نابلس
للفرش المنزلي
أصفهاني
09-2374601
Jordan Commer
مكة

Paltel
لمدة 4 شهور مجاناً
رفعنا سرعتك
والأزرق بخدمتك

Charred eggplant with tahini and herbs
M'tabbal

If Tara were to take ten things to her desert island, to live off forever, this is what the list would look like: eggplants, tahini, garlic, lemons, olive oil, pomegranate seeds, fresh mint, dried mint, parsley, and salt. M'tabbal, then—quite literally a roll-call of her top ten—is one of Tara's favorite dishes. Serve it either as a side to some pan-fried fish or grilled meat or as part of a larger spread.

Keeping notes: This keeps well in the fridge for up to five days. As always, serve it at room temperature rather than fridge-cold.

Serves four to six as part of a mezzeh spread

4 large eggplants, charred (see page 336; 2 lb 2 oz/1kg)
3 tbsp tahini
2 large garlic cloves, crushed
¼ cup/60ml lemon juice
Salt
2 tbsp pomegranate seeds
¼ tsp dried mint
About 10 mint leaves
¼ cup/5g parsley leaves, roughly chopped
About 1 tbsp olive oil

Scoop the flesh out of the charred eggplants; you should have about 1 lb 2 oz/500g. Set this aside in a colander in the sink or over a bowl for at least 1 hour (or overnight, in the fridge) to drain.

Put the drained eggplant flesh into a large mixing bowl and, using your hands, pull it apart; you want to create long, thin strands. Add the tahini, garlic, lemon juice, and 1 tsp of salt and mix to combine. Spoon the mixture onto a serving plate with a lip (or into a bowl) and sprinkle with the pomegranate seeds, dried mint, and fresh herbs. Finally, drizzle with the oil and serve.

Pictured on page 85

Roasted red pepper and walnut dip
Muhammara

Serves four as part of a mezzeh spread

1 cup plus 2 tbsp/110g walnut halves
6–7 red bell peppers (2 lb 2 oz/1kg)
⅓ cup/80ml olive oil
1 red onion, finely chopped (1 cup/120g)
4 garlic cloves, crushed
2 tsp tomato paste
2 tsp ground cumin
2 tsp Aleppo chile flakes (or 1 tsp regular chile flakes)
½ cup/35g panko breadcrumbs
1½ tbsp pomegranate molasses
2 tsp lemon juice
Salt and black pepper
1 tbsp parsley leaves, roughly chopped

The word *muhammara* can mean both "roasted" and "red" and can also (though not here) refer to the use of paprika in a dish to bring a smoky depth of flavor and reddish color. Muhammara is Syrian in origin, moving freely to Palestine and Lebanon when the Levant was a single territory. It still moves freely now, across whichever table it is served at, acting as a dip, spread, or side in all sorts of contexts. Scoop it up with warm toasted pita, spoon it alongside some cooked lima beans or lentils or any roast meat, pair it with some creamy hummus or cheese, or use it as part of a mezzeh spread. You can't really go wrong.

Keeping notes: This keeps well in the fridge for up to three days.

Gluten-free note: Adding the panko makes the mix firm up and slightly dry, in a good way. For a gluten-free alternative, use an equal quantity of ground almonds or increase the quantity of walnuts by about 2 tbsp/20g.

Preheat the oven to 350°F. Line two baking sheets with parchment paper.

Spread the walnuts out on a prepared baking sheet and roast for about 8 minutes, until lightly toasted. Remove from the oven and set aside.

Increase the oven temperature to 450°F. Place the bell peppers on the second prepared baking sheet and toss with 1 tsp of oil. Bake for about 40 minutes, or until completely softened and charred. Transfer to a bowl, cover with a clean dish towel or a plate, and let cool for about 20 minutes. Once cool enough to handle, remove and discard the skins, stems, and seeds—the remaining flesh should weigh about 13⅓ oz/380g.

Put 2 tbsp of oil into a medium sauté pan and place over medium-high heat. Add the onion and cook for about 7 minutes, stirring a few times, until softened and browned. Add the garlic, tomato paste, and spices and cook for 30 seconds, stirring constantly. Remove from the heat and tip into a food processor, along with the roasted pepper, panko breadcrumbs, pomegranate molasses, lemon juice, 1 tbsp of oil, 1 tsp of salt, and a grind of black pepper. Blitz for about 30 seconds, to form a coarse paste, and then add 1 cup/90g of the walnuts. Blitz for another 20 seconds or so; not much longer than this, as you want the walnuts to just break down rather than form a paste. Transfer to a serving platter and drizzle with the remaining 2 tbsp of oil. Roughly crush the remaining 2 tbsp walnuts with your hands and sprinkle these and the parsley on top and serve.

Pictured on page 84

Butternut squash m'tabbal
M'tabbal qarae

The difference between m'tabbal and baba ganoush is the addition of tahini. For us, if it has tahini in it, then it's m'tabbal. Other opinions, as always, are available. Whatever you call this sort of dip, three rules remain absolute: it's all about the smokiness of the eggplants, lemons will be squeezed, and there will be garlic. The squash is our own (quite literally) sweet addition.

Serve this as a dip, to scoop up with warm pita, or as a side to all sorts of things—grilled meat or fish, for example, or a range of roasted veg.

Keeping notes: Double the batch and make more than you need, if you like; it keeps well in the fridge for up to three days. Just bring it back to room temperature rather than serving it fridge-cold.

Serves eight as a dip, or six as part of a spread

1 small butternut squash (2 lb/900g)
3 tbsp olive oil
Salt and black pepper
1 large head of garlic (about 2½ oz/70g)
4 large eggplants, charred (see page 336; 2 lb 2 oz/1kg)
¼ cup/75g tahini
3 tbsp lemon juice
½ red chile, thinly sliced into rounds
½ tsp dried mint
¼ cup/5g mint leaves, torn
1 green onion, thinly sliced (2 tbsp/10g)

Preheat the oven to 425°F. Line a baking sheet with parchment paper.

Cut the squash in half, lengthwise, and then scoop out and discard the seeds. Using a knife, make shallow crosshatch cuts across the flesh and then place cut side up on the prepared baking sheet. Drizzle each half with 1 tsp of oil and sprinkle with ⅛ tsp of salt and a good grind of black pepper. Bake for 50 minutes, or until the squash is very soft.

While the squash is roasting, slice the top off the head of garlic, horizontally, so that the cloves are exposed. Place in the middle of a square of aluminum foil and drizzle with ½ tsp of oil and sprinkle with salt and pepper. Wrap tightly in the foil and bake for 40 minutes (at the same time as the squash is in the oven), until the cloves are soft and golden brown.

Remove both the squash and the garlic from the oven and set aside to cool. Once cool, scoop out the flesh of the squash and mash it coarsely with a spoon or fork—this should weigh about 1 lb 2 oz/500g. Place the flesh in a mixing bowl and set aside. The skin can be discarded. Squeeze out the cooked garlic cloves, roughly chop them, and add to the bowl with the squash. The papery skin and the foil can be discarded.

Scoop the flesh out of the charred eggplant; you should have around 1 lb 2 oz/500g. Roughly chop to form a coarse mash. Add this to the bowl of squash and garlic along with the tahini, lemon juice, and 1½ tsp of salt. Mix well to combine—we like the texture rough, but use an immersion blender to blitz and make it a bit smoother, if you prefer—then spread out on a large serving platter or individual plates. Top with the chile, dried mint, mint leaves, and green onion. Drizzle with the remaining 2½ tbsp of oil and serve.

Pictured on page 85

Tahini sauce

Makes 1 medium jar

Rounded ½ cup/150g tahini, plus more as needed
½ cup/120ml water, plus more as needed
2 tbsp lemon juice, plus more as needed
1 garlic clove, crushed
¼ tsp salt

Tahini sauce: the creamy, nutty, rich addition to many a snack, dish, or feast. It's on every table in Palestine, ready to be dipped into or drizzled over all sorts of things—roasted vegetables, fish or meat, and leaf-, pulse- or grain-based salads. It keeps well in the fridge for up to four days, so always make the full recipe here, even if what you are cooking only calls for a few tablespoons.

Mix together all the ingredients. If it is too runny, add a bit more tahini. If it is too thick, add a bit more lemon juice or water. You want the consistency to be like that of a smooth, runny nut butter. It will thicken up when left to sit around, so just give it a stir and some more lemon juice or water every time you use it.

Tahini parsley sauce
Baqdunsieh

Makes 1 small jar

¼ cup/75g tahini
¼ cup/60ml water, plus more as needed
2 tbsp lemon juice, plus more as needed
2 garlic cloves, crushed
¼ tsp salt
1 cup/20g parsley, finely chopped

Like the tahini sauce above, this also keeps well in the fridge, so make the full quantity even if your recipe asks for less. You'll find it goes with pretty much whatever else you are eating in the next few days.

Put the tahini, water, lemon juice, garlic, and salt into a small bowl. Whisk well until smooth, then stir in the parsley. Thin it out with an additional 1 tbsp or so of water or lemon juice, if you need to, if it's been sitting around. You want it to have the consistency of creamy nut butter.

VEGGIE SIDES AND SALADS

No Palestinian table is considered set without vegetable sides and salads. Not one big bowl of salad and a veggie or two, but a great big array of dishes all served in their own little bowls. A simple chopped salad, of cucumbers, tomatoes, bell peppers, chiles, and fresh herbs, will always be there. Fattoush as well, using up yesterday's leftover bread, now pulled into chunks and bulking out today's salad. Sides of fried cauliflower and steamed carrots; cubes of roasted eggplant stirred into bulgur; lentils with tahini and crispy onions—the list goes on and on. For those who like their vegetables, it's a very happy sight.

So ubiquitous is the salad offering that, when eating out in the restaurants of Bethlehem, Haifa, Nazareth, Jenin, or East Jerusalem, for example, these dishes will arrive at the table spontaneously, at the beginning of a meal. Whether or not they've been ordered, they appear along with the bread and often won't feature on the bill. On the one hand, it's great that all these vegetables are as integral to the meal as bread. There's a downside to this ubiquity, though, and to the fact that the customers don't often expect to pay for these dishes. The offering can, in all honesty, get stuck in a rut and be made without a whole lot of *nafas*—heart and soul (see page 339)—or imagination being put into it.

It's completely understandable and the bind works two ways: customers know what they want and often want what they know, so are not always keen to experiment or suddenly start paying for something that has, previously, turned up by itself at the table. Chefs, therefore, either continue to stick to the status quo, saving their energy and imagination for the main dish, or run the risk of pushback if they try to elevate (and start charging for) a salad. This tension is touched upon in "A Tale of Two Restaurateurs" (page 164), but it's something we saw time and again on our travels, when a chef's imaginative approach to a salad or veggie side was, more often than not, quietly relegated to the "chef's special" board.

For our part, then, we have a real mix of dishes here. Some are traditional—the Chopped Salad: Three Ways (page 92), Braised Fava Beans with Olive Oil and Lemon (page 123), or shulbato (see page 140), for example. With others, we've taken the traditional but given it a twist: fattoush with a tangy buttermilk dressing (see page 99), three ways of tabbouleh (see pages 102–104), or roasted new potatoes with an injection of punchy flavor (see page 137).

Reflecting all the years Sami has spent working, eating, and shaping his palate in London, several of the salads will, however, be much more familiar to the Ottolenghi customer than they will be recognizable on the traditional Palestinian table. These are the dishes for which Sami has taken the ingredients of his hometown, ramped up their boldness, and put them on platters and plates so large they'd cast a shadow over all the little bowls they'd otherwise be served in. These are big and bold dishes in all senses, not just the platters. They're big on flavor, big in color, big in surprise. In salads such as Baby Gem Lettuce with Charred Eggplant Yogurt, Smacked Cucumber, and Shatta (page 96), or Roasted Figs and Onions with Radicchio and Goat Cheese (page 100), the ingredients are traditional—they're just shown in a deliciously new light.

There are also some salads we would have liked to include but haven't because the ingredients are hard to source outside Palestine. Green almonds, for example, picked young and fresh from the tree and eaten by the handful, mark the beginning of spring in Palestine. Their taste and texture is distinct: fuzzy-skinned and crunchy like an unripe apricot or peach but without any of the tartness you'd expect. Picked at this stage, green almonds are sold in big bags by the side of the road, ready to be snacked on as they are or cut into thin slivers to add to leafy salads. We tried to experiment with very firm apricots, peaches, or plums to make a substitute but nothing really came close. Other ingredients that we would have used if they were more widely available include vegetables such as akkoub—a prickly thistle that, when its spines are removed, is one of the most celebrated foods of village cuisine—or yaqteen, a smooth long gourd that is shaped like a bottle with a nozzle on top. Colocasia—a root vegetable with a pink stem poking through—is another, as is molokhieh, the much-loved jute leaves that are widely grown. We came up with a substitute for these in besara (see page 150)—a molokhieh soup—and in our recipe for chicken meatballs in molokhieh (see page 239) but didn't feel happy with any of the uncooked alternatives we could have used.

A lot of the salads and sides here are robust enough to handle being played around with, though, alternatives are suggested in each recipe depending on what is in season or what you have. Likewise with the dressings and the amount of chopping you want to do, play with alternating a tahini or yogurt dressing where a lemony one is suggested and vice versa. And so with the chopping, if you don't like the idea of chopping a large bunch of vegetables into ½-inch/1cm dice, then don't. It will still taste good if everything is roughly chopped. Start with the ripest, sweetest ingredients you can get a hold of, cook what's in season, and you can't go wrong. And, if ever in doubt, just add cubes of tangy feta or some chunks of creamy avocado and a great big squeeze of lemon. "Everything's better with feta!" as Tara says, nearly every day.

Chopped salad: three ways
Salata Arabieh

Salata mafrumeh, salata na'ameh, salata baladiye, salata fallahi: whatever name this goes by, it's the same fresh chopped Palestinian salad. It's as ubiquitous as it is compulsory alongside every meal. It's there at breakfast, to have with hummus and falafel. It's there at lunch, inside a warm pita stuffed with kofta. It's there at supper, alongside the spread of pickles and olives and a rich meat stew. There are many versions on the theme, we've offered three. One as it is, allowing the ingredients to really sing, one with a nutty tahini dressing, and one with a yogurt dressing. Play around as you like, though, cubes of tangy feta, black olives, or creamy avocado are a really nice addition, as is a sprinkle of za'atar. Just two rules: start with vegetables as ripe and sun-kissed as possible and a knife as sharp as you can get it. It's a simple salad but one that requires a lot of chopping.

Getting ahead: Do all your chopping a few hours in advance, if you like (it can take a while, particularly if you are scaling up the recipe to feed a crowd), but don't assemble this too long before serving. It'll get watery if it sits around.

Serves four as a side

Original version

- 4 small Persian cucumbers, or 1 large English cucumber, quartered lengthwise, seeds removed, and cut into ¼-inch/6mm dice (2 cups/300g)
- 14¾ oz/420g ripe tomatoes (either 2 large heirlooms or 6 plum tomatoes), cut into ¼-inch/6mm dice
- 1 red bell pepper, cut into ¼-inch/6mm dice (1 cup/140g)
- 2 green chiles, seeded and finely chopped
- 7 green onions, finely sliced (scant 1 cup/70g)
- 1½ cups/30g parsley, very finely chopped
- ¾ cup/15g mint leaves, finely shredded
- 1 large garlic clove, crushed
- 2 lemons: finely grate the zest to get 2 tsp, then juice to get 3 tbsp
- 3 tbsp olive oil
- Salt and black pepper

Tahini version

- All the ingredients for the original
- Rounded ¼ cup/80g tahini
- 1 tbsp sumac

Yogurt version

- All the ingredients for the original
- 1 cup/250g Greek yogurt
- 1 tbsp dried mint

To make the original version, place all the ingredients in a large bowl along with 1¼ tsp of salt and a good grind of black pepper. Mix well to combine, then transfer to a serving platter or individual plates.

To make the tahini version, add the tahini, 1½ tsp of salt, and a good grind of black pepper to the bowl with all the other ingredients. Mix well to combine, transfer to a serving platter or individual plates, and sprinkle with the sumac.

To make the yogurt version, place the cucumbers, tomatoes, bell pepper, chiles, green onions, herbs, garlic, and ½ tsp of salt in a colander and set it over a bowl for 20 minutes, for the water to drain. Put the yogurt into a separate large bowl along with 2 tsp of dried mint, the lemon zest and juice, the olive oil, 1 tsp of salt, and a good grind of black pepper. Add the drained salad to the yogurt dressing and mix well to combine. Transfer to a large serving platter, or individual plates, sprinkle with the remaining 1 tsp of dried mint, and serve.

Pictured on page 94

Spicy herb salad with quick-pickled cucumber

This is a green leafy salad dialed right up to ten. It's packed with flavor, so keep what you're serving it with really simple. Pan-fried salmon or cod work really well.

Getting ahead: Make more of the seeds than you need; they keep well in an airtight container for a week or so and are lovely sprinkled over all sorts of salads or roasted vegetables.

If you want to get ahead with the salad, you can pick all the herbs and have them prepped. Don't assemble until just before serving, though; the leaves will wilt if they sit around for too long.

Serves four as a side

Seeds

1 tsp white sesame seeds, toasted
2 tbsp pumpkin seeds, toasted
1½ tsp coriander seeds, toasted and roughly crushed in a mortar and pestle
½ tsp Aleppo chile flakes (or ¼ tsp regular chile flakes)
½ tsp sumac
¼ tsp flaky sea salt

2 Persian cucumbers (1 lb 7 oz/650g)
Flaky sea salt
¼ cup/60ml cider vinegar
1 tbsp sugar
2 lemons: leave 1 whole, and juice 1 to get 1 tbsp
1 cup/20g parsley leaves (with some stem attached)
½ cup/10g tarragon leaves
¾ cup/15g dill leaves
¾ cup/15g mint leaves, roughly torn
6 green onions, thinly sliced at a sharp angle (¾ cup/60g)
2 cups/40g mâche
1½ tbsp olive oil
Black pepper

To prepare the seeds, place all the ingredients in a bowl. Mix to combine and then set aside.

Using a vegetable peeler, peel both cucumbers from top to bottom, to make long, wide, thin ribbons. Keep going until you get to the seedy center, which can be discarded (or eaten). Place the ribbons in a bowl with 1 tsp of flaky salt and mix well. Transfer to a sieve placed over a bowl and set aside for 15 minutes, for some of the liquid to drain. Put the vinegar and sugar into a separate bowl and whisk until the sugar dissolves. Add the cucumber, toss to combine, and set aside for 20 minutes, to lightly pickle.

Using a small, sharp knife, trim the top and tail off the whole lemon. Cut down along its round curves, removing the skin and bitter white pith. Release the segments from the lemon by slicing between the membranes, then roughly chop the lemon flesh. Put into a large bowl along with the lemon juice, parsley, tarragon, dill, mint, green onions, mâche, oil, 1 tsp of flaky salt, and a good grind of black pepper. Mix well to combine.

Drain the pickled cucumber, discarding its liquid, and add to the bowl along with half the seed mixture. Mix to combine, then transfer to a serving platter or individual serving plates. Top with the remaining seeds and serve at once.

Pictured on page 95

Baby gem lettuce with charred eggplant yogurt, smacked cucumber, and shatta

This works well either as a stand-alone starter or as part of a spread or side. It's lovely with some hot smoked salmon or trout. "Smacked" cucumbers sounds a bit dramatic but, really, it's just a way of bruising them to allow all the flavor to seep through to the flesh. Thanks to Ottolenghi chef Calvin Von Niebel for this salad.

Playing around: Some crumbled feta on top works very well, and if you don't have the Urfa chile flakes, just use a pinch of black nigella seeds or some black sesame seeds.

Getting ahead: Make all the elements well in advance, here, if you like; up to a day for the cucumber and the eggplant yogurt. The shatta needs to be made in advance, so you'll be all set here.

Serves four generously

Eggplant yogurt

2 large eggplants, charred (see page 336; 1 lb 2 oz/500g)
2 tbsp Greek yogurt
½ garlic clove, finely chopped
1½ tbsp lemon juice
1½ tbsp tahini
½ tsp salt

Smacked cucumber

1 medium English cucumber, peeled, sliced in half lengthwise, and watery seeds removed (6⅓ oz/180g)
1¼ cups/25g parsley, roughly chopped
1¼ cups/25g mint leaves, roughly chopped
½ garlic clove, roughly chopped
3 tbsp olive oil
¼ tsp salt

5–6 baby gem lettuces (1 lb 2 oz/500g), bases trimmed
Salt and black pepper
1½ tbsp shatta (red or green; see page 73) or rose harissa
½ tsp Urfa chile flakes (or a small pinch of black sesame seeds)

To make the eggplant yogurt, scoop the flesh out of the charred eggplant; you should have about 5¼ oz/160g. Place this in the bowl of a food processor along with the yogurt, garlic, lemon juice, tahini, and salt. Blitz for about 1 minute, until completely smooth, then set aside until needed. Clean the food processor.

To prepare the cucumber, place each half on a chopping board, cut side facing down. Using the flat side of a large knife, lightly "smack" them until bruised but still holding their shape. Cut the cucumber into roughly ½-inch/1cm dice and set aside.

Add the parsley, mint, garlic, olive oil, and salt to the food processor. Blitz for about 2 minutes, scraping down the sides a couple of times if you need to, to form a smooth paste, then add to the cucumber. Set aside for at least 20 minutes (and up to 1 day if kept in the fridge) for the flavors to infuse.

Slice each head of baby gem lengthwise to make eight long, thin wedges (per lettuce). Arrange the lettuce on a round platter, overlapping the outer and inner circles to look like the petals of a flower. Lightly sprinkle the wedges with salt and a grind of black pepper, then splatter with the eggplant yogurt. Spoon on the cucumber, drizzle with the shatta, sprinkle with the chile flakes, and serve.

Na'ama's buttermilk fattoush

Very few meals are complete in Palestine without bread. Very few dishes are served in Palestine without a chopped salad. That fattoush—which uses up day-old bread—is such a staple salad makes complete sense. You can use any flatbread—Turkish flatbread, naan, pita bread—torn into bite-size chunks. If you only have fresh flatbread that's also fine; just toast it a bit or broil it for a few minutes to dry it out. It'll firm up as it cools down.

The buttermilk is not a traditional addition, but it is the version of the salad Sami grew up on. Na'ama was Sami's mum—this was her version of the salad, and he would not change it for the world. It can be played around with, though, depending on what you have on hand—chunks of feta are, as ever, a nice addition, as are some black olives or green capers. For a more traditional version of the salad just follow the recipe, leaving out the buttermilk.

Getting ahead: Get all the chopping and prep done for this in advance if you like, and even mix the vegetables and herbs with the buttermilk, but don't assemble it with the bread until you are ready to serve. It's not a salad that likes to sit around for too long.

Ingredients note: Use Persian cucumbers (sometimes just called "mini cucumbers") if you can—they're much less watery than larger English cucumbers, so have a lot more flavor. If you have only English cucumber that's absolutely fine; just slice in half, lengthwise, scoop out the watery seed-filled core, and use the firm flesh you're left with.

Serves six

Sumac onions

½ onion, cut in half, then each half thinly sliced (¾ cup/100g)
1½ tsp sumac
1 tbsp olive oil
¼ tsp salt

2 large day-old naan, Turkish flatbread, or pita (see page 278), torn into roughly 1½-inch/4cm pieces (9 oz/250g)
1¼ cups/300ml buttermilk
3 large tomatoes, cut into roughly ½-inch/1.5cm dice (2 cups/380g)
10–11 radishes, thinly sliced (1 cup/100g)
2–3 small Persian cucumbers, or 1 medium English cucumber, peeled and cut into ½-inch/1cm dice (1⅔ cups/250g)
1 cup/20g mint leaves, roughly chopped
1 cup/20g parsley leaves, roughly chopped
2 tbsp thyme leaves
2 garlic cloves, crushed
3 tbsp lemon juice
¼ cup/60ml olive oil, plus more to serve
2 tbsp cider vinegar or white wine vinegar
1½ tsp sumac, plus ½ tsp to serve
Salt and black pepper

To make the sumac onions, place all the ingredients in a bowl. Mix well and set aside.

Put all the remaining ingredients into a large mixing bowl with 1½ tsp of salt and a good grind of black pepper. Mix well and set aside for about 10 minutes. Add half the sumac onions, mix to combine, then transfer to a large serving platter or individual plates. Sprinkle with the remaining onions, drizzle with additional olive oil, finish with the remaining ½ tsp of sumac, and serve at once.

Roasted figs and onions with radicchio and goat cheese

With figs, the riper the better when it comes to flavor and texture. The joy of roasting them, however, is that the sweetness and softness can be drawn out if the fruit is a little underripe. Here the figs and onions could be set aside to cool for 15 minutes before the salad is assembled, to prevent the cheese from melting. Don't build this pause in if you don't want to; the salad is wonderfully luxurious if you toss it straight away and let the goat cheese melt slightly.

Serve this as either a stand-alone starter or a side. It works particularly well with grilled meat or with a nutty grain salad.

Getting ahead: The dressing can be made up to three days in advance. Make more of it than you need, if you like, to have around for drizzling over other salads or dishes.

Serves four as a starter or side

Dressing
2½ tbsp balsamic vinegar
1½ tbsp pomegranate molasses
1½ tsp honey
2 garlic cloves, crushed
Flaky sea salt and black pepper
5 tbsp/75ml olive oil

12 figs, sliced in half lengthwise (15 oz/430g)
2 red onions, each sliced into 8 wedges (2⅔ cups/240g)
Flaky sea salt
1 tsp olive oil
½ head radicchio, core removed and leaves roughly torn (6⅓ oz/180g)
3 cups/60g arugula
½ cup/10g mint leaves
⅓ cup/40g walnut halves, toasted (see "Nuts," page 339) and roughly broken
Black pepper
4¼ oz/120g soft goat cheese, roughly crumbled into large chunks
1½ tsp lemon juice

Preheat the oven to 425°F. Line two baking sheets with parchment paper.

To make the dressing, mix together the vinegar, molasses, honey, garlic, ¼ tsp of flaky salt, and a good grind of black pepper. Slowly pour in the oil, whisking the whole time until combined and smooth.

Place the figs and onions in two separate bowls and add 1½ tbsp of the dressing, along with ⅛ tsp of salt and ½ tsp of oil, to each bowl. Toss well to combine, then transfer separately to the prepared baking sheets, cut side up for the figs. Both baking sheets can go into the oven at the same time: the figs need 20 minutes, or until softened and slightly caramelized, and the onions need 25–30 minutes, tossing once during baking, until they have softened and taken on some color. Remove from the oven and set aside to cool for about 15 minutes.

Put half the roasted onions into a large bowl along with the radicchio, arugula, mint, walnuts, ½ tsp of flaky salt, a good grind of black pepper, and half the remaining dressing. Toss well to combine, then transfer half the salad to a large serving platter or individual plates. Top with half the goat cheese and half the figs, cut side up. Repeat with the remaining salad, goat cheese, figs, and onions. Drizzle the remaining dressing and the lemon juice over the top and serve.

Green tabbouleh
Tabbouleh khadra

Tabbouleh is so ubiquitous across the Levant that we didn't feel the need to publish our own traditional take on this well-known salad. Rather than tweaking the bulgur and parsley version, we've offered three rather novel variations: this green one with kale, another that uses rice instead of bulgur (facing page), and a wintry-citrus-purple version (see page 104).

Sami's mother used to make a version of this to take on picnics in Jericho in the summer months. The salad was kept fresh by the addition of a few cubes of ice, wrapped up in newspaper, to the bottom of the basket. Picnics were, typically, an elaborate affair. Preparations would start the day before, with everyone coming together to chop and arrange for the movable feast.

This is as nice throughout the year as a side or part of a spread, as it is eaten on a picnic outdoors. The dressing is lemony and sharp, so it works particularly well with oily fish or rich meatballs.

Playing around: The kale can be replaced by all sorts of other cabbages, depending on what's in season; white cabbage, hispi (aka "pointed") green cabbage, spring greens, and young cauliflower with its tender leaves attached all work very well.

Getting ahead: You can prepare the salad in advance but don't add the dressing until serving, and shred (rather than chop) the herbs—this will prevent them from bruising and losing their color. The difference between chopping and shredding, for us, is the number of times the knife goes through the herb leaf. Chopping sees it getting cut many times—chop, chop, chop—whereas shredding sees the knife just go through once, in a cleaner motion.

Serves four

⅓ cup/50g bulgur (regular or whole wheat, for extra nuttiness)
5 tbsp/70ml boiling water

Dressing
⅓ cup/80ml lemon juice (from about 2 lemons)
2½ tbsp olive oil
⅛ tsp ground cinnamon
¼ tsp ground allspice
Salt and black pepper

1½ cups/100g kale leaves (or 6⅓ oz/180g if starting with kale on the stalk, which you then need to remove), finely shredded
4 cups/75g parsley (mostly leaves, not stems), finely shredded
1¾ cups/35g mint leaves, finely shredded
3 large (or 6 regular) green onions, very thinly sliced (¾ cup/60g)

Place the bulgur in a small bowl, pour in the boiling water, then set aside for about 20 minutes, or until the water has been absorbed.

To make the dressing, whisk together all the ingredients with ¾ tsp of salt and a grind of black pepper, and set aside.

Transfer the bulgur to a large mixing bowl and add all the remaining ingredients. Pour the dressing over the top, toss well, and serve.

Rice tabbouleh
Tabboulet ruz

Serves four to six

6 tbsp/75g basmati rice (or 1 cup/190g cooked rice, if starting with leftovers)
1½ tsp olive oil
¼ tsp ground turmeric
Salt
¾ cup/170ml water

Tabbouleh
4 cups/80g parsley leaves, finely chopped
1 cup/20g mint leaves, thinly shredded
2 medium very ripe tomatoes, finely chopped (1½ cups/270g)
2 small Persian cucumbers (or ½ medium English cucumber), finely chopped; no need to peel or seed (1¼ cups/180g)
6 green onions, thinly sliced (¾ cup/60g)
2 tbsp lemon juice
3 tbsp olive oil
¾ tsp salt
½ tsp ground allspice
¼ tsp ground cinnamon
1½ tsp sumac, plus ¼ tsp to serve

This is a great way to use up leftover cooked rice, if you have any (but also delicious enough to start from scratch if you don't!). If you do this you'll need to start with 1 cup/190g of cooked rice. Using leftover rice is fine, as long as you chill what you are not going to use soon after it's made, rather than letting it sit around at room temperature for too long. Take it out of the fridge about 20 minutes before you want to eat the tabbouleh, though; you don't want it to be fridge-cold. You won't need the olive oil, turmeric, or water here; just add the rice as it is with all the remaining ingredients.

Playing around: The rice can just as well be replaced by other grains, if you want. Quinoa is a gluten-free option, like the rice, and couscous and fregola also work well.

Getting ahead: Do all the chopping ahead of time, if you like—up to about 4 hours—and the rice can be made a full day ahead. It can be mixed in an hour or so before serving, but not much more than this.

Put the rice, oil, turmeric, and ⅛ tsp of salt into a small saucepan with a lid. Mix well, until the rice is well coated, then pour in the water. Bring to a boil over high heat, then decrease the heat to low. Cover the pan and cook for about 17 minutes, or until the rice is cooked. Spoon the rice onto a plate and set aside until completely cool.

To make the tabbouleh, place all the ingredients in a large mixing bowl. Add the cooked rice, mix well, then spoon onto a large serving plate. Sprinkle with the remaining ¼ tsp sumac and serve.

Winter tabbouleh with a blood orange dressing
Tabbouleh shatwieh

Blood oranges have a distinct color and tartness that make them really stand out in a salad or dressing. Their season is short, though, so regular oranges are absolutely fine for the rest of the year. As with our other tabbouleh salads (see pages 102 and 103), the bulgur can be replaced by an equal quantity of quinoa, if you like, for a gluten-free alternative. If you do this, then cook the quinoa as you normally do—in a pan of boiling water for 9 minutes or so, and rinsed under running water. Set it aside to dry, then add the olive oil and spices.

Getting ahead: This is a robust salad, so you can make it a good few hours before serving, if you want to get ahead. Leftovers are also lovely the next day.

Serves six to eight

Blood orange dressing

1 blood (or regular) orange, juiced to get 3 tbsp
2 tbsp lemon juice
¼ tsp ground cinnamon
¼ tsp allspice
2 tsp pomegranate molasses
1 tsp sugar
Salt and black pepper
½ cup plus 1 tbsp/130ml olive oil

1¼ cups/200g bulgur
½ tsp ground cinnamon
½ tsp ground allspice
1 tbsp olive oil
¾ cup plus 3 tbsp/225ml boiling water
Salt
9 oz/250g lacinato kale, stems discarded (or saved to chop up and pan-fry for another dish) and leaves roughly shredded (2¼ cups/150g)
½ small head red cabbage, core cut out and discarded, thinly sliced by hand or with a mandoline (4 cups/550g)
2 cups/40g parsley leaves, roughly chopped
1¼ cups/25g mint leaves, roughly torn
9 green onions, finely sliced (mounded 1 cup/90g)
4 blood (or 2 regular) oranges (1 lb 2 oz/500g), peeled and sliced into ¼-inch/6mm-thick rounds
Black pepper
Mounded ½ cup/85g pomegranate seeds (from ½ pomegranate)

To make the dressing, combine the orange juice, lemon juice, cinnamon, allspice, molasses, and sugar in a bowl with ⅛ tsp of salt and a good grind of black pepper. Whisk to combine, then continue to whisk as you slowly add the oil until thick and emulsified. Set aside.

Put the bulgur, cinnamon, allspice, 2 tsp of olive oil, the boiling water, and ¼ tsp of salt into a medium sauté pan with a lid. Bring to a boil over medium heat, then cover the pan, remove from the heat, and set aside for 30 minutes. Remove the lid, fluff the bulgur with a fork, and set aside to cool.

Put the kale into a bowl with the remaining 1 tsp of oil and a tiny pinch of salt. Using your hands, mix well, gently massaging the leaves, then set aside.

Tip the cooled bulgur into a very large bowl and add the cabbage, parsley, mint, green onions, oranges, ¾ tsp of salt, and a generous grind of black pepper. Mix well to combine, add the kale, and pour in the dressing. Mix just to combine, then transfer to a serving platter or individual plates. Finally, sprinkle with the pomegranate seeds and serve.

Vivien Sansour and the Palestinian Seed Library

Vivien Sansour is a strong woman. She has made a name for herself as a pioneering agriculturalist, botanist, and, perhaps most impressive, founder of the Palestinian Seed Library project. She's forty and feisty and has a vision for her country that she's growing, seed by seed. It's a vision that highlights the vital link between farmers and their land. It's a vision that suggests that the connection between people and place really means something and really matters—that it's not all just about making a quick, big buck.

The road to success was not always straightforward for Vivien. Born in Jerusalem and raised in Beit Jala, she moved with her family to North Carolina in the 1980s, to make the most of the job opportunities offered in the States. Vivien's family perhaps had some inkling of where her future interests would lie when she enrolled in a PhD program to study agricultural life sciences. Nonetheless, it came as a surprise to everyone—including Vivien herself—when she decided to drop out partway through the course and move back to her home village on the outskirts of Jerusalem. Her family thought she was crazy—she had no clear plan, nor had she prepared for the move. But Vivien had something more important than a plan—she had a vision, however indistinct in those early days, and she is a woman with the strength to stay true to her vision.

So what had sparked this new direction for Vivien? The journey all started, in fact, with a single seed. Two seeds, actually, and one slide of the herb za'atar, shown to her in a lecture hall in North Carolina.

First, the slide. Vivien was already slightly uneasy with the thrust of her PhD program. The emphasis seemed to be more on "this is what we need to be teaching farmers" rather than "this is what we should be learning from farmers." It was a slide of za'atar, though, pictured clinically alongside its botanical Latin name, that snapped her into realizing it was time to go "home." Vivien sat on a bench in the park and knew that she wanted to be smelling and feeling the za'atar she had grown up with rather than studying it from a distance. She wanted to be working with her hands, not her head. She wanted to be with the farmers, not the academics, of the world.

In Palestine, Vivien quickly landed on her feet, undertaking a two-year project while living in Jenin, in the north of the country. She'd connected with Nasser Abufarha, the owner of the Canaan cooperative (see page 250), who commissioned her to travel the region meeting, hanging out with, and writing about the cooperative's approximately thirty-five farmers.

Time and again, as Vivien traveled the region, she would hear stories about a certain large variety of watermelon called the Jadu'l. Everyone had clear memories of the Jadu'l, but it was no longer anywhere to be seen. Stories were told of people hiding in watermelon fields during the war, as the leaves were large enough to provide cover. But when Vivien tried to seek out the seed, she was told that she was "looking for a dinosaur."

Look for the dinosaur she did, though, eventually tracking down an elderly farmer/handyman in his garage workshop in Jenin. In a drawer full of nails and hammers and behind a mishmash of screws was a bag of dried-up heirloom Jadu'l watermelon seeds. They were no use to him anymore, he said—he was now working with hybrid seeds and fertilizers that were earning him more than these heirloom seeds—so Vivien was welcome to them. She put them in her bag and went on her way, feeling like a detective who'd solved her first case.

Her second "case" took place closer to home, in her local market in Bethlehem, shopping for vegetables. Vivien was seeking out the purple carrots her mother used to make for her, cooked in a tamarind sauce. Again, this vegetable of which she had such fond memories was nowhere to be found. She scoured the market, speaking to people as though she were trying to do a dodgy deal on the black market. "If I felt like a detective seeking out the Jadu'l watermelon," says Vivien, "I felt like a drug dealer looking for the purple carrots."

Eventually, she found a man who knew a man who lifted up the cloth draped over his table in the market to reveal a sack of the bounty. He couldn't give them all to her—they'd been promised elsewhere—but Vivien was allowed two carrots, which she raced home to plant in the ground, where they would sprout and produce flowers and seeds.

And so, off the back of these two heirloom vegetables, the Palestinian Seed Library was born. "Seed as metaphor for growth" might seem a bit cliché, but cliché it isn't in a place where the very existence of certain heirloom seeds and crops, and the way of life surrounding their farming, is in crisis. For those whose lives, livelihood, identity, and connection to the past are so tied up with the land, it all feels very unmetaphorical indeed. Preserving, archiving, protecting, and propagating individual heirloom seeds is a very real way to preserve, protect, and record the way of life of a people living under occupation. However tough, or even hopeless, something looks—or shriveled and dried out in the case of the Jadu'l watermelon seeds that Vivien was given—put it in the ground and nurture it and great things will happen: life will start all over again.

The threat and challenges faced by small farmers are many and complex and come from all sides. Accusations are leveled as much at the Palestinian authorities as they are at the Israeli government, for their setting up of industrial zones for which the main focus is short-term profit. The main challenge is the big incentives given to farmers to abandon their traditional way of farming—using a variety of heirloom crops and working in accordance with the seasons, for example—in favor of a mono-crop approach to farming. The choice between making a living in the short term versus holding out and preserving things for the benefit of the long term is not, for most Palestinian farmers, one they have the freedom to make. The advantages of mono-crop farming—producing strawberries year-round in greenhouses, for example—are obvious from an agribusiness and commercial point of view. The disadvantages to the land, though, and the way of life of those who farm in accordance with the seasons, are just as obvious to see, but only by those who want to see them. The outcome, in Vivien's words, is that "Palestinian farmers are being transformed from agents of their own choice to becoming day laborers on their own farms."

There are other challenges as well. Challenges that are controversial to talk about and that incite different opinions depending on to whom you talk. Vivien takes it back to 1948, when Israel was created (and even pre-1948), and points to the myth put forward by the Israelis of Palestine being a "dry area." Starting from this point, credit for the future fertility of the land—for "making the desert bloom"—can be taken by those who are seen to be farming the land, i.e., the Israelis.

Focusing instead on crops that don't need irrigation in the first place—ba'al crops (after the Canaanite fertility deity, worshipped for rain), such as figs, grapes, and olives—Vivien has no truck with this narrative. Her passion, instead, lies with the genius of her ancestors, those who were clever enough to develop a system of farming that was free, in large part, from the need for irrigation. "It kept us alive for millennia and gave the world wheat."

It's a passion she instills in the schoolkids and visitors who come to look at the seed library, which is now located in Battir, an agricultural village and UNESCO World Heritage Site just outside Jerusalem (see page 58). "So often these kids are taught to think of themselves as a colonized or victimized people; that they need to be white or English-speaking, for example, to succeed," Vivien says. She tells them, instead, what their ancestors gave to the world and sees them puff up with pride. "It's thanks to us that Italians eat pasta! Why do the kids who come in to see my seed library not know this?"

For such schoolkids, feeling proud of where you've come from is a great big step toward feeling pride and confidence in where you can go. For the farmers that Vivien met during her two years in Jenin, like Khadir Khadir (see page 250), the assistance they receive from the likes of Vivien and Nasser at Canaan enables them to feel supported, as well, in what they can do.

Conditions are tough, no doubt, and "the reality is true," says Vivien. "But it's also true that we have the seeds and in these seeds we have our DNA." In terms of messaging, it's all a long way from a dusty slide pulled up in a lecture hall that afternoon back in North Carolina. At the time of writing, Vivien was propagating three seeds: the white cucumber, the "tall dark" Abu Samra wheat, and an heirloom tomato. It's exciting to think how much more can be grown.

Roasted cauliflower and charred eggplant with tomato sauce

We spent three nights in Haifa on one of our trips and spent two of those eating supper at the same restaurant, Fattoush, in town. The reason we went back two nights in a row was because we ate a version of this salad the first night and then went to bed dreaming about it. We went back the next night and duly ordered a whole portion each. All the elements here are delicious in and of themselves; the combination of all three is positively wonderful.

Getting ahead: You can char and marinate the eggplant a day or two ahead, then finish the dish off on the day of serving.

Serves four generously

4 large eggplants, charred (see page 336; 2 lb 2 oz/1kg)
1 garlic clove, crushed
1½ tsp lemon juice
2 tbsp cider vinegar
Salt
1 large (or 2 medium) cauliflower, cut into roughly 1¼-inch/3cm florets (8 cups/800g)
3 tbsp olive oil
1 tsp coriander seeds
¾ tsp ground turmeric
Black pepper

Tomato sauce

3 large tomatoes, cut into ¼-inch/6mm dice (1⅓ cups/240g)
½ cup/10g parsley, roughly chopped
1 tbsp oregano leaves, roughly chopped
2 tbsp olive oil
2 tbsp lemon juice
½ tsp salt

¼ cup/5g mint leaves (small ones if you can, or larger ones, shredded)
¼ cup/5g parsley leaves, whole or roughly chopped

Scoop the flesh out of the charred eggplants; you should have about 1 lb 2 oz/500g. Place in a colander set over a bowl and set aside for at least 1 hour (or overnight, in the fridge), to drain. Put the drained eggplant flesh into a medium mixing bowl and, using your hands, pull it apart to create long, thin strands. Add the garlic, lemon juice, vinegar, and 1 tsp of salt. Mix to combine and then set aside (in the fridge if you are making this a day ahead).

Preheat the oven to 425°F. Line a baking sheet with parchment paper.

Put the cauliflower into a large bowl along with the oil, coriander seeds, turmeric, ¾ tsp of salt, and a good grind of black pepper. Mix well to combine, then spread out on the prepared baking sheet. Roast for 30 minutes, until the cauliflower is golden and tender. Remove from the oven and set aside to cool to room temperature.

To make the sauce, while the cauliflower is roasting, place all the sauce ingredients in a bowl. Mix to combine.

Spread the eggplant on a serving plate that has a lip and arrange the cauliflower on top. Spoon on the sauce, sprinkle with the mint and parsley, and serve.

Pictured on page 112

Roasted eggplant, feta yogurt, Aleppo chile, and pistachios

There are lots more sheep and goats than there are cows in Palestine, as cows are not traditionally reared. Much of the yogurt and cheese, therefore, is made from sheep or goat milk. It's tangy—sour, even—in a way that works well against the rich "meatiness" of roasted eggplant. The further the yogurt or cheese is taken—whether hung, in the case of labneh (see page 338), or fermented, in the case of kishek (see page 337)—the more intense the tanginess. Here—in this dish, which features often on the Ottolenghi menu—we use feta. It has a similar tangy-sour flavor profile at the same time as being instantly ready to use.

Playing around: The feta yogurt and other toppings work equally well on other roasted vegetables—roast wedges of beet or butternut squash, for example—as they do with the eggplant.

Getting ahead: If you want to get ahead, all the various elements can be made up to a day in advance. Keep the eggplant and the feta yogurt in the fridge, separately, returning the eggplant to room temperature before serving.

Serves four as a starter or side

4 large eggplants (2 lb 2 oz/1kg)
¼ cup/60ml olive oil
Salt and black pepper
2 tbsp pistachios, lightly toasted (see "Nuts," page 339) and roughly chopped
¼ cup/5g mint leaves
¼ cup/5g dill leaves
¼ tsp Aleppo chile flakes (or ⅛ tsp regular chile flakes)

Feta yogurt

2 tsp whole milk
1 tbsp lemon juice
2½ oz/75g feta, finely crumbled
1¼ cups/300g Greek yogurt
⅛ tsp salt

Preheat the oven to 450°F. Line a baking sheet with parchment paper.

Cut each eggplant, lengthwise, into wedges. They should be about ¾ inch/2cm wide at the base. Place them in a large bowl with the oil, ¼ tsp of salt, and a good grind of black pepper. Mix to combine, then spread out on the prepared baking sheet. Roast for 30 minutes, until cooked through and golden brown, then remove from the oven and set aside to cool.

To make the feta yogurt, put the milk, lemon juice, feta, yogurt, and salt into a bowl. Whisk well to combine, breaking apart the feta until it almost disintegrates, then keep in the fridge until ready to serve.

Arrange the eggplant wedges on a large platter or individual serving plates and spoon on the feta yogurt. Top with the pistachios, mint, dill, and chile flakes and serve.

Pictured on page 113

Roasted squash and zucchini with whipped feta and pistachios

This is great as either a starter or as part of a spread. It also works as a side dish, served alongside meatballs or roast chicken. Use yellow zucchini if you can; the clash of color looks great with the butternut squash.

Playing around: You don't need to do both the squash and the zucchini, if you'd prefer to have just one or the other. You can also play around with other vegetables—carrots work just as well as the squash.

Getting ahead: Roast the squash and zucchini a few hours before serving and mix them with the dressing, they're happy to sit around for up to 4 hours, at room temperature, before serving. The whipped feta and yogurt mix can also be made up to a day ahead and kept in the fridge until ready to serve.

Serves four

½ small butternut squash (unpeeled), sliced lengthwise, seeds scooped out, then each half cut crosswise into ¾-inch/1.5cm slices (1 lb 3 oz/550g)
2½ tbsp olive oil
Salt and black pepper
3–4 yellow (or green) zucchini (1 lb 2 oz/500g), sliced in half lengthwise and then crosswise (to get 4 pieces from each), then each piece cut in half again, lengthwise, to make wedges
1 tbsp honey
2 garlic cloves, crushed
1 tbsp cider vinegar
¼ cup/5g tarragon leaves, roughly chopped
1 cup/250g ricotta
3 tbsp Greek yogurt
3½ oz/100g feta, roughly crumbled
1 lemon: finely grate the zest to get 1 tsp, then juice to get 1½ tbsp
⅓ cup/50g pistachios, toasted (see "Nuts," page 339) and roughly chopped
1½ tsp coriander seeds, toasted and roughly crushed in a mortar and pestle
¾ tsp Aleppo chile flakes (or ½ tsp regular chile flakes)
About ¼ cup/5g small mint leaves

Preheat the oven to 475°F. Line two baking sheets with parchment paper.

Put the squash into a large bowl with 1½ tbsp of oil, ¾ tsp of salt, and a good grind of black pepper. Mix well, then spread out flat on a prepared baking sheet. Bake for 25 minutes, turning over halfway through so that both sides get some color. Remove from the oven and set aside to cool. Leave the oven on.

While the squash is cooking, grease a grill pan and place over high heat. Put the zucchini into a large bowl with the remaining 1 tbsp of oil, ½ tsp of salt, and a good grind of black pepper. Once the grill pan is smoking hot, add the zucchini, in two batches if you need to, and cook for about 3 minutes, rotating the wedges so that they have grill marks on all sides. Transfer to the second prepared baking sheet and bake for 5 minutes, or until they're cooked through but still retain a bite.

Put the honey, half the garlic, the vinegar, tarragon, and ⅛ tsp of salt into a large bowl and mix to combine. Add the squash and zucchini and stir very gently, to coat. Set aside until needed.

Put the ricotta, yogurt, 2¼ oz/60g of feta, the lemon zest and juice, the remaining garlic, ⅛ tsp of salt, and a good grind of black pepper into a bowl. Mix well until smooth, using a whisk to break apart the feta. Spread the mixture out on a large serving platter and top with the zucchini and squash. Scatter with the remaining 1¼ oz/40g feta, followed by the pistachios, coriander seeds, and chile flakes. Top with the mint leaves and serve.

Yogurt-roasted cauliflower with quick-pickled chiles, golden raisins, and red onions

Roasting cauliflower florets in spiced yogurt makes them feel almost tandoori-like. It creates a lovely crisp crust that works so well against everything else in the dish—the soft sweetness of the golden raisins, the creamy crunch of the pine nuts. This works well either as a stand-alone salad or served along with some chicken and rice.

Getting ahead: The cauliflower can be roasted ahead of time, but don't mix the salad together until you are ready to serve; the herbs will wilt if they sit around for too long.

Serves four as a side

⅓ cup/85g Greek yogurt
2 garlic cloves, crushed
¼ tsp ground turmeric
1½ tsp paprika
2 tsp ground cumin
5 tbsp/75ml olive oil
3 tbsp lemon juice
Salt and black pepper
1 large head cauliflower, leaves and all (2½ lb/1.2kg)
¼ cup/30g golden raisins
½ red chile, seeded and thinly sliced (1 tbsp/10g)
½ red onion, cut into thin rounds (mounded ½ cup/60g)
4 tsp cider vinegar
¼ cup/25g pine nuts, toasted (see "Nuts," page 339)
½ cup/10g parsley leaves
¼ cup/5g mint leaves

Preheat the oven to 475°F. Line two baking sheets with parchment paper.

Put the yogurt, garlic, turmeric, paprika, cumin, 2 tbsp of oil, 1 tbsp of lemon juice, 1 tsp of salt, and a good grind of black pepper into a large bowl. Whisk well to combine, then set aside.

Pull the leaves away from the cauliflower; they'll have different lengths, but keep their shape intact. Slice the larger leaves down the middle, vertically, and place them (with all the other leaves) in a medium bowl with 1½ tsp of oil, ⅛ tsp of salt, and a good grind of black pepper. Mix to combine, then spread out on a prepared baking sheet. Set aside.

Remove the stalk from the cauliflower and slice it into roughly ¼-inch/6mm-thick pieces. Cut the cauliflower into large florets, about 2½ inches/6cm, and add, along with the stalks, to the bowl of yogurt. Mix until well coated, then transfer to the second prepared baking sheet, spreading the pieces out so they're not overlapping. Transfer both sheets to the oven. Bake the leaves for 15 minutes, until they're softened and charred, and the cauliflower for 30 minutes, or until cooked through and charred in places. Remove from the oven and set both aside to cool completely.

While the cauliflower is roasting, put the golden raisins, chile, onion, vinegar, and a tiny pinch of salt into a large bowl (the cauliflower will all be added to this). Mix to combine, then set aside for about 20 minutes, to pickle.

Once the cauliflower is completely cool, add it, with the leaves, to the bowl along with the pine nuts, herbs, remaining 2½ tbsp of oil, and remaining 2 tbsp of lemon juice. Mix well to combine, then transfer to a serving platter and serve at once.

Chunky zucchini and tomato salad
Mafghoussa

Serves six

2 lb 2 oz/1kg zucchini (either 10 small pale green ones, ideally, or 5 large darker green ones), trimmed and sliced in half lengthwise (or quartered lengthwise, if large)
5 large very ripe tomatoes (1¾ lb/800g), cut in half crosswise
3 tbsp olive oil
Salt and black pepper
1¼ cups/300g Greek yogurt
1 large garlic clove, crushed
1 lemon: finely grate the zest to get 1 tsp, then juice to get 2 tbsp
1 tbsp date molasses, plus 2 tsp
2 red chiles, seeded and finely chopped
¼ cup/5g mint leaves, roughly chopped, plus 1 tbsp small leaves
¾ cup/15g parsley, roughly chopped, plus 1 tbsp chopped

Mafghoussa, meaning "mashed" in Arabic, is more of a spread than a salad. We've kept our version nice and chunky but, if you want a spread, the vegetables can be lightly crushed. Either way, it's delicious as it is—spooned up with some pita—or served alongside all sorts of grilled meats, rice dishes, and other salads. Some lightly toasted and roughly chopped walnuts mixed in are also a really nice addition.

The vegetables for mafghoussa are traditionally charred on the embers in a taboon oven, the clay (and often communal) oven found outdoors in Palestinian village homes (see page 341 for more on taboon). The dish is great at a summer barbecue, when tomatoes and zucchini are at their best and the grill will be out and ready. In the absence of either a taboon oven or the right weather for a barbecue, a grill pan set over high heat on the stove also, happily, works very well.

Getting ahead: The vegetables can be grilled, chopped, and left to drain the day before serving, if you want to get ahead. Mix them with the yogurt and herbs on the actual day, though.

Preheat the oven to 425°F. Line two baking sheets with parchment paper, place a ridged grill pan over high heat, and ventilate the kitchen well.

Spread the zucchini and tomatoes on the prepared baking sheets, cut side up. Brush with 2 tbsp of oil (in total) and season with ½ tsp of salt and plenty of black pepper.

By now the grill pan should be piping hot. Place a few of the zucchini on the pan, cut side down, and cook for 4–5 minutes; the zucchini should be nicely charred on one side. If you've quartered your zucchini lengthwise, adjust them on the grill pan halfway through so that both exposed sides get charred. Return them to the baking sheet, arranging them all cut side up, and continue with the remaining zucchini and tomatoes in the same way—the tomatoes just need a minute or so less on the grill. Transfer the vegetables to the oven and roast for 20 minutes, until the zucchini are very tender and the tomatoes are cooked through but still retain their shape. Remove the baking sheets from the oven and allow the vegetables to cool down slightly. Chop them roughly into 1-inch/2.5cm pieces and let drain in a colander for 15 minutes.

Meanwhile, whisk the yogurt, garlic, lemon zest, lemon juice, 1 tbsp date molasses, and two-thirds of the chiles in a large mixing bowl. Add the chopped vegetables, ¼ cup/5g mint, ¾ cup/15g parsley, 1 tsp of salt, and plenty of pepper. Stir well, then transfer to a large, shallow serving plate. Spread it all over, then garnish with the remaining 1 tbsp parsley, one-third chile, and 1 tbsp mint leaves. Finally, drizzle with the remaining 2 tsp of date molasses and remaining 1 tbsp of oil and serve.

Roasted eggplant with tamarind and cilantro
Batinjan bil tamer hindi

Tara's kids are always asking which of them is her favorite child. "I have a favorite daughter," she tells only daughter, Scarlett. "And definitely a favorite oldest son," she explains to Scarlett's twin brother, Theo. "And, of course, my favorite youngest child will always be Casper," she says to the little one, before he punches the air and runs off to make some noise. When it comes to vegetable "favorites," though, no such qualifications are needed: it's eggplant all the way. So loved is the mighty eggplant, and in this dish in particular, that they swiftly became Tara's new screensaver for her phone when they were shot for the book. Tara's favorite daughter—who'd previously taken the coveted screensaver spot—was distinctly unimpressed to have been bumped out by a vegetable.

This can be served either as a veggie main, with some rice and yogurt spooned alongside, or as a side to all sorts of things—some pan-fried tofu, for example, or a lamb chop.

Getting ahead: This is a dish that can be made and assembled a good few hours before serving; it's happy to sit around for up to 5 hours. It can even be made the day before, if you like. Keep it in the fridge overnight, and either warm it through for a few minutes (before sprinkling with the fresh cilantro) or bring it back to room temperature before serving.

Serves six as a side or part of a spread, or four as a main

3½ oz/100g tamarind pulp (or 6 tbsp/70g tamarind paste, if starting with ready-made)
½ cup/120ml boiling water
4 large eggplants, sliced in half lengthwise (2 lb 2 oz/1kg)
6 tbsp/90ml olive oil
Salt and black pepper
4 large garlic cloves, crushed
2 lemons: finely grate the zest of both to get 1½ tsp, then juice to get ¼ cup/60ml
2 tsp sugar
½ tsp coriander seeds, lightly toasted, then roughly crushed in a mortar and pestle
¼ cup/5g cilantro leaves

Preheat the oven to 425°F. Line a baking sheet with parchment paper.

Place the tamarind pulp in a bowl and pour in the boiling water. Set aside for 20 minutes or so, stirring or squeezing the pulp into the water from time to time. (If starting with ready-made paste, just place in a bowl.)

Use a small, sharp knife to make four or five deep, parallel incisions in the cut side of each eggplant half. Don't go so far through the flesh that you reach the skin on the other side. Repeat at a 45-degree angle to create a diamond pattern. Place the eggplants on the prepared baking sheet, cut side up, and brush evenly with ¼ cup/60ml of oil. Sprinkle with ¾ tsp of salt and a good grind of black pepper and roast for about 35 minutes, turning the sheet around halfway through roasting, until the eggplants are cooked through, soft, and golden brown.

While the eggplants are roasting, pass the tamarind mixture through a fine-mesh sieve into a bowl; it should weigh about 2½ oz/70g. The seeds and pulp left behind in the sieve can be discarded. Add the remaining 2 tbsp of oil along with the garlic, lemon juice, sugar, ¾ tsp of salt, and a grind of black pepper to the tamarind. Mix well and then, when the eggplants have been roasting for 35 minutes, generously spoon this sauce on their cut sides. Sprinkle with the coriander seeds and return to the oven for a final 5 minutes. There will be a bit of excess sauce on the baking sheet but that's fine; you can just spoon this over the eggplants when serving.

Remove the eggplants from the oven and allow to cool for 10 minutes (or longer if serving at room temperature) before transferring to a serving platter or individual plates. Sprinkle with the lemon zest and cilantro and serve.

Summer squash and chickpeas cooked in yogurt
Kousa bil laban

Cooking vegetables in yogurt is common all over Palestine but particularly characteristic in the north, due to the Syrian and Lebanese influences. Cooking things in a sauce of yogurt (rather than, say, a tomato sauce) happens due to practical reasons—there is so much yogurt around that it's a building block of the traditional cuisine—but, also, because it's such a good way to enrich a dish and make it luxurious. Here, for example, two thoroughly humble ingredients—chickpeas and summer squash—are totally transformed into something rich and comforting. Don't start with a large summer squash, they can taste bitter and their flesh can be watery. If you can't find summer squash, use an equal weight of zucchini. If you do this, they'll just need a couple of minutes less cooking.

Serve this either warm or at room temperature, as a side or as part of a spread.

Getting ahead: This is best eaten the day it's made. Leftovers are fine for a couple of days, though. Just bring back to room temperature or gently warm through before eating.

Serves four to six

- 1 small summer squash or zucchini (1¾ lb/800g)
- 5 tbsp/75ml olive oil
- 1 onion, roughly chopped (1 cup/140g)
- 1 green chile, finely chopped
- 1⅔ cups/400g Greek yogurt
- 1 egg yolk
- 1 x 14-oz/400g can cooked chickpeas, drained and rinsed (1¾ cups/240g)
- Salt and black pepper
- 2 large garlic cloves, crushed
- 1 cup/20g cilantro leaves, finely chopped
- ½ tsp Aleppo chile flakes, or ¼ tsp regular chile flakes (optional)

Top and tail the summer squash, then quarter the whole squash lengthwise. Using a small knife, cut away and discard the core flesh and seeds. Cut the remaining firmer flesh into ½-inch/1.5cm dice and set aside.

Put 2 tbsp of oil into a large saucepan, about 8 inches/20cm wide, and place over medium heat. Add the onion and cook for 5 minutes, stirring a few times. Add the chile, cook for 1 minute, then add the summer squash. Cook for another 5 minutes, stirring a few times, until the squash has become slightly greener and starts to soften.

Put the yogurt and egg yolk into the small bowl of a food processor (or a countertop blender) and blend for 30 seconds, until smooth and runny. Pour into a small saucepan and place over high heat for about 3 minutes, stirring constantly with a wooden spoon, until the yogurt starts to bubble. Take care it does not come to a boil, as this will cause the yogurt to split. Once hot, add this to the pan of summer squash, along with the chickpeas, 1½ tsp of salt, and a grind of black pepper. Cook gently over low heat, stirring from time to time, for another 5 minutes. Keep an eye on the yogurt toward the end of cooking; it will split if it gets too hot.

Meanwhile, put the remaining 3 tbsp of oil into a small saucepan and place over medium heat. Once hot, add the garlic and cook for 1–2 minutes, stirring frequently, until the garlic is a very light golden brown. Add the cilantro, stir for 5 seconds, and then set aside.

Spoon the summer squash and sauce into a deep bowl (or individual serving bowls) and top with the garlic-cilantro mix. Sprinkle with the chile flakes, if desired, and serve either warm or at room temperature.

Zucchini, garlic, and yogurt
M'tawaneh

M'tawaneh is traditionally made with the scooped-out flesh of zucchini after they've been hollowed in order to be stuffed. Here, however, we're short-cutting the process by starting with the whole zucchini, skin and all. It has a bit more texture as a result, which we love, making it more of a veggie side or condiment than a completely smooth dip. The result is rich, light, and comforting all at once.

Serve this either as it is, scooped up with some warm pita for a light lunch with some black olives, or as a side to all sorts of things. Pan-fried fish, grilled chicken, or roasted beets, for example, all work particularly well.

Keeping notes: This keeps well in the fridge for up to three days.

Serves four as a dip or side

2 tbsp olive oil, plus more to serve
1 onion, finely chopped (1 cup/150g)
4 large zucchini, chopped into ½-inch/1cm dice (6⅔ cups/800g)
Salt
⅔ cup/200g Greek yogurt
3 large garlic cloves, crushed
½ tsp dried mint
1 tsp dried pink peppercorns (not the kind in brine), roughly crushed in a mortar and pestle

---

Put the oil into a medium sauté pan and place over medium-high heat. Add the onion and cook for about 5 minutes, stirring from time to time, until it has started to soften. Add the zucchini and ½ tsp of salt, and cook for 10 minutes or so, stirring a few times, until the zucchini are soft. Remove the pan from the heat and set aside to cool.

Put the yogurt, garlic, and ¼ tsp of salt into a large bowl and mix to combine. Once the zucchini are cool, add to the yogurt and stir to combine. Transfer to either a serving platter with a lip or a shallow bowl. Sprinkle with the dried mint and peppercorns, drizzle with some olive oil, and serve.

Braised fava beans with olive oil and lemon
Foul akdar

This is a very simple dish but, thanks to the generous amount of lemon juice and the even more generous olive oil, also wonderfully sharp and rich. It's lovely as it is, warm or at room temperature, with a bowl of rice or some plain yogurt alongside, or as a side or as part of a mezzeh spread. Leftovers are also delicious and keep well for a couple of days, so double or triple the batch if you have a glut of beans.

Ingredients note: For those used to taking fava beans out of both their pods and their individual fibrous skins, braising them whole will be a revelation. The younger and more tender the beans that you start with, the more melt-in-the-mouth they will feel.

Serves four as a side or part of a spread

6 tbsp/90ml olive oil
1 onion, finely chopped (1 cup/150g)
3 garlic cloves, crushed
1 lb 5 oz/600g fresh fava beans, stalks trimmed and stringy part removed, then cut on the diagonal into roughly 1½-inch/4cm-long pieces
¾ cup plus 2 tbsp/200ml chicken or vegetable stock
Salt and black pepper
1 lemon: finely grate the zest to get ½ tsp, then juice to get 2 tbsp
¼ tsp dried mint
½ cup/10g parsley leaves, roughly chopped
½ cup/10g mint leaves, roughly chopped just before serving

Put the oil into a large sauté pan with a lid and place over medium-high heat. Add the onion and cook for about 7 minutes, stirring occasionally, until soft and golden brown. Add the garlic and cook for another 30 seconds, until fragrant, then add the fava beans, stock, 1½ tsp of salt, and a good grind of black pepper. Bring to a simmer, then decrease the heat to medium-low and cook for about 25 minutes, covered, until the beans are very soft.

Stir in the lemon juice and dried mint and set aside for just 10 minutes, if serving warm, or to cool, if serving at room temperature. Scatter the parsley, chopped mint, and lemon zest on top and serve.

Spiced chickpeas
Balilah

As a kid, Sami used to snack on balilah on the way home from school in East Jerusalem. Traditionally, it's a street-food piled into cone-shaped newspaper packages and served warm, but it also works as a salad, served warm or at room temperature. As a salad, it works with all sorts of things: some grilled fish or chicken with a simple green salad or just wedges of roasted butternut squash, for example.

Getting ahead: This is served either warm, soon after assembly, or at room temperature; it can happily sit around for a few hours. Leftovers are also great for the lunchbox the next day. Keep in the fridge overnight and bring back to room temperature before eating.

Serves four as a salad, or six as part of a spread

1 cup plus 2 tbsp/200g dried chickpeas, soaked overnight in twice their volume of water and 1 tsp baking soda (or 2 x 14-oz/400g cans cooked chickpeas)
Salt
2 lemons
1½ tsp cumin seeds, lightly toasted and roughly crushed in a mortar and pestle
1½ tsp coriander seeds, lightly toasted and roughly crushed in a mortar and pestle
5 tbsp/75ml olive oil
½ cup/10g parsley leaves, roughly chopped, plus a few leaves
½ cup/10g mint leaves, roughly torn, plus a few leaves
3 green onions, thinly sliced (⅓ cup/30g)
¾ tsp Aleppo chile flakes (or ½ tsp regular chile flakes)
½ red onion, very finely chopped (½ cup/70g)
Black pepper

Drain the chickpeas, place in a large saucepan, and cover with plenty of cold water. Bring to a boil over high heat, then decrease the heat to medium-low. Simmer for 40–60 minutes (or 5–10 minutes, if starting with canned), skimming any foam off the surface of the water a few times, until the chickpeas are very soft but still retain their shape. Toward the end of the cooking time—5–10 minutes before they are ready—add ½ tsp (or ¼ tsp, if starting with canned) of salt.

Meanwhile, finely zest one of the lemons to get 2 tsp zest. Set this aside in a large bowl (the chickpeas will end up here). Peel the same lemon, cutting away the bitter white pith. Roughly chop the flesh, removing any seeds, and add this, along with all of the juices, to the bowl with the zest. Halve the remaining lemon, lengthwise, and squeeze the juice of one half into the bowl. Slice the remaining half into very thin slices, discarding any seeds as you go along, and add to the bowl as well.

Drain the chickpeas once they are cooked and, while they are still hot, add them to the lemon in the bowl. Add the cumin seeds, coriander seeds, oil, chopped herbs, green onions, half the chile flakes, half the onion, 1½ tsp of salt (or just 1 tsp if starting with canned chickpeas), and a good grind of black pepper. Mix well to combine, then transfer to a serving platter. Top with the remaining onion and chile flakes and the remaining parsley and mint leaves. Serve either warm or at room temperature.

Lentils with tahini and crispy onions
Adass bil tahineh w al basal

This is a really useful and completely addictive side to all sorts of grilled vegetable, meat, or fish dishes. It's nutty and creamy from the tahini and almonds, hearty and wholesome from the lentils, and, thanks to the crispy fried onions, very hard indeed to stop eating.

Getting ahead: You can make the lentils a day ahead, if you like, adding the nuts and crispy onions just before serving. Keep the lentils in the fridge but, as always, bring them back to room temperature before serving. The onions can also be made a day ahead (and stored separately from the lentils). They need to be kept at room temperature, in an airtight container.

Serves six to eight

1¾ cups/350g green lentils

Crispy onions

About 1⅔ cups/400ml sunflower oil
2 onions, cut in half, then each half thinly sliced (2½ cups/300g)
1½ tbsp cornstarch
Salt

¼ cup/60g tahini
2 large garlic cloves, crushed
2 large green chiles, finely chopped
¼ cup/60ml lemon juice (from about 2 lemons)
2½ tsp ground cumin
Salt
Mounded ½ cup/60g sliced almonds, toasted (see "Nuts," page 339)
¾ cup/15g parsley leaves, roughly chopped
¼ cup/60ml olive oil
½ tsp paprika

Put the lentils into a large saucepan and pour in 6⅓ cups/1.5L of water. Set aside for 1 hour, to soak.

To make the crispy onions, put the oil into a large frying or sauté pan—you want it to rise about ¾ inch/2cm up the side of the pan. Place over medium-high heat. Line a plate with paper towels. Mix the onions with the cornstarch, then, when the oil is hot, add about one-third of the onions. Cook for 8–14 minutes (timing varies greatly depending on how hot your oil is), stirring from time to time, until the onions are really golden and crispy. Transfer to the prepared plate—spread them out to not get soggy—and sprinkle lightly with salt. Set aside while you continue with the remaining onions.

Bring the pan of lentils to a boil over high heat, then decrease the heat to medium-low and cook for about 15 minutes, until the lentils are soft but still retain a bite. Drain the lentils and rinse straightaway under cold water, to stop the cooking. Drain again, then tip into a large mixing bowl along with the tahini, garlic, chiles, lemon juice, cumin, and 1½ tsp of salt. Mix well to combine, then set aside for 10 minutes.

When ready to serve, put half the crispy onions, most of the toasted almonds, and a third of the parsley into a wide serving bowl. Mix to combine, then add the lentils. Give everything a gentle stir, and top with the remaining onions, almonds, and parsley. Drizzle with the olive oil and sprinkle with the paprika.

Sautéed tomatoes
Galayet banadoura

Serves four as part of a mezzeh spread

1¾ lb/800g plum tomatoes (8 or 9)
6 tbsp/90ml olive oil
1 green chile, halved lengthwise, then roughly chopped, seeds and all
8 garlic cloves: 2 crushed, 6 very thinly sliced lengthwise
Salt and black pepper
½ tsp dried mint
2 tbsp pine nuts
¼ cup/5g mint leaves, shredded
¼ cup/5g parsley leaves, roughly chopped

This is somewhere between a tomato dip and stewed tomatoes. Either way, it's rich, silky, and really versatile. Serve it either as part of a mezzeh, with some crusty white bread to mop it all up, or as a side to myriad dishes. Any grilled meat or fish, some pan-fried tofu, and all sorts of grain and pulse dishes work well. It's also really delicious as a pasta sauce.

Getting ahead: The cooked tomatoes keep well in the fridge for up to four days. The garlic and pine nuts can also be prepared well ahead and kept at room temperature, ready to be spooned on when assembling the dish.

Core the tomatoes and score the base with an "X"—this makes it easier to remove their skins. There are two ways to do this. The first is to bring a medium saucepan of water to a simmer over medium-high heat, and lower in the tomatoes. Cook for 1–2 minutes, or until the skins start to shrink back, then remove them with a slotted spoon. While the tomatoes are still warm, peel off and discard the skins. The second way is to place them in a large bowl and cover with boiling water. Let soak for 1–2 minutes, then drain. Again, while the tomatoes are still warm, peel off and discard the skins. Once peeled, slice each tomato into six wedges and set aside.

Put 3 tbsp of oil into a large sauté pan and place over medium-high heat. Add the tomatoes, chile, crushed garlic, 1 tsp of salt, and a good grind of black pepper. Cook for about 18 minutes, stirring occasionally, until the tomatoes have broken down and the sauce has thickened. Stir in the dried mint and transfer to a serving platter. Set aside to cool slightly.

Meanwhile, put the sliced garlic and remaining 3 tbsp of oil into a small frying pan and place over medium heat. Cook for about 4 minutes, or until the garlic starts to become lightly golden. Add the pine nuts and cook for another 3 minutes, or until they have taken on some color. Pour the mixture, along with the oil, over the tomatoes and garnish with the mint and parsley leaves. Serve warm or at room temperature.

The Tent of Nations: one family's story of peaceful resistance

Sumud is the Arabic word for "steadfastness": the stubborn, patient insistence that, despite the odds, things will work out. The Tent of Nations, a small farm 7 kilometers southwest of Bethlehem, is a case study in Palestinian sumud. The tale of the farm is one-of-a-kind but only by degree. The issues at the heart of the story—namely the threat Palestinians feel to their autonomy over, ownership of, and freedom within the land of their ancestors—play out for family after family, day after day, all throughout the Occupied Palestinian Territories (see page 339).

The Tent of Nations is home to the Nassar family. Daoud and Amal are husband and wife and they live on the land with their extended family, including Amal's brother, Daher, and their mother, Milada. It's been their home since 1916, when Amal's grandfather bought the land. Amal's father, Bishara, was born in one of the eight caves within the land. The family has been living there, simply, ever since. At the same time, they've been in court since the early 1990s—around thirty years at the time of writing—peacefully and legally defending their right to stay there. Steadfast, they remain.

At the heart of the long-standing case is the question of land ownership. This goes back to the Oslo Accords, written up in 1993, which stated that the West Bank was to be divided into three distinct areas: A, B, and C. On paper, the thinking was simple; dividing the land up this way would make it clear who was allowed to be where, and who was responsible for the upkeep, protection, and governance of each particular area. Area A, 18 percent of the West Bank, remained under Palestinian Authority (PA) control and security authority. Area B, about 22 percent of the West Bank, was to be shared responsibility, with civil administration under PA control, and exclusive security control under the Israeli jurisdiction (with limited cooperation from Palestinian police). Area C, by far the biggest chunk of land at 63 percent of the West Bank, remained under full direct Israeli civil and security control. According to those who drew up the accords, this all made sense and seemed pretty fair, with a plan in place to ensure that full Palestinian governance was achieved by 1999.

Twenty years later, that goal has clearly been missed along the way, and the effects are felt far and wide. Palestinians in Area C feel particularly let down by a system that does little to protect their services and needs. Area C contains most of the West Bank's natural resources and open areas, but the distribution of these

resources—most noticeably water and the freedom to build—is far from equal. If a Palestinian in Area C needs a police car or an ambulance or trash collection, chances are there won't be one rushing to them anytime soon.

The Tent of Nations is in Area C. It's surrounded by five Israeli settlements. The nearest is close enough that the Nassar family can hear the voices of the settlers on the farm, carried down the valley. The largest settlement, Beitar Illit, has a population of more than 40,000. The settlements are all deemed illegal under international law, a fact refuted by the Israeli government. If the feeling of being encroached upon was mainly visual for the Nassar family, as the settlements were built and expanded throughout the 1980s, it became actual in the early 1990s, when the military authorities declared that more than 90 percent of the farm belonged to the State of Israel. A loophole had been found in the system and was set to be exploited. Unfortunately for the Israelis, however, the Nassars had the faith and, crucially, the paperwork to start their long, determined but peaceable battle. Both their deep faith and robust paperwork were thanks to Amal's grandfather, who'd had the unusual foresight to register the land in 1924.

The loophole was a piece of legislation dating back to the Ottoman Empire, which said that if a piece of land is considered "uncultivated" for over three years (even if this is due to its owners being denied the access to cultivate it) then "ownership" will revert automatically to the state. The Nassars received their first of many demolition orders. Peacefully, they refused to budge. Peacefully, they have been in court ever since.

This is just one of the cases keeping them in court. Two others are against the military, following the destruction of their fruit trees in 2014 and the hundreds of olive trees that have since been uprooted. Demolishing these trees is an act of destruction in two ways. On one hand, it's an actual way of preventing the land from being properly cultivated, thus creating "facts on the ground" that can be used by the Israeli authorities in court. And on the other hand, in a land where olive trees are so deeply rooted in the identity and livelihood of the people, it's also, symbolically, as well as literally, devastating.

Again, the frustrating irony for a Palestinian trying to take action in Area C is that, because the officials call the shots, the officials can, and do, make it as madly difficult as possible for the family to proceed in court. The situation is Kafkaesque. Amal has lots of stories about attempts that have been made to thwart their legal efforts and progress. After ten years in the military courts, for example, they were told that their Palestinian lawyer was not eligible to contest the case in Israel's Supreme Court because he carried West Bank identity papers. "Consequently," Amal says, "we found an Israeli firm willing to take it on." On a separate occasion, they were asked to bring witnesses to support the claim that the land had been farmed over three generations. They rented a bus for more than thirty local villagers to go to the military court near Ramallah. After they waited for five hours in the heat of the sun, a single soldier came out and told them, "We don't want witnesses; go home."

"At every turn," says Daoud, "we are given the option to get violent or to resign and leave. At every turn we choose not to take these options. Nobody can force us to hate. We refuse to be victims and we refuse to be enemies. We want to live in peace and dignity on our own land." If this all sounds a bit syrupy, then we are not doing a good enough job conveying the contrast between the reality Amal and Daoud have to put up with on a daily basis, and the grace, hope, and faith with which they do so.

The family has a strong Christian faith, rooted in the "turn the other cheek" line of thinking rather than the "eye for an eye" school of thought. Their faith is also strengthened by the steady stream of volunteers and visitors—both international and local—who support their efforts in various ways. Volunteers, for example, can come and stay for a number of days or weeks and provide support with farm work, particularly during times of harvest, after which jams are made, fruit and nuts are dried, and olives are pressed. It took twelve years to get their first volunteer to come to the farm in 2011, says Daoud. Now, they get about 8,000 a year. "No one believed we could withstand the system but we kept going. It's this—something coming from nothing—that gives us hope."

Some visitors stay for weeks to work, while others, just as important, come for day trips to see the farm, have a meal cooked for them by Bishara's widow, Milada, and hear from Amal and Daoud about the work being done to fight peacefully for justice. "COME, SEE, TELL" is written on a sign as you enter the farm. It's a powerful reminder of the importance of visiting, of bearing witness to and then telling people who don't know (or aren't listening) about it, to propel them in turn to take action. Local schoolkids also visit, either for day trips or for longer summer camps.

Donations also help, whether large or small. A solar-energy system is thanks to German sponsorship, for example. On a smaller scale, individuals are able to sponsor single or multiple olive trees to replace those that have been destroyed. This all goes an enormous way to restoring not only the land but also the spirits of those who live on it—but of course there is still a long, long way to go.

The Tent of Nations is one-of-a-kind, but, in a land where the number of settlements continues to grow, it's a testament more widely to the power of a Palestinian family's faith, sumud, and desire to stay rooted to the land they feel so part of. It's not just about the actual plot of land and it's certainly not about the money. "The last check we received [from a settler, to buy the land] was blank," says Daoud. "We were told by an anonymous caller that we could write out the check with any amount we wanted." It's about the principle, about doing the right thing, about not accepting that the only options open to them are violence or resignation.

Amal's name means "hope" in Arabic. "*Inshallah hasam*: tomorrow will be better," she says. Their eldest daughter has just graduated from school, after studying international human rights law. The next generation stands ready to take on the battle; the battle that the Nassar family calls active hope and peaceful resistance.

Spicy roasted new potatoes with lemon and herbs
Batata bil filfil

Sometimes—oftentimes!—all a dish needs alongside it is some roasted new potatoes. This is the side for the job.

Getting ahead: Take this up to the point before the potatoes are ready to go into the oven, if you want to get ahead; the potatoes and tomatoes can sit around on the baking sheet for a couple of hours. Don't put them into the oven ahead of time; they want to be eaten freshly roasted.

Serves four as a side

3 tbsp olive oil
1 tsp cumin seeds, lightly crushed in a mortar and pestle
1 tsp coriander seeds, lightly crushed in a mortar and pestle
7 large garlic cloves, thinly sliced (3 tbsp/20g)
1 large red chile, thinly sliced (¼ cup/20g)
7 oz/200g cherry tomatoes, sliced in half
1 lb 10 oz/750g baby new potatoes, quartered
½ tsp sugar
Salt and black pepper
1 large lemon: finely grate the zest to get 2 tsp, then juice to get 2 tbsp
½ cup/10g cilantro leaves, roughly chopped
¼ cup/5g dill, roughly chopped

Preheat the oven to 425°F. Line a baking sheet with parchment paper.

Put the oil into a large sauté pan and place over high heat. Add the cumin seeds and coriander seeds and cook for 1 minute, stirring frequently. Add the garlic and cook for another 1 minute, until the garlic starts to color. Add the chile and tomatoes and cook for another 2 minutes, stirring from time to time, until the tomatoes have started to soften. Add the potatoes, sugar, 1 tsp of salt, and a generous grind of black pepper. Give everything a good stir, then transfer the mixture to the prepared baking sheet. Roast for about 40 minutes, tossing once halfway through, until the potatoes are crispy and cooked and the tomatoes are breaking down.

Remove from the oven and set aside to cool for 5 minutes before adding the lemon zest, lemon juice, cilantro, and dill. Toss gently and serve at once.

Mashed turnip with greens, caramelized onions, and feta

This started off as a way to use up all the turnip and potato flesh we generated from recipes in which turnips and potatoes were stuffed. The turnips made the cut (see page 241); the potatoes did not. The resulting mash turned out so good, though, that it soon became a reason to buy the vegetables in the first place! Necessity (not to discard good food) was indeed the mother of great invention here (along with Noor Murad, of course, our crucial right-hand lady on the book, who created the recipe!). If you are making the stuffed turnips, and do have all that spare flesh, save it to make this the next day. Just cover it with water until ready to use, to prevent discoloration.

Playing around: Don't be too precious with what herbs and greens you add here; try to keep the amounts the same, but if you have more spinach than kale to use up, for example, or parsley rather than dill, that's absolutely fine. It's meant to be a bit of a fridge-raid recipe.

Serves four to six as a side

½ cup/120ml olive oil
2 onions, thinly sliced (2½ cups/300g)
1 lb 10 oz/750g turnips, peeled and cut into roughly ¾-inch/2cm chunks
1 lb 5 oz/600g russet potatoes, peeled and cut into roughly 1¼-inch/3cm chunks
6 tbsp/100g Greek yogurt
4 garlic cloves, crushed
1 tbsp cumin seeds, roughly crushed in a mortar and pestle
7 oz/200g lacinato kale, woody stems discarded and leaves roughly torn (2¼ cups/140g)
Salt and black pepper
5 cups/100g baby spinach
¼ cup/5g parsley leaves, roughly chopped, plus more to garnish
¼ cup/5g dill, roughly chopped, plus more to garnish
4¼ oz/120g feta, roughly crumbled into large chunks

Put 2½ tbsp of oil into a large sauté pan and place over medium heat. Once hot, add the onions and cook for about 35 minutes, stirring only every so often, until deeply browned and caramelized.

While the onions are cooking, put the turnips, potatoes, and 2 tsp of salt into a large saucepan with a lid. Fill the pan with water so that the vegetables are covered and bring to a boil over medium-high heat. Decrease the heat to medium-low, cover, and cook for 15 minutes, or until the vegetables are easily pierced with a knife. Drain through a sieve and return to the pan along with the yogurt, 2 tbsp of oil, ½ tsp of salt, and a good grind of black pepper. Use a potato masher to create a chunky mash, and transfer to a serving platter.

Scrape the onions into a bowl and return the pan to medium-high heat. Add 1½ tbsp of oil, followed by the garlic, and cook for 1 minute, stirring continuously. Add the cumin seeds and cook for another 30 seconds, or until fragrant. Add the kale, ¼ tsp of salt, and a good grind of black pepper and cook for about 5 minutes, stirring often, until softened and lightly charred. Add the spinach and cook for about 1 minute, until just wilted. Transfer to a bowl and stir in the herbs.

Scatter half the feta and half the onions over the top. Pile the greens into the center and top with the remaining onions and feta and the remaining herbs. Drizzle all over with the remaining 2 tbsp of oil and serve.

Bulgur, tomato, and eggplant pilaf
Shulbato

This makes either a simple lunch, served with some thick Greek yogurt, or a side to all sorts of things; grilled chicken, pan-fried tofu, salmon fillet—they all work well.

Playing around: Cubes of creamy avocado or tangy feta are a nice addition, dotted on top before serving. Also, if you're looking for an alternative to the eggplant, zucchini can be used. Cut them into roughly ¾-inch/2cm dice and add to the pan at the same time as the bulgur.

Getting ahead: The eggplant cubes can be roasted ahead of time, if you like, and warmed through with the bulgur before serving.

Serves four as a light meal or side

2 medium eggplants, cut into roughly ¾-inch/2cm dice (5 cups/420g)
5 tbsp/75ml olive oil
Salt
1 onion, thinly sliced (1½ cups/180g)
1 garlic clove, crushed
1 tbsp tomato paste
1 tbsp sugar
3 medium tomatoes, roughly chopped (2 cups/380g)
2 green chiles, seeds and all, finely chopped
1⅔ cups/400ml boiling water
2¼ cups/350g coarse bulgur
1 tsp ground cumin
¼ tsp ground cinnamon
Black pepper
½ cup/10g cilantro leaves, roughly chopped
About ½ tsp Aleppo chile flakes (or ¼ tsp regular chile flakes)
Greek yogurt, to serve (optional)

Preheat the oven to 450°F. Line a baking sheet with parchment paper.

Place the eggplants in a large mixing bowl with 3 tbsp of oil and ½ tsp of salt. Mix well, then spread out on the prepared baking sheet. Roast for 20 minutes, or until soft and golden brown. Remove from the oven and set aside.

While the eggplants are roasting, put the remaining 2 tbsp of oil into a large saucepan with a lid, and place over medium heat. Add the onion and cook for about 8 minutes, or until the onion has softened and started to color. Add the garlic and cook for another 2 minutes, then add the tomato paste and sugar. Stir for 30 seconds, then add the tomatoes, chiles, and water. Bring to a boil, then add the bulgur, spices, 1¼ tsp of salt, and a good grind of black pepper. Return to a boil, then decrease the heat to low. Cook for 15 minutes, covered, then remove the pan from the heat. Keep the lid on and set aside for 10 minutes.

Add the eggplants to the pan and gently stir in.

Spoon onto a serving platter or individual plates, sprinkle with the cilantro and chile flakes, and serve with a spoonful of yogurt, if desired.

Buttery rice with toasted vermicelli
Ruz bil sh'arieh

Serves four as a side

1½ cups/300g basmati rice
3 tbsp unsalted butter
1 cinnamon stick
1¾ oz/50g vermicelli wheat noodles or spaghetti, roughly broken into 1¼-inch/3cm pieces
2¼ cups/520ml hot water or hot chicken stock (optional)
Salt and black pepper

There's a theory that a woman used to add pasta to rice only if she was an unconfident cook or couldn't cook rice properly. The old wives' tale was that adding pasta was a guaranteed way to prevent the rice from sticking together. True or otherwise, it's a guaranteed way to get it seriously fluffy and it's a good few steps up from regular steamed rice. Here, the pasta brings texture, the butter brings comfort, and the cinnamon brings a hint of spice.

Ingredients note: Don't get the flat Asian rice noodles; you want the Italian wheat vermicelli nests. They are like spaghetti, but thinner. Regular spaghetti makes a fine alternative.

Place the rice in a bowl and allow tap water to run over it until the water is clear. Set aside to soak for at least 1 hour (or overnight, if you are getting ahead). Transfer the soaked rice to a sieve placed over a bowl and let drain for about 15 minutes.

Put 2 tbsp of butter and the cinnamon into a medium saucepan with a lid and place over medium-high heat. Add the vermicelli and cook for 3 minutes, stirring continuously, until deeply golden. Mix in the rice for about 30 seconds, then add the water, along with 1½ tsp of salt (or slightly less—about 1 tsp—if using stock and it is salty) and a good grind of black pepper. Cover the pan tightly with aluminum foil and put the lid on top of this. Decrease the heat to low and cook for 15 minutes. Turn off the heat and set aside for 15 minutes, covered, to steam.

Remove the lid and foil and dot with the remaining 1 tbsp of butter. Set aside for another 10 minutes, covered with the foil and lid, or just the lid, before serving.

SOUPS

You don't need to grow up eating soup for it to always, somehow, take you straight back home. It's an inherently comforting thing to eat, nurturing and reassuring at the end of the day. For Sami, growing up, what was made into soup at home reflected what was being grown in the fields and sold in the market. Batches were big and the cost of feeding a large family was kept in check. Spring meant besara, making use of all the fava beans, molokhieh, and soft herbs in season. Autumn and winter meant dark green chard and lentil soup or something hearty, like freekeh with chicken meatballs (see page 156).

For all their power to comfort and soothe, soups can also be made to surprise and delight. This can either be from a great big squeeze of lemon (which we've reached for in all but one of our soups in this chapter) or a texture-giving topping. Fried crispy onions are a frequent addition to lots of soups in Palestine—it makes them quite addictive—but we've only used this winning trick once in this chapter, on the Chard, Lentil, and Preserved Lemon Soup (page 157). Layers of texture and topping have been brought about in other ways—with caramelized pistachios (see page 153), for example, or spicy pumpkin seeds (see page 149). A mix of roasted eggplant cubes and chopped walnuts also works well (see page 152), as does leaving some fava beans whole to stand out from those that are blitzed in besara (see page 150). As well as bringing crunch and contrast, these sorts of toppings are also a way to bulk out a soup, making it into a meal in itself, served with, of course, the ubiquitous bread (or rice), olives, or pickles.

A clash in color, as well as texture, can also work to bring an element of surprise to a soup; such as a green herb oil drizzled over an orange butternut squash soup (see page 153) or the addition of finely diced tomatoes to a green cucumber soup (see page 149).

Another great thing about soups is how un-precious they are—as happy to be made ahead of time, waiting in the fridge or freezer to be eaten, as they are to be spooned up there and then. They're also robust enough to be played around with in terms of toppings and garnishes. They can be dressed down for a midweek supper, or dressed up for a stand-alone meal or impressive starter with friends. There's a soup for all occasions, a soup for all seasons, and a soup for all sorts of reasons. It's the ultimate home-cooked food.

ראש-פינה
ראש-פינה
ראש-פינה

Chilled cucumber and tahini soup with spicy pumpkin seeds

If you want something to be rich and creamy and vegan all at once, tahini is often the big secret, ingredient-wise. Swirled in a sauce, a dressing, or a soup, as here, tahini is a wonderful way to enrich a dish. With the cucumber, lemon, and herbs doing all the work at the other end to freshen and lighten things up, this is a perfect meal for a summer day.

Playing around: Double or triple the batch for the pumpkin seeds, if you like; they keep for a week in a sealed container, at room temperature, and are lovely sprinkled over all sorts of salads and roasted vegetables.

Getting ahead: The soup can be made up to a day in advance; it keeps well and doesn't lose its color. Just give it a stir before serving, as there'll be a little water separation.

Serves four

Spicy pumpkin seeds
3 tbsp olive oil
¼ cup/40g pumpkin seeds
1 tsp ground cumin
¼ tsp chile flakes
⅛ tsp salt

3 large cucumbers (2 lb 2 oz/1kg), peeled
¼ cup/65g tahini
2 tbsp olive oil, plus more to serve
2 lemons: finely grate the zest to get 2 tsp, then juice to get ¼ cup/60ml
2 large garlic cloves, crushed
½ cup/10g dill, roughly chopped, plus a few fronds
¾ tsp Aleppo chile flakes (or ½ tsp regular chile flakes)
3½ oz/100g ice cubes
1 cup/20g mint leaves
1 cup/20g parsley, roughly chopped
Salt and black pepper
1 tomato, cut into ¼-inch/6mm dice (½ cup/80g)

To prepare the pumpkin seeds, put all the ingredients into a small sauté pan and place over medium heat. Cook for about 8 minutes, stirring frequently, until the seeds begin to color lightly and pop. Transfer to a bowl (or to an airtight container if making a batch) and set aside to cool.

Cut off a roughly 3-oz/80g chunk of cucumber and slice in half. Scoop out the seedy core and put this in a countertop blender (or a deep bowl if you are using an immersion blender), then finely chop the remainder into 1½-inch/1cm dice. Set this aside. Roughly chop the remaining 2 cucumbers into ¾-inch/2cm chunks and transfer to the blender along with the tahini, oil, lemon zest, lemon juice, garlic, chopped dill, chile flakes, ice cubes, half the mint, half the parsley, 1 tsp of salt, and a good grind of black pepper. Blitz for about 2 minutes, until completely smooth, then keep in the fridge until ready to serve.

Divide the soup among four deep bowls and spoon the reserved cucumber and diced tomato on top. Shred the remaining mint and sprinkle this over each portion, along with the remaining parsley, the dill fronds, the spicy pumpkin seeds, and a final drizzle of oil and serve.

Molokhieh soup with fava beans
Besara

Besara is somewhere between a soup and a thick, warm dip. Fava beans are the main ingredient, pointing to the dish's Egyptian origins before it spread across the Levant. By the time it got to Palestine, the herbs in the Egyptian version—cilantro and parsley—were matched by Palestine's flavor-packed green leaf, molokhieh. Wherever it is made across the Levant, the presence of fried onion, chile, lemon, and olive oil is a constant.

Molokhieh is a bit like spinach but its texture is distinct—slimy, almost (without the word putting people off; see page 339). It's used a lot in the Middle East but the leaves, fresh or frozen, can be hard to find outside of Middle Eastern stores. We've come up with an alternative of spinach cooked with a bit of okra, which is then all blitzed together. Texture-wise, the result comes pretty close.

Getting ahead: This keeps in the fridge and keeps its color for two days, or longer if frozen.

Serves four

9 oz/250g frozen chopped molokhieh, or 5¼ oz/150g okra, sliced into ⅛-inch/3mm rounds, plus 14 oz/400g spinach, stems discarded (7 oz/200g)
2 tbsp olive oil
1 onion, finely chopped (1 cup/150g)
3 large garlic cloves, crushed
1½ lb/700g frozen shelled fava beans
1 tsp cumin seeds, lightly toasted and roughly crushed in a mortar and pestle
2 tsp coriander seeds, lightly toasted and roughly crushed in a mortar and pestle
3 cups/700ml chicken or vegetable stock
¾ cup/15g cilantro leaves, roughly chopped, plus a few chopped leaves to serve
¾ cup/15g parsley leaves, roughly chopped, plus a few chopped leaves to serve
¾ cup/15g dill leaves, roughly chopped, plus a few chopped leaves to serve
Salt and black pepper
1 large red chile, thinly sliced (½ oz/15g)
1 lemon, cut into wedges
Warm bread, to serve (optional)

If using just the molokhieh, put the oil into a large saucepan, about 8 inches/20cm wide, and place over medium-high heat. Add the onion and cook, stirring from time to time, for about 8 minutes, or until golden brown. Add the garlic and cook for 1 minute. Take half this mixture out of the pan and set aside; this will be used when serving. Add the molokhieh to the mixture remaining in the pan—it should go in frozen—along with most of the fava beans and all the cumin seeds and coriander seeds. Pour in the stock and bring to a gentle boil over medium heat, skimming any foam from the surface as you go. Cover the pan and simmer over low heat for 5 minutes, then add all the herbs, 1½ tsp of salt, and a good grind of black pepper. Return to a boil and simmer gently for a final 5 minutes, with the pan covered.

If using the combination of okra and spinach, put the oil into a large saucepan, about 8 inches/20cm wide, and place over medium-high heat. Add the onion and cook, stirring from time to time, for about 7 minutes, or until softened and lightly browned. Add the garlic and cook for 1 minute. Take half this mixture out of the pan and set aside; this will be used when serving. Add the okra to the mixture remaining in the pan and cook for 3 minutes, then add the spinach, spices, stock, 1½ tsp of salt, and a good grind of black pepper. Bring to a boil, then decrease the heat to medium and cook for 20 minutes, or until the okra has completely softened. Add the herbs and most of the fava beans, and cook for another 5 minutes.

Using a blender (immersion or countertop), roughly blitz the soup—you don't want to blitz too much, as you still want to see pieces of fava bean.

Ladle the soup into bowls, and top with the reserved fried onions and whole fava beans, followed by a sprinkle of sliced chile and the additional herbs. Serve with lemon wedges alongside and some warm bread, if you like.

Charred eggplant and lemon soup

The more you char your eggplants here, the smokier and better the soup will taste.

Getting ahead: Both elements here—the soup and the fried eggplant topping—can be made a day or two in advance. Keep them in the fridge, separately, and just warm through before serving.

Serves four

6 eggplants (3⅓ lb/1.5kg): 4 charred (see page 336)
Salt
1 qt/1L chicken or vegetable stock
6 tbsp/90ml lemon juice (from about 4 lemons)
4 garlic cloves, crushed
1 tsp ground cinnamon
2½ tsp ground cumin
Black pepper
3 tbsp olive oil
About 1¼ cups/300ml sunflower oil
1 red chile, finely chopped (1 tbsp/10g)
½ cup/10g cilantro leaves, finely chopped
1 cup/100g walnut halves, roughly chopped
½ cup/150g Greek yogurt
2 egg yolks
2 tsp cornstarch

Scoop the flesh out of the charred eggplants. Set this aside in a colander in the sink or over a bowl for about 1 hour to drain. Finely chop the drained flesh; it should weigh about 14 oz/400g.

Cut the remaining 2 eggplants into roughly ¾-inch/2cm cubes. Place them in a sieve set over a bowl or in the sink, sprinkle with 1 tsp of salt, mix well, let drain for 30 minutes, then pat dry with paper towels.

Put the charred eggplant flesh into a large saucepan along with the stock, ¼ cup/60ml of lemon juice, the garlic, cinnamon, 2 tsp of cumin, 2 tbsp of olive oil, 2 tsp of salt, and a good grind of black pepper. Bring to a boil over medium-high heat and, once boiling, decrease the heat to medium and simmer for 30 minutes; the liquid will reduce by about a third.

Meanwhile, put the sunflower oil into a medium sauté pan and place over medium-high heat. Line a plate with paper towels. Once the oil is hot, add the cubes of eggplant (in three or four batches, so as to not overcrowd the pan) and fry for 5–6 minutes, until they are a deep golden brown. Transfer to the prepared plate while you continue with the remaining batches. Put all the eggplant into a bowl along with the remaining 2 tbsp of lemon juice and 1 tbsp of olive oil, the chile, cilantro, and walnuts. Mix to combine, then set aside.

Put the yogurt, egg yolks, and cornstarch into a medium bowl and whisk well until smooth. Spoon a ladleful of the hot soup into the yogurt and stir well to combine. Repeat this one more time before stirring the yogurt mixture into the soup. Doing this prevents the yogurt from splitting when it's added to the hot soup. Cook over medium-low heat for 2 minutes, stirring continuously, until the soup has come together and slightly thickened.

Divide the soup among four bowls and sprinkle with the remaining ½ tsp of ground cumin. Top with the fried eggplant–walnut mix and serve at once.

Pictured on page 154

Butternut squash and saffron soup with caramelized pistachios and herb oil

This is the soup to launch your autumn cooking, whether you're looking for a comforting midweek meal or an impressive starter for a feast. Don't make both toppings if you don't want to; the soup works well with either the pistachios or the herb oil alone. The combination of all three, though, is a special one.

Getting ahead: All the elements can be made well in advance. The soup keeps in the fridge for up to three days (or longer in the freezer). The herb oil can also be made a day or two ahead; it keeps its color well. The pistachios keep well in a sealed container at room temperature; they'll get less crunchy with time but still taste good. Double the batch for these, if you can; they're lovely sprinkled over salads or just to have around to snack on.

Serves four generously, or six as a starter

2½ tbsp olive oil
2 large onions, roughly chopped (2⅓ cups/320g)
5 garlic cloves, crushed
1 large butternut squash, peeled, seeded, and cut into roughly ½-inch/1.5cm dice (2 lb 2 oz/1kg)
1 large potato, peeled and chopped into roughly ½-inch/1.5cm dice (mounded 1 cup/250g)
1 tsp paprika
¼ tsp saffron threads
1 qt/1L vegetable stock
Salt and black pepper

Caramelized pistachios

1 cup/150g pistachios or pumpkin seeds
1 tsp Urfa chile flakes (or ½ tsp regular chile flakes)
1 tsp orange blossom water (optional)
2 tsp light corn syrup
2 tsp maple syrup
1 tbsp olive oil
¼ tsp flaky sea salt

Herb oil

¾ cup/15g parsley leaves, finely chopped
½ cup/10g oregano leaves, finely chopped
1 shallot, finely chopped (⅓ cup/50g)
½ tsp chile flakes
½ cup/120ml olive oil
1 tbsp cider vinegar
Salt and black pepper

Preheat the oven to 350°F. Line a baking sheet with parchment paper.

Put the oil into a large saucepan with a lid, and place over medium heat. Add the onions and cook for about 12 minutes, stirring often, until soft and golden brown. Add the garlic and cook for 30 seconds, until fragrant, then add the squash, potato, paprika, saffron, stock, 2 tsp of salt, and a good grind of black pepper. Bring to a boil over medium-high heat, then decrease the heat to medium-low and simmer for about 25 minutes, covered, or until the vegetables are completely soft and cooked through. If you like your soup smooth, use a blender (immersion or countertop) to blitz it as much as you want. We like to half-blitz it so that some texture remains; if using a countertop blender, transfer half the soup to this, blitz until smooth, then return this to the un-blitzed soup in the pan. Keep warm until ready to serve.

To make the caramelized pistachios, while the soup is cooking, put all the ingredients into a bowl and mix well to combine. Tip out onto the prepared baking sheet and bake for about 15 minutes, stirring halfway through, until the nuts are golden and bubbling. Remove from the oven, set aside until completely cool, then roughly chop the nuts. Set aside (or keep in an airtight container if making in advance) until needed.

To make the herb oil, put all the ingredients into a bowl with ¼ tsp of salt and a grind of black pepper. Stir to mix, then set aside until ready to serve.

Ladle out the soup and top with a generous spoonful of the pistachios. Drizzle with the herb oil and serve at once.

Pictured on page 155

Freekeh soup with chicken meatballs
Shorbet freekeh

It's hard to talk about any form of chicken soup without talking about comfort. Pulling this back from the brink of slippers and Sunday night, though (not that anyone ever needs to resist), is the freekeh (see page 336 for more). Adding this smoked cracked wheat, with its nutty bite, to this soup makes it the best of all worlds: comforting *and* classy.

Getting ahead: The meatballs can be made and pan-fried a day in advance. The soup also keeps well, once cooked, for up to three days in the fridge.

Ingredients note: You can ask your butcher to grind the chicken thighs, or you can pop them into the freezer for half an hour, to firm up, then put them into the bowl of a food processor and blitz until finely ground. Firming them in the freezer helps them to grind cleanly, but skipping this stage is also fine.

Serves four

Chicken meatballs

1 large slice sourdough bread, crusts removed, cut into roughly ½-inch/1cm dice (1¾ cups/55g)
3 tbsp buttermilk
10½ oz/300g ground chicken thighs or turkey thighs
3 green onions, finely sliced (⅓ cup/30g)
¼ cup/5g parsley, finely chopped
½ cup/10g mint, finely chopped
1 green chile, seeded and finely chopped
½ tsp ground cinnamon
½ tsp ground allspice
Salt and black pepper
2 tbsp sunflower oil

2 tbsp olive oil
1 large leek, trimmed, cut in half lengthwise and finely sliced (2 cups/200g)
3 celery stalks, trimmed and finely sliced (1¼ cups/150g)
1 tsp cumin seeds, roughly ground in a mortar and pestle
1 tsp ground cinnamon
½ tsp ground allspice
4 garlic cloves, crushed
1 tbsp tomato paste
1 cup/170g freekeh
1½ cups/30g cilantro, roughly chopped
1 cup/20g parsley, roughly chopped
6⅓ cups/1.5L chicken stock
Salt and black pepper
3 green onions, finely sliced (⅓ cup/30g)
¼ cup/60ml lemon juice (from about 2 lemons)
½ cup/120ml buttermilk
¼ tsp dried mint

To make the meatballs, put the bread and buttermilk into a large bowl. Set aside for about 5 minutes, then use your hands to squish the mixture into fine crumbs. Add the ground chicken and all the remaining ingredients for the meatballs, along with ¾ tsp of salt and a generous grind of black pepper, except the sunflower oil. Mix to combine, then form the mixture into small balls, each weighing about ½ oz/15g; you should make about 30 balls.

Put the sunflower oil into a large frying pan and place over high heat. Line a plate with paper towels. Once the oil is hot, add the meatballs and fry for about 3 minutes, turning throughout, so that they are nicely browned on all sides but not cooked through. Remove from the pan and set aside on the prepared plate until needed.

Put the olive oil into a large saucepan with a lid, and place over medium heat. Add the leek and celery and cook for about 12 minutes, stirring from time to time, until the vegetables are soft but not taking on any color. Add the spices, garlic, and tomato paste and cook for 1 minute, until fragrant. Add the freekeh, 1 cup/20g of cilantro, the parsley, stock, 2 tsp of salt, and a good grind of black pepper. Simmer for about 40 minutes, with the pan partially covered, or until the freekeh is soft and the liquid has reduced by a third. Add the meatballs and simmer for 10 minutes, with the pan covered, until they are cooked through. Stir in two-thirds of the green onions, the remaining ½ cup/10g of cilantro, and 3 tbsp of lemon juice and keep warm until ready to serve.

Combine the buttermilk with the dried mint, the remaining 1 tbsp of lemon juice, and ¼ tsp of salt and stir well to mix.

Divide the soup among four bowls, drizzle with the buttermilk mixture, sprinkle with the remaining green onions, and serve at once.

Chard, lentil, and preserved lemon soup
Shorbet adass w sliq

If something is verging on the holier-than-thou in the kitchen, top with some crispy fried onions, we say. They work particularly well when paired with that most virtuous of all things—the lentil!—in something such as mjaddarat el burgul (see page 178), rummaniyya (see page 176), or, as here, this soup. For those happy feeling holy, though, the soup also works well as it is, without the onions. If you still want a crunch, then some pumpkin seeds (see page 93 for herb-salad ones or page 149 for spicy ones), caramelized pistachios (see page 153), or croutons all go really well.

Getting ahead: The soup can be made well ahead—up to three days if keeping in the fridge, or longer if you are going to freeze it—and the onions also keep well in a sealed container at room temperature for a couple of days. Make more of the onions than you need, if you like—they are lovely to have to sprinkle on all sorts of things: lentils and rice, oven-roasted veg, or grilled meat.

Serves four

1 cup/200g green or brown lentils
2 tbsp olive oil
1 onion, finely chopped (1 cup/150g)
3 garlic cloves, crushed
1½ tsp cumin seeds
1 tsp coriander seeds, roughly crushed in a mortar and pestle
½ tsp ground turmeric
¼ tsp chile flakes
9 oz/250g Swiss chard, stalks removed and finely chopped, leaves roughly torn
Salt and black pepper
3 cups/750ml chicken or vegetable stock
1 preserved lemon, seeds discarded, skin and flesh finely chopped (2 tbsp/20g)
½ recipe Crispy Onions (see page 126)
1 lemon, cut into wedges (optional)

Rinse the lentils in plenty of cold water and place them in a medium saucepan. Cover with 1 qt/1L of water and bring to a boil over high heat. Decrease the heat to low and simmer for 30 minutes, or until the lentils are just soft. Drain and set aside.

Put the oil into a medium saucepan—about 8 inches/20cm wide—and place over medium heat. Once hot, add the onion and cook for 10 minutes, stirring occasionally, until soft and golden brown. Add the garlic, cumin seeds, and coriander seeds and cook for 1 minute, then add the turmeric, chile flakes, chard stalks, 1½ tsp of salt, and a good grind of black pepper. Mix well to combine, then add the lentils and stock. Bring to a boil, then decrease the heat to medium-low and simmer for 10 minutes before adding the chard leaves and preserved lemon. Cook for 4 minutes, then remove from the heat.

Transfer about half the soup to a countertop blender (or to a separate bowl, if using an immersion blender) and blitz until smooth. Return the blitzed soup to the un-blitzed soup in the pan and set aside until ready to serve.

Warm the soup through and divide among four bowls. Top with the crispy onions and a squeeze of lemon, if you like, and serve.

VEGGIE MAINS

How food is cooked at home in Palestine is very different from the way that it is cooked in restaurants. In restaurants, the emphasis is on food that can be cooked fast: marinated and skewered meat, for example, ready to be quickly grilled. Ground meat shaped into kofta, ready to be fried or baked. This sort of cooking—quick-on-and-off-the-heat—is called *mashawi*. It's something that restaurants in Palestine are really good at. All the work can be done in advance, ready to be quickly whipped up when the order comes through. These are the kebabs and shawarma joints, the falafel, kofta, and pita stands, seen on many a street corner in the cities (and in chapters two, six, and seven in this book).

Restaurants are also good at maza, or mezzeh, the spread of little bowls and dishes that take over the table (and much of chapters two and three) at the beginning of a meal. These, again, are all dishes that can be prepared, in bulk if needed, in advance: carrots can be chopped and steamed, cucumbers and tomatoes can be diced, eggplants can be charred and drained for baba ganoush. Lemons are squeezed, bread is made and ready to be warmed through, olives are pickled and ready to be portioned up, labneh is hung. This is all food that is as happy to appear at the table, at the snap of a finger, as it is to sit around for a day or so if service is slow and the food needs to go back into the fridge overnight. No time, money, or food is wasted. It's an efficient, delicious, often grilled or fried business.

Home cooking, on the other hand, is different. Home cooking is about sheet-pan recipes or stews, about stuffed vegetables or meats, about roasts and things that take a bit more time to make. This sort of cooking—*tabeekh*—is the opposite of the "grab-and-eat" style of restaurant cooking; it's slower and more comforting. This can be the stuffed dishes, *mahashi*—vegetables that need coring and hollowing out before being stuffed and cooked. Or it can be the category of cooking known as *sawani*—the roasts, braises, and sheet-pan recipes—dishes that use up the vegetables and herbs you have in the fridge and that, when served from the pan they are baked in, are often described as "rustic." These are the dishes that start with the ingredients often called "humble"—pasta, chickpeas, wilted spinach, and rice. These are the recipes for easy, comforting, everyday cooking and are what this chapter—and so much of Palestinian home cooking—is all about.

Pan-fried okra with tomato, olives, and haloumi
Bamia bil siniyhe

Given the difference between home and restaurant cooking (see page 160), this is a dish that blurs any such distinction. Although it feels "rustic" and "homey," it's one we first ate and were inspired to re-create after a meal at Daher Zeidani's Alreda restaurant in Nazareth. The fact that the dish blurs the restaurant/home distinction says a lot about Daher himself (see page 166), as much a seasoned chef as he is host, focal point, and bringer together of community. People spend time at Alreda not just to eat (though eat very well they do); they come to the restaurant to meet with their neighbors, to talk, drink, listen to music, and debate. This is a dish with bold flavors, which is quick and easy to make. It works as well as a main—served with bread or rice—as it does as a side or as part of a spread.

Getting ahead: This is a quick and easy dish but you can make it a few hours in advance, if you like, up to the point before it goes under the broiler. That way you can just finish it off in the oven for 10 minutes before serving.

Ingredients note: If you see bags of small frozen okra in a Middle Eastern supermarket, grab them. Not needing to be trimmed, smaller okra don't run the risk of their seeds being exposed (which is what gives okra its reputation for being "slimy"). Starting with regular okra is absolutely fine, though; trim the tips but not so far that you can see the seeds.

Serves two as a main, or four as a side

3 tbsp olive oil, plus more to drizzle
4 garlic cloves, thinly sliced
¾ tsp ground cumin
½ tsp paprika
1 tbsp shatta (red or green; see page 73) or rose harissa
1 tbsp cider vinegar
1 tsp sugar
¼ cup/60ml water
Salt
14 oz/400g okra, trimmed (see headnote), or frozen baby okra, defrosted
6⅓ oz/180g cherry tomatoes (about 15), sliced in half
Mounded ⅓ cup/70g pitted Kalamata olives
4¼ oz/120g haloumi cheese or feta, broken into roughly ½-inch/1cm chunks
1 green chile, thinly sliced
¼ cup/5g parsley, roughly chopped
1 lemon, cut into wedges

Preheat the broiler.

Put the olive oil into a large ovenproof frying or sauté pan, about 12 inches/30cm wide, and place over medium heat. Add the garlic and cook for just under 1 minute, or until it starts to color. Add the cumin, paprika, and shatta and cook for 30 seconds, then add the vinegar, sugar, water, and 1 tsp of salt. Bring to a boil, then add the okra and cook over medium heat for 5 minutes, stirring once or twice. Add the tomatoes, olives, and haloumi to the pan and cook for another 2–3 minutes, shaking the pan from time to time so that things don't get stuck to the base.

Place the pan directly under the broiler for 10 minutes—you want the cheese and okra to take on lots of color and even blister in parts. Remove from the oven and set aside to cool for 5 minutes.

Top the okra with the chile, parsley, and a good drizzle of oil and pass the wedges of lemon alongside.

A tale of two restaurateurs: the politics (or not) of food

We ate one night in Haifa, up north from Tel Aviv, on the coast. The next night, in nearby Nazareth, we were eating again. The same central activity, but the two evenings could not have been more different. Both chef/owners were Palestinian and they both served us great food. What made the two experiences so polar opposite, though, was the chef/owners' relationships to their food and customers, and what they saw as the purpose of having a restaurant in northern Israel.

Contrasting the two really shows how different opinions can be about the role of food in the region and how strongly these opinions are held. After sitting at their respective tables, over the course of two nights, we walked away thinking two things. One was that both ways of seeing food in northern Israel, from a restaurateur's point of view, are entirely valid; that we, as guests at their tables, should restrict any judgments we might have to their food. The second was that we were getting to eat very, very well. This is a tale of two restaurateurs, then: one in Haifa and the other in Nazareth.

First, "hip" Haifa. Haifa is a port city, rising steeply up from the Mediterranean Sea on the slope of Mount Carmel. It's home to a lot of start-ups and has the feel of a real technological hub. Through the city stretches a long, wide main road. It reaches from the coast right up to the incongruously coiffed, vibrant green terraces of the Bahá'í Gardens, backdrop to many a selfie.

In Haifa, we had supper at the then newly opened Lux restaurant. Located on the port road in Haifa's lower city, Lux is as bustling as the Independence Road it looks out onto. It was Sami's partner Jeremy's birthday the night we were there, and we feasted to celebrate. The open kitchen was in full swing, the music was playing, the bar stools were high, and all the food that came our way was excitingly tasty and something fresh. Chef/owner Alla Musa (pictured opposite) was creating a stir locally, taking the ingredients of the area—the fish, spices, yogurt, and nuts—and giving them to his customers in a sexy, different, and very delicious way. Standouts, for us, were pan-fried seafood on a spread of herbed labneh, and a fillet of sea bass with charred eggplant and baby okra. We'd gone to Haifa in search of something new and noteworthy being done with fish, and this was the night we found it.

We'd chatted with Alla the day before in El Marsa, the other restaurant he owns and runs in Akka. Akka is a really pretty fishing port close to Haifa. With a steady flow of tourists and locals on their days off, El Marsa—a seafood

restaurant—caters to what his customers want. In the early days, Alla tried to push the boat out and experiment with the menu, but there was no point. People wanted seafood linguine and a kids' menu, not the foams and finishes Alla had learned while working at a Michelin-starred restaurant in Sweden. "People just didn't want it," he said. With rent and salaries to pay and plans to expand both his family and his business, Alla's goal is to make great food that makes enough money to allow him to carry on making great food. Giving the market what it wants and letting the food speak for itself is not any sort of cop-out, says Alla, it's just plain good business sense.

Alla Musa couldn't have been more generous with his time, beer fridge, and bottle of arak. He was happy as anything to sit around and chew the food-related fat, and the conversation flowed as steadily as the drinks, until one topic came up that was evidently out of bounds: politics. Tara asked whether the local Palestinian fishermen were affected by restrictions on the water they could fish in, and she was met by an affable diversion. Sami asked the seemingly impartial question whether Alla's business partner at Lux, Ahmad Asadi, was an Israeli or a Palestinian Arab. "He's local," said Alla. "How would you describe yourself?" followed up Sami.

"I don't want to talk politics," Alla replied. "And saying whether someone is an Arab or Palestinian or Israeli just turns everything into politics."

Alla's determination not to talk about politics does not mean he doesn't know the lay of the political land. He's politically savvy enough to know that when there is tension at the Gaza border it affects who his customer base will be for the next few days and weeks. His Israeli regulars, who normally sit side by side with Haifa's Arabs, just don't turn up. Alla is young, ambitious, and completely nuts about his food. If he upped the politics of it—if he made it into a question of identity and struggle and connection to the land—he'd be reducing the flow of customers who come through the door. Israeli, Palestinian, Palestinian-Israeli, Arab-Israeli, Arab of the Negev, the people of the north, people of the West Bank, 48ers, Inside Arab, the Shamenet Arab, Arab al beseder: whatever his customers call themselves, Alla just wants them to come and eat, drink, and be merry. No politics, no tension, no problem; let's party! With that, Alla finds out that it's Jeremy's birthday, and the shot glasses appear.

The following night we are in Nazareth, pulling up our chairs at the Alreda restaurant, opened by Daher Zeidani in 2003. After the previous night's celebrations, we'd resolved to have a night off booze. Chef/owner Daher pulled up a chair to talk with us before we ordered our food. "Don't you think it's so rude," he opened with, "when customers go to a restaurant and don't have a drink? Who are these people who think it's okay to just ask for water all night? I am the host and I want my guests to sit back and eat what I give them and have a drink." Cripes, we thought, that'll be three beers then. It was just one of Daher's very many strong opinions.

If Alla Musa's food was all about the food, then Daher's food was food being served with a very large side order of politics. This was food with a strong Arabic identity, served in a restaurant that felt like an old Arabic house made by a chef/owner who didn't give two hoots about whose feathers he might be ruffling. The Germans! The English! The Japanese! Israelis! Never let it be said that national stereotypes don't live on! Having ruled out half of Europe, Asia, and the Middle East, Daher clarifies his position, unashamedly, "This is not a superficial place. This is a place for enlightened liberals." The very irony of his position—having such a fixed (i.e., illiberal) view on what constitutes being a liberal customer—hangs, with the cigarette smoke, in the air.

The customers that Daher is interested in and keen to serve and please are his local, Arab regulars, about 80 percent of whom he knows by name. The restaurant feels as much like a social club as it does a formal restaurant, with lots of hand shaking and back-patting as Daher pulls up a chair at one of the tables whenever he feels like it. "I am the host. Why is it odd for me to pull up a chair, tell my guests what they should be eating, and then later sit down and ask them if they like the food and what they think?"

Do-as-we-were-told we duly did, then, welcoming the food that Daher made for us. A salad of "flowers and fruit" was followed by a spread of dishes, including the okra baked in tomatoes that inspired us to make our own version once back home (see page 162). We also tried Daher's famous Nazareth salsiccia, long thin beef or pork sausages that have been soaked in white wine and then cooked in a tangy red pepper sauce flavored with cloves, allspice, garlic, slices of lemon, pine nuts, and parsley. It was all packed full of flavor and wonderful to eat.

Daher explained how difficult it is to please his Israeli customers, using the flowers and fruit salad as an example. If he were to make a traditional "Arabic salad," with chopped vegetables, white cheese, and a lemony dressing, people visiting from Tel Aviv would say, "Why have we come all the way for this? We could have had this at home; show us something new." Adding his twists—the flowers and raisins—to traditional dishes, though, means that the next table of Israelis to sit down might balk at the idea that this is "allowed" to be called an Arabic salad. We'd seen this tension time and again on our travels; certain salads and dishes stuck in a traditional rut, on the one hand, but then, on the other hand, not "allowed" to be played around with or moved forward if they were still to be called an "Arabic salad." Trying to open the point up more generally—suggesting that this tension is as likely to be observed by local Arabs as it is by visiting Israelis and acknowledging all the reasons why this might be the case—does not generate much conversation at the table.

For all his talk, though, you get the impression that Daher is really not too bothered what anyone, apart from his regulars, might think. Unlike Alla Musa in Haifa, Daher has been in the restaurant game for several decades and his priorities have changed. Unlike Alla, when asked about the day-to-day logistics of running a restaurant and whether life is made inconvenient for him, Daher takes a deep breath, pulls in his chair, and pours out a drink. We hear about the Israeli health minister who forced Daher to cancel so many of his dishes due to ingredients that weren't "allowed" to be used. We hear about his sister's freshly picked olives and olive oil needing to be replaced by canned olives from an Israeli factory. The traditional unpasteurized Arabic cheese he loved had to be replaced by a more industrially made version. The chicken wing pastilla for which he was known had to be taken off the menu, as the three days it takes to actually make a pastilla was too long. And on it goes; the obstacles put in the way of running his restaurant are part of Daher's everyday. "They only come every four years, though," Daher says, referring back to the visits of the health minister, "so we can hide."

This is a guy who is not afraid to air his opinions, no matter who might hear them or whose toes he might be treading on. "Did you hear about the Palestinian chef who sold out and set up shop in London with an Israeli chef?" he remarks. "That was me!" says Sami, before they burst into shared laughter and raise hands for a high five. And for just a moment, around that table of shared food and time, not a single opinion in the world matters.

EXEMPTION
ENTRANCE TO
ALREDA
IS NOT CONDITIONED BY
CURSE OR CONDEMNATION OF:
CHURCHILL, THE QUEEN,
HER FATHER, HER SON AND
THEIR SPIRIT

Eggplant, chickpea, and tomato bake
Musaqa'a

Echoes of Greek moussaka are correctly heard here, both in the name and the feel of the dish. It's a vegetarian take on the hearty, humble, healthful, and completely delicious sheet-pan dish. It works well either as a veggie main or as a side with all sorts of things—piled into a baked potato, for example, or served alongside some grilled meat, fish, or tofu. It's just the sort of dish you want to have in the fridge ready to greet you after a day at work. It's also lovely at room temperature, so it's great for an on-the-go lunch.

Getting ahead: You can make and bake this in advance; it keeps in the fridge for up to three days, ready to be warmed through when needed.

Serves four as a main, or six as a side

5 medium eggplants (2¾ lb/1.25kg)
½ cup/120ml olive oil
Salt and black pepper
1 onion, finely chopped (1 cup/150g)
6 garlic cloves, crushed
1 tsp chile flakes
1 tsp ground cumin
½ tsp ground cinnamon
1½ tsp tomato paste
2 green bell peppers, seeded and cut into 1¼-inch/3cm chunks (1⅓ cups/200g)
1 x 14-oz/400g can chickpeas, drained and rinsed (1¾ cups/240g)
1 x 14-oz/400g can chopped tomatoes
1½ tsp sugar
¾ cup plus 2 tbsp/200ml water
1 cup/20g cilantro, roughly chopped
4 plum tomatoes, trimmed and sliced into ½-inch/1.5cm rounds (12¼ oz/350g)

Preheat the oven to 450°F. Line two baking sheets with parchment paper.

Use a vegetable peeler to peel away strips of eggplant skin from top to bottom, leaving the eggplants with alternating strips of black skin and white flesh, like a zebra. Cut crosswise into round slices, ¾ inch/2cm thick, and place in a large bowl. Mix well with 5 tbsp/75ml of oil, 1 tsp of salt, and plenty of black pepper and spread out on the prepared baking sheets. Roast for about 30 minutes, or until completely softened and lightly browned. Remove from the oven and set aside.

Decrease the oven temperature to 400°F.

While the eggplants are roasting, put 2 tbsp of oil into a large sauté pan and place over medium-high heat. Add the onion and cook for about 7 minutes, until softened and lightly browned. Add the garlic, chile flakes, cumin, cinnamon, and tomato paste and cook for 1 minute, or until fragrant. Add the bell peppers, chickpeas, canned tomatoes, sugar, water, 1¼ tsp of salt, and a good grind of black pepper. Decrease the heat to medium and cook for 18 minutes, or until the bell peppers have cooked through. Stir in ¾ cup/15g of cilantro and remove from the heat.

Spread out half the plum tomatoes and half the roasted eggplants in a large baking dish, about 9 x 13 inches/23 x 33cm. Top with the chickpea mixture, then layer with the remaining tomatoes and eggplants. Drizzle with the remaining 1 tbsp of oil, then cover with aluminum foil and bake for 30 minutes. Remove the foil and bake for another 20 minutes, or until the sauce is bubbling and the tomatoes have completely softened. Remove from the oven and let cool for about 20 minutes. Top with the remaining ¼ cup/5g cilantro and serve either warm or at room temperature.

Beet and feta galette with za'atar and honey

Beet, feta, ricotta, honey, and thyme: some flavor combinations are just a match made in heaven. All wrapped up in some short, flaky, golden pastry and you're welcome! Our work here is done. Serve this with a green salad (the spicy herb salad on page 93, for example) alongside.

Getting ahead: There are lots of ways to get ahead here; the beets can be baked and sliced a day in advance, the onion can be prepared in full a day ahead, and the crust also keeps well in the fridge for up to three days (or frozen for longer). Once assembled, the galette can wait in the fridge for a good 6 hours before going into the oven. Once baked, it's best eaten the same day, either slightly warm or at room temperature.

Ingredients note: A mix of purple and golden beets looks great here, but don't worry if you can't find golden. Just increase the purple beet to 10½ oz/300g.

Serves four

2 small purple beets (7 oz/200g)
1 small golden beet (3½ oz/100g)
Salt and black pepper
1½ tsp olive oil

Crust
⅔ cup/80g all-purpose flour
⅓ cup/35g whole wheat flour
1½ tsp sugar
½ tsp flaky sea salt
1 tbsp oregano leaves, finely chopped
1½ tsp thyme leaves, finely chopped
½ cup/115g unsalted butter, fridge-cold and cut into ½-inch/1.5cm cubes
¼ cup/60ml ice-cold water

1 tbsp unsalted butter
1 tbsp olive oil, plus 1½ tsp
1 large red onion, cut into ¼-inch/6mm-thick slices (1½ cups/170g)
2 tsp sugar
2 tbsp cider vinegar
Salt
1 tbsp za'atar
¼ cup/5g parsley leaves, finely chopped
¼ cup/5g oregano leaves, finely chopped
¼ cup/60g ricotta
2 garlic cloves, crushed
Black pepper
3¼ oz/90g feta, crumbled into roughly ¾-inch/2cm chunks
1 egg, beaten
1 tbsp honey
½ tsp thyme leaves

Preheat the oven to 450°F.

Wrap the beets individually in aluminum foil and bake for 1–1½ hours, or until completely soft and cooked through; timing can vary quite a lot, depending on the size of your beet. Remove from the oven and let cool for 10 minutes, then use an old dish towel to gently rub away the skins. Slice each beet into ⅛-inch/3mm slices and (if you are starting with a mix of purple and golden) place in two separate bowls. Combine the golden beet with ⅛ tsp of salt, a good grind of black pepper, and ½ tsp of oil. Combine the purple beet with ¼ tsp of salt, a good grind of black pepper, and 1 tsp of oil. Set both aside until needed.

To make the crust, put both flours into a large bowl along with the sugar, salt, and herbs. Add the butter and use your fingers to rub it into the flour. Don't overwork the butter—you want chunks of it throughout the dough. Add the water and use your hands to gather the dough together into a shaggy ball. Transfer to a well-floured surface and roll out into a rough rectangle, about 11 x 7 inches/28 x 18cm. The dough here is fairly wet and sticky, so you'll need to flour your hands, rolling pin, and work surface often. This is the way it is meant to be, though (and it makes for a wonderfully short and flaky pastry).

Fold the shorter ends in toward each other so that they meet at the center, then fold the dough in half, like a book. Roll out the dough once with a rolling pin and then just fold once in half again. Cover with plastic wrap and refrigerate for 1 hour (or overnight).

Put the 1 tbsp of butter and 1 tbsp of oil into a medium sauté pan and place over medium-high heat. Add the onion and cook for about 10 minutes, stirring occasionally, until softened and browned. Add the sugar, vinegar, and ⅛ tsp of salt and cook for 1 minute, or until most of the liquid has evaporated. Set aside to cool for about 15 minutes, then stir in 1 tsp of za'atar, the parsley, and the oregano.

Continued

Put the ricotta, garlic, ⅛ tsp of salt, and a good grind of black pepper into a bowl and set aside.

Generously flour a 12-inch/30cm square of parchment paper.

Transfer the crust dough to the prepared parchment paper and roll out to form a rough circle. It will have uneven edges but should be about 11 inches/28cm wide. Lifting up both the baking parchment and the dough, transfer to a baking sheet; you don't want to be lifting it onto the sheet once filled.

Spread the ricotta mixture over the base of the dough, leaving a ½-inch/1cm rim clear around the edges. Top with half the feta, then the onions. Next, and this time leaving a 1½-inch/4cm rim clear around the outside, top with the beets, alternating between purple and golden, with a little overlap between each piece. Wash your hands well (so that the feta does not turn red!), then scatter the remaining feta on top.

Using a knife, make ¾-inch/2cm incisions spaced about 3¼ inches/8cm apart around the edge of the galette. Creating these "strips" will allow for the beets and cheese to be encased. Take a resulting dough strip and fold it over the beet, in toward the center of the galette. Repeat with the next strip, pulling gently to slightly overlap and seal the last fold. Continue this way with the rest of the strips, then refrigerate the galette for 30 minutes (or up to 6 hours, if you are getting ahead).

Preheat the oven to 425°F.

Brush the edges of the pastry with the beaten egg and bake for 30 minutes, or until deeply golden and cooked through. Drizzle with the honey and the remaining 1½ tsp of oil, then scatter with the remaining 2 tsp of za'atar.

Transfer to a wire rack so that the bottom remains crisp and let cool for about 15 minutes. Garnish with the thyme leaves and serve.

السيوري للمكسرات
AL SYOURI NUTS
AL SYOURI NUTS

Pomegranate-cooked lentils and eggplants
Rummaniyya

Rummaniyya means "pomegranatey" in Arabic. It can refer to a dish either garnished lightly with pomegranate seeds or, as here, made rich and tart from an abundant use of pomegranate molasses in the cooking sauce. This is great as a main, served with lots of bread to dip into the juices, or as part of a mezzeh spread. Leftovers are also lovely for breakfast, with a poached or fried egg on top.

Getting ahead: This keeps well in the fridge, for up to three days, ready to be warmed through or eaten at room temperature. If you are making it ahead, just hold back on the onions, these can be stirred in as you warm up the dish.

Serves four as a main, or six as a mezzeh or side

2 eggplants, cut into 1¼-inch/3cm dice (6 cups/500g)
4 tbsp/60ml olive oil, plus 1½ tbsp
Salt and black pepper
¾ cup/150g green or brown lentils
4 garlic cloves, crushed
1 green chile, seeded and finely chopped
1 tbsp ground cumin
1½ tsp fennel seeds or dill seeds, roughly crushed in a mortar and pestle
1 tsp ground coriander
1 tbsp cornstarch
¼ cup/80g pomegranate molasses
2 tbsp lemon juice
1 tbsp tahini
1 recipe Crispy Onions (see page 126)
¼ cup/5g parsley, roughly chopped
¼ cup/40g pomegranate seeds
2 red chiles, with seeds, thinly sliced

Preheat the oven to 450°F. Line a baking sheet with parchment paper.

In a large bowl, mix the eggplants with 2 tbsp of oil, ½ tsp of salt, and a good grind of black pepper. Tip them onto the prepared baking sheet so that they are spaced well apart. Roast for 25 minutes, stirring once or twice throughout. Remove from the oven and set aside.

Rinse the lentils and put them into a medium saucepan with 1 qt/1L of water. Bring to a boil over high heat. Once boiling, decrease the heat to medium and simmer for 20 minutes, until the lentils are almost cooked. Drain the lentils over a bowl—you want to keep 1½ cups/350ml of the cooking liquid—and set both the lentils and liquid aside.

Pour 2 tbsp of oil into a large sauté pan and place over medium-high heat. Add the garlic and green chile and fry for 2 minutes, stirring frequently, or until the garlic is a light golden brown. Add the cumin, fennel seeds, and coriander and stir continuously for 30 seconds. Stir in the cornstarch for 1 minute, then add the lentils, 1½ cups/350ml of reserved cooking liquid, ¾ tsp of salt, and plenty of pepper. Bring to a boil and cook for 5–6 minutes, stirring frequently, until the liquid has thickened to the consistency of a thick porridge. Add the pomegranate molasses, lemon juice, tahini, eggplants, and half the crispy onions. Stir well, then remove from the heat.

Either serve from the pan or transfer to a large shallow bowl. Sprinkle with the remaining crispy onions, the parsley, pomegranate seeds, and sliced red chile, and drizzle with the remaining 1½ tbsp oil.

Bulgur mejadra
Mjaddarat el burgul

For many Palestinians and Arabs around the world, the answer to the question "What is your ultimate comfort food?" is mejadra. It's the food a lot of kids grow up on and, for Sami, it will always take him straight back home. Like so many comfort foods, it's a humble dish—lentils, sometimes chickpeas, spices, and then a grain in the form of rice, most typically, or the bulgur or freekeh we've suggested here. In terms of what makes it so addictive, though, the crispy onions are the secret weapon.

Serve this warm or at room temperature with some yogurt (either plain or with some diced cucumber and shredded mint stirred in) alongside. If you have some pomegranate seeds, these look lovely sprinkled on top.

Getting ahead: The bulgur and lentils keep well in the fridge for a couple of days, ready to be warmed through or brought back to room temperature before eating.

Serves six

1½ cups/300g green lentils
1½ tsp cumin seeds
1½ tbsp coriander seeds
1¾ cups/300g coarse bulgur or freekeh or basmati rice (see headnote)
3 tbsp olive oil
½ tsp ground turmeric
1 tsp ground allspice
½ tsp ground cinnamon
Salt and black pepper
3¼ cups/750ml just-boiled water
1½ recipes Crispy Onions (see page 126)

Place the lentils in a medium saucepan with a lid, cover with plenty of water, and set aside to soak for 30 minutes.

Place the saucepan with the lentils and their soaking liquid over high heat and bring to a boil. Decrease the heat to medium and cook for 10–12 minutes, or until the lentils have softened but still retain a bite. Drain in a colander and set aside.

Wipe the pan clean and add the cumin seeds and coriander seeds. Place over medium heat and toast for a minute or two, until fragrant. Add the bulgur, olive oil, turmeric, allspice, cinnamon, 1 tsp of salt, and plenty of black pepper. Stir so that everything is coated, then add the cooked lentils and just-boiled water. Bring to a boil, then decrease the heat to low. Cover and simmer for 15 minutes.

Remove the pan from the heat, lift off the lid, and quickly cover the pan with a clean dish towel. Seal tightly with the lid and set aside for 10 minutes, to steam.

Finally, add half the crispy onions to the bulgur and lentils and stir gently with a fork. Pile up in a shallow serving bowl, or individual serving plates, top with the rest of the crispy onions, and serve.

Rice with yogurt, roasted cauliflower, and fried garlic
Labaniet alzahar

Serves four as a main, or six as a side

1 large cauliflower, cut into roughly 2½-inch/6cm florets (6½ cups/650g)
2 tbsp olive oil
Salt
1⅔ cups/400g Greek yogurt
1 egg yolk
1½ tsp cornstarch
3 cups/700ml whole milk
1 cup/200g arborio rice, rinsed and drained
White pepper

Fried garlic
5 large garlic cloves, thinly sliced
¼ cup/60ml olive oil
2 tsp coriander seeds, lightly crushed in a mortar and pestle

About ¼ cup/5g parsley leaves (optional)

This feels like a rich risotto or even, if you play around with the toppings as suggested, a thick congee. Either way, it's the most comforting of dishes, to be eaten either as a main, as Sami used to with his family, from a bowl with a spoon, or as a side to slow-cooked lamb, beef, or some roasted root veg.

Playing around: Instead of (or in addition to) the cauliflower, try roasting some little turnips or wedges of squash. For the congee theme, put all sorts of toppings into lots of different bowls—some thinly sliced green onions, for example, a drizzle of shatta, a spoonful of pan-fried ground lamb, charred cherry tomatoes, thin slivers of garlic fried until golden in oil. People can then make up their own bowl as they like.

Getting ahead: Ideally you want to cook the cauliflower, rice, and garlic all at the same time (rather than waiting for one element to be finished before going on to the next), so that everything is warm and ready at once.

Preheat the oven to 425°F. Line a baking sheet with parchment paper.

Put the cauliflower into a large bowl with the oil and ½ tsp of salt. Mix well to combine, then spread out on the prepared baking sheet. Roast for 25–27 minutes, until golden brown and tender.

While the cauliflower is roasting, place the yogurt, egg yolk, and cornstarch in a countertop blender and blend on medium speed for 1 minute, until the mixture is smooth and runny. You can also do this by hand but, if you do, mix it really well to prevent the sauce from splitting when cooked. Set aside.

Put the milk and rice into a large saucepan with a lid, along with 1 tsp of salt and a pinch of white pepper. Bring to a boil over high heat, then decrease the heat to medium-low. Cook for 20 minutes, covered, stirring from time to time, until the rice is almost cooked. Add the yogurt mixture and cook for another 7 minutes, until the rice is tender.

To make the fried garlic, put all the ingredients into a small saucepan and place over medium-low heat. Cook for 2 minutes, until the garlic is golden, then remove from the heat and set aside.

Spoon the rice into a shallow serving dish or individual bowls. Arrange the cauliflower pieces randomly on top and spoon on the garlic. Garnish with the parsley, if desired, and serve at once.

Spinach and toasted orzo with dill and chile yogurt

This is a quick, easy, and satisfying dish to make for a midweek supper. It works either as a veggie main or as a side to something such as grilled salmon or chicken.

Playing around: Some cubes of feta or black olives also work well, dotted over the orzo, either along with or instead of the yogurt.

Serves four

1⅓ cups/250g orzo
5 tbsp/70ml olive oil, plus more to drizzle
2 onions, roughly chopped (mounded 2 cups/300g)
1 lb 2 oz/500g baby spinach
Salt and black pepper
2 cups plus 2 tbsp/500ml water

Dill and chile yogurt
⅔ cup/200g Greek yogurt
1 green chile, seeded and finely chopped
1 garlic clove, crushed
½ cup/10g dill, finely chopped
1 tbsp lemon juice
1½ tbsp olive oil
¼ tsp salt

1½ cups/30g cilantro, finely chopped
1 lemon, cut into wedges

Place a large sauté pan with a lid over high heat. Add the orzo and toast for 10 minutes, stirring very frequently. Tip the toasted orzo into a bowl and set aside.

Return the same pan to medium heat and add the olive oil and onions. Cook for about 8 minutes, stirring a few times, until the onions start to turn golden. Add the spinach, in batches, stirring each batch until wilted. Add 2 tsp of salt and a good grind of black pepper, then pour in the water. Bring to a gentle boil, then add the orzo to the pan, stirring it in and pushing it down with the back of a spoon. Decrease the heat to low and cook, covered, for 10 minutes, until the orzo is just cooked but still retains a bite.

To make the yogurt, meanwhile, mix together all the ingredients and then set aside.

Just before serving, stir the cilantro into the orzo. Divide among four bowls and top with the yogurt. Serve with a final drizzle of oil and lemon wedges alongside.

Pasta with yogurt and parsley breadcrumbs
Ma'caroneh bil laban

Pasta was a favorite of Sami and his older brother Azam when they were kids. Sami's mother, Na'ama, used to make it two ways. The first was ma'caroneh bil foroun, a kind of Palestinian pasta al forno—juicy thick macaroni soaked in a meaty tomato sauce. Azam and Sami used to tussle over who got to the crispy bits on top first, then race to see who could slurp the tubes of pasta the fastest. Na'ama's second pasta staple was lighter and more refreshing, baked this time with yogurt and nuts. This is our take on that. It can be served warm or at room temperature.

Getting ahead: The parsley breadcrumbs can be made a day ahead and kept in a sealed container at room temperature. Everything else should be freshly cooked. It's a quick dish to make, though, perfect for a comforting midweek supper.

Serves four

5 tbsp/75ml olive oil
4 tbsp/65g unsalted butter
⅔ cup/40g breadcrumbs
Salt and black pepper
¾ cup/15g parsley, roughly chopped
½ tsp chile flakes
½ cup/60g pine nuts
½ tsp smoked paprika
2 cups plus 2 tbsp/500g Greek yogurt
3 garlic cloves, crushed
1 tsp ground cumin
2 egg yolks
1 lb 2 oz/500g orecchiette, penne, or conchiglie pasta
¼ cup/5g basil leaves, roughly torn

Line a plate with paper towels.

Put 1 tbsp of oil into a medium sauté pan along with 1 tbsp of butter. Place over medium heat and, once bubbling, add the breadcrumbs, ⅛ tsp of salt, and a good grind of black pepper. Cook for about 8 minutes, stirring often, or until lightly golden. Add ¼ cup/5g of the parsley and the chile flakes and continue to cook for another 5 minutes, or until deeply crisp and golden. Transfer to the prepared plate (or an airtight container, if making in advance) and set aside.

Wipe the pan clean and add the remaining 3 tbsp of butter. Place over medium heat and, once bubbling, add the pine nuts. Cook for 3 minutes, stirring often, then add the paprika. Cook for another 3 minutes, continuing to stir, until the pine nuts are deeply golden. Pour the mixture into a bowl and set aside.

Put the yogurt into a large bowl (large enough to hold the pasta once it's cooked) with the garlic, cumin, egg yolks, and remaining ¼ cup/60ml of olive oil. Whisk until smooth and set aside.

Bring a large pot of salted water to a boil and add the pasta. Cook for about 10 minutes (or according to the package instructions), until al dente. Reserve ¼ cup/60ml of the cooking liquid, then drain the pasta. Add the hot pasta to the bowl of yogurt, along with the reserved cooking liquid and the remaining ½ cup/10g of parsley. Stir well to combine, then divide among four shallow bowls. Spoon on the pine nut butter, sprinkle with the breadcrumbs, top with the basil, and serve at once.

FISH

Growing up in East Jerusalem, on the verge of the Judean desert, Sami didn't encounter many fishmongers in his day-to-day. There was one fishmonger his family would go to, in contrast to the dozens of butchers around. Fish feasts were saved for family trips up north in the summer months, to the coastal towns of Haifa and Akka. When we were traveling and eating our way around Palestine for *Falastin*, it was, still, really only in Haifa and Akka that we found fresh fish. The West Bank is landlocked, obviously, and entry to Gaza, with its once thriving fishing community (see page 196) is barred.

Still, that didn't stop us pushing the boat out and coming home with all sorts of catches.

One of the reasons fish is so great and so easy to cook is that it takes very little time. With just a bit of preparation—making a batch of Fish Spice Mix (page 190), or making a sauce in advance—many of the dishes in this chapter can be on the table less than ten minutes after you've started making them; Spiced Za'atar Squid with Tomato Salsa (page 191), for example, Roasted Cod with a Cilantro Crust (page 204), or Baked Fish in Tahini Sauce (page 208).

At the same time, fish always carries with it a sense of occasion. From little stuffed sardines (see page 194) to Whole Baked Mackerel in Vine Leaves (page 211), bringing fish to the table will always be accompanied by a little "ta da!" It's not all five-minute fast-food snacks and suppers, though, there are some real showstoppers here as well—the Prawn and Tomato Stew with Cilantro Pesto (page 212), or sayyadieh (see page 215), which showcases what the fisherman has brought home that day.

In terms of sauces, we've gone two ways. White firm fish often likes to be paired with a rich tahini sauce. Cod, haddock, pollack, and so forth, these are all made comforting and hearty when baked in tahini or finished with a drizzle of this wonderful nutty, creamy paste. Oily fish or seafood, on the other hand, is often best paired with a sharp tomato sauce. A fresh tomato dagga (see page 194) can cut through the richness of sardines or mackerel. Most fish, though—as long as it is fresh and firm—is very often happy to be served as it is, packed with herbs or lightly spiced, quickly cooked, and dressed with little more than just a great big squeeze of lemon.

Fish spice mix
Baharat samak

This mix is used throughout the chapter—in dishes such as the fish kofta, roasted cod, spiced fish, and baked mackerel—so double or triple the batch, if you like. It keeps well in an airtight container at room temperature for up to a month, and much longer in the freezer. It's also great to use as a rub for all sorts of things—cubes of chicken or tofu, prawns for the barbecue, or roasted mixed vegetables.

Makes 7 tsp

2 tsp ground cardamom
2 tsp ground cumin
2 tsp ground turmeric
1 tsp paprika

Place all the spices in a bowl and mix well to combine. If making more than you need, transfer to a sealed container.

Spiced za'atar squid with tomato salsa
Habar bil za'atar

This works well either as a punchy starter or snack, or as a light meal in itself, served with a crisp green salad. If having it as a snack and eating it with your hands, the salsa can happily be replaced with just a squeeze of lemon.

Getting ahead: You don't really need to get ahead here—this is such a quick meal—but there are still steps you can take if you want to. The salsa can be made up to a day ahead and kept in the fridge, the fish can be scored, and the two bowls with the various spices can be prepared in advance. With this all done, you're then looking at a less-than-5-minute meal.

Serves four as a starter, or two as a light meal

Tomato salsa (optional)
2 tomatoes, roughly chopped (mounded 1 cup/200g)
1 green chile, seeded (if you don't want the heat) and roughly chopped
¼ cup/5g cilantro, roughly chopped
1½ tbsp lemon juice
1 tbsp olive oil
Salt and black pepper

1 lb 2 oz/500g medium squid, cleaned
⅓ cup/50g cornstarch
2 tsp ground coriander
2 tsp ground cumin
1 tsp ground allspice
3 tbsp za'atar
1 tsp flaky sea salt
About 1 cup/240ml sunflower oil
1 lemon, cut into wedges

To make the salsa, put all the ingredients into a food processor with ⅛ tsp of salt and a good grind of black pepper. Blitz for just 10 seconds—don't take it too far, as you still want it to be chunky. Transfer to a bowl and set aside until ready to serve.

Slice through each squid tube lengthwise to create two rectangular halves. With the lines spaced about ¼ inch/6mm apart, lightly score the outside of each half to make a crisscross pattern. Once scored, cut the squid into long vertical strips, each about ¾ inch/2cm wide, and place in a bowl. Cut the tentacles in half, or leave them whole if they're not too large, and add them to the bowl as well. Pat the squid dry with paper towels, removing as much moisture as possible.

Put the cornstarch, coriander, cumin, and allspice into a large bowl. Mix to combine, then set aside.

In a separate large bowl (big enough to hold all the squid once cooked), combine the za'atar and flaky sea salt.

Just before serving, put the oil into a large sauté pan and place over medium-high heat. Line a plate with paper towels.

While the oil is heating up, add half the squid to the cornstarch mixture and toss well to combine. Shake off the excess and, once the oil is hot, carefully lower in the squid and cook for 1–2 minutes, or until golden brown and just cooked through. Using a slotted spoon, transfer to the prepared plate and set aside while you continue with the remaining batch.

Once all the squid is cooked, put it into the bowl of za'atar salt and toss well to coat. Serve at once, with lemon wedges and the tomato salsa alongside.

Fish kofta with yogurt, sumac, and chile
Koftet samak

These herb-and-spice-packed kofta make a lovely starter, or a light meal in themselves, packed into a pita and served with a chopped salad. They're a winner with kids as well—you might just want to leave out the chile. Play around with the herbs that you add; cilantro, parsley, and mint (in any combination) also work. Just keep the total amount of herbs about the same.

Getting ahead: These can be made in advance—a day, if you like—up to the point where they are about to go into the oven. Once cooked they can be eaten the next day—the flavors actually improve—either at room temperature or warmed through.

Serves four

6 tbsp/90ml olive oil
2 large onions, finely chopped (2½ cups/360g)
6 garlic cloves, crushed
1½ lb/700g cod fillet, skinless and boneless, chopped into 1¼-inch/3cm chunks
2 red chiles: 1 finely chopped, 1 finely sliced
¾ cup/15g parsley leaves, roughly chopped
¾ cup/15g dill, roughly chopped, plus a few leaves
1 lemon: finely grate the zest to get 2 tsp, then cut into 4 wedges
1 egg
2 tsp Fish Spice Mix (page 190)
1 tbsp sumac
Salt and black pepper
⅔ cup/200g Greek yogurt

Preheat the oven to 450°F.

Put 3 tbsp of oil into a large sauté pan and place over medium-high heat. Once hot, add the onions and cook for 12–14 minutes, stirring occasionally, or until softened and golden. Add the garlic and cook for another 3 minutes. Remove from the heat and set aside until completely cool.

Put the fish into a food processor and pulse a few times until finely chopped but not a complete paste. Transfer to a large bowl and add the cooled onion mixture, chopped chile, ¾ cup/15g of each herb, lemon zest, egg, fish spice mix, 2 tsp of sumac, 1 tsp of salt, and a good grind of black pepper. Mix well to combine, then, using your hands, shape the mixture into about 15 kofta—they should each be about 2 inches/5cm wide and weigh about 2⅓ oz/65g.

Put 2 tbsp of oil into a large frying pan and place over medium-high heat. Line a baking sheet with parchment paper.

Once the oil is hot, add the kofta in batches of two or three and fry for about 4 minutes, turning halfway through so that both sides are golden brown. Transfer to the prepared baking sheet and bake for 4 or 5 minutes, until just cooked through. Remove from the oven and set aside for 5 minutes or so, to slightly cool.

Spread the yogurt evenly among four serving plates and top each with three fish kofta, saving any extra for seconds. Sprinkle the kofta with the remaining 1 tsp of sumac, the additional dill, and sliced chile. Drizzle with the remaining 1 tbsp of oil and serve, with lemon wedges alongside.

Stuffed sardines with spicy tomato dagga
Sardine ma' daggit banadora

Green chile, garlic, dill seeds, sardines—this is a roll call of ingredients that typify Gazan cuisine. As well as being the general term for all pounded dressings or sauces, *dagga* is also the name of Gaza's famous spicy tomato salad. It's traditionally paired with oily fish—sardines, mackerel, salmon—to offset their richness, but really, it can be eaten in abundance alongside anything. It's wonderful with Baked Fish in Tahini Sauce (page 208), Kofta with Tahini, Potato, and Onion (page 234), or Chicken Shawarma Pie (page 260).

Getting ahead: You can prepare the stuffing a couple of days ahead and even stuff the sardines in advance; they'll keep well in the fridge for a day. The dagga can also be made up to a day in advance and kept in the fridge until serving.

Serves six

Stuffing

1 cup/20g parsley leaves, finely chopped
¾ cup/15g cilantro leaves, finely chopped
2 tbsp pistachios, finely chopped
3 garlic cloves, crushed
1 large green chile, finely chopped (2½ tbsp/25g)
3 tbsp lemon juice
1½ tsp ground cumin
¾ tsp ground allspice
1½ tbsp sumac
Salt and black pepper

Tomato dagga

4 large tomatoes, cut into ¼-inch/6mm dice (2½ cups/450g)
2 small green chiles, seeded and finely chopped (1 tbsp/10g)
1 cup/20g cilantro leaves, roughly chopped
2 tsp dill seeds or celery seeds
1 tsp ground coriander
¼ cup/60ml lemon juice (from 2 lemons)
5 tbsp/70ml olive oil
Salt and black pepper

18 large sardines, cleaned and butterflied (ask your fishmonger to do this; about 1⅔ lb/730g)
Salt
3 tbsp all-purpose flour
2 eggs, lightly beaten
3 tbsp olive oil

To make the stuffing, place all the ingredients in a small bowl along with ¾ tsp of salt and a good grind of black pepper. Mix well to combine and set aside.

To make the tomato dagga, place all the ingredients in a medium bowl with ½ tsp of salt and a good grind of black pepper. Mix to combine and set aside.

Wash the sardines and pat dry, then lay 9 of the fillets flat on a large baking sheet or chopping board, skin side down. Season lightly with salt, then divide the stuffing equally among the fillets, spreading it all over the fish. Lightly season the other 9 fillets and arrange them on top of the stuffed fillets, to sandwich them together.

Spread the flour out on one plate or in a wide shallow bowl and put the eggs into another.

Put the oil into a large frying pan and place over medium-high heat. Line a plate with paper towels.

Working with one fish "sandwich" at a time, carefully lift and dip it lightly into the flour, turning so that both sides get covered, then dip it into the egg. Put it into the pan and fry for about 5 minutes, turning once so that both sides are crisp. Transfer to the prepared plate while you continue with the remaining sardines. Serve warm or at room temperature, with the dagga spooned on top or served alongside.

Fishing in Gaza: the catch-22 of the sea

Writing *Falastin*, we've tried to strike a balance between telling it like it is in Palestine (which is not, clearly, always great) and conveying the upbeat spirit and ambition of the people we've met (which *is*, generally, always great). Looking at Gaza, though, it's hard to be upbeat. We say "looking" but, actually, we haven't been able to look for ourselves. Getting in and out of the city is, for the vast majority, a process totally frustrated by barriers and bureaucracy. The barriers are concrete—the city is surrounded by a large military wall—and the bureaucracy is complex. Apart from journalists and those associated with certain international organizations, the process of obtaining a travel permit to Gaza from either Israel or Egypt is frequently thwarted from beginning to end.

If getting in and out of Gaza is hard, then life inside the wall is even harder. Gaza is a very small strip of land on the eastern coast of the Mediterranean Sea. It's about 40 kilometers long and between 5 and 11 kilometers wide. It borders Egypt in the southwest, and Israel for about 48 kilometers on its eastern and northern borders. With a population of around 2 million, about 80 percent of whom are refugees, the Gaza Strip is one of the world"s most densely populated places. It's often described as the world's "largest open-air prison."

It's not just the people of Gaza who, since 2000 and the closing of borders during the second intifada, haven't been able to move freely to the West Bank or Israel for their daily work. It's the free movement of goods and produce that also faces severe restrictions. Although Israel physically withdrew from Gaza in 2005, its control over the Strip, border, and commerce has been maintained. The results of this—of people not being able to get in and out of the city to work, and barriers to the movement of goods being so many—are dire.

There are, in short, just not enough resources to go around the massively overcrowded city. Jobs, money, electricity, food, effective sewage maintenance—these are just some of the crucial things in short supply. Long power outages are part of the Gazan people's every day, as are inflated prices for gasoline and food, a dependence on food rations, and high unemployment. Industries that were once thriving are now under threat. The economies of many families and businesses have collapsed, malnutrition has become widespread. What was once a fertile, productive, and sustainable territory has turned into one with no autonomy, a dependence on aid, and, frankly, very little hope for the future.

From a culinary point of view, fishing is the main business caught up in the great big knotty net that has entangled Gaza since 2005, when Israel, which had conquered the Strip in 1967, withdrew unilaterally. In 2006, Hamas, a declared enemy of Israel, took control of Gaza, and cross-border attacks on Israel escalated. In retaliation, Israel imposed restrictions on movement at the border, starting what is in effect a blockade of the Gaza Strip that still continues today. In the eyes of the United Nations and Britain, though, Israel's occupation and legal responsibility for Gaza and its people still continues.

Just some of the casualties of this political game are the fishermen, whose fathers and their fathers before them sourced the sea to support their families. As Laila El-Haddad and Maggie Schmitt detail in their book *The Gaza Kitchen: A Palestinian Culinary Journey*, Gaza was once famous for its fish. Just nine nautical miles off its shores there is a deep channel used by large schools of fish as they migrate between the Nile Delta and the Aegean Sea. The channel supplied Palestinian fishermen with more than they needed to make a wage. This was crucial to both the nutrition of the people of the Gaza Strip and, of course, for the income brought in through exporting much of the catch to Israel, the West Bank, and Jordan. The income generated by these exports supported more than 30,000 people. Being in a fishing boat was a good, prosperous, and safe place to be.

The big issue for fishermen today, by contrast, is the many restrictions placed on how far out to sea they are allowed to sail. Before any such restrictions were in place, a fisherman was able to sail as far as he wanted to get a good catch. It was the Oslo Accords that, in 1993, set up a fishing zone of twenty nautical miles. This was under the guise of detailing Palestinian autonomy and was meant to be an interim agreement. Twenty miles was the line drawn, as this was the point where sardines could be caught as they migrated from the Nile Delta up toward Turkey during the spring. The designated zone was deemed to be enough to support a fishing industry of some 4,000 boat-owning families.

There had not previously, however, been any sort of zone or border, so the very fact of one being imposed only set a precedent that could then be squeezed in the years to follow. Since 1993, the border has shrunk from twenty to twelve to ten to six to three miles. This is a result of Israeli naval ships imposing their own limits as part of the tightening pressure on Gaza that came after the election victory of the Hamas Islamist movement in early 2006. With so much of the fishing grounds cut off, those sardines are now a good few miles out of reach.

Reducing the fishing space but sharing it among the same original number of boats means, furthermore, that the reserves of fish there continue to dwindle. In a horrible catch-22, today's fishermen are often forced to cull from the shallow waters close to the shore. Here, they catch the small and young fish that, if left alone as nature dictates they should be, would ensure future prosperity. A day on the sea, then, can yield barely enough fish to feed a family, let alone take to market to sell. Once the pot is shared between all those on board, and the fuel to power the boat in the first place has been factored in, many fishermen are barely breaking even.

It's not even always about making a living, though, it can just be about staying safe. If fishermen from Gaza sail over the appointed border line, the understanding is that they might be approached, targeted, arrested, or shot at by patrolling Israeli military boats coming from the Israeli city of Ashkelon, ten miles away. What is even less understood is how these approaches and attacks can still take place when a fisherman is clearly within the appointed zone. On board with very few things that would be needed to pass the most basic of health and safety tests—a VHF radio, life jackets, safety equipment—such goings-on make for a very uncertain livelihood.

There are other things, too, all challenging the sustainability of this once-thriving Gazan industry. The sewage system in the city—built to serve just 400,000 people and which collapsed because of war damage and lack of maintenance—has failed, and hundreds of thousands of gallons of only partially treated waste water go straight into the sea every day. This, obviously, affects the quality of the fish being caught. Furthermore, export restrictions are firmly in place, dictating what can and cannot leave the city walls with a view to being sold.

It's all, in short, a great big mess. Israel is under constant threat from Hamas attack so it then retaliates in response. It's hard to see what good targeting the Gazan fisherman does, though. For a city dependent in large part on international aid organizations and donors, the situation is a cruel inversion of the Chinese proverb about teaching a man to fish. "Give a poor man a fish and you feed him for a day," the proverb goes. "Teach him how to fish and you give him an occupation that will feed him for a lifetime." "Put that man under occupation and take away his means to fish," we might chip in for debate, "and for both a day and all his lifetime he will remain hungry."

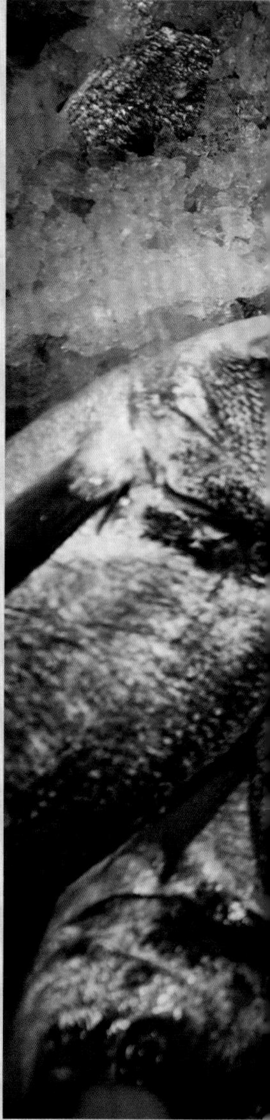

Baked fish kubbeh
Kubbet samak bil siniyeh

Kubbeh in its traditional form—shaped like little torpedoes, with the bulgur casing pressed around the filling (see page 71)—is wonderful to make but does take a bit of time. Here, the same ingredients are simply baked together in a dish before being cut into individual slices. Doing this allows for the benefits of combining all the kubbeh ingredients with only a fraction of the work involved.

Getting ahead: This should be eaten the day it is baked, either warm or a couple of hours later at room temperature.

Serves four generously

½ cup/120ml olive oil, plus more for brushing
1 cup plus 3 tbsp/190g fine bulgur
¾ cup plus 2 tbsp/200ml boiling water
2 onions, finely chopped (2¼ cups/320g)
4 garlic cloves, crushed
1 lb/450g haddock fillets (or another sustainably sourced firm white fish), skinless and boneless, chopped into roughly ¾-inch/2cm chunks
1 egg, lightly whisked
1 tsp ground cumin
½ tsp ground coriander
½ tsp ground allspice
¼ tsp ground turmeric
¾ tsp ground cinnamon
1 cup/20g cilantro leaves, roughly chopped, plus a few leaves
1 cup/20g parsley leaves, roughly chopped
1 green chile, seeded and finely sliced
Salt and black pepper
2 lemons: finely grate the zest of 1 to get 1½ tsp, then juice to get 1 tbsp, and cut the other into wedges
2 tsp sumac
3 tbsp tahini
¼ cup/60g Greek yogurt
2 tbsp cold water

Preheat the oven to 450°F. Brush the base and sides of an 8-inch/20cm square pan lightly with oil.

Place the bulgur in a large bowl and pour in the boiling water. Cover the bowl with a clean dish towel or a large plate and set aside for 15 minutes. Remove the towel or plate, fluff up the bulgur with a fork, and set aside to cool.

Put 2 tbsp of oil into a large sauté pan and place over medium-high heat. Add the onions and cook for about 10 minutes, stirring a few times, until soft and nicely browned. Add the garlic and cook for 1 minute. Remove from the heat and set aside to cool. Once cool, add half of the onion to a food processor along with 9 oz/250g of fish, the egg, cooked bulgur, cumin, coriander, allspice, turmeric, ½ tsp of cinnamon, ½ cup/10g of each herb, ¼ cup/60ml of olive oil, 1½ tsp of salt, and a good grind of black pepper. Blend for about 1 minute, until the mix comes together in a sticky ball, and then set aside.

Put the remaining onions in a bowl with the remaining fish, half of the chile, all the lemon zest, 1 tsp of sumac, the remaining ¼ tsp of cinnamon, the remaining ½ cup/10g of each herb, 1 tbsp of oil, ¼ tsp of salt, and a good grind of black pepper. Mix to combine, then set aside.

Put half the bulgur-fish mixture into the base of the prepared pan and press down firmly; it should rise about ¾ inch/2cm up the side of the pan. Top with the sumac-fish mixture and press down firmly. Top this with the rest of the bulgur-fish mixture, using your hands to spread it out, pressing down as you go, so that it is even and smooth. Use a small sharp knife to score the top with a crosshatch or "spider web" pattern, spaced about 1½ inches/4cm apart. Drizzle with the remaining 1 tbsp of oil and bake for 18 minutes, then increase the oven temperature to 500°F and bake for 7 minutes, or until golden. Remove from the oven and set aside to cool for 15 minutes before gently transferring to a serving platter.

While the kubbeh is baking and cooling, put the tahini into a bowl with the yogurt, lemon juice, cold water, and ⅛ tsp of salt. Whisk until smooth, then set aside.

Drizzle half of the tahini yogurt over the kubbeh and sprinkle with the remaining 1 tsp of sumac, the remaining chile, and the additional cilantro leaves. Cut into squares and serve, with the lemon wedges and remaining tahini yogurt in a bowl alongside for people to spoon over as they like.

Spiced salmon skewers with parsley oil

These skewers are quick and easy to prepare and a winner with all when served. Allow one skewer as a starter, or one or two for a main, bulked out with some rice and a green salad.

Getting ahead: You can get the salmon marinating a day ahead, if you like, ready to go on the skewers and be cooked. The parsley oil is also fine made a day ahead.

Equipment note: You will need six metal or wooden skewers (about 10 inches/25cm long). If wooden, soak them in water for 1 hour before using.

Makes 6 skewers; serves six as a starter, or four as a main

1¾ lb/800g salmon fillet, skinless and boneless, cut into roughly 1½-inch/4cm chunks (ideally, you want 24 pieces of salmon)
1 tbsp Fish Spice Mix (page 190)
2 tsp sumac
3½ tbsp olive oil
Salt and black pepper
2 onions, halved lengthwise and each half quartered into 4 big chunks (10½ oz/300g)

Parsley oil
2 cups/40g parsley
1 garlic clove, finely chopped
6 tbsp/90ml olive oil
Salt and black pepper
1 lemon

12 cherry tomatoes (about 5¼ oz/150g)
1 lemon, cut into wedges

Put the salmon into a large bowl along with the fish spice mix, sumac, 2 tbsp of olive oil, ¾ tsp of salt, and a generous grind of black pepper. Mix well to combine, then set aside in the fridge for 1 hour.

Put the remaining 1½ tbsp of olive oil into a large sauté pan and place over medium-high heat. Add the onions and cook for about 5 minutes, stirring a few times, until they are slightly softened but have not taken on any color; don't worry if they fall apart a little bit and are no longer whole chunks. Remove from the heat and set aside.

To make the parsley oil, put the parsley, garlic, olive oil, ¼ tsp of salt, and a good grind of pepper into the small bowl of a food processor. Blitz for about 1 minute, until smooth, then transfer to a small bowl. Use a small, sharp knife to trim off the top and tail of the lemon. Cut down along its round curves, removing the skin and white pith. Release the segments by slicing between the membranes, then roughly chop the segments. Add these to the oil, stir well, and set aside until needed.

Preheat the oven to 475°F.

To assemble the skewers, start with a tomato and then alternate the salmon chunks and onion pieces. If you have a thinner, end piece of salmon, fold it in half to form a sort of cube. Finish each skewer with a second tomato.

Place a well-greased grill pan over high heat. Line a baking sheet with parchment paper.

Once the grill pan is smoking hot, add the skewers, in two batches, and grill for 3–4 minutes, turning throughout so that all sides are charred. Transfer to the prepared baking sheet and continue with the remaining skewers. Transfer to the oven and bake for 6–7 minutes, or until the salmon is just cooked through.

Transfer the skewers to a large serving platter (or individual serving plates) and drizzle with the parsley oil. Serve at once, with lemon wedges alongside.

Roasted cod with a cilantro crust
Samak mashew bil cozbara w al limon

The combination of fish and tahini is one we find hard to resist, but this works just as well without the tahini sauce if you're looking for a shortcut or want to keep the focus on the lemon. Either way, this is as close to fast food as you can get. It's a 15-minute meal to make, beginning to end. Possibly even less time to eat.

If you are using the tahini sauce, make the whole quantity of the master recipe. It keeps in the fridge for about four days and is lovely to have around to drizzle over all sorts of roasted vegetables, meat, fish, and salads.

Playing around: Any other meaty white fish works just as well here; sea bass or halibut, for example. Salmon also works well.

Serves four

4 tbsp/60ml olive oil
4 garlic cloves, crushed
2½ cups/50g cilantro, finely chopped
2½ tsp Fish Spice Mix (page 190)
½ tsp chile flakes
Salt and black pepper
4 large cod fillets (or another sustainably sourced white fish), skin on (about 1½ lb/700g)
4 large fresh bay leaves (optional)
2 lemons: 1 cut into 8 very thin slices, 1 quartered lengthwise into wedges
About ¼ cup/65g tahini sauce (see page 87; optional)

Preheat the oven to 500°F. Line a roasting dish with parchment paper.

Put 2 tbsp of oil into a small saucepan and place over medium-low heat. Add the garlic and cook for 10 seconds, then add the cilantro, fish spice mix, chile flakes, ¼ tsp of salt, and a grind of black pepper. Cook for 4–5 minutes, stirring frequently, for the garlic to really soften, then remove from the heat.

Place the cod in the prepared roasting dish, skin side down, and brush with the remaining 2 tbsp of oil. Season lightly with salt and pepper, then spoon the cilantro mix on top of each fillet. Spread it out so that the whole top is covered, then top each one with a bay leaf (if using), along with 2 slices of lemon. Roast for 7–8 minutes, or until the fish is cooked through. Serve at once, with about 1 tbsp of tahini sauce drizzled over, if desired, and lemon wedges alongside.

Pictured on page 206

Seared sea bass with lemon and tomato sauce

This is our favorite sort of quick fish supper, particularly if you've made the sauce in advance. Serve with some rice, crusty white bread, or just a spoon, if you prefer, to scoop up all the lovely juices.

Starting with a can of plum tomatoes and blitzing it up (rather than starting with canned chopped tomatoes or uncooked tomato puree in the first instance) is well worth doing; the flavor of the blitzed plum tomatoes is wonderfully intense. With the emphasis of this dish as much on the rich sauce as it is on the fish, it's worth taking this extra step here.

Getting ahead: The tomato sauce keeps well in the fridge for up to three days or can be frozen.

Serves four

7 tbsp/100ml olive oil
4 tsp Fish Spice Mix (page 190)
Salt and black pepper
8 sea bass fillets, skin on and lightly scored, halved crosswise at a slight angle (1½ lb/680g)
1 onion, thinly sliced (1¼ cups/150g)
5 garlic cloves, crushed
1-inch/2.5cm piece ginger, peeled and finely grated (2 tbsp/25g)
1 green chile, seeds and all, finely chopped (1½ tbsp/15g)
1 tbsp tomato paste
1 x 14-oz/400g can peeled plum tomatoes, blitzed in a food processor until smooth (see headnote)
1½ tsp sugar
1 cup/20g dill, roughly chopped
1¼ cups/25g cilantro, roughly chopped, plus leaves to garnish
1⅔ cups/400ml chicken stock
5¼ oz/150g cherry tomatoes
½ lemon, very thinly sliced into rounds, seeds discarded

Combine 2 tbsp of oil, 2½ tsp of fish spice mix, 1 tsp of salt, and a good grind of black pepper in a shallow dish. Add the scored sea bass, turning to coat, and set aside to marinate. You can do this up to 3 hours in advance, if you are getting ahead, but not for much longer than this, otherwise the fish will start to break down.

Put 2 tbsp of oil into a large sauté pan and place over medium-high heat. Once hot, add the onion and cook for about 8 minutes, stirring occasionally, until softened and browned. Add the garlic, ginger, and chile and cook for another minute or two, until fragrant. Add the remaining 1½ tsp of fish spice mix along with the tomato paste and cook for another 30 seconds. Add the canned tomatoes, sugar, two-thirds of the dill and chopped cilantro, the stock, 1 tsp of salt, and a good grind of pepper. Bring to a boil, then decrease the heat to medium and cook for 20 minutes, stirring occasionally, or until the sauce is thick and rich. Keep warm over low heat until needed.

In a small bowl, toss the cherry tomatoes with 1 tbsp of oil. Place a large frying pan over high heat and, once very hot, add the tomatoes. Cook for about 4 minutes, shaking the pan a few times, until charred all over. Add the lemon slices and cook for another 2–3 minutes, shaking the pan a few more times. Add this to the pan of tomato sauce along with the remaining chopped herbs and keep warm until ready to serve.

Wipe the frying pan clean, place it over medium-high heat, and add 1½ tsp of oil. Once hot, add a fourth of the sea bass fillets, skin side down, pressing gently on the flesh so that the fish doesn't curl. Cook for 4 minutes, or until the skin is crisp and browned, then flip the fish over in the pan. Cook for another 30 seconds, then transfer to a plate. Continue with the remaining three batches, adding another 1½ tsp of oil to the pan before searing each batch.

Divide the sauce among four plates and top each with 4 pieces of sea bass. Sprinkle with some cilantro leaves and serve at once.

Pictured on page 207

Baked fish in tahini sauce
Siniyet samak bil tahineh

Preparing fish with dairy products is not common in Arabic cuisine, as it's not considered healthful. Tahini often steps in, therefore, to fulfill the role butter or cream might otherwise have played—to enrich the fish and make the dish one to comfort. We ate far too much of this for lunch in Akka one day, minutes before Tara decided to break the "boys only" rule when it comes to jumping off the harbor wall (see pages 186–7 for a photo of the boys). Joining the locals in a leap, Tara can confirm, is not recommended from a digestion point of view. Pair the fish, instead, with a crisp fresh green salad, or the spicy tomato dagga on page 194.

Getting ahead: Both the tahini sauce and the caramelized onions can be made up to three days in advance, if you want to get ahead. That way you're all set for a very quick-to-make supper.

Serves four to six

Tahini sauce
Rounded ½ cup/150g tahini
2 garlic cloves, crushed
2 tbsp lemon juice
¼ cup/60 ml water
½ tsp salt

Caramelized onions
¼ cup/60ml olive oil
2 very large (or 3 large) onions, very thinly sliced (3⅓ cups/400g)
3 tbsp water

6 cod fillets (or another sustainably sourced white fish; such as hake or halibut), skin on (2 lb/900g)
3 lemons: 2 finely grated to get 1 tbsp zest, then juiced to get 2 tbsp; 1 cut into wedges
1½ tsp ground cumin
Salt and black pepper
3 tbsp olive oil
About 3 tbsp all-purpose flour
2 green chiles (seeded or not, depending on whether you like things spicy), thinly sliced
3 tbsp pine nuts
½ cup/10g parsley leaves, roughly chopped
1 tsp sumac

To make the tahini sauce, place all the ingredients in a medium bowl. Mix well to combine—you want the consistency to be that of thick cream—and set aside.

To caramelize the onions, put the oil into a large sauté pan and place over medium-low heat. Add the onions and cook for about 10 minutes, stirring from time to time. Add the water and cook for another 8 minutes, until the onions have completely softened but have not taken on any color. Remove from the heat and set aside.

Preheat the oven to 425°F.

Place the fish in a large shallow bowl and add the lemon zest, lemon juice, cumin, ½ tsp of salt, and a good grind of black pepper. Mix well with your hands and set aside to marinate for 10 minutes, at room temperature. Don't leave it for much longer than this, otherwise the fish will start to break down.

Put 1½ tbsp of oil into a medium frying pan and place over medium-high heat. Sprinkle the flour onto a flat plate and, one at a time, lift the fish pieces and lightly dip them into the flour. Add half of the fish to the oil and cook for about 4 minutes, turning once halfway through so that both sides are golden. Transfer to a baking dish, about 9 x 13 inches/23 x 33cm, skin side down, and set aside. Add the remaining 1½ tbsp of oil to the pan and repeat with the remaining fish.

Stir the caramelized onions into the tahini sauce, along with the chiles, then pour the sauce evenly over the fish. Sprinkle with the pine nuts and roast for 8 minutes, or until the fish is just cooked. If you want some extra color on top, switch the oven to the broiler setting and broil for another 3 minutes.

Serve warm or at room temperature, sprinkled with the parsley and sumac and lemon wedges alongside.

Whole baked mackerel in vine leaves
Samak bil waraka

As befits all sorts of things wrapped up in a package before being presented, this is a dish for a celebration! It's impressive to make, and mackerel is always rich so sides can be kept simple—some roast potatoes and a simple green salad are all that you need.

Getting ahead: This is very dinner-party-friendly, as all the prep work can be done up to about 4 hours in advance. Take the fish to the point where it's sitting on the baking sheet ready to go into the oven and it can wait around from there.

Serves four

2 lemons, sliced into ¼-inch/6mm-thick rounds
2½ cups/50g cilantro leaves, roughly chopped, plus ¼ cup/5g leaves
1¼ cups/25g parsley leaves, roughly chopped
1 onion, roughly chopped (1 cup/140g)
6 garlic cloves, crushed
2 red chiles, roughly chopped (2 tbsp/20g)
1 tbsp Fish Spice Mix (page 190)
7 tbsp/100ml olive oil
Salt and black pepper
4 whole mackerel (about 8 oz/225g each) or whole seabass, trout, sea bream, or snapper, cleaned and gutted
About 36 jarred vine leaves, drained (about 6⅓ oz/180g)
5¼ oz/150g cherry tomatoes

Roughly chop half of the lemon slices, discarding any seeds as you find them, and place in a food processor along with the 2½ cups/50g of cilantro, the parsley, onion, garlic, chiles, fish spice mix, 5 tbsp/70ml of olive oil, 2 tsp of salt, and a good grind of black pepper. Blitz for about 20 seconds, to form a coarse mix, and set aside.

Preheat the oven to 400°F. Line a baking sheet with parchment paper.

Pat the fish dry and thinly score the outside about three times on each side. Sprinkle the inside and outside of the fish with salt—about ¼ tsp per fish—then fill and cover the fish with the herb paste; about half in the cavities and half rubbed over the outside.

Working on a clean work surface, lay three vine leaves in a horizontal line—don't worry about removing the stems—shiny side down and one slightly overlapping the next. Repeat with another two rows of vine leaves, again three per row, to form one large rectangle of vine leaves, about 11 x 10¼ inches/28 x 26cm, with no gaps in between.

Place one mackerel in the center of the vine leaves, belly facing toward you and head and tail lying on either side of the rectangle. Gently fold the vine leaves over the mackerel, rolling over and wrapping the body of the fish completely, with the head and tail exposed on either end. Transfer to the prepared baking sheet and repeat with the remaining vine leaves and mackerel. Once all the mackerel are on the sheet, space them about 1½ inches/4cm apart and scatter the tomatoes and reserved lemon slices over the top. Drizzle with the remaining 2 tbsp of olive oil and bake for 35 minutes, or until the fish is cooked through and the vine leaves have taken on some color.

Transfer the packages to a serving platter and pour on any juices. Garnish with the ¼ cup/5g cilantro leaves and serve at once. The paper-thin vine leaves will be charred and crisp, so eat this with your hands, if you are happy to be informal, sandwiching together a chunk of fish between two of the charred leaves.

Prawn and tomato stew with cilantro pesto

This is another fish dish where the holy trinity of Gazan cuisine—dill, garlic, and chile—makes it sing so boldly and loud. Big thanks to Noor Murad for this one. Serve this as it is, with some crusty white bread to mop up the juices, or dot some cubes of white feta or black olives (or both) on top. A crisp green salad with a lemony dressing on the side and you're all set.

Getting ahead: Batch-make the base for the stew here, if you like; this freezes well and keeps in the fridge for a good few days. That way you can just char your cherry tomatoes and pan-fry the prawns in minutes. The cilantro pesto can also be made up to three days in advance and kept in the fridge.

Serves four

Cilantro pesto

1½ cups/30g cilantro, roughly chopped
1 green chile, finely chopped
⅓ cup plus 1 tbsp/50g pine nuts, lightly toasted (see "Nuts," page 339)
1 lemon: finely grate the zest to get 1½ tsp, then cut into wedges
⅓ cup/80ml olive oil
Salt and black pepper

9 oz/250g cherry tomatoes
4 tbsp/60ml olive oil
1 large onion, finely chopped (1¼ cups/180g)
4 garlic cloves, crushed
¾-inch/2cm piece ginger, peeled and finely grated (1½ tbsp/15g)
1 green chile, finely chopped
2 tsp coriander seeds, lightly crushed in a mortar and pestle
1½ tsp cumin seeds, lightly crushed in a mortar and pestle
8 cardamom pods, lightly bashed in a mortar and pestle
1 cup/20g dill, finely chopped
2 tsp tomato paste
6 plum tomatoes, roughly chopped (2¾ cups/500g)
1¼ cups/300 ml water
Salt and black pepper
1 lb 5 oz/600g raw king prawns, peeled

To make the cilantro pesto, put the cilantro, chile, and pine nuts into a food processor and pulse a few times, until the pine nuts are roughly crumbled. Transfer to a bowl and add the lemon zest, oil, ¼ tsp of salt, and a grind of black pepper. Mix to combine, then set aside.

Place a large sauté pan over high heat. Toss the cherry tomatoes with 1 tsp of oil. Once the pan is very hot, add the tomatoes. Cook for about 5 minutes, shaking the pan once or twice, until blistered and heavily charred on all sides. Remove from the pan and set aside.

Wipe the pan clean, add 2 tbsp of oil and place it over medium-high heat. Add the onion and cook for about 8 minutes, stirring occasionally, until softened and lightly browned. Add the garlic, ginger, chile, spices, dill, and tomato paste and cook for 2 minutes, until fragrant. Add the plum tomatoes, water, 1½ tsp of salt, and a good grind of black pepper. Bring to a simmer, then decrease the heat to medium and cook for about 25 minutes, or until the sauce has thickened and the tomatoes have completely broken down.

Pat the prawns dry and mix them in a bowl with ¼ tsp of salt, 1 tbsp of oil, and a good grind of black pepper.

Put 2 tsp of oil into a large frying pan and place over high heat. Once hot, add the prawns in batches and fry for 1 minute on each side, until cooked through and nicely browned. Set each batch aside while you continue with the remaining prawns. When the sauce is ready, stir in the prawns and charred tomatoes and cook over medium heat for about 3 minutes, to heat through.

Serve either straight from the pan or spoon into wide shallow bowls. Scoop out the cardamom pods, if you like, they are there to flavor the dish rather than to be eaten. Dot with about half of the pesto and pass the lemon wedges and remaining pesto in a bowl alongside.

Fisherman's dish
Sayyadieh

Sayyadieh translates as "fisherman's catch" or "fisherman's dish." The combination of spiced rice and pan-fried fish is a Palestinian favorite in the coastal towns of Jaffa, Haifa, and Akka. The choice of fish depends, traditionally, on what's been caught that day. Here, we've used a medley of white fish and prawns, but other combinations—calamari and prawns or two kinds of white fish, for example—also work well.

Playing around: Tahini sauce (see page 87) is lovely drizzled on top before serving, for a rich addition.

Getting ahead: The nuts can be toasted and the onions can be caramelized with the cinnamon sticks a day ahead, if you like. Doing this will take 30 minutes off your prep time when it comes to making the dish.

Serves six

3 tbsp unsalted butter, diced
¼ cup/30g pine nuts
¼ cup/30g sliced almonds
7 tbsp/100ml olive oil
4 large onions, thinly sliced (5¾ cups/700g)
3 cinnamon sticks
1 green chile, finely chopped (2 tbsp/20g)
4 garlic cloves, crushed
¾ tsp ground allspice
Mounded 1⅓ cups/280g basmati rice, rinsed until the water runs clear, then drained well
2¾ cups/650ml boiling water
¼ tsp saffron threads
Salt and black pepper
1 lb 5 oz/600g grey mullet (or another sustainably sourced firm white fish, such as halibut, cod, or monkfish), skinless and boneless, chopped into 1½-inch/4cm pieces
¼ tsp ground cinnamon
¾ tsp ground cumin
12 large raw tiger prawns, head and tail intact but shell and back vein discarded (about 1 lb 2 oz/500g)
2 lemons: juice 1 to get 1½ tbsp, cut 1 into 6 wedges
½ cup/10g parsley leaves, roughly chopped

Place a small frying pan over medium heat and add 1½ tsp of butter. Line two plates with paper towels. Once the butter has melted, add all the nuts and fry for about 7 minutes, stirring almost constantly, until golden. Transfer to a prepared plate and set aside.

Put 3 tbsp of oil and 2 tbsp of butter into a large, high-sided sauté pan with a lid, and place over medium-high heat. Add the onions and cinnamon sticks and cook for about 30 minutes, stirring often, or until sweet, softened, and deeply browned. Add the chile, garlic, and allspice and cook for 1 minute. Add the rice, stir well, and cook for another 90 seconds, to toast. Add the water, saffron, 1½ tsp of salt, and a good grind of black pepper. Bring to a boil, then decrease the heat to low and cook, covered, for 12 minutes.

While the rice is cooking, put 1½ tsp of oil into a large frying pan and place over high heat. Put the fish into a large bowl and add the ground cinnamon, ¼ tsp of cumin, ¾ tsp of salt, and a good grind of black pepper. Once hot, add half the fish and fry for 2–3 minutes, turning halfway through, or until golden on both sides but not cooked through. Transfer to the second prepared plate, then add another 1½ tsp of oil to the pan and continue with the remaining fish. Wipe out the pan, you'll be using it again for the prawns.

Once the rice is ready, uncover the pan and add the fish, gently pushing the rice around to tuck half the fish into the rice—the rest can sit on top. Increase the heat to medium, cover, and cook for another 5 minutes. Remove from the heat, add the remaining 1½ tsp of butter, and set aside, covered, for 10 minutes.

In a large bowl, mix the prawns with 1 tbsp of oil, the remaining ½ tsp of cumin, ½ tsp of salt, and a good grind of pepper. Place the frying pan over high heat, add the remaining 2 tbsp of oil, and fry the prawns, in two batches, for 2–3 minutes, until golden and cooked through. Transfer to a medium bowl, mix in the lemon juice and half the parsley, and set aside.

Transfer half the rice to a large serving platter along with the white fish. Top with half the nuts and half the prawns and follow this with the remaining rice, nuts, and prawns. Sprinkle with the remaining parsley and serve, with the wedges of lemon alongside.

الشهيد البطل
فراس اديب حسين مبروكة
استشهد بتاريخ ١٦-٢-٢٠٠٣
مفروشات العايدي
0569
0599 335 421

MEAT

AL.QASABA MUSEUM
Ad-Darajeh public Bath
Al-Aqaba Quarter
Housh Al-Jitan
Al- Qaryoun Quarter
Al-Qaryoun Stream
Eastern Market
Khan At-Tojjar
Al-Jadid Khan
An- Naser Street
Al- Manara Plaza
An- Naser Mosque

As a kid, Sami used to be sent to the neighborhood butcher by his mother, Na'ama, with a bag full of meat chunks, a peeled onion, a bunch of parsley, and some mixed spices. Sami's job was to take the ingredients, all wrapped up in a paper package, to their butcher, who'd then grind them up in his shiny electric machine. Na'ama had her own manual meat grinder at home but it wasn't big enough to grind the amount needed to feed everyone sitting around the large family table. Such was the quality of the ground meat that Sami could never resist sneaking a few mouthfuls of the mix as he strolled back. Once it was home, the meat would be shaped into kofta or meatballs, spooned into dumplings or cored-out vegetables, piled into pitas or onto open pies, or spread out in an easy sheet-pan dish.

Well over half our recipes in this chapter start with ground meat. This is a tribute, in part, to the memory of Sami's strolls and the food he ate growing up. More generally, though, it's a testament to how convenient ground meat is for the home cook. It's a good way to stretch meat out, it cooks easily and quickly and lends itself to all sorts of family-friendly dishes. Sheet-pan dishes and pasta (see pages 254 and 256), chicken arayes (see page 228), shush barak (see page 220), meatballs (see pages 239 and 243), kofta (see pages 230 and 234); these are just some of the dishes in *Falastin* that can be eaten with simply a fork or a spoon. And there's something about this—about the lack of need for a knife to cut with, and all the "formal table manners" a double set of cutlery suggests—that just makes these things so inherently comforting and nurturing.

If ground meat recipes are those to fall back on for everyday cooking, starting with a whole chicken, lamb shoulder, lamb neck, or oxtail is, generally, associated more with celebratory meals. These are very often the signature dishes of Palestine; the upside-down dish maqlubeh (see page 264) or Gaza's sumaqqiyeh (see page 273). Maftoul (see page 267) is another dish whose appearance at the table so often marks a celebration, signaling to those around the table that the cook has been in the kitchen for a good while.

It doesn't all need to be too epic on the part of the cook, though. As with so much cooking, it's so often just about getting a bit organized and planning in advance. Open the freezer of all home cooks in Palestine and it will be full of sealed bags of dumplings, for example, ready to be cooked in yogurt, or sfiha (see page 226), the open pies topped with various things, ready to go straight into the oven when needed. If not the freezer, then there are all those dishes that are happy to sit in the fridge for two or three days, ready to be eaten over several meals. The stews and slow-cooked chicken thighs (see page 260), the meatballs and kofta; these are so often the dishes whose flavor actually improves when all the ingredients have had time to sit around together overnight.

As with all ingredients, but particularly with meat, start with the best quality you can.

كيلو الكبده
والكلاوي ب
(١٢) شيكل فقط

Meat dumplings in yogurt sauce
Shush barak

These ravioli-like dumplings, cooked in a rich yogurt sauce, go by a couple of other names: taqiyet elyahoodi, which means "Jew's hat," or dinein qtat, which means "cat's ears." Whichever their shape resembles more—hats or cats—few dishes take Sami so quickly back home. They're his real madeleine moment. They're a labor of love, but, as is often the case with the food that reminds us of home, the result is pure comfort and nurture.

Getting ahead: You can make these in advance, as they freeze well. Put them straight into the yogurt from frozen; they'll just need a couple more minutes in the pan.

Serves four

Filling
1 tbsp olive oil
½ onion, finely chopped (½ cup/70g)
7 oz/200g ground beef (or lamb, or a combination of both)
½ tsp baharat (see page 335)
¼ tsp ground turmeric
Salt and black pepper
¼ cup/5g cilantro leaves, finely chopped

Dough
1¼ cups/150g all-purpose flour, plus more for dusting
1 tbsp sunflower oil
About ¼ cup/60ml lukewarm water
¼ tsp salt

Yogurt sauce
4 cups plus 3 tbsp/1kg Greek yogurt
1 egg yolk
1 tbsp cornstarch
1¼ cups/300ml chicken stock
1½ tsp salt

Adha
¼ cup/60ml olive oil
5 garlic cloves, crushed
1½ cups/30g cilantro leaves, roughly chopped

1 tsp Aleppo chile flakes (or ½ tsp regular chile flakes)

To make the filling, put the olive oil into a medium frying pan and place over medium heat. Add the onion and cook for about 6 minutes, stirring a few times, until slightly golden. Add the meat, baharat, turmeric, ¼ tsp of salt, and a grind of black pepper and continue cooking for about 5 minutes, stirring and breaking up the meat with a wooden spoon so that it does not form into clumps, until the meat is cooked through and any liquid released has evaporated. Stir in the cilantro and set aside until completely cool.

To make the dough, put the flour, sunflower oil, water, and salt into a medium mixing bowl. Using your hands, gather the dough together into a shaggy and somewhat sticky ball. Transfer to a lightly floured work surface and knead for about 4 minutes, until the dough is elastic and smooth. Shape into a ball, cover, and let rest for about 10 minutes, at room temperature.

Line a baking sheet with parchment paper.

On a lightly floured surface, roll out the dough to form a 14 x 18-inch/35 x 45cm rectangle; it should be quite thin, about ⅛ inch/3mm. Using a 3-inch/7cm cookie cutter, cut the dough into circles—re-rolling the scraps three or four times, you should be able to make about 25 rounds. Working with one piece at a time, take a round of dough and flip it over so that the stickier underside, without any flour on it, is now facing upward. Doing this will make it easier to seal the dumplings. Spoon about ½ tsp of the meat filling into the center of each circle. Fold the dough in half and then pinch tightly around the outside to form a half-moon shape. Next, pinch together the edges so that they overlap slightly, resembling tortellini. To help you with this, either keep a bowl of water beside you, dipping your fingers once or twice as you go along, to prevent them from becoming sticky, or use a clean brush on the rim, dipped in water, to help with the seal. Arrange the dumplings on the prepared baking sheet while you continue with the remaining batch.

Preheat the broiler.

Once all the dumplings are shaped, broil them for 8 minutes—placing them in the middle of the oven rather than directly under the broiler, to prevent them from burning—or until slightly golden.

To make the yogurt sauce, meanwhile, put the yogurt, egg yolk, cornstarch, and stock into a countertop blender. Blend on medium speed for about 1 minute, until the mixture is smooth and runny, then transfer to a large saucepan, along with the salt, and place over medium-low heat. Cook for about 5 minutes, stirring often, until the yogurt comes to a gentle boil.

Add the dumplings to the sauce and continue cooking for about 18 minutes, stirring gently a few times and keeping an eye on the sauce to make sure it does not split, until the dumplings have cooked through and the sauce resembles a thin béchamel.

To make the adha, put the oil and garlic into a small frying pan and place over medium-high heat. Cook for about 4 minutes, stirring often, until the garlic is lightly golden. Remove from the heat, transfer to a bowl, and stir in the cilantro.

Divide the dumplings and sauce among four bowls and drizzle the adha on top. Sprinkle with the chile flakes and serve at once.

Cooking in Aida refugee camp, Bethlehem

Islam Abu Aouda lives in a refugee camp in Bethlehem. Her firstborn is severely disabled, and her home is humble. The needs of her husband and six children come before her own. Frankly, it would be easy to feel sorry for Islam. Spending time with her, though, you don't feel sorry. You feel inspired, energized, and happy. This is a lady with the best hug in town who sure knows how to giggle.

To make ends meet, Islam, along with five other ladies in Aida Camp, gives cooking lessons and hosts home-stays once or twice a month to interested visitors. Their group, formed in 2010, is called the Noor Women's Empowerment Group. The money they make from these lessons and home-stays goes toward making life better for the disabled kids in the camp. They might buy some equipment a child needs to get around, or use the money to give a group of kids an experience they've never had. The visitors, in return, get a slice of Palestinian kitchen life and a good meal to boot. Women rule the roost, stockpots are enormous, and, regardless of how many guests are expected, enough food is made to feed a small wedding. In time-honored fashion, the world is set right over a chopping board.

Going to Aida Camp for the first time, a visitor can be struck by how normal it all feels. The very foundations of the camp are abnormal, clearly—refugee camps only exist for those who've been uprooted from their home—but, with everyone going about their business, it all feels strangely everyday. Socioeconomic conditions are poor, population density is high, basic infrastructure is insufficient, and the smell of tear gas is familiar but, still, kids go to school, parents do what work they can, babies are born, the elderly are cared for, plays are put on, pictures are painted, meals are cooked. Just like every other teenager in the world, the older kids hang around on street corners, hankering after cool sneakers and mobile phones.

It is this apparent ordinariness that results in the incredulity frequently voiced by visitors when they see a refugee doing something as "everyday" as pulling out their mobile phone. "Yes, I'm a refugee," they find themselves having to explain, "and yes, I have a mobile. Yes, I am on Instagram." Their circumstances may be irregular and not normal but refugee camps are full of regular people doing normal things. To an outsider, it's what makes people such as Islam seem so extraordinary.

When we spent the morning with Islam, we prepared shush barak, little lamb-filled dumplings that Sami had been craving. Dough was made, rolled, shaped, filled, and then cooked in a yogurt sauce made from kishek (see page 337), a sharp-tasting fermented yogurt. It's a Marmite ingredient—people either love

it or hate it. For Tara, the jury is still out. For Sami, it's the Proustian "madeleine moment" that takes him straight back home.

Islam's husband, Ahmed, was with us in the kitchen, not necessarily getting his hands covered in flour but obviously supportive of his wife. He gave Sami a semi-jovial hard time, undermining Sami's great success as a chef and traveler by saying that none of it meant anything unless a man had "a wife and lots of kids." As Sami and Ahmed discussed the respective paths of "tradition" versus "passion," Tara and Islam looked on smiling, as they rolled and shaped and filled their dumplings, entertained by two grown men having the conversation about whether one can truly "have it all"—a conversation women are themselves so well versed in.

In terms of having it all—or just getting to dream a little—a visitor might expect Islam to voice the dream of all refugees: "the right to return" to the place they call home. For today, though, Islam's bucket list is more the kind you take to the beach. Her dream is to make a trip to the sea, to watch the sun set over the horizon. She may live just a two- or three-hour drive from the coastal town of Haifa but, in her mid-thirties, an ocean is still something Islam has never actually seen with her own eyes. Freedom to travel from A to B (quite literally, in the case of the region's division into Areas A, B, and C—see "The Tent of Nations" on page 130, which goes into more detail on this) is limited for people such as Islam. Getting in the way is the paperwork needed, the visa often denied, the checkpoint lines so long and humiliating, the regular and real demands of her family. For now, then, the horizon that Islam is focused on is closer to home: feeding visitors to make money to provide for her extended family in the camp.

This is just a snapshot of Islam's story. She is just one of about 3,000 refugees living in Aida Camp. Aida is just one of the three camps in Bethlehem. These camps are themselves just three of the fifty-eight recognized refugee camps throughout the region of Jordan, Lebanon, the Syrian Arab Republic, the Gaza Strip, and the West Bank, including East Jerusalem. These camps are home to about 5 million refugees, and 5 million different life stories.

Open meat or cauliflower pies
Sfiha

These easy-to-make "open" pies are loved by kids and grown-ups alike. They are perfect party food: great to snack on and also really practical, as they can be batch-made and then baked from frozen. They're also lovely for a light meal, served with fattoush (see page 99) or any other salad.

Thanks to Sami's sister Sawsan for creating the recipe for the dough here. It turned out so well that it's revised for Za'atar Bread (page 285) and sambousek (see page 294).

Playing around: There are two toppings to choose from here—one meat and one veggie. Make either one or the other, or a mixture of the two. If you want to serve both, you'll need to either double the quantity of dough or halve the quantities for the toppings.

Getting ahead: The dough can be made up to two days in advance and kept in the fridge after rising. Just bring it back to room temperature the day you are rolling it out. You can also make the pies up in full, topping and all, and freeze them before baking. They can go into the oven straight from the freezer.

Makes 12 pies; serves four to six as a snack or lunch

Dough

1½ tsp fast-acting dried yeast
1 tsp sugar
¾ cup/170ml lukewarm water
2½ cups/320g all-purpose flour
1 tbsp milk powder (also known as dried skimmed milk)
⅛ tsp ground turmeric (optional)
¾ tsp salt
3 tbsp sunflower oil
4 tbsp olive oil

Meat topping

9 oz/250g ground lamb
1 small onion, chopped (¾ cup/100g)
1 medium tomato, finely chopped (⅔ cup/120g)
3 tbsp tahini
½ tsp ground cinnamon
¾ tsp ground allspice
¾ tsp Aleppo chile flakes (or ½ tsp regular chile flakes)
¾ cup/15g parsley, finely chopped
1 tbsp lemon juice
1 tbsp sumac
¼ tsp salt

To make the dough, put the yeast, sugar, and water into a small bowl and whisk to combine. Set aside for 5 minutes, until it starts to bubble.

Put the flour, milk powder, turmeric (if using), and salt into the bowl of a stand mixer fitted with the dough hook. Mix for 1 minute, just to incorporate, then add the yeast mixture, sunflower oil, and 3 tbsp of olive oil. Mix on low speed for about 2 minutes, to bring everything together, then increase the speed to medium. Continue to mix for 5–6 minutes, until the dough is soft and elastic. It will feel very soft and almost sticky, but this is how it should be. Tip the dough onto a clean work surface and bring together to form a ball. Grease the mixing bowl with the remaining 1 tbsp of olive oil and return the dough to the bowl. Turn it a couple of times so that it's completely coated in oil, then cover and set somewhere warm for 1 hour, until it's doubled in size.

Roll the dough out into the shape of a sausage, about 12 inches/30cm long, and cut into 12 even pieces, about 1½ oz/45g each. Roll each piece into a ball, place on a large plate, cover, and set aside for 20 minutes, to rest.

If making the meat topping, put all the ingredients into a large bowl and mix well to combine; doing this with your hands is the best way. Set aside.

If making the veggie topping, preheat the oven to 400°F. Line a baking sheet with parchment paper.

Put the cauliflower, onion, bell peppers, oil, and spices into a large bowl with ¾ tsp of salt. Mix well, then spread out on the prepared baking sheet. Bake for 25 minutes, or until the vegetables are golden brown and tender. Remove from the oven and allow to cool slightly, then chop the cauliflower into ¼-inch/6mm chunks. Finely chop the bell peppers—there is no need to peel them—and place all the vegetables in a medium mixing bowl along with the tahini, lemon juice, parsley, and ¼ tsp of salt. Mix to combine, and set aside.

Preheat the oven to 425°F. Line two baking sheets with parchment paper.

Arrange the dough balls on the prepared baking sheets, spaced well apart. Using your fingers, flatten each ball into a round disc, about 4 inches/10cm wide and ⅛ inch/3mm thick. Spoon a heaped 2 tbsp (about 1¾ oz/50g) of whichever topping you are using into the center of each disc and spread it out evenly, leaving a ½-inch/1cm border clear around the edge. Sprinkle with the pine nuts, if you are doing the meat topping, and set aside for another 10 minutes. Bake for 17–18 minutes, rotating the sheets halfway through (or even switching the position of the sheets if it looks like the pies on the top sheet are taking on too much color), or until the pies are cooked and the edges are golden brown. Remove from the oven and serve warm or at room temperature, with lemon wedges alongside.

Veggie topping

1 medium cauliflower, cut into roughly 2-inch/5cm florets and any stalk cut into roughly ½-inch/1cm pieces (5 cups/500g)
1 large onion, thinly sliced (1½ cups/180g)
2 red bell peppers, halved, core and seeds removed, and then thinly sliced (1⅓ cups/200g)
¼ cup/60ml olive oil
¾ tsp Aleppo chile flakes (or ½ tsp regular chile flakes)
¾ tsp baharat (see page 335)
¼ tsp ground turmeric
Salt
2 tbsp tahini
2 tbsp lemon juice
¼ cup/5g parsley, finely chopped

¼ cup/25g pine nuts
2 lemons, cut into wedges

Spiced chicken arayes

Arayes is the plural of the word for "bride" in Arabic, which is *aroos*. There are various tales as to why this particular name is given to this snack; one is that the white bread represents the white dress of the bride wrapped around the dark tuxedo (typically a lamb filling) of the groom in a deep embrace. Thinking slightly more practically, for those with an appetite, arayes are essentially pan-fried pita bread sandwiches. They're great either for snacking on before a meal or as a meal in themselves, served with a fresh chopped salad (see page 92) and some sumac yogurt (see page 259).

Getting ahead: The filling can be made ahead of time—up to three days if you just make the tomato sauce and up to a day if you've added the chicken—ready for the arayes to be filled and fried to serve.

Serves four as a snack

4 tbsp/60ml olive oil
2 onions, finely chopped (2 cups/300g)
Salt
6 garlic cloves, crushed
1½ tsp caraway seeds, roughly crushed in a mortar and pestle
1½ tsp cumin seeds, roughly crushed in a mortar and pestle
¾ tsp ground cinnamon
½ tsp chile flakes
2 tsp tomato paste
2–3 plum tomatoes (9 oz/250g), coarsely grated and skins discarded (mounded 1 cup/200g)
12¼ oz/350g ground chicken thighs (see headnote, page 156)
1¼ cups/25g cilantro leaves, roughly chopped
Black pepper
4 pitas (see page 278)
3 tsp unsalted butter
1 lemon, cut into wedges
Tahini sauce (see page 87; optional), to serve

Put 2 tbsp of oil into a large sauté pan and place over medium-high heat. Add the onions and ½ tsp of salt and cook for about 8 minutes, stirring often, until soft and golden. Add the garlic, spices, and tomato paste and cook for 1 minute, until fragrant. Stir in the plum tomatoes and cook for about 8 minutes, stirring often, until they have completely broken down and the mixture is quite thick. Remove from the heat and set aside to cool. Once cool, transfer the mix to a medium bowl along with the chicken, cilantro, 1 tsp of salt, and a good grind of black pepper. Mix well to combine and set aside.

Preheat the oven to 400°F. Line a baking sheet with parchment paper.

Using a serrated knife, slice the pitas open to create two separate rounds. Place them on a clean work surface, cut side up. Spread one of the rounds with about 5 oz/150g of the chicken mix—it should be about ¼ inch/6mm thick—then place an unfilled pita on top, pressing down gently to make a sandwich. Continue with the remaining chicken mixture and pita rounds to make four sandwiches in total.

Put 1½ tsp of butter and 1 tbsp of oil into a large frying pan and place over medium-high heat. Add two of the sandwiches to the pan and cook for 2–3 minutes, flipping after a minute or so, until both sides have taken on some color. Transfer to the prepared baking sheet and blot gently with some paper towels to soak up any excess oil. Continue with the remaining two sandwiches, adding the remaining 1½ tsp of butter and 1 tbsp of oil to the pan. Once they are all pan-fried, transfer the baking sheet to the oven and bake for 7 minutes, or until cooked through. Remove from the oven and set aside to cool for about 5 minutes before slicing each pita in four pieces.

Serve warm, with lemon wedges and some tahini sauce alongside to dip into, if desired.

Baked kofta with eggplant and tomato
Kofta bil batinjan

Kofta are something of an obsession throughout the Middle East. These meat patties can be baked, fried, grilled, braised; stuffed into pita and drizzled with tahini; or baked in a tomato sauce and served with rice. We offer two versions: this one baked with tomato, and another, richer version, baked in a tahini sauce (see page 234). They are both simple meals, to comfort—perfect for a midweek supper served with some bread or rice to mop up the juices—rather than to wow with their elegant looks.

Getting ahead: The tomato sauce (which can be easily doubled or tripled, if you want to freeze a batch) keeps well in the fridge for up to four days. The meat mix can also be made a day ahead, kept in the fridge and waiting to be cooked. Once baked, these are also lovely (or even better, as is often the case with meatballs) the next day. Either warm them through or just bring back to room temperature.

Makes 12 kofta; serves six as a main, or eight as a side

2 very large (or 3 large) eggplants, as wide as possible (1 lb 14 oz/850g), peeled in alternate long strips (to look like a zebra), then cut crosswise into 12 slices, about 1 inch/2.5cm thick
Salt and black pepper
¼ cup/60ml olive oil

Tomato sauce
2 tbsp olive oil
1 onion, finely chopped (1 cup/150g)
6 garlic cloves, crushed
2 tsp tomato paste
1 x 14-oz/400g can chopped tomatoes
¼ tsp sugar
1 tsp dried mint
½ tsp Aleppo chile flakes (or ¼ tsp regular chile flakes)
¼ cup/60 ml water
Salt and black pepper

Kofta
12¼ oz/350g ground beef (15–20% fat)
12¼ oz/350g ground lamb (15–20% fat)
1½ cups/30g parsley, very finely chopped
1 onion, coarsely grated (¾ cup/120g)
2 garlic cloves, crushed
3–4 plum tomatoes, coarsely grated and skins discarded (mounded 1 cup/200g)
1 tsp tomato paste
2 tsp ground cinnamon
1 tbsp ground allspice
¼ tsp grated nutmeg
½ tsp Aleppo chile flakes (or ¼ tsp regular chile flakes)
1 tbsp olive oil
Salt and black pepper

Preheat the oven to 450°F. Line a baking sheet with parchment paper.

Place the eggplant slices in a large bowl. Sprinkle with ½ tsp of salt and a good grind of black pepper and pour in the oil. Mix well to combine, then spread out on the prepared baking sheet. Bake for 25 minutes, or until golden brown and cooked through. Remove from the oven and set aside.

Decrease the oven temperature to 425°F.

To make the tomato sauce, while the eggplants are roasting, put the oil into a medium saucepan and place over medium-high heat. Add the onion and cook for about 6 minutes, stirring occasionally, until it has softened and lightly browned. Add the garlic and tomato paste and cook for another 30 seconds. Stir in the canned tomatoes, sugar, mint, chile flakes, water, ½ tsp of salt, and a good grind of black pepper. Bring to a boil, then decrease the heat to medium-low. Cook for 20 minutes, stirring occasionally, until the sauce is thick and rich. Remove from the heat and set aside until ready to use.

To make the kofta, put all the ingredients into a large bowl, along with 1¾ tsp of salt and a good grind of black pepper. Mix well, then divide the mixture into 12 large balls. Shape into patties—about 3 inches/7cm wide—and set aside.

3 large tomatoes, cut crosswise into 12 slices, about ½ inch/1cm thick (1 lb 2 oz/500g)
1 large green chile, thinly sliced (2 tbsp/20g)
¼ cup/5g cilantro leaves, roughly chopped
12 small basil leaves, whole (or larger leaves, shredded)
¼ cup/25g pine nuts, toasted (see "Nuts," page 339)

Arrange the slices of eggplant in a single layer in the bottom of a large, deep baking dish, about 9 x 13 inches/23 x 33cm. Place one kofta patty on top of each slice and place a slice of tomato on top of this, to create a kind of sandwich. Spoon a generous 1 tbsp of the thick tomato sauce on top of each sandwich, spreading it out slightly so that it drizzles down the sides. Sprinkle with the green chile, cover the dish tightly with aluminum foil, and bake for 20 minutes. Then increase the oven temperature to 475°F, remove the foil, and bake for a final 18 minutes.

Remove the dish from the oven and, using a spatula, lift the kofta out of the liquid (don't discard the liquid, though), trying to keep the eggplant slices intact. Place on a large platter or individual serving plates, then pour the cooking juices from the pan into a medium sauté pan. Bring to a boil over high heat and cook for 7 minutes, stirring frequently, until the liquid has thickened and reduced by half. Spoon this sauce over the kofta and sprinkle with the cilantro, basil, and pine nuts. Serve warm or at room temperature.

Pictured on page 233

Kofta with tahini, potato, and onion

Playing around: This is a rich dish, thanks to the tahini. If you want to lighten things up, the potatoes can be replaced with florets of cauliflower. Other vegetables also work, including cubes of butternut squash or pumpkin. If you do this, the cauliflower will need 5 minutes less in the oven than the potatoes and the squash or pumpkin will need about 5 minutes more.

Serves four

3 russet potatoes (1 lb 2 oz/500g), peeled and cut into roughly ½-inch/1.5cm dice (2 cups/470g)
3 tbsp olive oil
Salt and black pepper

Kofta
9 oz/250g ground lamb (at least 20% fat)
9 oz/250g ground beef (at least 20% fat)
½ onion, coarsely grated (½ cup/75g)
1 large plum tomato, coarsely grated and skin discarded (½ cup/90g)
1 tsp tomato paste
2 tsp olive oil
¾ tsp ground allspice
¾ tsp ground cinnamon
¾ tsp Aleppo chile flakes (or ½ tsp regular chile flakes)
½ cup/10g parsley, roughly chopped
2 garlic cloves, crushed
Salt and black pepper

7 tbsp/125g tahini
⅓ cup/80g Greek yogurt
1½ tbsp lemon juice
¾ tbsp cider vinegar
2 garlic cloves, crushed
½ cup/120ml water
Salt and black pepper
1 onion, thinly sliced (1¼ cups/150g)
¼ cup/5g parsley leaves
¼ cup/25g pine nuts, lightly toasted (see "Nuts," page 339)
½ tsp Aleppo chile flakes (or ¼ tsp regular chile flakes)

Preheat the oven to 450°F. Line a baking sheet with parchment paper.

In a medium bowl, toss the potatoes with 2 tbsp of oil, ¾ tsp of salt, and a good grind of black pepper. Transfer to the prepared baking sheet and bake for 25 minutes, tossing halfway through, until golden and cooked through. Remove from the oven and set aside.

Increase the oven temperature to 475°F.

To make the kofta, meanwhile, put all the ingredients into another medium bowl with 1 tsp of salt and a generous grind of black pepper. Shape into 12 little torpedo-shaped pieces, each weighing about 2 oz/55g. Set aside.

Put the tahini, yogurt, lemon juice, vinegar, garlic, and water into a medium bowl with ¾ tsp of salt and a good grind of black pepper. Whisk together well, until smooth and slightly runny, and set aside until needed.

Put the remaining 1 tbsp of oil into a large ovenproof sauté pan and place over medium-high heat. Add the kofta and the sliced onion and cook for about 5 minutes, or until the kofta are lightly colored and the onion has softened. Transfer the pan to the oven and bake for 4 minutes, or until the kofta are cooked through and the onion has lightly browned. Remove from the oven, stir in the potatoes, and pour on the tahini sauce. Swirl the pan, so that the sauce gets distributed, and return to the oven for a final 4 minutes, or until the sauce is bubbling. Remove from the oven and let cool for 5 minutes before topping with the parsley, pine nuts, and chile flakes. Serve directly from the pan.

Lamb bolognese with okra
Sinniyat bamia bil lahmeh

This is essentially a ground lamb bolognese baked with okra. It's simple, comforting, and completely delicious. Eat it as it is, with a salad alongside, or with some plain rice or spaghetti.

Getting ahead: This is a lovely one to bake ahead and have in the fridge for the workweek. It keeps well in the fridge, for up to three days, ready to be warmed through before serving.

Ingredients note: As always with okra (if you don't want a dish to become "slimy"), don't trim the pods so much that you end up seeing the seeds. If you can see them, they'll be able to seep out. If you can't, then they won't, and anyone accusing okra of being "gloopy" can be called out as just plain wrong.

Serves four to six

5 tbsp/70ml olive oil
1¾ oz/50g okra, lightly trimmed (see headnote)
1 onion, sliced in half, then each half cut into 4 wedges (1½ cups/160g)
10 garlic cloves: 5 crushed, 5 very thinly sliced
½ tsp chile flakes
1½ tsp coriander seeds, roughly crushed in a mortar and pestle
1½ tsp cumin seeds, roughly crushed in a mortar and pestle
½ tsp ground allspice
10½ oz/300g ground lamb (at least 20% fat)
1¼ cups/300g uncooked tomato puree
6 plum tomatoes (1 lb 3 oz/550g): 2 roughly chopped, 4 sliced into ½-inch/1cm-thick rounds
2 tsp sugar
½ cup plus 2 tbsp/150ml water
Salt and black pepper
1 cup/20g cilantro leaves, roughly chopped

Preheat the oven to 400°F.

Put 1½ tsp of oil into a large frying pan and place over high heat. Once smoking hot, add half the okra and cook for 3 minutes, shaking the pan once or twice, until nicely colored on all sides. Transfer to a plate, then repeat with another 1½ tsp of oil and the remaining okra. Set aside until needed.

Put 2 tbsp of oil into a large sauté pan and place over medium-high heat. Add the onion and cook for 5 minutes, stirring a few times, until soft and lightly colored. Add the crushed garlic, chile flakes, coriander seeds, cumin seeds, and allspice and cook for another 1 minute, until fragrant. Add the ground lamb and cook for 2–3 minutes, using a spoon to break up any chunks, or until no longer pink. Add the tomato puree, chopped plum tomatoes, sugar, water, 1¼ tsp of salt, and a good grind of black pepper. Decrease the heat to medium and cook for 20 minutes, stirring occasionally, until the sauce is thick and rich.

Stir ¾ cup/15g of the cilantro, half the sliced tomatoes, and half the okra into the sauce, then spread out in a large baking dish, about 11 x 8 inches/ 28 x 20cm. Top with the remaining okra and tomatoes, scattered roughly over, cover with aluminum foil, and bake for 30 minutes. Increase the oven temperature to 450°F, remove and discard the foil, and cook for another 20 minutes, or until the okra and tomatoes have taken on some color and the sauce is bubbling. Remove from the oven and set aside to rest for 10 minutes.

Meanwhile, put the sliced garlic and remaining 2 tbsp of oil into a small frying pan. Set over medium heat and cook for about 10 minutes, stirring from time to time, until the garlic is golden and crispy. Drain into a sieve set over a bowl and set aside; you don't need the oil for this dish, so either discard it or save it to add to your next salad dressing.

When ready to serve, sprinkle the bolognese with the fried garlic and remaining ¼ cup/5g cilantro.

Chicken meatballs with molokhieh, garlic, and cilantro

This is somewhere between a stew and a soup. A "stoup," maybe. Comforting and hearty, certainly, served with some rice or crusty white bread.

Playing around: If you want to make this dish gluten-free, replace the breadcrumbs in the meatballs with an equal weight of grated zucchini. The resulting meatballs aren't quite as firm as those made with bread, but this, arguably, makes them even more comforting.

Getting ahead: The meatballs can be made up to a day in advance and kept in the fridge, ready to fry. The molokhieh can also be made a day or two in advance. You can make up the whole thing well before serving; it keeps in the fridge for two days.

Serves four

Meatballs

1¾ oz/50g crustless sourdough bread, finely blitzed into crumbs, or 1 large zucchini (½ lb/220g), coarsely grated
1 lb 2 oz/500g ground chicken or turkey thighs (see headnote, page 156)
2 garlic cloves, crushed
1½ tsp ground cumin
1 tsp ground cinnamon
½ tsp ground allspice
¼ tsp chile flakes
½ cup/10g cilantro leaves, roughly chopped
½ cup/10g parsley leaves, roughly chopped
½ cup/10g mint leaves, roughly chopped
1 lemon: grate finely to get 1½ tsp zest, then cut into wedges
Salt and black pepper
2 tbsp olive oil

2 garlic cloves, crushed
1 lemon: shave the rind to get 4 strips, then juice to get 1½ tbsp
1¾ cups/450ml chicken stock
1¾ lb/800g frozen molokhieh (or 1¾ lb/800g frozen chopped spinach plus 7 oz/200g okra, thinly sliced—see pages 150 and 339)
½ tsp ground cinnamon
Salt and black pepper
½ cup/10g parsley leaves, roughly chopped
1 cup/20g cilantro leaves, roughly chopped

Chile adha

¼ cup/60ml olive oil
6 garlic cloves, crushed
½ tsp chile flakes
½ cup/10g cilantro leaves, roughly chopped

To make the meatballs, place the breadcrumbs in a small bowl and cover with water. Stir, then drain through a colander, squeezing out most of the moisture from the bread. (If using grated zucchini, toss it with ½ tsp of salt and place in a sieve set over a bowl. Let to sit for 20 minutes, then use your hands to squeeze out as much liquid as possible.)

Transfer the crumbs to a large bowl with the chicken, garlic, spices, herbs, lemon zest, ¾ tsp salt, and plenty of black pepper. Using well-oiled hands, shape into about 30 small balls; roughly a scant 1 oz/25g each.

Put 1 tbsp of oil into a large nonstick sauté pan with a lid, and place over high heat. Once hot, add half the meatballs and cook for 2–3 minutes, turning throughout, until golden brown all over. Transfer the meatballs to a baking sheet and set aside. Keep the pan on the heat and continue with the remaining 1 tbsp of oil and remaining meatballs in the same way.

Return the same pan to medium-high heat. Add the 2 garlic cloves, lemon rind, and stock and bring to a boil—this should take about 3 minutes. Add the molokhieh (or the spinach and okra combination), cinnamon, 2 tsp of salt, and plenty of black pepper, then decrease the heat to medium and cook, covered, for about 20 minutes, or until the molokhieh is bubbling and completely defrosted. Add the meatballs, parsley, and ½ cup/10g of cilantro and cook, covered, for another 10 minutes, or until completely cooked through. Stir in the lemon juice.

To make the adha, meanwhile, put the olive oil into a small frying pan over medium-high heat. Add the garlic and cook for about 3 minutes, stirring occasionally, or until golden and crispy. Add the chile flakes, then remove from the heat and pour into a bowl. Stir in the cilantro and set aside.

Divide the soup among four bowls and top with the fried garlic and remaining ½ cup/10g cilantro. Serve at once, with lemon wedges alongside.

Stuffed turnips with turkey, freekeh, and spicy tamarind sauce
Mahshi lift

Serves six

Stuffing

½ cup/80g cracked freekeh (see page 336), rinsed well, drained, and picked of any stones
9 oz/250g ground turkey thighs
¾ tsp baharat (see page 335)
¾ tsp ground cumin
¾ tsp ground cinnamon
½ cup/10g dill leaves, roughly chopped, plus 1 tbsp to serve
½ cup/10g parsley leaves, roughly chopped, plus 1 tbsp to serve
½ cup/10g tarragon leaves, roughly chopped, plus 1 tbsp to serve
1½ tbsp olive oil
1 lemon: finely grate the zest to get 1½ tsp
1½ tsp tomato puree
Salt and black pepper

4½ lb/2kg turnips
6 tbsp/90ml sunflower oil

Tamarind sauce

3 oz/80g dried tamarind pulp (see page 341), soaked in 1 cup/240ml boiling water for 30 minutes
1 onion, finely diced (1 cup/150g)
6 garlic cloves, crushed
1 large green chile, seeded and finely chopped (2 tbsp/20g)
2 tbsp olive oil
½ tsp ground cumin
½ tsp ground coriander
½ tsp ground cinnamon
1 tsp baharat (see page 335)
6 plum tomatoes, coarsely grated and skins discarded (2¼ cups/400g)
1½ tsp tomato paste
Salt and black pepper
1 tbsp sugar
2 cups plus 2 tbsp/500 ml water

Stuffing vegetables is commonplace in Palestinian cooking. As well as being delicious, celebratory, and comforting, the resulting dishes are often a practical way of making meat stretch further than it would otherwise do. Stuffing vegetables is, however, time-consuming—sauces and fillings need to be made, vegetables need to be hollowed out, the cooking time required is often relatively long. This is not to dissuade you from making a recipe like this—the results are wonderful—but to explain why there are not lots more recipes for stuffed vegetables in *Falastin*. Traditionally, coring and stuffing vegetables is done as a group activity, with the time spent divided between (equally important) coring and chatting duties.

Getting ahead: The turnips can be cored up to a day in advance; just keep them in plenty of cold water with some lemon juice squeezed in (to prevent discoloration). The whole dish can also be cooked a day ahead of serving, if you like, then just warmed through to serve—the flavors actually improve the next day.

To make the stuffing, bring a medium pan full of water to a boil. Add the freekeh and cook for about 15 minutes, or until just cooked through. Drain through a sieve, rinse under cold water, then set aside for about 15 minutes, to drain completely.

While the freekeh is cooking, put the remaining stuffing ingredients into a bowl along with 1 tsp of salt and a good grind of black pepper. The freekeh can be added once it is drained and dried. Mix well to combine and set aside.

Peel the turnips, trim the top ends so that they sit flat, then, using a manakra (see page 338) or a swivel peeler (as opposed to a Y-shaped peeler), core them. Pierce through one end of each turnip with your manakra or peeler, then twist to increase the cavity's circumference as you go along. Stop short before you get to the base, though, you don't want to pierce it all the way through. You should end up with a cavity about 1¼ inches/3cm wide, with edges about ¼ inches/6mm thick. Don't worry too much if you do pierce through the bottom; the trimmings can be used to seal the ends if needed. (Any trimmings beyond this can be used to make turnip mash; see page 138).

Line a baking sheet with paper towels.

Pour the sunflower oil into a large sauté pan. Place over medium-high heat and, once hot, carefully add the turnips, in batches of two or three. Fry for 7–10 minutes, turning occasionally to brown on all sides. Transfer to the prepared baking sheet and continue with the remaining batches. Once the turnips are cool enough to handle, use your hands or a small spoon to fill the cavities with the freekeh stuffing, pushing it down gently as you go.

Continued

To make the sauce, use your hands to break apart the tamarind pulp as much as possible. Strain the mixture through a sieve, pushing gently with a spoon, to get out as much tamarind liquid as you can; you should have about 1 cup plus 1 tbsp/260ml. The pulp and seeds can be discarded. Put the onion, garlic, and chile into a food processor and pulse a couple of times—you want the mixture to be finely ground but not to become a complete paste.

Put the oil into a large sauté pan with a lid, and place over medium-high heat. Add the onion mixture and cook for about 7 minutes, stirring from time to time, until softened and lightly colored. Stir in the spices and cook for a few seconds, then add the tomatoes, tomato paste, 2 tsp of salt, and a good grind of black pepper. Cook for another 5 minutes, for the mixture to thicken, then add the sugar, tamarind liquid, and water. Cook for another 10 minutes, stirring occasionally.

½ cup/60g pomegranate seeds (from ½ pomegranate)
1½ tbsp olive oil
½ cup/150g Greek yogurt, (optional)

Remove the pan from the heat and gently lower in the turnips, filling side up. Return to medium-low heat and let simmer gently, covered, for about 70 minutes, or until the turnips are easily pierced with a knife. Remove from the heat and set aside, uncovered, for about 10 minutes, to slightly cool.

While the turnips are cooking, combine the pomegranate seeds, 1½ tbsp olive oil, and remaining 1 tbsp of dill, parsley, and tarragon in a bowl. Spoon this over the turnips before serving them, straight from the pan, with a spoonful of yogurt, if desired.

Meatballs and peas in tomato sauce

This is a dish to both comfort and surprise. Comfort in a way that only baked meatballs can, and a surprise at the amount of flavor packed into both the balls and the sauce. Serve with some plain rice, mashed potato, or crusty white bread to mop up the juices, along with a crisp green salad.

Getting ahead: The sauce can be made in advance—it keeps well in the fridge for up to three days or can be frozen for longer—and the meatballs can be shaped in advance and either kept in the fridge overnight or pan-fried, ready to be warmed through. You can also just make the whole dish up to a day in advance, ready to warm through before serving.

Playing around: Meatballs often call for a bit of bread, to keep them spongy and light. If you want to, the bread can be replaced with an equal amount of coarsely grated zucchini. Once grated, place the zucchini in a sieve or colander and give it a good squeeze to extract some of the liquid. If you use the zucchini, you won't need the milk.

Serves four

Meatballs

2 slices of white bread, crusts removed, torn into roughly ½-inch/1cm chunks (1¾ cups/60g)
3 tbsp whole milk
1 onion, roughly chopped (1 cup/140g)
2 garlic cloves, crushed
1 lb 2 oz/500g ground beef (at least 15% fat)
2 tsp ground cinnamon
1 tsp ground allspice
¾ cup/15g parsley, roughly chopped, plus a few leaves to serve
½ cup/10g mint leaves, roughly chopped
1 large lemon: finely grate the zest to get 1½ tsp
Mounded ⅓ cup/70g pitted green olives, roughly chopped
Salt and black pepper

3 tbsp plus 1 tsp olive oil
1 onion, finely chopped (1 cup/150g)
4 garlic cloves, crushed
1 tsp cumin seeds, roughly crushed in a mortar and pestle
6 cardamom pods, lightly crushed in a mortar and pestle
1 cinnamon stick
½ tsp chile flakes
2 tsp tomato paste
8 plum tomatoes (1¾ lb/800g), coarsely grated and skins discarded (3⅓ cups/600g)
1 cup/240ml chicken stock
1½ tsp sugar
Salt and black pepper
2½ cups/300g frozen peas, defrosted
5¼ oz/150g feta, roughly broken into 1½-inch/4cm chunks
2 green onions, thinly sliced (¼ cup/25g)

To make the meatballs, put the bread and milk into a large bowl, mash together with your hands until the bread has completely disintegrated, then set aside.

Put the onion into the bowl of a food processor and pulse a few times until very finely chopped but not liquidized. Tip the onion into the bowl of bread and add the garlic, beef, spices, herbs, lemon zest, olives, 1¼ tsp of salt, and a good grind of black pepper. With lightly oiled hands, shape the mixture into golfball-size balls, about 1½ oz/40g in weight; you should be able to make about 22 balls.

Put 2 tbsp of oil into a large sauté pan and place over high heat. Add the meatballs in batches—you don't want to overcrowd the pan—and cook for about 3 minutes, turning so that all sides get nicely browned. Transfer the balls to a separate plate and set aside while you continue with the remaining batches.

Preheat the oven to 450°F.

Return the same pan to medium-high heat and add 1 tbsp of oil. Add the onion and cook for about 6 minutes, scraping the pan for any flavor gathered at the bottom, until softened and nicely browned. Add the garlic, cumin seeds, cardamom pods, cinnamon, chile flakes, and tomato paste and cook for 1 minute, or until fragrant. Add the plum tomatoes, stock, sugar, 1¼ tsp salt, and a good grind of black pepper and cook for about 20 minutes, until reduced by a third. Remove from the heat, stir in the peas, then transfer the mixture to a large ovenproof dish, about 11 x 8 inches/28 x 20cm. Top with the meatballs, scatter on the feta, and drizzle with the remaining 1 tsp of oil. Bake for 20 minutes, or until the meatballs are cooked though, the sauce is bubbling, and the feta has taken on some color. Let sit for about 10 minutes, then sprinkle with the green onions and additional parsley leaves and serve.

Stuffed eggplants and zucchini in a rich tomato sauce

Baatingan w kusaa bil banadoura

Stuffing vegetables is such an everyday event in the Palestinian kitchen that most cooks have a special knife to help them with the task. It's called a manakra, with a thin blade curved into a semicircle and both sides serrated. You can get them online or in specialty shops but, for a good alternative, a swivel peeler (a straight one, as opposed to a Y-shaped one) or a corer both work very well. Sami and Tara were also shown how to use a power drill, by some ladies serving lunch out of a garage in a parking lot in Jerusalem, to core carrots and zucchini, but such a recommendation comes with obvious health and safety warnings!

Serve these either as a side or as a main, with a salad or some other cooked vegetables alongside. Some bread is also good, to mop up the juices.

Getting ahead: The stuffing mixture can be made up to a day ahead. The tomato sauce keeps well in the fridge for up to three days, and also freezes well. Double the recipe for the sauce, if you can, so that you have a batch ready to go when you next need it.

Serves six as a main, or twelve as a side

Sauce
2½ tbsp olive oil
2 onions, finely diced (2½ cups/350g)
4 cups/1kg tomato puree
12¼ oz/350g ripe tomatoes (2 large), coarsely grated
3¼ cups/750ml chicken stock or water
1 tbsp sugar
Salt and black pepper

Stuffing
¾ cup plus 2 tbsp/175g Egyptian rice (see page 336)
9 oz/250g ground lamb (or ground beef or a mixture of both)
¼ cup/60ml olive oil
½ tsp ground cinnamon
¾ tsp ground allspice
½ tsp ground cumin
About 3 green onions, finely sliced (⅓ cup/35g)
¾ cup/15g mint leaves, roughly chopped
¾ cup/15g parsley leaves, roughly chopped
1 cup/20g dill, roughly chopped
1 red chile, seeded and finely diced (1 tbsp/10g)
1 lemon: finely grate the zest to get 1 tsp
3 tbsp water
Salt and black pepper

1½ lb/700g eggplants (between 3 and 6, depending on size)
1½ lb/700g zucchini (between 3 and 6, depending on size)

To make the sauce, put the oil into a saucepan or casserole pan with a lid—about 10 inches/25cm wide—and place over medium heat. Add the onions and cook for about 10 minutes, stirring frequently, until soft and caramelized. Add the rest of the sauce ingredients, along with 2½ tsp of salt and a good grind of black pepper. Simmer over medium heat for about 10 minutes, stirring from time to time, then remove from the heat and set aside.

To make the stuffing, while the sauce is cooking, place all the ingredients in a large bowl with 1½ tsp of salt and a good grind of black pepper. Mix well, using your hands to make sure that everything is well incorporated. If making in advance, keep in the fridge until ready to use.

Trim the stalks from the eggplants, then insert a manakra (or peeler or corer) into the eggplant; you want it to be very close to the skin—about ⅛ inch/3mm away—but not so close that it tears and won't hold its shape when it's stuffed. Scoop out the flesh to create a generous cavity. You don't need the flesh anymore, but keep it for another recipe; it can be cut into cubes and steamed or added to your next omelette. If your eggplants are particularly large, slice them in half, crosswise, and scoop out the flesh using a regular small serrated knife—be sure to keep one end of each half intact, so that the stuffing does not fall out!

Use the manakra or a swivel peeler to scoop out the zucchini flesh. Keep about ⅛ inch/3mm of flesh attached to the skin inside the zucchini and about ½ inch/1cm from the end intact—they need to be robust enough to keep the stuffing inside. Again, keep the scooped-out flesh to use elsewhere.

Using your hands, so that you can push in a bit of stuffing at a time, fill all the eggplant and zucchini cavities. Stop filling them about ½ inch/1cm from the top of each vegetable; the stuffing needs some space to expand inside the vegetables when they are cooking.

Gently lower the stuffed vegetables into the sauce. They won't fit in a single layer, but try to avoid too much overlap and submerge them in the sauce as much as you can. Return the sauce to medium heat and, once simmering, decrease the heat to low. Cover the pan and simmer very gently for 90 minutes, or until the rice is completely cooked through and soft—test if it is ready by sticking a knife into the middle of one of the vegetables; it should go in very easily. Don't worry if some of the rice/stuffing spills into the tomato sauce, this can happen and it will be fine when served.

Coriander adha

7 tbsp/100ml olive oil
6 garlic cloves, finely chopped
1 tbsp coriander seeds, lightly crushed in a mortar and pestle
1 red chile, seeded and finely diced (1 tbsp/10g)

¼ cup/5g parsley leaves, roughly chopped
¼ cup/5g mint leaves, roughly torn
¼ cup/5g dill leaves
1 green onion, thinly sliced (2 tbsp/10g)
1 cup/250g Greek yogurt

To make the adha, meanwhile, put the oil into a small frying pan and place over medium heat. After about 1 minute, add the garlic and decrease the heat to medium-low. Cook for about 5 minutes, stirring very often, until the garlic is golden and crispy. Keep a close eye on the pan here; you don't want the oil to get too hot and for the garlic to burn. Reserving the oil as you pour, strain the garlic through a sieve. Set the garlic aside—it will crisp up as it cools down—and return the oil to the pan. Add the coriander seeds and chile and cook for about 1 minute, stirring a few times, until fragrant. Remove from the heat, transfer to a separate bowl, and set aside until needed.

When the vegetables are cooked and the sauce is thick and rich (but still pourable), use a slotted spoon to carefully lift the vegetables out of the pan. Pour the sauce onto a large serving platter (or individual serving plates) with a rim and top with the stuffed vegetables. Spoon on the adha—the coriander-chile oil first, followed by the fried garlic slices—then sprinkle with the fresh herbs and green onion. Serve warm or at room temperature, with the yogurt spooned alongside.

Chicken musakhan

Musakhan is the hugely popular national dish of Palestine. Growing up, Sami ate it once a week, pulling a piece of chicken and sandwiching it between a piece of pita or flatbread. It's a dish to eat with your hands and with your friends, served from one pot or plate, for everyone to then tear at some of the bread and spoon on the chicken and topping for themselves.

Traditionally, musakhan was made around the olive oil pressing season in October or November to celebrate (and gauge the quality of) the freshly pressed oil. The taboon bread would be cooked in a hot taboon oven (see page 341) lined with smooth round stones, to create small craters in the bread in which the meat juices, onion, and olive oil all happily pool. Musakhan is cooked year-round, nowadays, layered with store-bought taboon or pita bread, and is a dish to suit all occasions—easy and comforting enough to be the perfect weeknight supper as it is, but also special enough to stand alongside other dishes at a feast.

Playing around: The chicken can be replaced with thick slices of roasted eggplant or chunky cauliflower florets, if you like (or a mixture of both), for a vegetarian alternative. If you do this, toss the slices or florets in the oil and spices, as you do the chicken, and roast at 425°F for about 25 minutes for the cauliflower and about 35 minutes for the eggplant.

Serves four

1 chicken (about 3¾ lb/1.7kg), cut into 4 pieces (3 lb/1.4kg), or 2 lb 2 oz/1kg chicken breasts with the wing-tips left on (between 4 and 6, depending on size), skin on, if you prefer
½ cup/120ml olive oil, plus 2 or 3 tbsp
1 tbsp ground cumin
3 tbsp sumac
½ tsp ground cinnamon
½ tsp ground allspice
Salt and black pepper
¼ cup/30g pine nuts
3 large red onions, thinly sliced ⅛ inch/3mm thick (mounded 4 cups/500g)
4 taboon breads (see headnote), or any flatbread (such as Arabic flatbread or naan bread; ¾ lb/330g)
¼ cup/5g parsley leaves, roughly chopped
1¼ cups/300g Greek yogurt
1 lemon, cut into wedges

Preheat the oven to 425°F. Line a rimmed baking sheet with parchment paper, and line a bowl with paper towels.

Place the chicken in a large mixing bowl with 2 tbsp of oil, 1 tsp of cumin, 1½ tsp of sumac, the cinnamon, allspice, 1 tsp of salt, and a good grind of black pepper. Mix well to combine, then spread out on the prepared baking sheet. Roast until the chicken is cooked through. This will take about 30 minutes if starting with breasts, and up to 45 minutes if starting with the whole chicken, quartered. Remove from the oven and set aside. Don't discard any juices that have collected in the pan.

Meanwhile, put 2 tbsp of oil into a large sauté pan, about 10 inches/25cm, and place over medium heat. Add the pine nuts and cook for 2–3 minutes, stirring constantly, until the nuts are golden brown. Transfer to the prepared bowl (leaving the oil behind in the pan) and set aside. Add the remaining ¼ cup/60ml of oil to the pan, along with the onions and ¾ tsp of salt. Return to medium heat for about 15 minutes, stirring from time to time, until the onions are completely soft and pale golden but not caramelized. Add 2 tbsp of sumac, the remaining 2 tsp of cumin, and a grind of black pepper and mix well, until the onions are completely coated. Remove from the heat and set aside.

When ready to assemble the dish, preheat the broiler and slice or tear the bread into fourths or sixths. Place under the broiler for 2–3 minutes, to crisp up, then arrange on a large platter. Top the bread with half the onions, followed by all the chicken and any chicken juices left in the pan. Either keep each piece of chicken as it is or roughly shred it, into two or three large chunks, as you plate up. Spoon the remaining onions over the top and sprinkle with the pine nuts, parsley, remaining 1½ tsp of sumac, and a final drizzle of olive oil. Serve at once, with the yogurt and lemon wedges alongside.

Olive trees and olive oil

Palestinian olive oil is delicious. It's rich, it's green, it's grassy, it's all sorts of words one normally associates with the tasting of fine wines. So why does no one, really, know about it outside Palestine? Why is the terrain of extra-virgin olive oil generally held to be Italy, or Greece, or Spain?

The answer lies in logistics—more particularly, the logistics of getting to be a well-known product in an export market. It's about marketing, selling, pricing, and all sorts of other practical factors. But if out-and-out quality were the judge in a simple blind taste test of "which olive oil really knocks your socks off," a lot more people would know a lot more about Palestinian olive oil.

It *is* there, though, and it is available outside Palestine, so that's the good news. The less good news is that challenges are also there: challenges to the trees themselves, to the farmers who pick the olives, and to the producers who make, distribute, and export the oil. As always, there are as many stories and challenges as there are trees. Just a snapshot, then, here, telling the story from the points of view of an olive tree guardian, an olive oil producer and distributor, an olive farmer, and finally a small social enterprise company in the United Kingdom that imports and sells Palestinian olive oil.

To start with: the tree. Half of the farmed land in Palestine is planted with olive trees. Some of them are very old—around 1,000 years—so they play a huge part in the link between the people, their history, and their land. With the olives generating nearly a quarter of Palestine's agricultural output, they also play a huge part in the country's productivity and economy.

The olive harvest, from mid-October to early November, is a crucial time, and every year all the farmers, along with their families and visitors, head to the groves for long days of picking. Everyone gets involved, kids too, pulling at the low-hanging olives or climbing up little ladders leaning on the trees to reach for the higher branches. A big net stretches out on the ground, collecting and protecting those olives that have fallen down by themselves. It's an event that goes on for about three weeks, with everyone stopping all together for a big lunch under the shade of one of the trees.

It all sounds rather idyllic. Indeed, it *would* be idyllic were it not for the extent to which these trees (and therefore this way of life) are threatened. The main threats come in the form of bulldozers or intentional fires, both of which are employed to make way for the building of Israeli settlements or as a means to destroy Palestinian income. Furthermore, particularly ancient trees are being dug up for sale to the

highest Israeli or international bidder, who then replants them in, say, their garden. The irony of the situation—that olive trees are being dug up from the land they've been part of and nurturing for so many years in order to showcase, precisely, an ancient connection with the land—is intense.

Another reason olive trees are being destroyed is to make way for the continued building of the separation wall. A tree said to be one of the oldest olive trees sits in the village of al-Walajeh, located near the Green Line (see page 337), south of Jerusalem. At about 12 meters high and 25 meters wide, it's ten times the size of an average olive tree. It's believed to be over 4,000 years old. Salah Abu-Ali's family has been farming the land since the 1960s. After observing the threat to the existence of the tree by the building of the wall, Salah has taken it upon himself to sit guard as the tree's protector. Now known locally as "the guardian of the olive tree," his post under the shade of its wide branches is near permanent. It's clear, doing the math, that Salah spends more time in the company of his tree than that of his wife. His wife's presence (and presumably, if plates of food could speak, support) makes itself known only in the form of a large dish of stuffed vine leaves, rolled long and thin, which appear to accompany our time spent with Salah in the shade of his tree. As well as protecting the tree, and making oil from the large olives he harvests in the autumn, he also hosts visitors who make a pilgrimage to his shrine, to hear his story and, in so doing, spread the word far beyond the reach of the branches. "Post my story on Facebook," Salah calls out, as we go on our way.

Notwithstanding these threats and challenges, the story is not all doom and gloom. As always, the vision, commitment, and enthusiasm of just one individual can be enough to transform the status quo. In the world of olives, in the world of Palestine, Nasser Abufarha—olive oil producer and distributor (pictured opposite)—is one such man.

Trained as an anthropologist and having worked in the United States for many years, Nasser returned to Palestine around the beginning of the year 2000, to set up Canaan Fair Trade. Canaan is, as the name suggests, a fair trade organization and social enterprise project that works with local farmers to produce some of the best olive oil, almonds, maftoul, and freekeh the country has to offer. It started in 2004 and began exporting in 2008. Today, Canaan has a network that, collectively, works with fifty village-based cooperatives of farmers and women across Palestine.

Very much wearing two hats at once, Nasser manages to bring together the needs of the farmers to have productive conditions to work in and, at the same time, the needs of a business to make a profit in order to grow and market itself to the outside world. Walking around Canaan, there's a real buzz. The factory is there, of course, doing its work to press olives and sort almonds, but there's also an impressive shop selling olive oil, tapenade, almonds, and grains to visitors. A big café space is being developed to host workshops and provide a venue for functions. Working alongside this profit-generating and thoroughly "modern" buzz, though, sits the large and very traditional working taboon oven (see page 341), all lit up inside and on the go. Stopping by to whip up some open pies for a midmorning snack, Nasser brings *baladi* ("from the land") eggs, wild asparagus, zalabeed (the tender and sweet shoots of the middle of the onion), and fresh za'atar from his bag. Munching on the pies fresh from the taboon oven, watching the building work for the new café going on, the possibility of combining the best of all worlds—the traditional and the future-looking—feels very real. It's all about olives, yes, but it's also about so much more. "Olive oil is important for our food security and our cultural representation," says Nasser. "It is [also] a symbol of our identity. The trees connect us to our land, to the place, to the history, and to past generations. [. . .] They represent the continuity of a nation and our rootedness in the land."

Just one of the farmers producing olives (among other things) for Canaan is Khadir Khadir (pictured on page 252), living and working in the village of Nus Ijbail. Khadir came to farming initially as a means to get out of working in (and sleeping on the floor of) an Israeli plastics factory. Conditions were tough and life was not good, so Khadir had to find a plan B. After an uncle asked him to help him out with the harvest, Khadir quickly got the farming bug and now has, while still being one of the youngest members of the village, something of the "unelected mayor" feel about him. The village population is only about 350 and, also, is

aging, as most young people have left. Khadir sees it as his mission to stay and help, though. Making the village productive and viable is not just about keeping alive the old ways of cooperative farming. It's about keeping alive the old ways of people looking out for each other and caring and holding on to a sense of identity and pride.

The logistical challenges to productivity and morale for farmers such as Khadir, working the land under the conditions of occupation, are very real. The three main challenges Khadir faces day-to-day are demolition orders, insufficient access to water, and the lack of freedom of movement. He remains, though, upbeat and resilient. "I consider myself a very lucky man," he says. Again, the symbolism of the olive tree—a tree so resilient and independent that it is able to both self-pollinate and live off little or no water—is hard not to note. The trees play as big a part in the Palestinian sense of identity and spirit—which has resilience at its core—as they do in the agricultural output of the country.

After people such as Khadir have picked the olives, and people at Canaan have produced and packaged the oil, the challenge is then to get over and around all the logistics that get in the way of selling it to the export market. One importer of Palestinian Fair Trade products is a social enterprise company called Zaytoun (which translates from Arabic as, appropriately, "olive").

Zaytoun was set up in 2004 by Manal White and Heather Masoud. It started off as a grassroots volunteer initiative with a focused task to import products such as olive oil, almonds, za'atar, freekeh, and dates from Canaan and sell these to the UK market. For all the challenges of getting it to market, Manal is enthusiastic about the continued and expanding demand for Palestinian olive oil (among other products) in markets outside Palestine.

The market is there, then, as are the olives, farmers, producers, distributors, and importers. The product is incredibly good and the passion is very real. With barriers to export and other logistical, political factors looking like they are not going to change anytime soon, it's up to the customer to use their purchasing power to seek it out. It is there—online, in specialty stores, in well-stocked produce markets—and, if it's not, ask for it. Create the market, which the supplier will then want and need to supply. Buy Palestinian olive oil not just because it is deliciously rich, green, and grassy. Buy it because it's a way to keep oiling the logistical cogs that could be turning a lot more smoothly to get this product to market.

Lemon chicken with za'atar

As anyone who has cooked the chicken sheet-pan recipes from Sami's previous cookbooks—*Ottolenghi: The Cookbook* and *Jerusalem*—knows, the secret weapon behind so many (seemingly) effortless dinners is a make-ahead chicken dish that can just be put into the oven when needed. All the work is done in advance, which means that at dinnertime there is little fuss, and happy feasting. It's a complete winner every time.

Ingredients note: We tend to start with a whole chicken (so that chicken stock can be made from the carcass), but it's absolutely fine, of course, to start with chicken breasts, with the wing-tips left on, or legs, if you prefer.

Serves four

3 lemons
1 whole chicken (2¾ lb/1.3kg), cut into legs, thighs, and breasts with the wing-tips left on (or about 2 lb 2 oz/1kg of chicken legs or breasts with the wing-tips left on), skin on, if you prefer
2 onions, sliced in half, then each half cut into 3 wedges (2¾ cups/260g)
2 heads of garlic, skin on, sliced in half, crosswise
2 tsp sumac
¾ tsp ground allspice
4 tbsp/25g za'atar
6 tbsp/90ml olive oil
¾ cup plus 2 tbsp/200ml chicken stock or water
Salt and black pepper
¼ cup/5g parsley, finely chopped
¼ cup/30g sliced almonds, toasted (see "Nuts," page 339)

Cut 2 of the lemons into ¼-inch/6mm-thick slices and place in a large mixing bowl. Finely grate the zest of the remaining lemon (to get 1½ tsp of zest) and set this aside for later. Squeeze the same lemon to get about 1½ tbsp of juice and add this to the mixing bowl along with the chicken, onions, garlic, sumac, allspice, 2 tbsp of za'atar, 2 tbsp of oil, the stock, 1½ tsp of salt, and a good grind of black pepper. Mix well to combine, then cover with a large plate and let marinate in the fridge for at least 2 hours (or overnight, if you have time).

Half an hour or an hour before baking, take the chicken out of the fridge; it should be at room temperature before going into the oven.

Preheat the oven to 425°F.

Transfer the chicken to a large rimmed baking sheet, skin side up, and pour on all the marinade and lemon slices. Drizzle the chicken with 1 tbsp of oil and bake for about 45 minutes, giving everything a bit of a stir halfway through, until the chicken is golden and cooked through and the onions have taken on some color.

Toward the end of the cooking time for the chicken, combine the parsley, lemon zest, remaining 2 tbsp of za'atar, and remaining 3 tbsp of olive oil in a bowl.

Transfer the chicken to a serving platter along with the lemon slices and any juices that have collected at the bottom of the pan. Some people will love to eat the lemon slices and others won't. Either way, serve them up with the chicken—they look great.

Spoon the parsley mixture on the chicken, finish with the almonds, and serve.

Spicy pasta bake

Sami, like so many kids—Middle Eastern or otherwise—did a lot of his growing up at home on pasta bakes. There's quite a kick in our version, but the chile flakes can be decreased or left out if you prefer. Don't skimp on the time the bolognese sauce sits on the stove, though. It's what gives the dish such depth and makes the house smell like home.

Getting ahead: The bolognese sauce can be made up to two days before assembling the dish, and it also freezes well. Bring it back to room temperature or gently warm through before adding the cooked macaroni—it will be too firm to mix if you don't. The whole dish can be assembled a day in advance as well, ready to go into the oven, and, again, also freezes well. If you are baking from frozen it will need 5 to 10 minutes longer in the oven.

Serves six generously

Bolognese sauce

1 onion, roughly chopped (1 cup/140g)
3 celery stalks, roughly chopped (1¼ cups/150g)
2 green bell peppers, stem, core, and seeds removed, flesh roughly chopped (1 cup/150g)
1½ tbsp unsalted butter
2 tbsp olive oil
5 garlic cloves, crushed
1 tbsp tomato paste
2 tbsp oregano leaves, finely chopped
1 tbsp ground cumin
1 tbsp ground cinnamon
2 tsp ground allspice
1¼ tsp chile flakes
2 bay leaves
1 lb 2 oz/500g ground beef (15–20% fat)
1 x 14-oz/400g can chopped tomatoes
5–6 plum tomatoes (1 lb 2 oz/500g), coarsely grated and skins discarded (2¼ cups/400g)
2 red bell peppers, stem, core, and seeds removed, flesh cut into roughly 1¼-inch/3cm dice (1¾ cups/260g)
1 tsp sugar
7 tbsp/100ml water
Salt and black pepper
1 cup/20g parsley, roughly chopped

Béchamel sauce

3 tbsp unsalted butter
6 tbsp/60g all-purpose flour
2 cups plus 2 tbsp/500ml whole milk
A pinch of ground nutmeg
1 tsp salt
½ cup/130g Greek yogurt
2 egg yolks

12¼ oz/350g macaroni pasta
6⅓ oz/180g feta, roughly crumbled
¾ tsp Aleppo chile flakes (or ½ tsp regular chile flakes)
Olive oil, to drizzle

To make the bolognese, put the onion, celery, and green bell peppers into a food processor and pulse a couple of times, until finely chopped. Put the butter and oil into a large cast-iron saucepan with a lid, and place over medium-high heat. Tip in the onion mixture and cook for about 7 minutes, stirring from time to time, until softened. Add the garlic, tomato paste, oregano, spices, and bay leaves and cook for 1 minute, until fragrant. Add the beef and cook for 3 minutes or so, using a spoon to break the meat apart into fine crumbles, until no longer pink. Add the canned and plum tomatoes, red bell peppers, sugar, water, 2¼ tsp of salt, and a good grind of black pepper. Bring to a simmer, then cover the pan, decrease the heat to medium-low, and simmer very gently for 2½ hours, stirring every half hour or so, until the sauce is thick and rich. Lift out and discard the bay leaves, stir in the parsley, and set aside until needed.

To make the béchamel, put the butter into a medium saucepan and place over medium-high heat. Once melted, whisk in the flour and cook for 1 minute or so, until pale golden and beginning to smell like popcorn. Gradually pour in the milk, whisking continuously as you do so to avoid any lumps. Decrease the heat to medium, add the nutmeg and salt, and cook for 5 minutes, whisking continuously, until the flour has cooked out and the sauce is completely smooth. Remove from the heat and set aside for about 10 minutes, then stir in the yogurt and egg yolks until fully incorporated.

Preheat the oven to 425°F.

Bring a large pot of salted water to a boil and add the macaroni. Cook for about 7 minutes, or according to the package instructions, until al dente. Reserving ¼ cup/60ml of the cooking water, drain the macaroni through a sieve and then add it to the bolognese sauce along with the reserved cooking water. Mix well to combine, then transfer to a baking dish, about 9 x 13 inches/23 x 33cm and 3½ inches/9cm deep, then pour in the béchamel and spread it out evenly. Sprinkle with the feta and bake for 25 minutes, or until golden and bubbling. Let cool for 10–15 minutes, then serve, with a final sprinkle of the chile flakes and a drizzle of oil.

Pulled lamb shawarma sandwich

Slow-cooked lamb, piled into a warm pita with all the condiments you care for—this is the ultimate shawarma sandwich. Once cooked, the lamb keeps in the fridge so don't worry if there are fewer than eight of you for that first sandwich. The lamb is also great as a proper meal, rather than a sandwich, served as it is with a selection of sides; fattoush (see page 99), butternut squash (see page 86), and a crisp green salad makes just one great combination.

Getting ahead: The lamb can be cooked a day or two ahead, ready to be warmed through when serving.

Serves eight

3 onions: 1 roughly chopped, 2 cut into wedges
2 heads of garlic: 1 cut in half, horizontally, 8 cloves from the second head roughly chopped
1-inch/2.5cm piece ginger, peeled and roughly chopped (2 tbsp/25g)
1 cup/20g parsley, roughly chopped
1½ tbsp ground cumin
1½ tbsp ground coriander
2 tsp smoked paprika
2 tsp ground turmeric
2 tsp ground cinnamon
¼ tsp ground cloves
3 tbsp cider vinegar
¼ cup/60ml olive oil
Salt and black pepper
4½–5½ lb/2–2.5kg lamb shoulder, bone in
3 cups/700ml chicken stock
½ lemon

Sumac yogurt
⅔ cup/200g Greek yogurt
¼ cup/60g tahini
1½ tbsp lemon juice
2 tbsp water
2 tsp sumac
½ tsp salt

2 plum tomatoes, thinly sliced (mounded 1 cup/200g)
1 red onion, thinly sliced into rounds (1 cup/120g)
½ cup/10g parsley leaves
¼ cup/5g mint leaves
7 tbsp/100g shatta (red or green; see page 73)
8 pitas (see page 278)

Put the chopped onion into a food processor along with the chopped garlic and ginger. Pulse until finely minced, then add the parsley and spices. Pulse for about 10 seconds, until just combined. Scrape down the sides, then add the vinegar, oil, 2¼ tsp of salt, and a generous grind of black pepper. Pulse to form a coarse paste, then transfer to a nonmetallic container large enough to hold the lamb.

Pat the lamb dry and pierce liberally all over with a small, sharp knife. Add it to the spice paste and coat generously, so that all sides are covered. Cover with aluminum foil and let marinate, refrigerated, overnight.

Take the lamb out of the fridge about 1 hour before going into the oven; you want it to be closer to room temperature than fridge-cold.

Preheat the oven to 325°F.

Put the quartered onions and halved garlic into the center of a large roasting pan and pour in the stock. Sit the lamb on top of the vegetables, cover tightly with foil, and bake for 4 hours. Remove from the oven, discard the foil, and bake for 90 minutes more, increasing the oven temperature to 350°F toward the last 30 minutes of cooking time. The lamb is ready when it is fork-tender and easily pulls away from the bone. Set aside to cool slightly, about 15 minutes, before using two forks to roughly shred the lamb directly in the pan, gathering as much of its juices as possible. Transfer the shredded lamb, onions, garlic cloves, and any of the pan juices to a serving bowl. Squeeze the lemon juice over the top and set aside.

To prepare the sumac yogurt, while the lamb is in the oven, put the yogurt, tahini, lemon juice, water, sumac, and salt into a bowl and whisk well to combine.

When ready to serve, lay out the tomatoes, red onion, parsley leaves, mint, shatta, and sumac yogurt, along with the pita, to let everyone make up their own shawarma sandwich.

Chicken shawarma pie

Spiced, marinated chicken thighs, slow-cooked until meltingly tender, layered with baked potato slices and rich tahini sauce, all wrapped up in thin-as-a-feather butter-brushed filo. This is a *wow* of a pie. Serve it either warm or at room temperature, with a crisp green salad and some pickles alongside.

Playing around: The layer of potatoes at the base makes this pie comforting and hearty but, for a slightly lighter version, you can leave them out. You can also just make the chicken part of the dish. As it is, it makes a delicious stew, served with steamed rice or piled into a pita or wrap. If you do this, keep the tahini sauce—it's always a welcome addition.

Getting ahead: The chicken can be made a day or two ahead of assembling the pie. Keep it in the fridge and just bring it back to room temperature before putting the dish together.

Serves six

1 lb 10 oz/750g chicken thighs, skinless and boneless
4 garlic cloves, crushed
¾-inch/2cm piece ginger, peeled and finely grated (1½ tbsp/15g)
2 tsp ground cumin
2 tsp ground coriander
¾ tsp smoked paprika
½ tsp ground turmeric
¾ tsp ground cinnamon
⅛ tsp ground cloves
6 tbsp/90ml olive oil
2 tbsp cider vinegar
Salt and black pepper
2 russet potatoes (1 lb/450g), unpeeled and cut into ¼-inch/6mm-thick rounds
3 tbsp unsalted butter
1 onion, thinly sliced (1¼ cups/150g)
¾ cup plus 2 tbsp/200ml chicken stock
¼ cup/5g parsley leaves, roughly chopped
¼ cup/5g cilantro leaves, roughly chopped

Tahini sauce

3 tbsp tahini
⅓ cup/80g Greek yogurt
2 garlic cloves, crushed
1 tbsp lemon juice
2 tbsp water
⅛ tsp salt

8 (12 x 15-inch/30 x 38cm) sheets good-quality filo (6 oz/170g)
1 tsp black sesame seeds
¾ tsp Aleppo chile flakes (or ½ tsp regular chile flakes)

Put the chicken into a large bowl with the garlic, ginger, ground spices, 1 tbsp of oil, the vinegar, 1 tsp of salt, and a generous grind of black pepper. Mix to combine, then let marinate for at least 30 minutes (or overnight in the fridge).

Preheat the oven to 400°F. Line a baking sheet with parchment paper.

Mix the potatoes with 1½ tbsp of oil, ¾ tsp of salt, and a good grind of black pepper. Transfer to the prepared baking sheet and spread out so that they are not overlapping. Bake for 20 minutes, then increase the oven temperature to 450°F. Remove the sheet from the oven, carefully flip over each potato slice, and return to the oven for another 10 minutes, or until golden. Remove from the oven and set aside until needed.

Decrease the oven temperature to 400°F again.

Put 1 tbsp of butter and 1½ tbsp of oil into a large sauté pan and place over medium-high heat. Once hot, add the onion and cook for 5 minutes, stirring occasionally, until softened. Add the chicken and cook for about 10 minutes, until lightly brown, then add the stock, ¼ tsp of salt, and a good grind of black pepper. Bring to a boil, then decrease the heat to medium. Simmer gently for 25 minutes, or until the chicken is just cooked through. Increase the heat to medium-high and continue to cook for about 8 minutes, or until the liquid has thickened and reduced to about ¼ cup. Remove from the heat and let cool for about 10 minutes, then use two forks to shred the chicken into large chunks. Stir in the herbs and set aside.

To make the tahini sauce, put the tahini, yogurt, garlic, lemon juice, water, and salt into a bowl. Whisk together until smooth, then set aside.

Melt the remaining 2 tbsp of butter and combine with the remaining 2 tbsp of oil. Line the base of a 9-inch/23cm springform cake pan with parchment paper and lightly grease the sides with some of the butter mixture. Lay a sheet of filo out on a clean work surface and brush with some butter mixture. Transfer this to the pan so that the base is covered and the filo rises up and over the pan's sides. Repeat with the next sheet of filo, brushing it first with butter mixture, then arranging it in the pan, rotating it slightly so that the excess hangs at a different angle. Continue in this fashion, brushing each piece generously as you go, until you have used up 6 pieces of filo in total and the base and sides are all covered.

Next, add the potato slices, overlapping slightly, so that the base of the pie is completely covered. Top with the chicken mixture and gently push down to even out. Last, spoon in the tahini sauce, spreading it gently to coat the chicken layer. Brush a piece of filo with butter mixture and fold it in half horizontally, like a book. Place this over the tahini layer, tucking in the filo around the filling. Brush the top with the butter mixture, then repeat with the last piece of filo, angling it to cover any exposed areas. Now fold over the overhang, crinkling up the filo to create a nice "crumpled" effect on the top. Brush the top with the remaining butter mixture, sprinkle with the sesame seeds, and place on a baking sheet. Bake at 400°F for 1 hour, or until deeply golden.

Let cool for about 15 minutes before removing from the pan. Sprinkle with the chile flakes and serve.

Pictured on page 262

Upside-down spiced rice with lamb and fava beans
Maqlubet el foul el akdhar

Maqlubeh is one of Palestine's key national dishes. This "upside down" dish, made in one pot before being inverted onto a plate to serve, carries with it a real "ta da!" thrill. However many times you've made it (or if you're making it for the first time), there's always a moment of "eeek" before the pot gets flipped. Tap the base, count to three, and be quick and confident that all will be well! Serve with a chopped salad (see page 92), some pickles, if you like, and a spoonful of thick yogurt.

Getting ahead: You can make the stock and cook the lamb a day ahead. Keep it in the fridge overnight, and just warm through before proceeding.

Serves eight

- 1¾ cups/350g basmati rice
- Salt
- 7 tbsp/100 ml olive oil
- 1 lb 10 oz/750g lamb neck (4–5 pieces), bone in
- Black pepper
- 1 onion, sliced ½ inch/1cm thick (1 cup/150g)
- 8 garlic cloves, peeled
- 10 cardamom pods, roughly bashed in a mortar and pestle
- 20 black peppercorns, roughly crushed in a mortar and pestle
- 3 bay leaves
- 2 dried Iranian limes (see page 336; if you can find them, or else leave them out), roughly pierced with a small knife
- 5 plum tomatoes (1 lb/450g), roughly chopped
- 2 tsp tomato paste
- 2 green chiles, halved lengthwise
- 2½ tsp ground allspice
- 2½ tsp ground cinnamon
- ¾ tsp ground turmeric
- 10½ oz/300g butternut squash, unpeeled and cut into ½-inch/1cm-thick half-moons
- 14 oz/400g butter beans, trimmed, then cut at an angle into 1½-inch/4cm pieces
- 1 green bell pepper, seeded and cut into roughly 1¼-inch/3cm cubes (1 cup/150g)
- 1 large onion, cut into ½-inch/1cm-thick rings (1½ cups/100g)
- 3 tbsp unsalted butter, cut into ½-inch/1cm dice
- 1 large lemon, cut into 1/16-inch/2mm-thick slices, seeds discarded (¾ cup/100g)

Begin by rinsing the rice until the water runs clear, then allow it to soak in plenty of cold water with 2 tsp of salt for at least 2 hours (or overnight).

Put 2½ tbsp of oil into a large saucepan, about 10 inches/25cm wide and 4 inches/10cm high with a lid, and place over medium-high heat. Toss the lamb pieces with ½ tsp of salt and a good grind of black pepper and, once the saucepan is hot, add along with the onion, garlic, cardamom, peppercorns, bay leaves, and limes. Cook for about 8 minutes, stirring occasionally, or until the lamb has taken on some color and the onion is soft and golden. Add the tomatoes, tomato paste, chiles, and ground spices and cook for about 4 minutes, until slightly thickened and fragrant. Add 6 cups/1.4L of water and 2 tsp of salt, bring to a boil, then cover with the lid, decrease the heat to medium-low, and cook for 1 hour and 40 minutes, or until the lamb is tender and practically falling off the bone. Remove from the heat and use a pair of tongs to pick out the lamb, transferring it to a bowl and letting it cool slightly before pulling the meat apart into large chunks, discarding the bones. There is a fair amount of fat here, but don't discard it; it can be added to the meat. Leave the stock and aromatics in the pan.

Line a baking sheet with parchment paper.

While the meat is cooking, put 1½ tbsp of oil into a large sauté pan over medium-high heat. Add the squash, ⅛ tsp of salt, and a grind of black pepper and cook for about 10 minutes, turning as needed, until golden and softened. Transfer to the prepared baking sheet. Add another 1½ tsp of oil to the same pan, followed by the butter beans, green bell pepper, ¼ tsp of salt, and a good grind of black pepper. Cook for 8–9 minutes, stirring often, until the vegetables have charred and softened. Transfer to the same baking sheet, keeping them separate from the squash. Add another 1½ tsp of oil to the pan, along with the onion. Cook for about 3 minutes, until browned and slightly softened, before transferring to the baking sheet, separate from the rest.

Drain the rice through a sieve. Return the stock and aromatics to the stove and place over medium heat. Bring to a simmer, add the rice, and cook for 6 minutes, or until al dente, draining it through a sieve set over a bowl. Measure out ½ cup plus 2 tbsp/150ml of stock, saving the rest for another use.

Mounded 1 cup/150g green peas, fresh or frozen and defrosted
7 oz/200g fava beans (podded but still in their shells), fresh or frozen and defrosted
1 tbsp olive oil
¼ cup/30g whole blanched almonds
3 tbsp pine nuts
1 red chile, finely chopped
½ cup/10g cilantro, roughly chopped
1¼ cups/300g Greek yogurt

Wipe out your saucepan, then coat the bottom and sides with 1 tbsp of oil and 1 tbsp of butter. Spread the lemon slices out over the base of the pan, followed by the squash, onion, chunks of meat, butter beans and green bell pepper, and, finally, the peas and fava beans. Sprinkle with ⅛ tsp of salt and a grind of black pepper, then give everything a good press, pushing down to compact the vegetables. Top with the rice and push down again to compress. Use the skinny handle of a wooden spoon to make four or five small holes through the rice, then pour in the reserved stock. Cover the pan tightly with aluminum foil, followed by the lid, and place over medium-high heat, cooking for about 7 minutes before decreasing the heat to low and cooking, undisturbed, for 40 minutes. Uncover, dot with the remaining 2 tbsp of butter, then replace the lid and let cook for 10 minutes more. Remove from the heat and let sit for about 20 minutes to cool slightly.

Meanwhile, put the remaining 1 tbsp oil into a small frying pan placed over medium-high heat. Once hot, add the almonds and cook for 3–4 minutes, stirring continuously, until golden. Add the pine nuts and cook for another 30–60 seconds. Using a slotted spoon, remove the nuts from the pan and set aside to cool. The oil can be discarded.

Remove the pan's lid and place a large flat serving dish over the open pan. Quickly invert the pan, so that the plate is now at the base. Tap the bottom of the pan (which is now at the top!) to gently help the maqlubeh slide out. Garnish with the nuts, red chile, and cilantro and serve, with a spoonful of yogurt alongside.

Pictured on page 263

Fragrant Palestinian couscous
Maftoul

Maftoul is one of the key players in Palestinian cuisine. It's the centerpiece of whatever table it arrives at, turning a family meal into a feast. It's big on flavor, great on looks, and wonderfully satisfying to eat.

Getting ahead: The chicken can be marinated a day ahead (but does not need to be).

Serves four generously

4 chicken legs (or breasts with the wing-tips left on, if you prefer), skin on (2 lb 2 oz/1kg)
2 tbsp olive oil
Salt and black pepper
1½ tsp ground cumin
1 tsp ground coriander
1 tsp ground cinnamon
¾ tsp ground turmeric
2 tsp fennel seeds, slightly crushed

Maftoul
3 tbsp olive oil
2 medium onions, each cut into 8 wedges (3½ cups/350g)
2½ tsp salt
1 tbsp tomato paste
½ tsp sugar
2 large carrots, peeled and cut into ¾-inch/2cm-thick slices (2¼ cups/320g)
½ butternut squash (14 oz/400g), peeled, seeded, and cut into 1¼-inch/3cm chunks
1 x 14-oz/400g can cooked chickpeas, drained and washed (1¾ cups/240g)
8 large garlic cloves, sliced in half lengthwise (1 oz/30g)
3¼ cups/750ml chicken stock
1⅔ cups/250g maftoul or fregola
2 tbsp lemon juice
¼ cup/5g parsley leaves, roughly chopped

Preheat the oven to 425°F.

Place the chicken in a large bowl and add the oil, 1 tsp of salt, and a good grind of black pepper. Toss to coat, then transfer to an oven dish (or baking sheet lined with parchment paper), skin side up. Put the cumin, coriander, cinnamon, turmeric, and fennel seeds into a small bowl and mix to combine. Sprinkle just a fourth of this over all the chicken, then roast for 45 minutes, or until nicely browned and cooked through.

To make the maftoul, while the chicken is in the oven, put the oil into a large pot (about 10 x 5 inches/25 x 12cm) with a lid, and place over medium-high heat. Add the onions and salt and cook for about 5 minutes, stirring from time to time. Add the tomato paste and sugar and cook for 1 minute. Add the carrots and squash and cook for 3 minutes, stirring a few times, then add the chickpeas, the remaining three-fourths spice mix, the garlic, and stock. Bring to a boil, then decrease the heat to low and simmer for about 15 minutes, covered, or until the vegetables are just cooked. Making sure you reserve the stock, strain the vegetables and keep them somewhere warm. Return the stock to the same pot—you should have about 2½ cups/600ml—then add the maftoul and bring to a boil. Decrease the heat to low, then cover and cook for 10 minutes, or until the maftoul is just cooked. Turn off the heat and set aside for 10 minutes, with the pot still covered. After 10 minutes, fluff up the maftoul with a fork and add the vegetables to the pot, along with the lemon juice and half the parsley.

Spoon the maftoul into a large deep serving dish. Top with the chicken, sprinkle with the remaining parsley, and serve.

Baseema Barahmeh and the Anza PFTA Cooperative

Baseema Barahmeh lives in a village called Anza, southwest of Jenin. She is a wife and a mother of four. She's also a farmer, a board member of the Palestinian Fair Trade Association (PFTA), a village council member, an expert in hand-rolled maftoul, and coordinator of the Anza women's cooperative. *Anza* means "the hard rock," a description that could as well apply to Baseema, in fact, a serene but independent force of nature who is making good things happen in her village. How on earth does she fit it all in, we wondered aloud. She starts her day at 4 a.m., we're told.

Established in 1992, the Anza cooperative rolls maftoul, sun-dries tomatoes, shells and cracks almonds, blends za'atar, and supplies olive oil to Canaan Fair Trade (see page 250), who then sell it to the local and international markets. More locally, they bake savory manakeesh (see "Playing around," page 278) and other pastries to sell to schools. It was Baseema's idea to do this, seeing it as a way to give the kids access to healthful food and, also, for the cooperative to have year-round work rather than be tied to the olive or za'atar harvesting season.

She needed government funding to subsidize the plan and, after a bit of persuasion, the government agreed. Other cooperatives are now taking Baseema's lead and seeking to roll out similar programs in their own districts.

At its biggest, the cooperative had 100 members, all between forty and sixty years old. As government funding for it decreases year after year, though, so too does the number of women. When we met, there were just twenty-five. The women of Anza village are well educated, so most of those under forty are choosing jobs in government rather than working with their hands. It's not just about the work, though, it's about the community and women coming together. "And laughing," says Baseema. "We arrange ourselves into groups of four and make sure that each group has both an organized person and a funny person who tells all the stories. It's this balance that ensures productivity!"

The problem with dwindling numbers for the cooperative is not just the loss of camaraderie and productivity in the short term. It's about a loss of traditional skills in the long term. Hand-rolling maftoul is a skilled art. There's no better way to feel foolish, in fact, than trying your hand at rolling maftoul with someone who's been doing it all her life. Maftoul is made by adding flour and water to tiny balls of bulgur and rolling it in the palms of your hands until it becomes slightly less tiny. It seems simple enough. Predictably, it's not. In the time that it took Tara to fail to make a tablespoon of maftoul, Baseema had pretty much made lunch for twenty. Even by Palestinian standards, though, Baseema sets the bar high. There are only twelve women in the cooperative who are able to make maftoul properly, and even within those twelve there are some whose job it is to just steam rather than roll the grain.

The Palestinians' reputation for hospitality, and for showing this hospitality through food, is well known. The quantity of food offered by Baseema, however, along with her son and daughter-in-law, was frankly intimidating. There were just three of us at the table eating. There was enough food for twenty. Small bowls of molokhieh, large trays piled high with manakeesh, pasta, pastries, stuffed vine leaves, steamed rice, warm pita, one large bottle of Coke, another of Fanta, and a large thermos of strong Arabic coffee squeezed in between. Hard as we tried to make a dent, our efforts literally didn't register.

We talked, among other things, about Fair Trade. Having been a member of the PFTA since 2008, Baseema is a proud advocate. The model provides financial security and sustainable work for farmers, cooks, and producers such as herself. Fair trade premiums enable members to buy tools and materials for harvesting, which they wouldn't otherwise be able to do. It also enables women to become independent, to provide for their families. "I don't have to ask my husband's permission," Baseema says. "I can just go ahead and do things for myself." It's unusual for a family to be represented on the village council by a woman, but, says Baseema, "I wanted the independence, and to see the results of my work. I am proud of my work; I want it to be in my name." Her son agrees, leaning back on his chair and lighting another cigarette. He is proud, clearly, but also worries that his mother takes on too much and does not look after herself. "And she wakes up at 3 a.m., not 4," he says.

Meaty vine leaf pie

Rolling individual vine leaves stuffed with meat and rice is wonderful—the leaves melt in the mouth and their making often signals a celebration—but it's a time-consuming business. Here, we've taken a fair bit of the work out of the equation by making one big pie. Serve with any (or all) of the following: a spoonful of yogurt, a squeeze of lemon, or some flatbread.

Getting ahead: This can be served warm or at room temperature, the day it is made or for up to two days after.

Ingredients note: Brining vine leaves—we don't always boil our leaves before using them, but here we do. This is because the leaves and stems remain intact (rather than the stems being discarded) and we want everything to be super soft and tender when eaten.

Serves eight

1 x 16-oz/450g jar vine leaves in brine, drained (9 oz/250g)
4½ tbsp/65ml olive oil
⅓ cup/50g blanched whole almonds, roughly chopped
⅓ cup plus 1 tbsp/50g pine nuts
4 plum tomatoes, sliced into ½-inch/1cm-thick rounds (14 oz/400g)
1 onion, finely chopped (1 cup/150g)
3 large garlic cloves, crushed
12¼ oz/350g ground beef
5¼ oz/150g ground lamb
2 tbsp tomato paste
2½ tsp baharat (see page 335)
1¾ cups/350g Egyptian rice or arborio rice
Salt and black pepper
1½ cups/30g mint leaves, finely shredded
2½ cups/50g parsley, finely chopped, plus whole leaves

Sauce

3¾ cups/900ml boiling water
⅓ cup/80ml lemon juice (from about 2 lemons)
1 tbsp olive oil
Salt and black pepper

1 cup/250g Greek yogurt (optional)

Preheat the oven to 400°F. Line a plate with paper towels. Line a baking sheet with parchment paper. Line the base of a high-sided 9 x 13-inch/23 x 33cm baking dish (or 10-inch/25cm round baking dish) with parchment paper and set aside.

Fill a medium saucepan three-fourths full of water and bring to a boil over medium-high heat. Loosely unravel the clumps of vine leaves—it's fine that they're stuck together—and add them to the pan. Decrease the heat to medium and simmer for 15 minutes. Drain the leaves through a sieve and run under cold water for about 2 minutes, until the leaves are no longer warm to the touch. Set aside to drain completely.

Put 1 tbsp of oil into a small frying pan and place over medium heat. Add the almonds and cook for 2 minutes, stirring often. Add the pine nuts and cook for another 4–5 minutes, stirring frequently, until golden. Tip the nuts out onto the prepared plate and set aside.

Mix the tomatoes with 1½ tbsp of oil and spread out on the prepared baking sheet. Roast for 12 minutes, until softened but still retaining their shape. Remove from the oven and set aside until needed.

Put the remaining 2 tbsp oil into a large sauté pan and place over medium-high heat. Add the onion and cook for 5 minutes, stirring from time to time, until it is golden brown. Add the garlic and cook for another 30 seconds, then add the beef and lamb. Continue to cook for another 6 minutes or so, stirring and breaking up any lumps of the meat so that it is browned all over. Add three-fourths of the nuts, the tomato paste, baharat, rice, 2 tsp of salt, and a good grind of black pepper. Continue to cook for 2–3 minutes, stirring frequently. Remove from the heat and set aside to cool for 10 minutes before stirring in the mint and chopped parsley.

Continued

Transfer the cooked tomatoes from the baking sheet to the prepared baking dish. Place them side by side, so that the base of the dish is covered. Next, line the base and sides of the baking dish with just fewer than half the vine leaves, shiny side down, overlapping the leaves so that there are no gaps or holes in between. Spoon in a third of the meat and spread it out in an even layer. Add another layer of leaves, overlapping them slightly to just cover the filling, then repeat the process so that you have three layers of filling in total. Finish with the vine leaves, this time letting them drape over the sides of the dish. Tuck them into the dish, like you're wrapping them around the pie, so that the filling is totally sealed.

To make the sauce, whisk together all the ingredients with 1 tsp of salt and a good grind of black pepper.

Pour the sauce very gently over the bake—it will almost cover the top—and seal the dish tightly with aluminum foil. Put the dish on a rimmed baking sheet (in case there is any leakage) and bake for 80 minutes, until the liquid is mostly absorbed and the rice is completely cooked through. Remove from the oven—don't remove the foil yet—and set aside for 20 minutes. Remove and discard the foil, then invert the dish onto a large platter or board. The best way to do this is to place a chopping board or large platter on top of the pie, then boldly flip it over so that the board or platter is at the bottom. The pie should detach itself easily from the parchment paper—don't worry if any tomatoes have stuck to the parchment, just remove these by hand and place on top of the pie. Sprinkle with the remaining nuts and a handful of parsley leaves and set aside for 15 minutes. Serve warm or at room temperature, with a spoonful of yogurt, if desired.

Oxtail stew with chard, sumac, and tahini *Sumaqqiyeh*

Serves four generously

2 onions, roughly chopped (2 cups/300g)
6 garlic cloves, roughly chopped
2 green chiles, seeded and thinly sliced (¼ cup/40g)
1 tbsp sunflower oil
3⅓ lb/1.5kg oxtail
Salt and black pepper
2 tbsp olive oil
2–3 plum tomatoes, finely chopped (1⅔ cups/300g)
1 tbsp tomato paste
1 tbsp ground cumin
1 tbsp ground cinnamon
1 tbsp baharat (see page 335)
1½ tsp sugar
6⅓ cups/1.5L water

Tahini sauce
¼ cup/75g tahini
5 tbsp/75ml water
1½ tbsp lemon juice
⅛ tsp salt

1 x 14-oz/400g can chickpeas, drained and rinsed (1¾ cups/240g)
1 lb 2 oz/500g Swiss chard, stalks removed and roughly chopped into 1-inch/2.5cm pieces, leaves roughly shredded
1 tbsp dill seeds or celery seeds
¾ cup/15g parsley, roughly chopped
2 tbsp sumac
1 cup/20g dill, roughly chopped

The green chile, the dill seeds, the tahini sauce—the roll call of typical Gazan ingredients makes this a classic Gazan dish. In Gaza, the tahini would be red tahini, which is nuttier and richer than regular tahini. The difference between the two is the sort of heat the sesame seeds are roasted with; steam heating in the case of regular tahini, and roasting with direct heat in the case of red tahini. As long as you are starting with what we call "proper tahini," though (see page 288 for the sermon), any regular creamy Arabic tahini is just fine.

Getting ahead: The oxtail needs a long cooking time—4 hours—to ensure that it falls off the bone as much as you want it to. You can make it a day or two in advance, though, taking it up to the point before the chard leaves and fresh dill get added. These should always go in at the last stage, so that they retain their color and freshness.

Put the onions, garlic, and two-thirds of the chiles into a food processor. Pulse a few times, until finely minced but not so much that it turns to a puree. Set aside until ready to use.

Put the sunflower oil into a large heavy-bottomed saucepan with a lid and place over medium-high heat. Pat the oxtail dry and sprinkle with ½ tsp of salt and a good grind of black pepper. In two batches, sear the oxtail for 5–6 minutes, turning so that all sides get nicely browned. Once all the meat is browned, transfer it to a separate plate, pour off the excess oil, and wipe the pan clean. Add the olive oil, onion, garlic, and chile mix and cook for about 4 minutes, stirring often, or until softened. Add the tomatoes and tomato paste and cook for another 4 minutes, or until the tomatoes have broken down. Stir in the spices, then add the oxtail, sugar, water, 2¼ tsp of salt, and a generous grind of black pepper. Bring to a boil, then decrease the heat to medium-low, cover the pan, and let simmer gently for 4 hours, stirring every so often, or until the meat is tender and almost falling off the bone.

To make the tahini sauce, put all the ingredients into a bowl. Whisk until smooth and set aside.

After about 4 hours, use a pair of tongs to remove the oxtail from the pan. Set it aside to cool slightly, and add the chickpeas and chard stalks to the pan. Increase the heat to medium-high and cook for 20–25 minutes, stirring often, until the sauce has thickened and reduced by half.

Meanwhile, once the oxtail is cool enough to handle, tear off the meat and fat in large chunks, discarding the bones; you should be left with about 1 lb 7 oz/ 650g. Return this to the pan, along with the chard leaves, dill seeds, parsley, 1½ tbsp of sumac, and all but a handful of chopped dill. Cook for about 5 minutes, or until the leaves have wilted and the meat has heated through.

Transfer the stew to a large serving platter and drizzle with a third of the tahini sauce. The remaining sauce can be served in a bowl alongside. Top with the remaining chopped dill, chiles, and 1½ tsp of sumac and serve at once.

BREADS AND PASTRIES

The idea of bread piled high doesn't really mean anything until you spend time in Palestine. Not a meal goes by without platters of flatbread in attendance, ready to be pulled apart and handed around to signal the start of a meal. There's often no need for cutlery once a piece of flatbread has been shaped into a scoop in one hand, ready for the other hand to pile food directly onto it. For those who like eating with their hands, it's a legitimized form of hands-on heaven. If the bread is not being used as a scoop, it's turned into a mini shovel plowed into bowls of warm, creamy hummus.

Just as bread is there on every table—icebreaker, utensil, scoop, and shovel—it's also there on every street corner. The sounds of ka'ak carts on the cobbled streets of East Jerusalem are near-permanent, accompanied by the cries of vendors selling their freshly baked goods from sunrise to sunset. Jerusalem sesame bread in the morning, pita bread and manakeesh as the day goes on. For Palestinians everywhere, bread is the sight, sound, smell, and taste of home. The Arabic word for this is *taghmees*. Bread is not just something to eat or something to help scoop up other food to eat. For Palestinians, it's a way of life.

Traditionally, flatbread is cooked in an outdoor oven called a taboon oven (see page 341). Lining the base of the conical or dome-shaped taboon oven are lots of little stones or pebbles, which get very, very hot. Once the flatbread is placed on top of the stones, the dough bakes very quickly and, also, takes on the shape made by the stones. It looks almost moon-like when it's pulled out from the oven with a long-handled paddle, indentations like mini craters all over. These then become little pools for olive oil or tahini to drizzle into and wallow. Taboon bread is divine in a dish such as Chicken Musakhan (page 247). Try as we might, though, taboon is not something we found easy to create without said outdoor oven and a sack full of stones. We tried the stones in a regular oven—Sami was a sight walking back from the garden center with his shopping bag spilling over with little rocks!—and also using our fingers to make indentations in the dough, but the results weren't good enough to showcase the bread. You'll just have to go to Palestine to try proper taboon bread for yourself! The dough is the same dough used to make pita (which in turn can lead you on to manakeesh—see page 278), so there's more than enough to get going with and share in the meantime—rolls filled with tahini and cinnamon (see page 287), Jerusalem sesame bread (see page 282), pies to snack on or take on a picnic (see page 296), little rolls filled with fresh oregano and za'atar (see page 285), big buns filled with sumac onions (see page 292). For everyone—everywhere—the smell of fresh bread baking is what makes a house a home.

Pita bread
Khubez

Who put the pocket in the pita? Pita is the Arab bread *khubez adi* ("ordinary bread") or *khubez kimaaj* (taken from the Turkish and translated as "bread cooked in the ashes"). Before indoor ovens became the norm, this "ordinary" dough would be quickly rolled into an oval shape and then thrown either against the very hot inside walls of the outdoor oven or into the ashes of the direct flame itself. The intense heat of the flame, and its rapidly vaporizing steam, then does the job that a leavener would otherwise do, creating lots of little air bubbles that cause the dough to rise quickly. It rises quickly and it also cooks really quickly, but, once out of the oven, deflates just as quickly! The speed with which all this rising and deflating happens is what causes the split between the two layers of dough and the empty "pocket" to form. It's this pocket that distinguishes pita from other flatbread and that, happily, makes it such a welcome home to all sorts of fillings: falafel (see page 62), shawarma (see page 259), ijeh (see page 24), and so on.

Playing around: Pita dough is the same dough used to make manakeesh, when the dough is rolled out as if making pita but is then brushed or topped with various things before being baked, as if making a pizza. For manakeesh za'atar, mix ½ cup/120ml of olive oil with 1 cup/100g of za'atar and brush about 1½ tbsp of this on top of each pita. Sprinkle with some finely chopped tomato, if you like, then carefully transfer to two or three preheated baking sheets. Bake at 500°F for 8–10 minutes, rotating the sheets halfway through, until slightly golden, and serve at once.

Getting ahead: Fresh pita is pillowy and soft and likes to be eaten the day it is baked. Anything older than a day, though, can be pulled apart to use in fattoush (see page 99), or pan-fried in a mix of olive oil and butter to add to any soup or leafy salad as you would a crouton. Make the full quantity here even if you are not going to eat all twelve at once. Pitas can be frozen once baked, then warmed through in the oven or toasted to serve.

Ingredients note: We've used 100 percent all-purpose flour, but you can use a mix of all-purpose and whole wheat, if you prefer. The result won't be as pillowy and soft but has a toothsome, wholesome bite that can be appealing.

Makes 12 pitas

2 tsp fast-acting dried yeast
1 tbsp sugar
About 1¾ cups/420ml lukewarm water
6 cups/750g all-purpose flour (or a mix of 4¾ cups/600g all-purpose flour and 1⅓ cups/150g whole wheat flour), plus more for dusting
¼ cup/35g milk powder (also known as dried skimmed milk)
2 tsp salt
2 tbsp olive oil

Put the yeast, sugar, and ¾ cup plus 2 tbsp/200ml of water into a small bowl. Mix to combine, then set aside for about 4 minutes, or until it starts to bubble.

Place the flour, milk powder, and salt in the bowl of a stand mixer fitted with the dough hook. Mix on low speed for just 1 minute, for the ingredients to combine. Increase the speed to medium, then, slowly, pour in the warm yeast mixture, followed by the oil; it will form a shaggy mess at first, but keep the machine running for about 7 minutes, slowly adding the remaining water, for the dough to come together as a ball. You want it to be smooth and elastic and for the dough not to stick to your fingers when pinched.

Transfer the dough to a lightly oiled bowl, cover, and place somewhere warm (on a stove with a pilot light, for example) for about 1 hour, until the dough has risen by a third.

Transfer the dough to a lightly floured work surface, cut into 12 pieces, and shape into round balls, each weighing about 3½ oz/100g. Cover with a clean, slightly damp dish towel and let rest for 10 minutes; you won't see any change in size or shape after 10 minutes but it's still important for the dough to have this rest.

After 10 minutes, flatten the balls of dough one at a time, first with your fingers and then using a rolling pin to shape them into 6–7-inch/15–18cm-wide circles. Use more flour to dust the work surface, if you need, to prevent them from sticking as you roll. Take care not to have any tears in the dough, as this will allow steam to escape in the oven and prevent the pitas from puffing up. Continue until all the balls of dough are rolled out, covering them with a damp dish towel once rolled, to prevent them from drying out. Set aside to rise for a final 20 minutes.

While the dough is rising, preheat the oven to 500°F. Line two baking sheets with parchment paper and place them in the oven to heat up.

When ready to bake, remove the hot sheets from the oven and place two or three pita rounds on each (depending on how many you can fit without any dough overlapping), top side down; flipping them over at this stage allows the baked pitas to be equally "pillowy" on both sides. Bake for 4–5 minutes, or until they puff up and their tops are slightly golden. You don't want them to take on too much color, as this will lead to the bread being hard.

Arrange the baked pitas in a large shallow bowl and cover them with a clean dish towel. Covering them with the towel is important for keeping the bread moist and pillowy while you continue with the remaining batch of dough. Serve warm.

Pictured on page 281

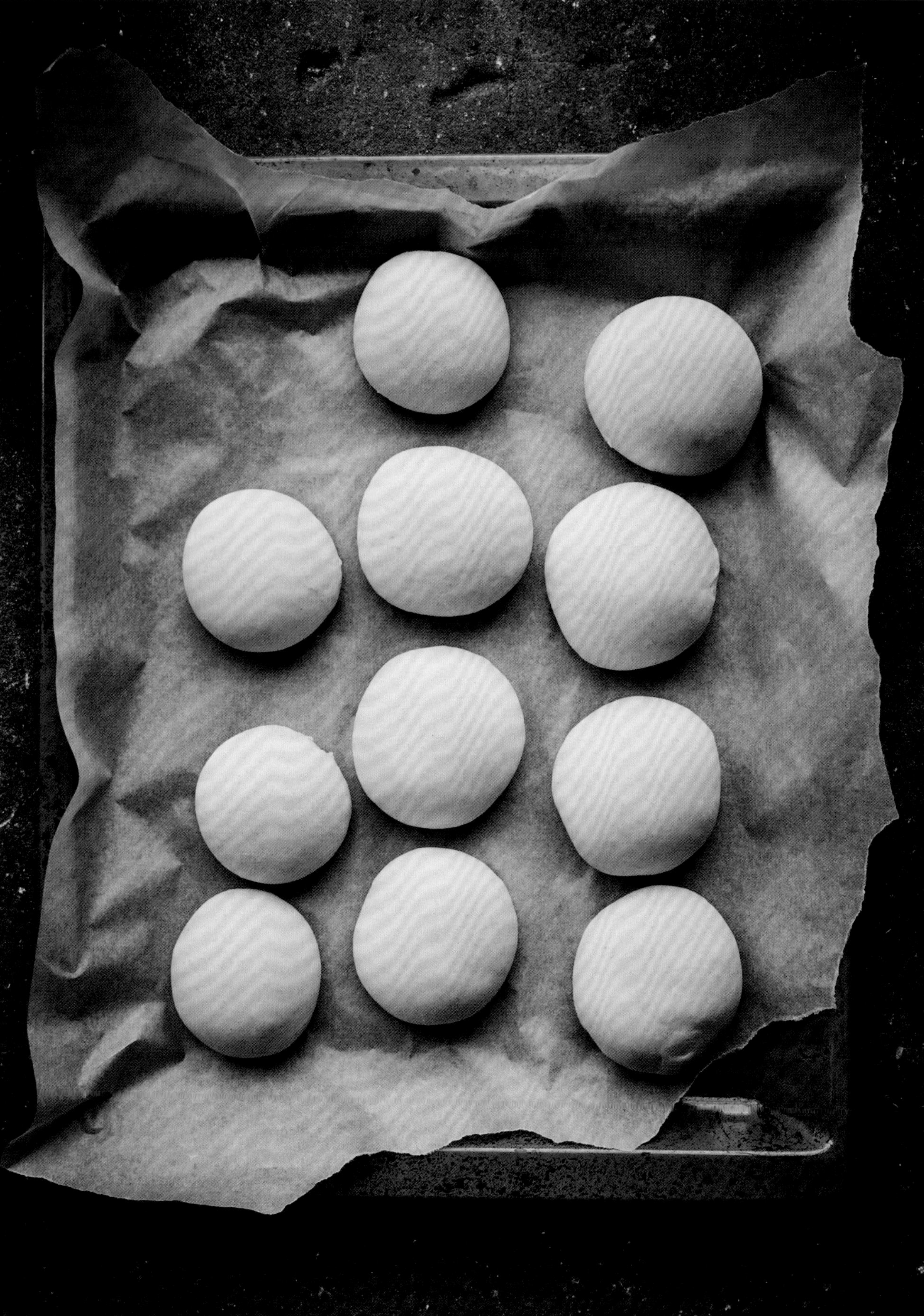

Jerusalem sesame bread
Ka'ak Al Quds

Ka'ak Al Quds are stacked high on street corners all over Jerusalem, sold by men young and old, from sunrise to sunset. Pomegranates or oranges often sit on a table alongside, ready to be freshly squeezed. This is breakfast on the go, Jerusalem-style. They are great for breakfast, eaten as they are, but just as good made into a sandwich for lunch or, as Sami used to, to snack on while walking home from school.

These breads are oval and thin (rather than round and thick) so, when shaping the dough, you'll need to pull a bit more than feels natural. The dough might want to spring back into a round shape, but be assertive and it will do what you want. Don't skip out on any of the resting stages, either; there are quite a few, so these are a good thing to make when you have something else to do at home or in the kitchen.

Keeping notes: In an ideal world these are eaten freshly made and warm from the oven. It doesn't always work like that, though, with all the rising and resting and so forth. Warmed through in the oven or lightly toasted the next day, they are also delicious. These are very happy to be frozen, once shaped into their oval rings. Baked straight from frozen, they'll just need a minute or two extra in the oven.

Makes 6 rings

Heaped 1 tbsp fast-acting dried yeast
2½ tbsp sugar
1 cup plus 2 tbsp/270ml lukewarm water
2 cups/250g all-purpose flour, plus more for dusting
2 cups/250g bread flour
2 tbsp milk powder (also known as dried skimmed milk)
1 tsp baking powder
Salt
3 tbsp sunflower oil, plus more for rubbing

Topping
6 tbsp/60g white sesame seeds
1 egg
2 tbsp whole milk or water

Put the yeast, sugar, and ½ cup/120ml of lukewarm water into a small bowl. Mix to combine, then set aside for 5 minutes, or until it starts to bubble.

Place both flours, the milk powder, baking powder, and 2½ tsp of salt in the bowl of a stand mixer fitted with the dough hook. (If you don't have a mixer you can knead by hand; it will just take a bit longer to work the dough.) Mix on medium-low speed for 1 minute, to incorporate, then add the oil, yeast mixture, and remaining ½ cup plus 2 tbsp/150ml of water. Mix on medium speed for 3 minutes, until the dough has come together and formed a smooth ball. Remove the dough from the bowl, gently form into a ball, and rub all over lightly with oil. Return it to the mixing bowl, cover, and set aside in a warm place for 1 hour or so, or until doubled in size.

When the dough has risen, punch it back down and turn it out onto a lightly floured work surface. Divide the dough into 6 pieces; each one should weigh just under 5¼ oz/150g. Shape one piece of dough at a time gently into a ball, tucking the dough under at the base to form the ball rather than rolling it between your palms, trying not to overwork it. Repeat with the remaining pieces of dough, then cover and set aside for 10 minutes, to rest.

Dig your finger into the center of one of the balls, to create a hole, then stretch the dough outward to create an oval ring. Use your fingers to pull and shape the dough into a large ring; it should be about 7 inches/18cm long on the outside (5 inches/12cm on the inside) and 3½ inches/9cm wide. The dough will want to spring back into a smaller shape, but be assertive here—you want it to be nice and long.

Continued

Transfer the ring to a piece of parchment paper as large as your baking sheet and continue forming the rest of the dough in the same way; you should be able to get two rings on each sheet of paper, spaced about 2 inches/5cm apart. Cover and set aside to rest for 15 minutes.

Preheat the oven to 450°F. Place two large baking sheets in the oven to warm up.

To prepare the topping, spread the sesame seeds out in a large shallow dish, about 9 x 13 inches/23 x 33cm, and set aside. In a small bowl, whisk together the egg and milk and set aside.

Brush the tops of each ring with the egg mixture, then dip them, egg-wash side down, into the sesame seeds so that the top is well coated. Return to the parchment, cover, and set aside to rest for another 10 minutes.

Remove the hot baking sheets from the oven, then drag the parchment, with the rings on top, carefully onto the sheets. Bake for about 15 minutes, rotating the sheets once during baking to ensure even cooking, until the rings are a deep golden brown.

Remove the rings from the oven and set aside for 10 minutes to serve warm, or longer, if serving at room temperature.

Za'atar bread
Aqras za'atar

Za'atar bread is also known as *fatayer fallahi*, which means "villagers' pie." Traditionally, it's made in spring, when the season for collecting fresh wild za'atar begins. We've used fresh oregano and dried za'atar, though, freeing up the option to make this year-round. The bread can be shaped all sorts of ways—into a flatbread, a loaf, or individual buns, as here. In any case, it should always be super soft—almost moist—in the middle, with a really crunchy crust. A mixture of black and white sesame seeds is preferable, but it's fine to use just white.

Serve this either warm, fresh from the oven, or at room temperature the same day, with some labneh (or feta), fresh chopped salad (see page 92), olives, or Hassan's easy eggs (see page 22).

Getting ahead: The dough can be made up to two days ahead and kept in the fridge, ready to be rolled and baked. Once baked, the buns also freeze well, ready to be toasted or warmed through in the oven straight from frozen.

Makes 12 rolls

1½ tsp fast-acting dried yeast
1 tsp sugar
¾ cup/170ml lukewarm water
2½ cups/320g all-purpose flour
1 tbsp milk powder (also known as dried skimmed milk)
1⅛ tsp ground turmeric
1¼ tsp salt
3 tbsp sunflower oil
4 tbsp olive oil
3 tbsp sesame seeds, plus 1½ tsp
¾ cup/15g oregano leaves
4½ oz/120g feta, crumbled
2 tbsp Greek yogurt
1 tbsp za'atar

Put the yeast, sugar, and water into a small bowl. Mix to combine, then set aside for 5 minutes, or until it starts to bubble.

Put the flour, milk powder, turmeric, and salt into the bowl of a stand mixer fitted with the dough hook. Mix for 1 minute, just to incorporate, then add the yeast mixture, followed by the sunflower oil and 3 tbsp of olive oil. Mix on low speed for about 2 minutes, to bring everything together, then increase the speed to medium. Continue to mix for 3 minutes. Add the 3 tbsp sesame seeds and oregano leaves and mix for another 4 minutes, until the dough is soft and elastic and the oregano leaves have been incorporated into the dough. It will feel very soft and almost sticky, but this is how it should be. Tip the dough onto a clean work surface and bring together to form a ball. Grease the mixing bowl with the remaining 1 tbsp of olive oil, then return the dough to the bowl. Turn it a couple of times so that it's completely coated in oil, then cover the bowl. Set aside somewhere warm for 1 hour, until the dough is doubled in size.

Roll the dough out into the shape of a sausage, about 12 inches/30cm long, and cut into 12 even pieces, about 1¾ oz/50g each. Roll each piece into a ball, place on a large plate, cover, and set aside for 20 minutes, to rest.

Preheat the oven to 425°F.

On a clean, lightly floured work surface, use your fingers to flatten each ball into a round disc, about 4 inches/10cm wide and ⅛ inch/3mm thick. Spoon a heaped 2 tsp (about ⅓ oz/10g) of the crumbled feta cheese into the center of each disc. Draw all the sides upward and press together to form a ball. Arrange the buns on a baking sheet, pinched side down and spaced well apart. Brush the balls all over with yogurt and sprinkle with the remaining 1½ tsp sesame seeds and za'atar. Set aside to rest for 5 minutes, then bake for about 20 minutes, or until the buns are cooked and the bottoms are golden brown. Remove from the oven and serve either warm, at once, or at room temperature.

Sweet tahini rolls
Kubez el tahineh

The journey of these rolls can be traced through Lebanon to Armenia, where kubez el tahineh comes from. They are simple to make, impressive to look at, and loved by all. They're a particular favorite with kids. Eat them as they are, or sliced and spread with *dibs w tahini*, the Palestinian equivalent of peanut butter and jam, where creamy tahini is mixed with a little bit of grape or date molasses.

Keeping notes: These are best eaten fresh on the day of baking but are also fine for up to three days once baked, warmed through in the oven. They also freeze well, after they've been baked and left to cool; you can pop them into the oven straight from the freezer until warmed through.

Makes 10 rolls

Dough
1½ tsp fast-acting dried yeast
1 tsp sugar
7½ tbsp/110ml whole milk, lukewarm
Olive oil, for greasing
2 cups plus 6 tbsp/300g all-purpose flour
Salt
5 tbsp/75g unsalted butter, melted
1 egg, lightly beaten

½ cup/100g sugar
1 tsp ground cinnamon
7 tbsp/120g tahini
1 egg yolk, beaten
1 tbsp white sesame seeds

To make the dough, put the yeast, sugar, and milk into a small bowl. Mix to combine, then set aside for 5 minutes, or until it starts to bubble.

Lightly grease a bowl with olive oil.

Put the flour and ½ tsp of salt into the bowl of a stand mixer fitted with the dough hook. Mix on low speed, then slowly pour in the yeast mixture. Add the melted butter and continue to mix for about 1 minute.

Add the egg to the mixer bowl, then increase the speed to medium and mix for 5 minutes, for the dough to get well kneaded. Using your hands, scrape the dough into a ball; it will be slightly sticky and elastic. Place it in the oiled bowl, turning it a couple of times so that the dough gets well greased. Cover the bowl and let rest in a warm place for about 1 hour, or until the dough is almost doubled in size.

Put the ½ cup/100g sugar and the cinnamon into a small bowl. Mix well to combine, then set aside.

On a lightly floured surface, roll out the dough into a large rectangle, about 14 x 20 inches/35 x 50cm. Drizzle the tahini over the dough, then, using the back of a spoon or a spatula, spread it out evenly, leaving ½ inch/1cm clear of tahini at both the shorter ends. Sprinkle the sugar mixture evenly over the tahini and let rest for 10 minutes, until the sugar looks all wet.

Starting from one of the long sides, roll the dough inward to form a long, thin sausage. Trim away about ¾ inch/2cm from each end, then slice the dough into 10 equal pieces; they should each be just over 1¾ inches/4.5cm long. Sit each piece upright, so that a cut side is facing upward, then, using your hands, gently flatten it to form a 3¼-inch/8cm-wide circle. Cover with a damp dish towel and let rest for 15 minutes.

Preheat the oven to 350°F. Line a baking sheet with parchment paper.

Transfer each roll of dough to the prepared baking sheet, spaced 1 inch/2.5cm apart. Brush the top and sides with the egg yolk, sprinkle with the sesame seeds, and bake on the middle rack of the oven for 18 minutes, or until cooked through and golden. Remove from the oven and set aside for about 20 minutes—you don't want them to be piping hot—then serve.

The art of tahini: one man's quest to get it just right

Behind every great Palestinian dish lies a swirl of tahini. Maybe not every *single* dish and maybe more or less than a swirl, but, still, it's the absolute golden stuff, very often there in the foreground, background, or alongside a dish.

In the foreground you'll see it drizzled over anything to come near it without an umbrella: baked kofta, grilled meat or fish, roasted vegetables, shakshuka. In the background, meanwhile, you won't see it but you'll be wondering how it is that a chilled cucumber soup, for example, can be so rich and nutty until you have that "ta-da! ta-ha-ini!" moment. All manner of dressings and sauces or spreads and stews will have a tablespoon or two of tahini in them, there to make the dish rich and creamy and utterly craveable. Sometimes it can just be sitting there alongside, providing the silky and luxurious element to a freshly fried fritter or falafel. It doesn't look like much, certainly, but—once loosened up with a bit of lemon juice and water, crushed garlic and salt—it becomes the thoroughly addictive secret behind so much of the country's cooking.

The challenge, with all this evangelical talk, is to make those who've never started with "proper" Middle Eastern tahini understand what on earth is being talked about. "Tahini, isn't that just what you add to chickpeas to make hummus?" Yes! And also to have around to drizzle on your toast and on your yogurt and ice cream and salad and salmon and lentils and, and, and. . . .

For us, the difference between the tahini made inside the Middle East and the tahini made outside the Middle East is enormous. Much of the tahini made outside the Middle East has, for us, both a "claggy" texture and a bitter taste that don't encourage very wide use in the kitchen. Even though the ingredients are the same—sesame seeds ground to form a thick paste—there are so many factors that lead one version of the product to be smooth, creamy, and rich, and another product to be, well, not.

Someone who knows the difference between one tahini and the next is Kamel Hashlamon. Kamel is a man on a mission. After a decade or so spent making his name and reputation in various hotel and restaurant kitchens in Jerusalem and Tel Aviv, he decided to step back, hone his craft, and become very, very good at one thing. Luckily, for those who love tahini, that one thing was the grinding of sesame seeds.

Becoming very good at grinding sesames requires several things. Using the best sesame seeds, for starters, commissioning the best millstone that

can then grind them, and, of course, providing the perfect conditions for the seeds to be ground as finely, smoothly, and gently as possible. The seeds are the Humera variety, from Ethiopia. The millstone would come from Syria, via Turkey. And the perfect conditions would include a temperature of 140°F, cold-pressing techniques, and a rate of production not much faster than a trickle. These are the steps that Kamel would perfect in pursuit of his mission—to make the best tahini around.

Kamel's first stop was Nablus, where he spent nine months learning the trade from one of the several old families in the city making tahini. Second stop was Turkey, to meet Mohammed Halabi, the Syrian stonemason who could make him the exact bespoke traditional millstone he was after. It had to be wider than the stonemason had ever made before and, using black granite, smoother than any baby's bum. Third stop: West Jerusalem, to find the right site. Not the obvious location for a Palestinian who grew up in Shuafat in East Jerusalem, of course. A very canny choice, however, for someone who wants to make the best possible tahini and wants to make enough of a buck to stay in business and be able to build on his dreams to grow. And in 2017, Kamel realized his dream and set up shop in Abu Ghosh, West Jerusalem.

The excellent tahini that Kamel produces on-site and sells in his shop is somewhere between a paste and a liquid and truly good enough to drink. He makes 30–40 liters a day (as opposed to the 2 metric tons a large factory would produce), and it is made so slowly and with such care that it does not "split" in the jar like most mass-produced tahini, where the oil separates and sits on top of the thick sesame paste. "Tahini splits when it's nervous," Kamel says gently. Alongside the tahini he makes on site, Kamel also sells an intoxicating range of halva, made off-site but using his tahini. It's beautifully displayed inside a glass counter, luring customers in off the street to try and buy.

Appealing to a primarily Israeli (but also Palestinian) market is enough to make some think Kamel has "sold out," but he is happy to take the observation on the chin and bat it right away. "We are all living in *the result* of the game," he says, "we are not in the game." It's a point of view that many who still see their day-to-day as a struggle or even a battle would take issue with, certainly. Talking about the situation for Palestinians as a "game" is not an expression you often hear. For a chef who has had a lot of challenges and barriers to the growth of his career, though, as a result of the politics of being Palestinian, Kamel's response to the situation is the equivalent of a massive cheffy charm offensive. Rather than bemoaning his lot or wringing his hands, Kamel has chosen to make the most irresistible product, package it beautifully, display it in a small stunning shop, and now be the artisanal producer selling it with a smile.

Israelis and Palestinians stand side by side at the counter, looking through the glass, debating little more than which halva to buy.

Sumac onion and herb oil buns

The inspiration for this recipe is less tradition itself than sumac onions; one of the sweet, sharp, and heavenly flavors of the very traditional chicken musakhan (see page 247).

Getting ahead: Get going the day before you want to eat these, so that the dough can rest in the fridge overnight. Once baked, they can be eaten warm or at room temperature for up to two days.

Makes 12 buns

Dough

Sunflower oil, for brushing
5⅓ cups/665g all-purpose flour, plus more for dusting
¼ cup/50g sugar
2¼ tsp fast-acting dried yeast
4 eggs
½ cup plus 2 tbsp/150ml water
½ tsp salt
¾ cup plus 1 tbsp/190g unsalted butter, at room temperature, cut into ¾-inch/2cm dice

Sumac onion filling

½ cup plus 2 tbsp/150ml olive oil
4 onions, finely chopped (5 cups/750g)
2½ tsp ground cinnamon
2 tsp sumac
2 cups/40g oregano leaves, roughly chopped
1 cup/20g thyme leaves, roughly chopped
1¼ tsp sugar
1 tsp salt

Herb oil

1 cup/20g parsley leaves, finely chopped
1 red chile, seeded and finely chopped (2 tbsp/20g)
1¼ tsp finely grated lemon zest
½ cup plus 2 tbsp/150ml olive oil
Salt

1 tsp sumac

To make the dough, brush a large bowl with sunflower oil. Put the flour, sugar, and yeast into the bowl of a stand mixer fitted with the dough hook. Mix on low speed for 1 minute. Whisk together the eggs and water and add to the bowl. Mix on low speed for just a few seconds, then increase the speed to medium. Continue to mix for 2 minutes, until the dough comes together. Next, add the salt and start adding the butter, a few cubes at a time, until it all melts together into the dough. Continue kneading for about 10 minutes, on medium speed, until the dough is completely smooth, elastic, and shiny. Place the dough in the prepared bowl, cover, and place in the fridge for at least half a day or, preferably, overnight. The dough will increase in volume by just under 50 percent.

To make the filling, put ¼ cup/60ml of olive oil into a large sauté pan and place over medium-low heat. Add the onions and cook for about 18 minutes, stirring frequently, until the onions are completely soft and golden. Add the cinnamon and cook for 1 minute. Remove from the heat and set aside to cool before adding the remaining 6 tbsp/90ml of olive oil, the sumac, oregano, thyme, sugar, and salt.

Line a 9 x 13-inch/23 x 33cm baking pan with parchment paper. On a lightly floured surface, roll the dough out into a rectangle, about 22 x 14 inches/ 55 x 35cm. Spread the sumac onion filling all over the dough, taking it right up to the edges.

With the long end facing toward you, gently roll up the dough as you would a jelly roll, using both hands to gently press the roll as you go along. Trim about ¾ inch/2cm off both ends so that it becomes a perfect sausage. Then cut crosswise into 12 even slices, each about 1½ inches/4cm wide. Carefully arrange the slices in the prepared baking pan, evenly spaced apart and cut side facing up so that the filling is showing. Cover with a slightly damp dish towel and let rise in a warm place (on a stove with a pilot light, for example) for 1½ hours. The rolls will rise by 20–30 percent.

About 30 minutes before the buns have finished rising, preheat the oven to 400°F.

Remove the dish towel and place the pan of buns on the middle rack of the oven. Bake for 30 minutes, until the buns are golden brown. Remove from the oven, cover loosely with aluminum foil, and return the buns to the oven for about 20 minutes, or until the dough is cooked through. Remove the buns from the oven and set aside to cool for 30 minutes.

To make the herb oil, combine all the ingredients in a bowl with a small pinch of salt.

Once the buns have cooled, evenly pour the herb oil over the top of them. Sprinkle lightly with the remaining 1 tsp sumac and serve.

Arabic samosas
Sambousek

Indian samosas, Hispanic empanadas, Cornish pasties, Bosnian burek: there are so many ways to encase various fillings with pastry before the whole thing gets baked or fried. Sambousek is the Palestinian way. Traditionally they're fried but we've baked ours here.

Getting ahead: These can be made in full in advance and kept in the freezer. You'll need to defrost them overnight (just transfer them to the fridge the night before baking) and bake them as normal.

Makes 12 samosas

Dough
1½ tsp fast-acting dried yeast
1 tsp sugar
¾ cup/170ml lukewarm water
2½ cups/320g all-purpose flour
1 tbsp milk powder (also known as dried skimmed milk)
⅛ tsp ground turmeric
¾ tsp salt
3 tbsp sunflower oil
4 tbsp olive oil

Filling
1 x 14-oz/400g can chickpeas, drained and rinsed (1¾ cups/240g)
3 tbsp olive oil
1 onion, finely chopped (1 cup/150g)
4 garlic cloves, crushed
1 sirloin steak (9 oz/250g), trimmed of most of the fat and finely chopped (6⅓ oz/180g)
1 tsp ground cumin
½ tsp ground ginger
¾ tsp baharat (see page 335)
½ tsp ground cinnamon
¼ tsp Aleppo chile flakes (or regular chile flakes)
¼ tsp ground turmeric
¾ tsp salt
½ cup/10g parsley, finely chopped

Mint yogurt (optional)
¾ cup/180g Greek yogurt
1 tsp dried mint
1 tbsp olive oil
1 tbsp lemon juice
¼ cup/5g mint leaves, roughly chopped
¼ tsp salt

1 egg, whisked together with 1 tbsp water, to make an egg wash
1 tbsp black or white sesame seeds (or a mix)

To make the dough, put the yeast, sugar, and water into a small bowl. Mix to combine, then set aside for 5–10 minutes, or until it starts to bubble.

Put the flour, milk powder, turmeric, and salt into the bowl of a stand mixer fitted with the dough hook. Mix for 1 minute, just to incorporate, then add the yeast mixture, followed by the sunflower oil and 3 tbsp of olive oil. Increase the speed to medium and mix for 6 minutes, until the dough is soft, sticky, and elastic. Tip the dough onto a clean work surface and bring together to form a ball. Grease the mixing bowl with the remaining 1 tbsp of olive oil and return the dough to the bowl. Turn it a couple of times so that it's completely coated in oil, then cover the bowl. Set aside somewhere warm for 1 hour, until doubled in size.

To make the filling, roughly crush the chickpeas with the back of a fork, leaving about half of them whole. Put the oil into a medium saucepan and place over medium-high heat. Add the onion and garlic and cook for 8 minutes, stirring a few times, or until softened and browned. Add the meat, spices, and salt and cook for 90 seconds, stirring constantly. Add the chickpeas and cook for another 2 minutes. Remove the pan from the heat, stir in the parsley, and set aside to cool.

To make the mint yogurt, place all the ingredients in a bowl. Mix to combine, and keep in the fridge until ready to serve.

Preheat the oven to 400°F. Line two baking sheets with parchment paper.

Cut the dough into 12 even pieces, about 1½ oz/45g each. Roll each piece into a ball, cover with a clean dish towel, and set aside for 20 minutes, to rest.

Taking one ball at a time, roll it into a circle, about 5 inches/12cm wide. Spoon 2 tbsp of the filling—about 1½ oz/40g—into the middle of the dough and fold the dough over itself to form a half-moon shape. Press down the edges with your fingers and seal with a fork. Arrange spaced well apart on the prepared baking sheets and continue with the remaining batch.

Brush the top of the sambousek with the egg wash and sprinkle evenly with the sesame seeds. Bake for about 20 minutes, until they are golden brown and cooked through. Rotate the position of the baking sheets halfway through for even browning. Let cool for about 10 minutes and then serve with the mint yogurt alongside.

Spinach pies
Fatayer sabanekh

These take Sami straight back home. He used to have them, once or twice a week, eaten fresh from the oven when he got home from school. The filling would vary—cheese, ground meat, mashed root vegetables—but spinach was always the firm favorite. If you want to make a meal of them, serve them with a simple chopped salad (see page 92) and a spoonful of plain yogurt.

Getting ahead: Both the dough and the filling can be made up to three days ahead and kept, separately, in the fridge. Once assembled, the pies freeze well and can be cooked from frozen; you'll just need to add an extra minute or more to the cooking time.

Batch cooking: The dough here is similar to the dough used to make sfiha pies (see page 226) and za'atar bread (see page 285), so make more than you need for this recipe and freeze what you don't use to have at the ready.

Makes 12 pies; serves four to six as a light lunch or snack

1½ tsp fast-acting dried yeast
1½ tsp sugar
7 tbsp/100ml lukewarm water
3 cups/375g all-purpose flour, plus more for dusting
4½ tsp baking powder
1 egg, lightly whisked
5 tbsp/75ml olive oil
¾ tsp salt

Filling

3 tbsp olive oil
2 onions, finely chopped (2½ cups/350g)
1 lb 1⅓ oz/500g frozen spinach, defrosted and squeezed well to get rid of any water (about 10½ oz/300g)
2½ tbsp sumac
2 tbsp lemon juice
¼ tsp chile flakes
4 tsp pomegranate molasses (optional)
1 tsp salt

1 egg, lightly whisked

Put the yeast, sugar, and water into a small bowl. Mix to combine, then set aside for 5–10 minutes, or until it starts to bubble.

Put the flour, baking powder, egg, the oil, yeast mixture, and salt into the bowl of a stand mixer fitted with the dough hook. Mix on low speed for about 2 minutes, to bring everything together, then increase the speed to medium-high. Continue to mix for 5–6 minutes, until the dough is soft and elastic. (If you are freezing the dough, now is the time to do it.) Cover the bowl and set aside somewhere warm for 30 minutes, until slightly risen. Roll the dough out into the shape of a sausage, about 12 inches/30cm long, and cut into 12 even pieces. Roll each piece into a ball and place on a large plate. Cover and set aside for 1 hour, to rest.

To make the filling, put the oil into a medium sauté pan and place over medium-high heat. Once hot, add the onions and cook for 4–5 minutes, stirring frequently, until the onions are soft but have not taken on any color. Remove from the heat and set aside for 10 minutes, then mix in the spinach, sumac, lemon juice, chile flakes, pomegranate molasses (if using), and salt.

Preheat the oven to 425°F. Lightly oil two large baking sheets.

Taking one ball of dough at a time, flatten and then roll it into a disc about 5½ inches/14cm wide and ⅛ inch/3mm thick. Dust with a little flour if needed to prevent the dough from sticking to your work surface.

Spoon 3 tbsp (about 1½ oz/40g) of the spinach mixture into the center of the disc and spread it into a 4½-inch/11cm-wide triangle. Draw the pastry in over the filling to form a triangle, press the middle to seal, then pinch the three points together firmly to form a triangle. Place on a prepared baking sheet and repeat with the remaining dough and filling, spacing the pies well apart on the sheets. Brush them with the whisked egg and bake for 12 minutes, until golden brown. Switch the position of the baking sheets halfway through for even browning. Don't worry if a few pies split open—rustic is a good look here!

Remove the sheets from the oven and set aside for about 15 minutes—you want to eat them warm rather than piping hot.

SWEETS

Palestinians, by and large, have a very sweet tooth. No get-together is complete without the offer of something sweet. A plate of fine-crumb cookies, for example, or squares of flaky filo, or slices of sugar-syrup-drenched semolina cake, all served with a short black coffee. It's a chicken-and-egg question of which came first: the ubiquity of the sweet treat or the near-permanence of Arabic coffee on tap. Either way, the combination is heady and heavenly.

As always, our offering is a mix of traditional recipes and those upon which we shine a new light. Leading the way on the traditional is knafeh (see page 302), popular throughout Palestine but a positive rock star in the city of Nablus (see page 78 for more), where its eat-me-now fragrance wafts around every street corner and down every alley. Ma'amoul (see page 310) and ghraybeh (see page 325) are also quintessential, for both midmorning coffee and at every family gathering or big get-together, romanticized with tales of why they're served at one particular religious or celebratory occasion or another. The joy of the simplicity of these cookies is that, on one hand, they can be made quickly to have around whenever needed, and on the other, they can also be scaled up in number for big occasions, so that batch after batch can be made and often frozen in advance of eating. Let it never be said that there will be a shortage of cookies whose name translates as "swoon" at a family wedding! Our No-Churn Strawberry Ice Cream (page 312) is also very typical, with its distinctly Arabic—almost chewy!—texture, thanks to the addition of mastic to the mix.

We have changed the angle on other recipes to make them more accessible to a non-Arabic audience. This can be done with specific ingredients, such as using a hibiscus tea bag to make a hibiscus syrup (see page 327), rather than the dried hibiscus flowers many Palestinians would take for granted as an ingredient. Or the creamy, silky ishta, so common in Palestinian desserts, is replaced by a cream cheese alternative in our flaky warbat (see page 306).

Fun and rewarding though making sweet treats is, there's a real culture of guests arriving at a house with boxes full of store-bought sweets as well. During Ramadan, for example, lots of shops close and are replaced by pop-up bakeries for the month, producing everything everyone wants to serve after the iftar, the "breaking of the fast" meal. So much so that it's actually more usual, for many, to buy rather than make certain things. As we discovered with atayef, the lace-like delicate pancakes rolled up and stuffed with ricotta. After our fourth or fifth attempt to get these perfect for *Falastin*, Sami put out an SOS phone call to his sister Sawsan in East Jerusalem. "Oh, no one makes these anymore!" she breezily assured her brother. "Everyone just buys them ready-made from the shops and then fills them up with whatever they want at home." Job done, then; available at all good Middle Eastern shops near you! Ditto mutabbaq khalili, the sugar-and-nut- or grated-cheese-and-spice-filled pastries particularly popular in Hebron and the southern West Bank.

Then there are the recipes where we've taken ingredients from the Palestinian pantry and created new dishes from them. These are the sweets with the distinct paw-prints of Noor Murad all over them. Noor has been with us every step and every stir of the way on the recipe development for *Falastin*.

Bahrain-made, New York–trained, and now London-based, Noor has brought her endlessly inspired twists and turns to so many of the recipes in this book. In just this chapter alone, the labneh cheesecake (see page 322), chocolate and qahwa torte (see page 317), baklava semifreddo (see page 314), and sticky date and halva puddings (see page 320) are Noor through and through: sweet of course, but at the same time punchy and totally distinct.

Knafeh Nabulseyeh

Knafeh is a national institution, made and served all over the Middle East, and no celebration is complete without it. It's particularly associated with Nablus, where the shredded filo pastry is filled with the city's trademark firm, white, salty Nabulsi cheese. A filling of just nuts and cinnamon is called knafeh Arabiyeh—"Arabic knafeh." Nabulsi cheese is not widely available, though, so we've used a combination of firm mozzarella and ricotta.

Getting ahead: These are best eaten the day they are drizzled with the sugar syrup. They can be made up to two days in advance, though, if you want to get ahead. If you do this, just skip the step where the syrup is poured on and then, when ready to serve, reheat the knafeh in the oven at 400°F. Once they are warmed through, pour on the syrup and serve while still warm. The sugar syrup can be made well ahead of using; it keeps in the fridge for weeks. You'll have a bit more syrup than you need here (you'll make 1⅔ cups/400ml and use 1 cup/240ml), but it's always good to have around, for when a touch of sweetness is needed.

Makes 15 pieces; serves six to eight

Sugar syrup
1 cup/240ml water
2 cups/400g sugar
2 tbsp lemon juice
1½ tbsp orange blossom water

13 oz/375g kataifi pastry (see page 337), defrosted and roughly pulled apart
¾ cup plus 2 tbsp/200g unsalted butter, melted
1 x 7-oz/200g block mozzarella (the firm kind), coarsely grated
6 tbsp/100g ricotta
5¼ oz/150g feta, finely crumbled
2 tbsp sugar
1 lemon: finely grate the zest to get 1 tsp
½ tsp flaky sea salt
1 tsp orange blossom water
3 tbsp pistachios, roughly blitzed in the small bowl of a food processor (or finely chopped)

To make the syrup, put the water and the sugar into a medium saucepan and place over medium-high heat. Bring to a boil and add the lemon juice, swirling the pan frequently until the sugar dissolves. Remove from the heat, stir in the orange blossom water, and set aside until completely cool.

Preheat the oven to 375°F. Liberally butter the base and sides of a baking dish, about 9 x 13 inches/23 x 33cm and 1½ inches/4cm high.

Place the pastry in a food processor, in three or four batches, and blitz a few times until the strands are about ¾ inch/2cm long. Transfer to a bowl, pour in the butter, and toss evenly so that all the kataifi is coated.

Put the mozzarella, ricotta, feta, sugar, lemon zest, salt, and orange blossom water into a separate bowl. Mix to combine and set aside.

Press about two-thirds of the kataifi mixture into the base of the prepared baking dish. Press down quite firmly; you want it to be as compact as possible. It should rise about ¾ inch/2cm up the sides of the pan. Evenly top with the cheese mixture, spreading very gently so that the kataifi layer is covered but doesn't get moved about. Finally, top with the remaining kataifi, pressing down firmly to cover any exposed cheese. Even out the top, then cover with a piece of parchment paper about the size of the sheet. Top with a separate baking dish, about the same size, so that the knafeh is compressed. Bake for 30 minutes, then remove the top dish and parchment and bake for another 25 minutes, or until deeply golden around the edges and browned on top.

Slide a knife around the edges of the tray and let cool for about 5 minutes before flipping over onto a platter or cutting board. Slowly drizzle with 1 cup/240ml of the sugar syrup, then set aside for 5 minutes, for the syrup to be absorbed. Sprinkle with the pistachios and serve warm, preferably, or at room temperature later on.

Filo triangles with cream cheese, pistachio, and rose
Warbat

Warbat is a popular snack during the month of Ramadan. Sami's childhood was spent crowding around the vendor selling them at the corner of the street. He'd barely make it home before the flaky pastry—dripping with thick and sticky syrup and always sprinkled with vivid green crushed pistachios—was finished. The filling is traditionally made with ishta—a kind of thick, milky, silky cream—which is then drizzled with rose water or rose water syrup. Ishta is not always easy to find, though, so we've created a cream cheese filling instead.

Keeping notes: Once assembled, these should be served on the same day—as soon as possible after the syrup is drizzled over them.

Makes 12 pastries

Rose syrup
¼ cup/60ml water
½ cup/100g sugar
1½ tsp lemon juice
¾ tsp rose water

Filling
1 lb/450g full-fat cream cheese
2 tsp cornstarch
¼ cup/50g sugar
½ tsp flaky sea salt
¼ tsp mastic gum (see page 338), or ½ tsp vanilla bean paste

10 sheets good-quality filo pastry (we use feuilles de filo), each sheet 12 x 15 inches/31 x 38cm (8½ oz/240g)
8½ tbsp/120g unsalted butter, melted
2 tbsp pistachios, finely crushed in a food processor or by hand
About 1½ tbsp dried rose petals (optional)

To make the rose syrup, put the water and sugar into a small saucepan and place over medium-high heat. Mix well, using a wooden spoon, and then, once it starts boiling, add the lemon juice. Simmer gently for 2 minutes, then stir in the rose water and remove straight away from the heat. Set aside.

Preheat the oven to 400°F. Line a baking sheet with parchment paper.

To make the filling, put the cream cheese, cornstarch, sugar, salt, and mastic gum into a medium bowl and whisk well to combine. Set aside.

Spread out one filo sheet on a work surface and brush evenly with some of the melted butter. Top with another sheet and brush with butter again. Repeat the process until you have five layers evenly brushed with butter. As is always the case when working with filo, you'll need to work fast when you start brushing and folding; the pastry will dry out if you don't. You should have used about one-fourth of the melted butter at this stage.

Now, using sharp scissors, cut the large layered sheet of pastry into 6 even squares, all 5 x 5 inches/12 x 12cm—you'll need to trim the sheets to get even squares. Taking one of these smaller squares at a time, spoon about 1¼ oz/35g (or 2 tbsp) of the thick filling into the center of each square, leaving a 1-inch/2.5cm border clear around the edge. Fold the pastry diagonally in half to form a triangle, press on the edges without reaching the filling (so that it stays well sealed within the pastry), then brush all over with more butter. Place all 6 triangle pastries on the prepared baking sheet and repeat the whole process (brushing one large filo sheet with butter, layering it five times, cutting it into 6 squares, filling and folding, and sealing each square) with the remaining pastry, butter, and filling.

Once all 12 pastries are made, bake for 22 minutes or until golden and crisp—some of them will pop open, but that's okay. Remove from the oven and set aside to cool for 10 minutes. Drizzle with the syrup, sprinkle with the crushed pistachios and rose petals, if desired, and serve.

Pistachio harisa

Harisa (not to be confused with harissa, the spicy North African chile paste!) also goes by the names basbousa or namoura, depending on where in the Levant it is being made. Either way, it's a sugar-syrup-soaked semolina cake, popular all over the Middle East. Traditionally, the dominant flavors are rose or orange blossom water, but we've augmented these flavorings with the less traditional combination of coconut and lemon zest. You only need a small piece, as you would baklava, with a strong black coffee.

Keeping notes: This keeps well for up to three days, stored in an airtight container. It also freezes well.

Serves eight to ten

Sugar syrup
1¼ cups/300ml water
2½ cups/500g sugar
2½ tbsp lemon juice
2 tbsp rose water

1⅓ cups/190g pistachios
½ cup plus 2 tbsp/125g sugar
7 tbsp/95g unsalted butter, at room temperature
½ cup/120ml sunflower oil
⅔ cup/200g Greek yogurt
3 eggs
2¾ cups/440g fine semolina
¾ cup/65g unsweetened shredded coconut
¾ tsp baking powder
¾ tsp flaky sea salt
2 large lemons: finely grate the zest to get 1 tbsp

To make the sugar syrup, put the water and sugar into a small saucepan and place over medium-high heat. Bring to a boil, then decrease the heat to medium and simmer for 10 minutes. Stir in the lemon juice and rose water and remove from the heat. Set aside to cool.

Preheat the oven to 400°F. Butter a 9 x 13-inch/23 x 33cm baking dish and set aside.

Put ½ cup plus ⅓ cup/120g of pistachios into the bowl of a food processor and blitz for 1 minute, until very fine. Transfer to a separate bowl and set aside.

Place the remaining ½ cup/70g of pistachios in the same food processor (there's no need to clean it) and pulse-blitz just a few times; you just want these pistachios to be coarsely chopped. Transfer to a separate bowl and set aside.

Put the sugar, butter, oil, and yogurt into the bowl of a stand mixer fitted with the paddle attachment and beat on high speed for about 3 minutes, until well combined and smooth. Decrease the speed to medium and add the eggs, one at a time. Mix for another 1 minute, then add the finely ground pistachios, semolina, coconut, baking powder, flaky salt, and lemon zest. Continue to mix until just combined—you don't want to overwork it—then tip the batter into the prepared baking dish. Even out with a spatula and sprinkle the coarsely chopped pistachios on top. Using your fingers, gently press the pistachios into the batter, without completely submerging them. Set aside for 10 minutes, to rest, then bake in the middle of the oven for 15 minutes, until the cake is almost set and the sides have taken on some color.

Remove the cake from the oven and, using a small sharp knife, make a diagonal crosshatch pattern across the top. Space the lines about 2 inches/5cm apart, doing five lines one way and five lines the other. Return to the oven for a final 10 minutes, until the surface is golden brown and a skewer inserted into the center comes out clean. Remove from the oven and set aside to cool for 10 minutes, then evenly pour the cooled sugar syrup over the cake. Set aside for 1 hour, until completely cool. When serving, follow the indentations to cut out individual pieces.

Ma'amoul bars
Ma'amoul maad

In the days leading up to Eid, to mark the end of Ramadan, Sami's aunties, mother, grandmother, and cousins would come together to make the very popular ma'amoul. Sitting on the floor in a circle, everyone would have their designated job: kneading or rolling the dough, stuffing or molding, baking, and packing. It seemed to go on for days, in Sami's imaginings, and led him to think that the process must be a long and complicated one. It was with some surprise then, when he made the cookies for himself years later, that he saw that the recipe couldn't be easier. Time set aside for festive catch-ups, Sami now sees, should be factored into the write-up of the recipe. These are traditionally cookies to mark Easter or Eid, but make them year-round. They have a wonderfully crumbly shortbread-like texture: crunchy, rich, and melt-in-the-mouth. Crumbs are part of the equation here, but that's how some things should be.

Playing around: We've given a choice of two fillings—one with dates and one with pistachios. If you want to make both versions, just double the quantity of the dough.

Getting ahead: The dough needs to rest for at least 4 hours, so it's a good idea to make this the day before you want to bake. Once made, the dough keeps well in the fridge for up to two days; you'll need to bring it back to room temperature before using, though, so that it is malleable. If you are using the dough the day you make it, then it does not need to go into the fridge. You can also make the fillings a day ahead. Once made, the bars keep in a sealed container, at room temperature, for up to a week.

Makes about 24 cookies

Dough
1 cup plus 7 tbsp/320g unsalted butter
2 cups/320g semolina
2½ cups/320g all-purpose flour
4 tsp baking powder
⅔ cup/80g confectioners' sugar
½ tsp fast-acting dried yeast
1 tsp mahleb (see page 338; or a tiny drop of almond extract)
2½ tsp ground aniseed
½ tsp salt

Date filling
1 lb 6 oz/625g Medjool dates, pitted and finely chopped
½ tsp mahleb (see page 338; or a tiny drop of almond extract)
¾ tsp ground cinnamon
¾ tsp ground cardamom
2½ tbsp sunflower oil

Pistachio filling
2⅔ cups/375g pistachios
¼ cup/75g honey
4 tsp orange blossom water
3 tbsp water
9 oz/250g natural marzipan, cut into ¾-inch/2cm chunks
1¼ tsp ground cardamom
1 tsp ground cinnamon
½ tsp salt

2½ tbsp rose water
2½ tbsp orange blossom water
2½ tbsp water
5 tbsp/75g ghee, melted
Confectioners' sugar, to dust

To make the dough, put the butter into a small saucepan and place over very low heat for about 2 minutes, just to melt.

Put the semolina, flour, baking powder, confectioners' sugar, yeast, mahleb, aniseed, and salt into the bowl of a stand mixer fitted with the paddle attachment. Mix on low speed for 1 minute, to combine. With the mixer still on low speed, pour in the melted butter, continuing to mix until well combined and the texture is that of sticky, wet sand. Cover the bowl with a plate and set aside for about 4 hours, at room temperature, for the semolina to really absorb the fat. Letting it rest for this long makes it much easier to work with.

Preheat the oven to 400°F. Grease well and line the base and sides of a 9 x 13-inch/23 x 33cm baking dish and set aside.

If making the date filling, put all the ingredients into a medium saucepan and place over low heat. Heat for 8 minutes, stirring a few times, to form a mushy, sticky paste. Remove from the heat and set aside. If you make this in advance, you'll want to warm it through a little when filling the pastry; it's much easier to spread when warm.

If making the pistachio filling, spread the pistachios out on a parchment-lined baking sheet and toast for about 8 minutes. Remove from the oven and set aside until completely cool. Put the honey, orange blossom water, and water into a small bowl. Mix well to combine and set aside. Once the pistachios are cool, transfer them to a food processor, along with the marzipan, and blitz for 2 minutes. You want them to turn into fine crumbs but still have a little bit of texture. Add the honey mixture, spices, and salt and pulse a couple of times to combine, to form a sticky paste.

Put the rose water and orange blossom water into a small bowl, along with the water and melted ghee. Mix to combine, then, while kneading with one hand, gradually pour the mixture over the dough. Continue to knead for about 5 minutes (either by hand or in a stand mixer fitted with the paddle attachment), until the dough is soft and comes together well and is pale in color. (Add a few more drops of water, if you need to, if the dough is too dry.)

When ready to assemble, divide the dough into two equal pieces and, working with wet fingers, press half the dough gently into the base and sides of the prepared baking dish.

Place the filling between two sheets of parchment paper (about 12 x 16 inches/ 30 x 40cm) and gently roll with a rolling pin to form a rectangle, about 9 x 13 inches/23 x 33cm—don't worry about getting the dimensions exact here, they can be adjusted in the baking dish.

Remove and discard the top layer of parchment from the filling and then, sliding your hand under the paste to help you, flip it upside down into the baking dish. With the paper still attached (and now facing upward), start pressing it gently in to and up the sides of the dish. Carefully pull away the paper and then flatten the filling to fill any gaps.

Repeat the process with the second half of the dough, spreading the remaining dough evenly over the filling, taking it right up to the edges. Pinch some of the excess pastry to fill any gaps and, using your fingers, seal the edges very well. Using a small, sharp knife, cut the dough (keeping it in its dish) into 4 rows and 6 columns, to make 24 squares. Take the knife right down to the bottom of the dish. The lines will close up as the dough bakes, but will help when it comes to finally cutting them. Next, use the back of a fork to press down gently into the middle of each square, to make line patterns with the tines of the fork.

Bake for 30–35 minutes, rotating the dish halfway through cooking, until the ma'amoul is golden brown and the edges are looking crispy. Remove from the oven and allow to cool completely before cutting.

Arrange the ma'amoul squares on a serving platter, dust generously with confectioners' sugar, and serve.

Pictured on page 318, middle right

No-churn strawberry ice cream
Bouza

After supper in Haifa one night on our travels, Sami stopped by an ice cream shop for something sweet. Opting for what Tara thought the least delicious option—the hallucinogenic-pink bubblegum-flavored ice cream—Sami proceeded to skip happily down memory lane, remembering the holiday treats of his childhood. Palestinian ice cream has a distinct texture, thanks to the mastic in the mix. It's unusual to those who haven't had it before, but the taste—that of licorice or anise—is soon acquired. Mastic is available in Middle Eastern grocery stores or online.

Keeping notes: Once made, this keeps in the freezer for a good two weeks.

Serves eight

1⅔ cups/400g strawberries, hulled
1 tbsp lemon juice
1½ tbsp sugar
1 tsp mastic gum (see page 338)
1¼ cups/300ml heavy cream
6 tbsp/120g condensed milk
1½ tsp orange blossom water
2 tsp sumac (optional)

Place half the strawberries in a food processor, along with the lemon juice and 1 tbsp of sugar. Blitz for 1 minute, until very smooth, then set aside.

Cut the rest of the strawberries into ½-inch/1cm cubes and place in a medium bowl. Add 4 tbsp of the strawberry sauce to the bowl, mix to combine, and keep in the fridge until ready to serve.

Put the mastic and remaining 1½ tsp of sugar into a spice grinder (or mortar and pestle). Grind for a few seconds, to form a fine powder, then transfer to the bowl of a stand mixer fitted with the whisk attachment. Add the cream, condensed milk, and orange blossom water, then whisk on high speed for 2–3 minutes, until the mixture is airy and creamy and soft peaks form. Pour the rest of the strawberry sauce into the whipped cream and then, by hand, gently swirl it through, taking care not to overmix. Spoon the mixture into a 1-qt/1L airtight container and freeze for at least 6 hours, or overnight.

Serve straight from the freezer. Scoop the ice cream into individual glasses or bowls. Spoon on the chopped strawberries and sprinkle with the sumac, if desired.

Orange blossom, honey, and baklava semifreddo

This is a real showstopper of a dessert. There are a few elements to it but none of them is complicated. The only thing to keep an eye on is timing, as the bubbling syrup needs to be added to the eggs halfway through their being whisked. Just follow the instructions and you'll be in for a treat that sees the best part of baklava—the sticky, nutty filling—layered in a simple semifreddo.

Getting ahead: This keeps for up to two weeks in the freezer, so you can make the whole thing well in advance.

Serves six to eight

Semifreddo

1 cup/240ml heavy cream
6 tbsp/75g sugar
2 tbsp honey
2 tbsp water
1 egg, plus 2 egg yolks
1½ tbsp orange blossom water

Baklava filling

⅔ cup/90g pistachios, toasted (see "Nuts," page 339)
⅔ cup/60g walnut halves, toasted (see "Nuts," page 339)
1 tsp ground cinnamon
10 cardamom pods, shells crushed and then discarded, seeds finely ground in a mortar and pestle (or ¾ tsp ground cardamom)
¼ tsp flaky sea salt
2½ tbsp honey
1 tbsp orange blossom water

Orange sauce (optional)

2 oranges
Mounded ½ cup/80g pomegranate seeds (from about 1 pomegranate)
¼ cup/5g mint leaves, roughly torn

Lightly grease and line the base and sides of an 8½ x 4½-inch/20 x 10cm loaf pan. Set aside until ready to use.

To make the semifreddo, put the cream into the bowl of a stand mixer fitted with the whisk attachment. Beat on medium-high speed for about 3 minutes, or until medium peaks form. Transfer to a separate bowl and keep in the fridge until needed. Wash the bowl and whisk and return them to the mixer; they need to be clean and ready to whisk the eggs halfway through the next stage.

Put the sugar, honey, and water into a small saucepan and place over medium-high heat. Bring to a boil, then decrease to a simmer, stirring often. After 3 minutes, add the egg and egg yolks to the bowl of the stand mixer. Beat on medium-high speed for about 3 minutes, until pale and creamy. Decrease the speed to medium-low and slowly pour in the bubbling hot syrup, which should be foamy and glossy. Once the syrup is completely incorporated, increase the speed to medium-high and continue to beat for about 6 minutes, until the mixture is pale and glossy and the bowl is cool to the touch. Using a spatula, fold in the orange blossom water and whipped cream until just combined. Put half the mixture—about 7 oz/200g—into the prepared loaf pan and smooth out the top. Wrap with parchment paper and freeze for 2 hours. Refrigerate the other half of the mixture in a separate bowl until needed.

To make the baklava filling, put the pistachios and walnuts into the bowl of a food processor and blitz roughly until crumbled. Transfer to a small bowl and stir in the spices, salt, honey, and orange blossom water. Once the semifreddo has been in the freezer for 2 hours, gently top with the baklava filling. Spread it out so that the top is covered, without pushing it in. Remove the reserved semifreddo from the fridge, give it a good whisk by hand, then pour it over the baklava filling. Spread it out until smooth, then rewrap the pan with parchment paper and freeze overnight.

To make the sauce, use a small, sharp knife to trim the tops and tails off the oranges. Cut down along their round curves, removing the skin and white pith. Release the segments by slicing between the membranes and transfer them to a bowl, discarding any seeds and squeezing what's left of the membranes to release any liquid into the bowl. Just before serving, add the pomegranate seeds and mint leaves to the sauce.

Either spoon the sauce in a line along the top of the semifreddo before slicing, or serve alongside.

Chocolate and qahwa flour-free torte

Qahwa means "coffee" in Arabic. Arabic coffee tends to be very strong and intense, consumed in small quantities and usually paired with something sweet, like a date or two. The Arabic coffee theme plays a strong note here, making this torte incredibly rich and intense. You only need a thin slice, served with some crème fraîche, vanilla ice cream, or plain yogurt alongside. No need for an extra caffeine shot.

Playing around: The saffron can be dropped, if this is not to your liking, and replaced with a pinch of cinnamon. Again with the rose water, decrease or remove it (or replace it with orange blossom water, or a teaspoon of vanilla extract) if you prefer.

Keeping notes: Once baked, this keeps for up to three days in the fridge.

Ingredients note: We've used two types of dark chocolate: one with 70 percent cocoa solids and the other (which can be called semisweet chocolate) with roughly 50 percent cocoa solids. You can use all 70 percent if you need to, but this will make the torte even more intense.

Serves ten to twelve

1 cup/220g unsalted butter, at room temperature, cut into ½-inch/1cm dice
7 oz/200g dark chocolate (50% cocoa solids), broken into roughly ½-inch/1cm pieces
1¾ oz/50g dark chocolate (70% cocoa solids), broken into roughly ½-inch/1cm pieces
2 tbsp instant espresso powder (also known as espresso instant coffee), plus ½ tsp
⅛ tsp saffron threads, roughly crushed in a mortar and pestle (optional)
10 cardamom pods, shells discarded and seeds finely crushed in a mortar and pestle (or ¾ tsp ground cardamom)
1¼ cups plus 2 tbsp/275g sugar
1 tbsp rose water
2 tbsp water
5 eggs
¼ tsp flaky sea salt
2 tsp cocoa powder
Vanilla ice cream, crème fraîche, or plain yogurt, to serve

Preheat the oven to 375°F. Grease and line the base and sides of a 9-inch/23cm springform cake pan and set aside.

Place the butter and both types of chocolate in a large heatproof bowl. Put the 2 tbsp espresso powder, saffron (if using), cardamom, sugar, rose water, and water into a small saucepan and place over medium-high heat. Bring to a boil, stirring continuously—this should take about 5 minutes—then pour this over the chocolate and butter. Stir everything together until the chocolate has melted and you are left with a thick but pourable sauce.

Separate 3 of the eggs, setting the whites aside. One at a time, add the yolks and the remaining 2 whole eggs to the chocolate sauce, stirring to incorporate.

Put the 3 egg whites and the salt into the bowl of a stand mixer fitted with the whisk attachment. Beat on medium speed for about 2 minutes, until stiff but not dry peaks form. In two batches, gently fold the egg whites into the chocolate until just incorporated; taking care not to overmix.

Pour the mixture into the prepared pan and bake for about 50 minutes, or until a skewer inserted in the center comes out clean. Let cool for about 1 hour, then refrigerate for at least 2 hours, or preferably overnight. Remove the torte from the fridge 30 minutes before serving; you want it to be room temperature. Transfer the torte out of the pan onto a serving platter.

Mix together the cocoa powder and remaining ½ tsp espresso powder in a small bowl. Using a fine-mesh sieve, sprinkle liberally and evenly over the torte, to coat. Serve with a spoonful of ice cream, crème fraîche, or plain yogurt alongside.

Palestinian Bakewell tart
Al mabroushy

This is our take on the Bakewell tart. Kids love these, adults love these, Mr. Kipling himself would have loved these, we're sure!

Keeping notes: Once baked, this keeps well in a sealed container for up to three days.

Makes 12 bars

Rose jam
¾ cup/250g strawberry jam
2 tsp rose water

Shortbread
1⅓ cups/165g all-purpose flour
⅔ cups/75g confectioners' sugar
¼ tsp flaky sea salt
1 lemon: finely grate the zest to get 2 tsp
½ cup plus 2 tbsp/150g unsalted butter, fridge-cold, cut into ½-inch/1cm dice

Halva spread
2¼ oz/60g halva
1 tbsp tahini
1½ tbsp water

¼ cup/25g sliced almonds
¾ oz/20g halva
1 tbsp sesame seeds
1½ tsp all-purpose flour
½ tsp flaky sea salt
2 tbsp confectioners' sugar (optional)

To make the rose jam, put the strawberry jam and rose water in a bowl. Mix well and set aside.

Preheat the oven to 375°F. Grease and line the base and sides of an 8-inch/20cm square baking dish and set aside.

To make the shortbread, put all the ingredients into a food processor and pulse for about 15 seconds, until the mixture has the consistency of coarse breadcrumbs. Remove 2¼ oz/60g of this—about an eighth—and keep in the fridge until needed. Press the remaining mixture into the prepared baking dish, so that it evenly covers the bottom, and bake for about 25 minutes, or until cooked through and lightly golden. Remove from the oven and set aside to cool for about 15 minutes.

To make the halva spread, put the halva, tahini, and water into a bowl. Beat with a fork until smooth.

Evenly spread the halva mixture over the cooled shortbread base. Top this with the jam and set aside.

Combine the reserved 2¼ oz/60g of shortbread in a bowl with the almonds, halva, sesame seeds, flour, and salt. Using your hands, rub together until this topping consistency is that of crumble.

Sprinkle the shortbread topping unevenly over the jam. Bake for a final 25 minutes, or until golden, then set aside for 1 hour, to cool. Remove from the pan and slice into 12 pieces. Dust with confectioners' sugar, if desired, and serve either warm or at room temperature.

Pictured opposite, middle left

Sticky date and halva puddings with tahini caramel

These little puddings—our take on sticky toffee pudding—are a knockout, best eaten warm with a spoon of crème fraîche, yogurt, or sour cream alongside.

Playing around: We love the tahini-rose caramel drizzled on top, but the puddings work well alone if you want to serve them with just the crème fraîche or yogurt. The rose water can also be replaced by water, if you don't like the flavor or don't have a bottle open.

Getting ahead: The puddings can be made ahead and stored in an airtight container for up to two days. Reheat in a microwave as they are or in a hot oven, wrapped in aluminum foil. They can also be frozen for up to two months.

Equipment note: Mini cake pans are widely available and useful to have, but, if you don't have them, a deep muffin tin with 8 molds or a regular 12-well muffin tin also work.

Makes 8 or 12 puddings

Tahini caramel
2½ tbsp tahini
2 tbsp rose water or water
2 tbsp water
¾ cup/150g sugar
½ cup/120ml heavy cream, at room temperature
3 tbsp unsalted butter, at room temperature
1 tsp flaky sea salt

Date puddings
6⅓ oz/180g Medjool (or other good-quality) dates, pitted and roughly chopped (5¾ oz/160g)
½ cup plus 1 tbsp/140ml boiling water
2 tbsp strong brewed coffee
½ tsp vanilla extract
¾ tsp baking soda
5 tbsp/75g unsalted butter, at room temperature
¾ cup/150g sugar
2 eggs
1⅓ cups plus 1 tbsp/175g all-purpose flour, sifted
2 tsp baking powder
2 tbsp white sesame seeds
3 oz/85g halva, roughly crumbled

1½ tsp white sesame seeds
About ½ cup/120g crème fraîche or yogurt or sour cream

Preheat the oven to 350°F. Liberally grease and line the base of eight 3-inch/7½cm mini cake pans with parchment paper and set aside. If using a muffin tin, line each well with a paper liner.

To make the caramel, put the tahini, rose water, and water into a small bowl. Whisk until smooth and set aside.

Place a medium saucepan over medium-high heat and, once hot, add a third of the sugar; it will begin to melt when it hits the pan. Give it a stir once or twice and, once the sugar has completely melted, add another third of the sugar. Continue in this way for 3–4 minutes, until all the sugar has been incorporated and has turned into an amber-colored caramel. Remove from the heat, add the cream and butter, and slowly whisk them in—the sauce will splutter, but this is normal. Return the pan to medium-low heat, whisking to smooth out any lumps, then add the tahini-rose mixture, along with the salt. Whisk until smooth and set aside.

To make the date puddings, place the dates in a bowl along with the boiling water, coffee, vanilla, and baking soda. Mix to combine and set aside.

Put the butter and sugar into the bowl of a stand mixer fitted with the paddle attachment (or alternatively use an electric hand mixer) and beat on medium speed for about 3 minutes, until pale and fluffy. Add the eggs, one at a time, beating to incorporate. Using a spatula, fold in the flour, baking powder, and sesame seeds. Last, stir in the date mixture, along with all its liquid, as well as the halva. The mixture will be quite wet.

Spoon the mixture into the prepared pans, filling them about two-thirds full. Bake for 22–25 minutes—depending on what size mold or muffin tin you are using—or until a skewer inserted into the center comes out clean. Let cool for 5 minutes, then, using a cloth to hold the pans so that you don't burn your hand, slide a small knife around the outsides to loosen them. Transfer them onto a baking sheet, then loosely cover with aluminum foil to keep warm.

Just before serving, return the tahini caramel to medium-high heat and bring to a simmer, stirring often. Place one pudding on each plate and pour on the caramel. Sprinkle with the 1½ tsp of sesame seeds and serve, with a spoonful of crème fraîche alongside.

Labneh cheesecake with roasted apricots, honey, and cardamom

Cheesecake is not, traditionally, a dessert eaten in Palestine, but all these ingredients are: the labneh and filo, the nuts and floral orange blossom. The base was Noor's idea; blitzing up the sheets of filo to make crumbs. Mixing this with the nuts calls baklava to mind. The result, we think, is distinct and special.

Playing around: Rose water or vanilla extract can be used instead of the orange blossom water, if you like. If using vanilla in the filling, use 1½ tsp of vanilla paste or the scraped seeds of half a vanilla pod, in addition to the vanilla extract already there. Lots of other fruits—stone fruits or otherwise—work as well as the apricots here; peaches, plums, cherries, and even strawberries. As always, with nuts, other nuts can be used apart from those we suggest. Brazil nuts or macadamia nuts both work in any combination in the base; just keep the net weight the same.

Getting ahead: If you are making your own labneh (which couldn't be easier; it just requires getting organized a day ahead), it needs to be made one to five days before using. To get the 2 cups plus 2 tbsp/500g of labneh called for, you'll have to start with 3½ cups/840g of Greek yogurt, mixed with ¾ tsp of salt. The cheesecake is best baked the day before serving, so that it can chill in the fridge overnight. The apricots are best roasted and put on top of the cake on the day of serving. Once assembled, the cake is best eaten the same day.

Serves ten to twelve

Base

5 sheets good-quality filo pastry (about 4 oz/110g)
6 tbsp/90g unsalted butter, melted
⅓ cup/40g walnut halves
½ cup/60g pistachios
1½ tbsp all-purpose flour
¼ cup/50g sugar
10 cardamom pods, shells discarded and seeds finely crushed in a mortar and pestle (or ¾ tsp ground cardamom)
1 tsp ground cinnamon
¼ tsp flaky sea salt

Filling

2 cups plus 2 tbsp/500g labneh (see headnote and page 48)
2 cups/500g ricotta
1 cup/200g sugar
½ tsp flaky sea salt
2 eggs, plus 3 egg yolks
2 tsp finely grated orange zest
1 tbsp orange blossom water
1¼ tsp vanilla extract
1½ tbsp cornstarch

¼ cup/75g honey
2 tsp orange blossom water
2½ tbsp orange juice
6 cardamom pods, shells on, seeds roughly bashed together in a mortar and pestle
12¼ oz/350g ripe apricots, pits removed, each cut into 6 wedges
A small handful of mint leaves (optional)

Preheat the oven to 350°F. Line a baking sheet with parchment paper. Grease and line the base and sides of a 9-inch/23cm springform baking pan and set aside.

To make the base, lay out one sheet of filo on a clean work surface. Measure 2 tbsp of the butter—this will be used for brushing the sheets—and set the remaining ¼ cup/60g aside for later. Brush the filo sheet with butter until well coated, then top a second sheet. Continue in this fashion until all the filo and butter have been used up, finishing the last layer with a coating of butter. Transfer the filo stack to the prepared baking sheet and bake for about 20 minutes, or until lightly golden and crispy. Remove from the oven and set aside to cool for 15 minutes (or longer) before breaking apart into large shards. In two batches, place the shards in a food processor and blitz for about 10 seconds, to form fine crumbs. Place in a medium bowl, then add all the nuts to the processor. Blitz for about 20 seconds, until fine but not powdery. Add the nuts to the filo along with the flour, sugar, spices, salt, and reserved ¼ cup/60g of butter and mix to combine. Tip the mixture into the base of the prepared baking pan and press it down firmly and evenly so that the whole bottom is covered. Bake for 12 minutes, or until golden. Remove from the oven and set aside to cool.

Continued

To make the filling, combine the labneh, ricotta, sugar, and salt in the bowl of a stand mixer fitted with the paddle attachment. Mix for just a few seconds. Scrape down the sides of the bowl, then add the eggs, egg yolks, orange zest, orange blossom water, vanilla, and cornstarch. Mix on medium speed for about 3 minutes, to combine.

Pour the filling into the cake pan. Bake for 60–70 minutes, or until the cake is beginning to take on some color around the edges but still has a slight wobble in the middle. Remove from the oven and let cool at room temperature for 1 hour before refrigerating for at least 4 hours or (preferably) overnight.

On the day of serving, preheat the oven to 425°F. Line a baking sheet with parchment paper.

Put the honey, orange blossom water, orange juice, and cardamom pods into a small saucepan and place over medium-high heat. Cook for 4–6 minutes, stirring often, until the mixture has reduced by half and is beginning to form a thin syrup. Spread the apricots out on the prepared baking sheet, on their sides, and drizzle with half the syrup. Bake for about 8 minutes, turning the apricots over halfway through baking, until completely softened but still retaining their shape. Remove from the oven and set aside for about 30 minutes, until completely cool.

Just before serving (or up to 1 hour, if you want to prepare ahead), release the cake from its pan and transfer to a round serving platter. Top with the apricots—there should not be any overlap—and drizzle with the remaining syrup. The bashed cardamom pods can be used for garnish as well—they look nice—but these are not to be eaten. Scatter with the mint leaves, if desired, and serve.

Shortbread cookies
Ghraybeh

Makes about 35 cookies

¾ cup plus 2 tbsp/200g ghee or clarified butter (see page 335), at room temperature
⅔ cup/80g confectioners' sugar, sifted
3 cups/370g all-purpose flour, sifted
¾ tsp salt
1½ tsp orange blossom water
1 tsp rose water
About 35 unsalted pistachios (enough for one to go on each cookie)

Ghraybeh means "swoon" in Arabic. Aptly, these little sugar cookies are often served at celebrations such as baptisms or weddings, when the air is thick with "swooning." They're a popular choice for large events for practical reasons—the recipe scales up wonderfully, if there are many mouths to feed, and they are quick and easy to prepare. Use them for everyday baking as well; they're lovely to have around to snack on.

Playing around: Play around with the shape and flavorings, if you like. We've gone for a thin bracelet with the ends "cemented" together with a nut, but a little round cake or a diamond also looks good. You can also stick two cookies together with any sort of jam—to create a sort of Palestinian Linzer cookie. Flavor-wise, the orange blossom and rose water can be replaced with vanilla extract and lemon zest.

Getting ahead: The dough can be made up to three days in advance and kept in the fridge (or longer in the freezer). The cookies can also be shaped and frozen, then baked straight from frozen; they'll just need an extra minute in the oven. Once baked, the cookies keep well in an airtight container for up to five days.

Put the ghee and confectioners' sugar into the bowl of a stand mixer fitted with the whisk attachment. Mix on medium-high speed for about 4 minutes, until pale and fluffy. Replace the whisk with the paddle attachment. Add the flour, salt, orange blossom water, and rose water and mix for another 3 minutes, until the dough is uniform and smooth. Using your hands, bring the dough together and shape into a ball. Place the dough in an airtight container and place in the fridge for about 1 hour, to rest. You'll need to remove it from the fridge about 10 minutes before you want to roll it out so that it has some malleability.

Preheat the oven to 350°F. Line two baking sheets with parchment paper.

Pinch off a bit of the dough, about ¾ oz/20g, and roll it into a sausage—it should be about 4 inches/10cm long and ¼ inch/6mm thick. Bring both ends together, slightly overlapping them and pressing down where the two ends meet. Press a single pistachio into the dough where the ends join and place on the prepared baking sheet. Repeat with the remaining dough and pistachios, spacing the rings ½ inch/1cm apart on the sheet. Bake for 15 minutes, until the cookies are cooked through but have not taken on too much color. Remove from the oven and set aside until completely cool before serving.

Pictured on page 318, top left

Muhallabieh with cherries and hibiscus syrup

This is basically Palestinian panna cotta—a simple set pudding—but even lighter and easier to make. Milky set puddings are traditionally served on New Year's Day as a symbol of prosperity and happiness. We can't vouch for the prosperity but they do make us happy. This takes minutes to prepare and is the perfect way to round off a meal.

Playing around: Figs can be used instead of the cherries, if you like, and all sorts of nuts work as well as (or instead of) the pistachios—walnuts are particularly good. A sprinkle of unsweetened shredded coconut, sliced almonds, or pomegranate seeds is also lovely.

Getting ahead: Both the puddings and the cherries can be made a day or two ahead of serving. Just keep them, separately, in the fridge, and assemble when ready to serve.

Ingredients note: Traditionally, dried hibiscus flowers are used to make the syrup. We've played around with hibiscus tea bags, instead, as an easier-to-find alternative.

Serves four

⅓ cup/50g cornstarch
2 cups plus 2 tbsp/500ml whole milk
¾ cup plus 2 tbsp/200 ml water
Rounded ¼ cup/60g sugar

Cherries and hibiscus syrup
1 pure-hibiscus tea bag
¼ cup/60ml boiling water
Rounded ¼ cup/60g sugar
½ tsp thyme leaves
½ vanilla bean, seeds scraped (¼ tsp)
1 tsp lemon juice
3½ oz/100g cherries, cut in half and pitted

2½ tbsp/25g pistachios, roughly chopped

Put the cornstarch into a small bowl along with 7 tbsp/100ml of milk. Whisk to make a smooth paste and set aside.

Pour the remaining 1⅔ cups/400ml of milk into a medium saucepan along with the water and sugar. Place over medium heat for 2–3 minutes, stirring a few times, until the sugar dissolves. When it starts to release steam, whisk in the cornstarch paste and keep whisking for another 3 minutes, until the mixture boils and has the consistency of thick custard. Remove from the heat and set aside for 5 minutes, then pour into individual glass bowls, wine glasses, or little tumblers. Cover with plastic wrap and chill in the fridge for at least 3 hours, or overnight, to set.

To make the syrup, place the tea bag in a small saucepan and pour in the boiling water. Set aside for 5 minutes, to steep, then lift out the tea bag. Add the sugar, thyme, vanilla seeds, and lemon juice to the pan and place over low heat for 3 minutes, stirring a few times, to help the sugar dissolve. Add the cherries, then remove from the heat and set aside to cool.

Top each pudding with a few pieces of cherry and about 1 tbsp (or more, if you have a sweet tooth) of the syrup. Garnish with the pistachios and serve.

THE
WALLED OFF
HOTEL
THE
WALLED OFF
HOTEL

The Walled Off Hotel, the separation wall, and the Balfour bungle

The Walled Off Hotel, in Bethlehem, is a work of Banksy genius. That's what we think, anyway. Other opinions are available. We'll get to those in a bit. For now, here's the pitch.

The Walled Off is a ten-room hotel that sits in the shadow of the eight-foot-high wall that separates Israel from the Palestinian Territories. From the name of the hotel—a play on "Waldorf"—onward, everything inside slightly skews reality and plays with the expectations of a typical hotel guest. Walking through the heavy red velvet curtains that hang at the entrance door, visitors feel as though they've entered some sort of colonial dystopian nightmare. Welcome to the hotel, the Walled Off boasts, with "the worst view in the world."

First impressions are of a space that feels incongruously old-school, embarrassingly English, unironically Empire-ish. Tea is imbibed from little china cups, teapots are silver, pictures sit in large gilded frames. The waitstaff wear waistcoats. A piano tinkles away, providing soothing background music.

Blink and look again, though, and the cracks soon appear. The cherubs floating over the piano are wearing gas masks. The kids on swings in the picture are flying around an Israeli military watchtower. The piano is eerily self-playing. The stuffed stag heads on the walls are not stag heads at all, but surveillance cameras.

The experience continues in the bedrooms, accessed via a secret door that looks, at first glance, like book-stacked shelves in a slightly dusty library. Frames hang on walls, empty of anything other than a written description of the picture you'd *expect* to see in a days-of-Empire drawing room. "Rural Landscape," says one; "Dog," says another. A montage of pictures hangs together around a velvet sofa and chair, showing a "Dog," a "Naval Battle," "Dog," "Dog," "Fruit," "Amateur Watercolor Done by Friend of the Owner," "Portrait of Race Horse," "Two Dogs."

The hotel's ten rooms are all very different from each other. One, the Budget Room, feels prison-like, filled with three sets of metal bunkbeds, each separated by a thin mosquito curtain. Other rooms are more plush. In the Banksy Room, a mural shows an Israeli soldier and a Palestinian protester having a great, big, fluffy pillow fight. The Presidential Suite is the most lavish and provocative of all. A mural of three leopards reclining is positioned above a zebra-print sofa where padded entrails snake out of the cushions. Next to the sofa is a large Jacuzzi set in the floor of the room. A pineapple-shaped ice container sits, in attendance, ready to chill the requisite sun-downers. It's disconcertingly bling, completely incongruous, and hugely thought-provoking. We think it is a little bit genius, a big bit stir-mongering, and all the more important and useful for that.

For anyone not quite getting the irony of it all, a visit to the small museum on the ground floor soon clarifies the hotel's genuine and serious perspective. The museum is small but massively hard-hitting in terms of the information packed in. The impact felt by visitors as they walk, read, listen, and watch their way around the range of pictures, video footage, and text is big. A three- or four-minute video at the outset, spoken in a plummy, military-style English-speaking voice, brilliantly summarizes the British bungle that kick-started this great big political, geographical conflict in the first place.

To summarize the summary (with an acknowledgment that doing so will only ever provide a reductive sweep over big events), there were two major things going on here—the Balfour Declaration of 1917 and the Second World War—and they came together eventually in the formation of the State of Israel in 1948, when Jewish survivors of Nazi persecution in Europe, desperate for a safe place to live, were granted a new homeland by the United Nations. Starting a national state for a population who had been persecuted, killed, and tortured over centuries was not just an understandable necessity; it was a global imperative. The big mistake, of course, was ignoring the rights of the Palestinians who were already living there.

From the late nineteenth century and the birth of the Zionist movement, there had been calls, from Jews facing anti-Semitism in Europe, for a Jewish homeland. This movement was given legitimacy with the Balfour Declaration, when Arthur Balfour, the British foreign secretary at the time, stepped in with his magic wand and said, "Look here, chaps, I know what, we can create a state for you here, the State of Israel, and you can all set up shop and be safe and well. Job done!" Or words to that effect.

The problem with this "magic solution," of course, was that this piece of land was already home to about 700,000 Palestinians. The words issued by Balfour at the time have to be read to be believed—suggesting, as they did, that it was somehow possible to *"view with favour the establishment in Palestine of a national home for the Jewish people"* at the same time as ensuring that *"nothing shall be done which may prejudice the civil and religious rights of existing non-Jewish communities in Palestine."* The two halves of the sentence just don't fit, Arthur! A new carving appeared on the separation wall outside the hotel in 2017 to coincide with the 100 years since Balfour's declaration. "ER," it says (to be read either as a hesitant "er" or as a more regal and reverent "Elizabeth Regina") on one line, with a one-word "SORRY" on the second. The great British Balfour bungle indeed.

The hotel has its critics. Banksy—the anonymous graffiti artist—will always generate a degree of controversy, but this is part of the point: to get people talking, discussing, disagreeing. The specific problem some locals have is the idea that the hotel, and the graffiti on the wall around and beyond the hotel, make art of (and therefore benefit from) the occupation. The view of some is that by making the occupation the subject of art, it somehow normalizes or trivializes it, rendering it acceptable to the tourists who just come to Bethlehem to "see the Banksy," "see the Church of the Nativity," and then scoot back in their bus or taxi to Jerusalem, where they are staying.

The question of Banksy benefiting from the hotel is one refuted by the facts. The hotel is locally run, with forty-five staff on the payroll, and all profits from the hotel and gift shop next door are plowed back into local community projects. The question of making Bethlehem a "two-stop shop" has a point, but it's a reality faced by lots of places people tend to visit for, frankly, one of two reasons. Pisa, for example, has more to offer than just its Leaning Tower. Is it not incumbent upon enterprising locals in Bethlehem to give tourists reason to venture on beyond the hotel and the church; to see the refugee camps, to have somewhere to go for a drink and some food afterward to take it all in? Getting a good meal in Bethlehem is, surprisingly, quite hard. Falafel and hummus—great, fine—but, at the time of writing, all the really tasty, interesting, and fresh cooking is being done inside people's homes rather than being available to visitors through restaurants.

The "making art of the occupation" question is complex but our take is that, surely, when there are so many issues in the world—where to start?—it's better to be one being talked about than one getting no airtime at all. If art helps get people to look at (and therefore think about, talk about, and tell people about) the separation wall, for example, is this really such a bad thing?

Next door to the hotel sits the "Wall Mart" shop. In it, Tara bought three T-shirts for her kids to wear back home in London. Each has an image of Banksy's Bethlehem-based art: a young girl floating upward, holding on to a bunch of balloons; a donkey having its papers checked by an armed soldier; a masked rioter throwing not a Molotov cocktail but a bunch of flowers. Does this make Tara an "occupation tourist," making light of what she has seen by a "been there, done that, got the T-shirt" attitude? Or does it mean that her six- and ten-year-old kids are now wearing them in south London and, as an absolutely direct result, knowing about Banksy and the wall, talking to their little friends about the situation and occupation? On one hand, these souvenirs are all too easy, too neat: the fridge magnet, the tote bag. But the questions and chats really do follow. "Do donkeys need passports in Palestine?" Tara hears her daughter's friend ask. "Why can't the girl just walk around the wall?" asks another. Getting people talking, getting kids asking questions; it's a really important part of the process of making change happen.

AKE
MMUS
WALLS
STOP THE WALL
Cream

VISIT
PALESTINE

Glossary: the pantry and politics of Palestine

Two notes. First, on content. The words in our glossary cover a lot of ground, all the way from the pantry to the politics of Palestine. When it comes to the politics, any attempt to compress very involved subjects down to just a line or two is, clearly, only ever going to be partial. The aim of this glossary, then, is to quickly and briefly inform; it does not do justice to the amount that can be said, from all perspectives, on all the various matters.

Second, on spelling. When Arabic words are transcribed into English, they are written out phonetically. This can lead to a lot of different ways to spell the same thing: pitta or pita, for example; hummous or humous or hummus or hummos! We have chosen the spelling that makes most sense to us and then stuck to it throughout.

ADHA means "pouring" or "spilling" in Arabic. A bit like tarka in Indian cuisine or the Turkish kızgın tereyağı, it's poured over a dish just before serving, to bring a final layer of flavor, aroma, and texture. Adha is made from a combination of garlic, spices, and fresh herbs that are brought to the point of sizzle in a little bit of butter, oil, or ghee. It can be drizzled over all sorts of dishes—stews, soups, or dips, for example—so make more of it than you need. It keeps well in a sealed container at room temperature for up to a week.

AKKAWI CHEESE originated in the port city of Akka. Akkawi is a slightly salty semihard cheese. It can be eaten either as it is—for breakfast or added to salads, as you would feta—or used in the making of sweet knafeh (see page 302), where the salty cheese contrasts so well with the sugar-syrup-drenched pastry. Before being used in a sweet dish, the cheese needs to be soaked in several changes of cold water. It's widely available in Middle Eastern grocery stores but, if you can't find any, a mixture of grated firm mozzarella and ricotta makes a good alternative. The ratio should be two-thirds mozzarella to one-third ricotta. In a savory context, substituting feta also works. See also **jibneh baida** and **Nabulsi cheese**.

AKKOUB is the Arabic name for the *Gundelia* plant, from the daisy family, which is native to the wild hills and mountains of the eastern Mediterranean and the Middle East. The vegetable (also known as tumbleweed), with its spiny leaves and prickly thistles, is hard to find outside the area, so it's not an ingredient used in *Falastin*. Still, it's an important part of Palestinian village cuisine, added to stews or salads, or pickled, once its spiny leaves and thistles have been removed.

ALEPPO CHILE FLAKES are named after the Syrian city of Aleppo. These dried chile flakes have a medium heat and sweet aroma, similar to the Turkish chile flakes, pul biber. Aleppo flakes can be sprinkled fairly liberally over all sorts of dishes. They work particularly well with eggs and are great, also, added to a bit of melted butter or heated oil, which is then drizzled over a stew or soup. If you can't find any, just substitute regular chile flakes—the hotter they are, the less you'll need.

ALLSPICE is an essential spice in the Palestinian pantry (as well as throughout the Levant), used in both savory and sweet contexts. It's made from the dried, unripe berries of the *Pimenta dioica* tree. Despite its Latin name, it's not related to either black pepper or capsicums. It's called "allspice" because of its ability to conjure up the flavors of many other popular spices: cinnamon and cloves, bay and black pepper, mace and hints of nutmeg. The berries are brown-green when picked and turn to a reddish brown when dried.

ANISEED is a versatile spice that can be used in a sweet or savory context. The small, pale brown seeds, which smell and taste sweet, are used either whole or ground in a range of cakes, custards, and cookies (see the ma'amoul recipe, page 310), as well as, for a savory example, fish stew. The flavor has warming notes of licorice, star anise, and fennel. Anethole is the principal essential oil and it's this that gives aniseed its distinct taste. It greets you head-on every time you have a sip of a drink such as Greek ouzo, French pastis, Lebanese raki, and Turkish arak.

AREAS A, B, AND C are the three areas into which the West Bank is divided. Each area has a different setup in terms of who leads on the governance, administration, and civil and security control in the area. Area A (18 percent of the West Bank) is under Palestinian Authority (PA) control. Area B (about 22 percent) is shared-responsibility; the PA is responsible for civil administration, and Israeli jurisdiction covers security control. Area C (at 63 percent, the largest chunk of land) is under full Israeli civil and security control. When the plan was written up in 1993 as part of the Oslo Accords, the measure was meant to be an interim one, with full Palestinian governance achieved by 1999. Twenty years on, the division of land into Areas A, B, and C is still in place.

BAHARAT translates literally from the Arabic as "spices." The combination of spices in a particular blend depends on what is championed by each region (and within each household in each region!), so no single flavor tends to dominate. Generally, though, it's an aromatic, warm spice made up of a combination of black peppercorns, coriander seeds, cardamom, cinnamon, cloves, allspice, cumin, and nutmeg. It brings a sweet depth and flavor to all sorts of savory and sweet dishes. It's widely available to buy, but if you want to make your own, place the following spices in a spice grinder or a mortar and pestle and grind until a fine powder is formed: 1 tsp black peppercorns, 1 tsp coriander seeds, 1 tsp cardamom pods, 1 small cinnamon stick, ½ tsp whole cloves, ½ tsp ground allspice, 2 tsp cumin seeds, and ¼ tsp ground nutmeg. Store in an airtight container, where it will keep for 2 months.

BALADI, translated literally, means "village," "country," or "land." The word conjures up more than that, though, it encapsulates the deep roots Palestinians have in their land and their feelings toward what grows out of it. The "i" in "baladi" makes it "my"—"*my* village," "*my* country," "*my* land."

BDS stands for "Boycott, Divestment, and Sanctions." The movement began in 2005, when a coalition of 170 Palestinian civil society groups issued a call for "people of conscience" to boycott (Israeli goods, universities, and cultural institutions), divest (from companies that provide goods and equipment to Israel), and support the application of sanctions by other countries on Israel. The movement elicits strongly opposing opinions—those who think it does as much harm as it does good—from both Palestinian and Israeli individuals and groups.

BESARA is somewhere between a soup and a thick, warm dip. The main ingredient is fava beans, pointing to its origins in Egypt before it spread to other Levantine countries. In Palestine, the herbs in the Egyptian version—cilantro and parsley—are matched by Palestine's flavor-packed dried leaf, molokhieh. Wherever it's made, a mixture of fried onion, chile, lemon, and olive oil is always spooned on top.

CARDAMOM brings its distinctive flavor and sweetness to all sorts of cakes and desserts. It works as well in a savory context, and we've also added some to our breakfast granola (see page 25). Throughout the Levant, cardamom pods are also often placed in the spouts of coffee pots to flavor the hot liquid as it is poured. The aroma is intense (a result of no fewer than twenty-five essential oils being present in the seeds), so a little bit goes a long way. If a recipe calls for ground cardamom, you can either source this preground or make your own. To make your own, bash open the pods in a mortar and pestle and discard the dry outer husks. Transfer the inner small black seeds to a spice or coffee grinder (or return them to the mortar and pestle) and grind until smooth. It might seem like a lot of work but the result is a real flavor-bomb—pungent, smoky, lemony, and floral—so it's well worth doing.

CHICKPEAS See **pulses**.

CLARIFIED BUTTER, known as ghee or samneh (or samna) in Arabic, is the pure fat left over from when butter has been separated from its milk solids. It has a long shelf life so was traditionally a key part of the Palestinian pantry (see **mooneh**). Nowadays, cooks are more likely to reach for regular butter, olive oil, or other vegetable oils as a healthier cooking fat.

DATE SYRUP, also known as date molasses, is the dark, sticky sweet syrup made from cooking down dates. A little bit goes a long way in both sweet and savory cooking. One teaspoon added to a meatball mixture or a stew, for example, brings a real depth of sweet flavor. It's wonderful paired with tahini, to be either spread on toast or spooned over yogurt (see page 25) in the morning. On toast, it's the equivalent of the classic peanut butter and jam combination.

DILL SEEDS smell like caraway, taste like anise, and bring a spicy warmth to dishes. They pair naturally with acidity—lemon juice, for example—and are ideal for pickling vegetables. Dill seeds (and dill weed) are widely used in Gazan cuisine, playing a leading role in Gaza's signature spicy tomato salad, dagga (see page 194). You can buy dill seeds online if you can't find them in a grocery store, but celery seeds or caraway seeds can be used as an alternative. The seeds should be crushed in a mortar and pestle before being used, in order to release their fragrance.

DRIED IRANIAN LIMES are small and rock-hard. They are lovely added to all sorts of soups, stews, or rice dishes, such as maqlubeh (see page 264), infusing them with their distinct and pungent sweet-sharp aroma. Puncture them here and there with the tip of a knife before adding to a dish, and remove them before serving—their job is to infuse rather than to be eaten.

EGGPLANTS: how to char The more you char your eggplants, the smokier the flesh, and the better your m'tabbal (see page 82), eggplant and lemon soup (see page 152), and cauliflower and eggplant with tomato sauce (see page 110) will taste. Unless you don't mind your whole house smelling of charred eggplants, ventilation is key. Open the windows, open the door, put on the fan! We char our eggplants in one of two ways. The first, if you have a gas flame on an open stove top (as opposed to an electric stove), is to put one eggplant over each gas ring, turn the flame on high, and leave it there for 15–20 minutes, turning halfway through with long tongs so that all sides get charred. The advantage of doing this is that it is a really quick and very effective way of getting the flesh smoky. The disadvantage is that it can cause a bit of a mess on your stove top if the eggplants leak once they've been turned and their skin gets pierced. This mess can either be cleaned up with a bit of elbow grease or minimized in the first place if you cover your stove top with aluminum foil. Make holes in the foil for the burners to pop through and then proceed. If you have an electric stove, you'll need to heat up a grill pan until it is very hot—place it over high heat for at least 5 minutes, until smoking—then add the eggplants directly to the pan. Pierce them a few times with a sharp knife before doing so. This method takes longer than the open-flame option—35 or 40 minutes, again turning throughout with long tongs so that all sides get charred—but you will get the same result. At the end of the 40 minutes, transfer the eggplants to a foil-lined baking sheet and place under a broiler for a final 10 minutes. Once charred (whether on a gas ring or in a grill pan), place the eggplants in a colander. Once cool enough to handle, slit them open to scoop out the flesh and place in a clean colander. Don't worry if some of the charred skin sticks to the flesh; this all adds to the smoky flavor. Set aside for an hour or so (or overnight), over a bowl, to drain. You're then all set for the smokiest of all smoky spreads, soups, and sauces.

EGGPLANTS: to salt or not to salt Opinion differs on whether or not eggplants should be salted (to release their bitterness) before cooking. For us it's more about whether we want moisture in the eggplants before cooking (rather than it being about bitterness, which we rarely find to be an issue these days). Our policy is to salt and drain when we are frying eggplant—getting rid of the moisture in the eggplant makes sense before it goes into hot oil—but not when we are roasting cubes or wedges of eggplant. In an oven, the steam generated by a bit of moisture trapped in the eggplant helps it cook for a long time without drying out.

EGYPTIAN RICE looks like short-grain rice but is creamier and holds its shape better. Because of this, it works particularly well in long-and-slow-cooked dishes and in dishes where vegetables or vine leaves are stuffed. It's fairly easy to source, in well-stocked supermarkets or specialty stores, but can be replaced by arborio rice, if need be.

A FALAFEL SCOOP is a good investment if you are planning to make a lot of falafel—it's not an expensive tool. But a small ice-cream scoop or just your hands can be used as an alternative to shape the falafel mix.

FATTEH, or fatta, means "crushed" or "crumbled" or "broken into pieces" in Arabic. It describes a type of food preparation practiced throughout the Levant and North Africa, where a piece of flatbread is torn into chunks and then layered into a dish. If the bread is fresh or untoasted, it will soak up the juices or sauce in a dish and collapse happily in with the other ingredients. If the pieces of bread are toasted, they will retain their shape and crunch, and can be used instead of a fork to scoop things up with and eat.

FAVA BEANS See **pulses**.

FREEKEH is a Middle Eastern whole grain or cracked wheat. The whole grain wheat is just called freekeh. The cracked version sometimes goes by the name "greenwheat." Either way, the wheat is harvested before it is fully ripe and then is roasted over an open fire so as to burn off the husks. This gives it a wonderfully smoky and nutty flavor. It's widely available in well-stocked supermarkets, in specialty stores, in health food shops, and online.

GLUTEN-FREE The "bulgur vs. quinoa" debate is one that Sami and Tara had many times during the writing of *Falastin*. "Please! Quinoa is just *not* an ingredient used in Palestine," Sami would point out, entirely reasonably, when discussing a dish such as Baked Fish Kubbeh (page 201). "But I don't eat bulgur wheat," Tara would respond, entirely selfishly, "and it does work here!" For all the tussles over traditional versus nontraditional ingredients and twists, the line was very firmly drawn, by Sami, at quinoa! While noting that quinoa is absolutely not used in traditional Palestinian kitchens, Tara would like to whisper that bulgur is often very happy to be replaced with the gluten-free alternative, if you are looking for one. Use the same amount of white quinoa as bulgur, throw it into boiling water for 9 minutes, then rinse under cold running water. In the case of that kubbeh, when mixing the cooked quinoa with the fish, add a couple of tablespoons of chickpea flour to the mix, to help everything bind together.

THE GREEN LINE is the generally recognized boundary or dividing line between Israel and the West Bank. It is properly referred to as the 1949 Armistice line; the ceasefire line of 1949. The exact borders of Israel and a future Palestinian state are subject to negotiation between the two parties. The Palestinians want a complete end to the Israeli occupation of the West Bank, Gaza Strip, and East Jerusalem, and use the phrase to mean a return to the pre–June 4, 1967, borders.

HARISSA (not to be confused with harisa—see page 309—the sugar-syrup-soaked semolina cake popular all over the Middle East!) is a spicy North African chile paste we use as an alternative to shatta if we don't have a batch ready-made. Rose harissa (we like the one produced by Belazu) is what we tend to use—the addition of the rose petals softens and sweetens the kick from the chile.

HAWADER, roughly translated as "ready to eat," is the practice of batch cooking or preparing food in advance that can then sit in the freezer or in jars on the shelf, ready to be served after heating through if needed. Hawader plays a big role in the seemingly effortless hospitality of Palestinian home cooks. If the freezer is full of ready-made kubbeh or fatayer, for example, food can always appear—as if by magic!—whenever someone turns up unexpectedly.

JAMEED, like kishek, is a dried and fermented yogurt. There are various ways to preserve and ferment yogurt; in the case of jameed, the yogurt is shaped into balls and dried in the sun. This method of preservation made its way into Palestine via the Bedouins of Jordan.

JIBNEH BAIDA is an umbrella term for the semihard, rindless, white, salt-brined Arabic cheeses that appear throughout the Middle East. They show up under various different names, depending on where they come from: jibneh Nabulsi from the city of Nablus or jibneh Akkawi from the port city of Akka. Their flavor is always pronounced, but varies according to the milk from which they are made (goat, ewe, sheep, cow) and the length and strength of the salt brine. These cheeses need to be soaked in water before using, to pull back on some of their saltiness.

JUTE MALLOW See **molokhieh**.

KATAIFI PASTRY, popular across the Levant (as well as Turkey and Greece), consists of long, thin strands of shredded filo pastry. It's what is used to make our Knafeh Nabulseyeh on page 302. Being in strands makes it easy for the pastry to get wrapped around or layered with various sweet or savory fillings before being baked or fried. This vermicelli-like pastry loves being drenched in melted butter, oil, or sugar syrup, and develops a wonderfully light crunch when cooked. It's not the easiest of ingredients to find but it should be stocked in the frozen section of a good Greek, Arab, or Turkish grocer.

KISHEK, also known as jameed, are preserved discs of fermented yogurt and (though not always) wheat. The discs are made at the end of summer in Palestine (and throughout the Levant), just after the wheat harvest. First, bulgur is made by boiling, drying, and crushing the wheat grain. This is then mixed with yogurt, spread out on a tray, and set aside until all the liquid has been absorbed into the grain. The kishek grains are then spread out on cloths and left to dry in the sun. Finally, these are rubbed together to produce a powder. This can then be added to soups and stews to both thicken them and bring a deep flavor. There are also wheat-free versions of kishek. These are just blocks of dried, fermented yogurt that are crushed and then reconstituted. With or without the wheat, kishek has a deep umami flavor similar to what you'd find in a mature cheese such as tart feta or Parmesan. The taste is totally distinctive, so it's worth hunting down in Middle Eastern markets, specialty stores, or online. If you can't get it, you can make a (very!) vague approximation by mixing together some sour cream or crème fraîche with some grated Parmesan and a few very finely chopped anchovies.

LABNEH is an Arabic cheese made by hanging yogurt (with salt, to draw out the liquid) until it's drained of all its liquid; the longer it is left to drain, the drier and firmer it becomes. If you are rushed, you can bring it about in 6 hours; you'll just need to squeeze the ball of yogurt a few times to help the process along. Ideally, it will hang for a couple of days. Once made, it can either be spread as it is on toast, sprinkled with za'atar or sumac and drizzled with olive oil, or rolled into balls that are then preserved in oil. It keeps in the fridge for up to 2 weeks (if not preserved in oil) or, as balls covered in oil, for about 2 months. Labneh can be made with either a combination of goat (or sheep or ewe) yogurt and Greek yogurt or, for a less "tangy" version, just Greek yogurt. For the recipe, to get the ratio of yogurt to salt, see page 48.

MAFTOUL, also known as Palestinian couscous or giant couscous, is made from sun-dried and cracked bulgur, which is then hand-rolled in flour. The little balls of pasta—like couscous, but larger—are then steamed and sun-dried. Maftoul is added to soups or stews, to bulk them out, or served as it is, itself bulked out with chickpeas, alongside a piece of meat or fish. It's fairly easy to find in well-stocked supermarkets but, as an alternative, fregola can be used instead.

MAHASHI, or mahsi, refers to stuffed food. The stuffing being the "hashwa" (derived from the same word). This can be anything from carrots, cucumbers, zucchini, and potatoes (which need to be cored) to cabbage and vine leaves (which will be rolled). Mahashi also refers to stuffed meat, from a whole lamb (or any part of the animal) to a whole chicken, which will be stuffed as it is. The stuffing can vary—a mixture of rice and meat is common, as is a mix of spiced ground meat, onion, and pine nuts, or a vegetarian stuffing of bulgur, tomatoes, and herbs—as can the cooking methods and sauces. Other mahashi include fish, seafood, eggs, and various parts of lamb, sheep, or cow.

MAHLEB, which has a nutty, slightly bitter-almond flavor, is made from grinding the pits of the black St Lucie cherry. The pits are sold whole or ground to use in bread and sweet baking. It's in our ma'amoul bars, but is lovely to have around for general use. Try adding a tiny bit to any butter cookies you are making, or adding it to sugar syrups for a fruit salad, or using to flavor whipped cream. A tiny drop of almond extract can be used as an alternative, if you are looking for one.

MANAKRA, also known as miqwarah or miqwar, are tools used to core out vegetables. They are small, long thin knives that have a thin, semicircular serrated blade. This blade makes easy work of removing the flesh from inside a vegetable. A swivel peeler (or a power drill, as we discovered over lunch one day when cooking and eating in a garage in a parking lot in Jerusalem!) works well as an (non-health-and-safety-compliant) alternative.

MANSAF is a stew of lamb braised in kishek, the fermented goat yogurt. It hails from the Levant, originated in Hebron, is the national dish of Jordan, and is a typical Bedouin dish. It's traditionally served at celebratory meals in Palestine—weddings and major feasts. The lamb and its tangy sauce tend to be assembled on a large serving platter, with buttery rice and paper-thin flatbread called shhrak layered in, and a garnish of toasted nuts, such as pine nuts and almonds. Guests either pull at the bread, using this in lieu of utensils to scoop up and eat the lamb and rice, or spoon some onto their own plate to eat with a fork.

MASHWI, or mashawi, means "grilled," referring to grilled food that uses skewered meats such as shuqaf (hunks of lamb), kofta (ground lamb), or shish taouk (marinated chicken). These (along with maza dishes; see **maza/mezzeh**) are the types of food more often served in restaurants in Palestine (as opposed to the more labor-intensive "tabeekh" cooking, usually confined to the home).

MASTIC GUM is a resin obtained from the mastic tree, found on the island of Chios in Greece. It is often called Arabic gum or Yemen gum (but not gum Arabic; which does not have the same taste). Mastic starts life as a sap that is then sun-dried into pieces of brittle and translucent resin. When chewed, this becomes a bright white and opaque gum. The taste is initially bitter, then transforms into something pine- or cedar-like. Added to things such as ice cream, jams, custards, or other set desserts, mastic brings its distinct, rich flavor—a combination of fennel, aniseed, and mint—and almost rubbery texture. In Gaza, it is also added to soups. It is available in health-food shops and online. There is no alternative!

MAZA/MEZZEH refers to the large number of small plates of salads, pickles, cured meats, and other appetizers that everyone can help themselves to at an informal meal or gathering. They are often served at room temperature, meaning that making them ahead works well.

MOLOKHIEH, also known as jute leaves or jute mallow, is a dark green leaf, a bit like spinach. The leaves are used widely throughout the Levantine region, added to soups and stews or cooked along with meat. It tastes rather bitter before it gets cooked. A bit like okra, it has a slightly gelatinous consistency that, when blitzed, thickens things up. The molokhieh plant is available fresh in the summer, and dried or frozen for the rest of the year. Outside Palestine, bags of frozen molokhieh are available in Middle Eastern supermarkets. If you can't find any, an approximation can be made by cooking together spinach and thinly sliced okra. The result, when blitzed together, is not the exact flavor of molokhieh but will get you somewhere close in terms of texture.

MOONEH translates literally as "pantry essential items," things such as rice, flour, grains, and sugar that always need to be well stocked, as they are used so much in the kitchen. It means more than this, though, referring to the whole process of preparing food well in advance of when it is going to be used—pickling, preserving, jamming, fermenting, and so forth. This is done as a way to make certain seasonal foods are available all year-round, and also allows the cook to make the most of a particular ingredient when it is abundant at a certain time of the year. This sort of mooneh, where the focus is on preserving food, is often prepared in groups—mooneh gatherings—when circles of women come together to sterilize jars, make brines, roll labneh, pickle vegetables, stack vine leaves, make jams, and so on. This sort of sociable batch cooking allows for many a short-cut to be taken in the making of everyday food.

MUSAKHAN is one of Palestine's national dishes, where chicken is cooked and served with layers of olive oil–drenched flatbread. It's traditionally made during the olive oil season, to test the quality of that year's crop. Sumac is also a key player, both in the marinade for the chicken and in the onions that are such a star of the dish. See page 247 for the recipe.

NABULSI CHEESE, like Akkawi cheese, is a slightly salty semihard cheese. It's made with a mix of milks (traditionally ewe and goat milk, in equal proportions). Authentic Nabulsi is perfumed with mastic and mahleb. In a savory context, it can be added to salads (grated or in cubes or slices) or eaten for breakfast with bread, as you would feta. In a sweet context, it comes into its own in knafeh (see page 302), where its tangy flavor offsets the syrup-doused pastry. See also **jibneh baida**.

NAFAS means "soul" in Arabic. In the context of the kitchen, the term translates loosely as "soul cooking"—cooking according to intuition, taste, and senses. Recipes are often passed on through talking and sharing and eating together, rather than being written down, so this element plays a key role in the beauty of homemade food.

NAKBA is the term used by Palestinians to refer to the displacement of more than 700,000 Palestinians and the establishment of Israel. It commemorates the end of the 1948 Arab-Israeli War, which Israelis refer to as the War of Independence. It is the name for the most traumatic collective memory for Palestinians, and literally means "a catastrophe" or "disaster." In the Palestinian consciousness, this date represents the displacement of Palestinians, their separation from their land, and the subsequent ban on their return to what they see as their homes and properties.

NUTS: how to toast The best way to toast nuts is to spread them on a baking sheet in the oven, preheated to 350°F. Timings vary depending on the nut. Slivered almonds get 6–7 minutes; pine nuts, walnuts, and pistachios about 8 minutes; and whole almonds 8–10 minutes. Always give them a stir halfway through cooking, or give the sheet a shake. Toasting them in the oven is better than in a pan on the stove, which can result in one side of the nut taking on a lot more color than the other. If you do need to toast in a pan, that's fine—just keep the heat low, stir often, and remove the pan from the heat a minute or so before the nuts are ready; the residual heat in the pan means they'll continue to cook.

OPT stands for "Occupied Palestinian Territories." The general phrase "occupied territories" refers to East Jerusalem, the West Bank, and, strictly speaking, the Golan Heights. Under international law, Israel is still the occupying power in Gaza, although it no longer has a permanent military presence there. The occupied territories are sometimes referred to as "Palestinian land" to explain why the construction of settlements is considered illegal by the UN. Critics of the phrase say that it is not accurate because, for example, the West Bank was captured from Jordan in the 1967 war. The phrase "Palestinian Territories" refers, strictly speaking, to the areas that fall under the administration of the Palestinian Authority. They are difficult to work out, though, because of the way the West Bank was divided into complex security zones under the Oslo Accords and because of on-the-ground changes since the outbreak of violence in September 2000.

ORANGE BLOSSOM WATER is a key ingredient in various Arab and Mediterranean cuisines. It is distilled water made from the macerated blossoms of Seville oranges. It can be used in savory cooking, a teaspoon or less added to a green leaf and herb filled soup, for example, but is most commonly used to flavor syrups, which are then used in the making and soaking of cakes and baklava, or to fold into creams for desserts. There are plenty of good brands around; we use the Cortas brand. See also **rose water**.

POMEGRANATE MOLASSES is made by cooking and reducing the juice of sour pomegranates to form a thick, dark syrup. It has a sweet-sour flavor that pairs brilliantly with all sorts of marinades, meatballs, sauces, salads, stews, stuffed vegetables, and sauces. There are lots of good brands available; we use either the Arabic brand Al-Rabih or the (more expensive and wonderfully astringent) Mymouné brand, which is made from 100 percent pomegranate molasses (with no added sugar).

PRESERVED LEMONS are a wonderful way to add a pop of flavor to all sorts of savory dishes. Preserving your own lemons is a lovely and easy thing to do—see Sami's book *Jerusalem*, if you have it (or you can look online), for the recipe—but here we use the thin-skinned Beldi preserved lemons produced by Belazu. They are widely available.

PULSES: dried vs. canned You can use either dried or canned pulses; the recipe will still work but the result will be different. Starting with dried pulses and soaking them overnight will bring about the "best" results (the creamier hummus, as you can use the cooking water when blitzing together the chickpeas), but using precooked chickpeas will always, of course, have the advantage of almost-instant readiness. When it comes to fava beans, though, we often prefer using already cooked canned beans rather than dried ones. For one thing, they are easier find, but the dried ones can also cook unevenly and require peeling.

QAHWA, or a'ahwah, means "coffee" in Arabic. It's strong and intense, often with a hint of cardamom, and is served at every gathering and social event in Palestine, before and after meals. It's usually served with something sweet—a date or a slice of baklava, for example—an idea we've run with in our chocolate and qahwa torte (see page 317).

QIDREH literally means "pot" in Arabic. Originally from Hebron, it refers to the richly spiced festive rice-and-meat dish (traditionally lamb, but beef or chicken can also be used) cooked in an unglazed copper pot. The pot sits over slow-burning coals either in the ground or in a stone oven. Cooks don't prepare this dish at home themselves; they fill their pot or urn and take it to a community qidreh oven, where the owner of the oven takes care of the cooking. The pots are tightly sealed, so, in order not to get all mixed up, they are individually named with chalk. Before serving, the urn is dramatically cracked open and the fragrant, buttery rice pours out. Qidreh cooking can be replaced with a cast-iron Dutch oven on a regular stove or oven.

ROSE WATER is the distilled water from the Damascus rose, or *ward jouri* in Arabic. As with orange blossom water, it can be used to flavor milk puddings, ice creams, cakes, and other sweets. A little bit goes a long way with these floral-flavored waters. Always start with less than you need, with the knowledge that you can add more but can't take it away. There are various brands around. We use either the Cortas or the Mymouné brand, both of which we recommend.

SAHLAB is a powder made from the tubers of wild orchids that grow in the mountains. It's used as a thickener in the making of many Arabic desserts—particularly set puddings—bringing about an almost elastic texture. It can also be dissolved in hot milk, along with some ground cinnamon, to make a thick, velvety, creamy drink. It can be found in most spice shops and Middle Eastern supermarkets. A (rough) approximation can be made by using 4–5 tbsp of cornstarch for each 1 tbsp of sahlab a recipe calls for (for every 1 qt/1L of milk).

SAHTEIN! is the Arabic equivalent of "bon appétit!" and translates as "two healths" or "may your health be redoubled." The response is often *al-albak*—"on your heart" or "same to you." At the end of a meal, guests might also say *sufra daymeh*—"may your dining room be eternally blessed." *Ahlan wa sahlan*, the cook will often reply, "welcome."

SAWANI are the equivalent of sheet-pan dishes and roasts in Palestinian cooking—dishes baked, roasted, or braised in large round baking pans where everything is tossed and cooked together.

THE SEPARATION WALL is the physical barrier that Israel started to build during the second intifada, between Israel and the West Bank. Some parts of the barrier consist of a fence and surrounding exclusion zone; others of a 26-foot-high concrete fence. What the wall is called and how it is perceived depends very much on which side someone is standing. From the Israeli side, the wall was built as a response to suicide bombings. The number of violent attacks has decreased since the "security wall" has gone up, confirming the legitimacy of the security concerns that gave rise to it. From the Palestinian side, the term "security wall" is offensive, as it implies that all Palestinians in the West Bank are a potential source of suicide or other violent attacks. The barrier both prevents freedom of movement and, because it diverges from the Green Line to encompass a number of settlements, effectively annexes Palestinian areas into Israel proper. There are a number of Palestinians, therefore, who refer to the wall as an "annexation wall," "segregation wall," or even "apartheid wall."

SHATTA, made from either fresh or semidried green or red chiles, is the must-have spicy condiment for every meal. Chiles are finely chopped, seasoned heavily with salt, then put in the fridge for 3 or 4 days before being blitzed up with some cider vinegar, or white wine vinegar, and lemon juice. See page 73 for the recipe.

STERILIZING JARS is a necessity when preserving foods; makdous, for example (see page 56), or shatta. It ensures that all bacteria and yeasts are removed from a jar so that the food remains fresh. There are various ways to sterilize a glass jar; including a water bath, where the jars go into water, with their lids added separately, the water is brought to a boil, and then the jars are "cooked" for 10 minutes, or filling the jars with just-boiled water and then rinsing and drying with a clean dish towel. We tend to just put ours into the dishwasher, though, and run it as a normal wash—it's a simple solution that works very well.

SUMAC is made from grinding down the dried sumac berry. This astringent, tangy spice is heavily used in Palestinian cooking. It can either be a seasoning—sprinkled over all sorts of egg dishes, or roasted vegetables, meat, or fish—or added to a batch of onions, cooked slowly for a long time before starring in a traditional dish such as musakhan.

TABOON OVENS are large outdoor (often communal) ovens made of stone. The heat is not sealed in with a door; instead it is the conical or domed shape of the oven that keeps the heat in. Little stones or pebbles line the base of the oven and, once these are incredibly hot, flatbread and other things are taken into the heart of the oven using a long flat paddle. Taboon bread takes on the shape of these pebbles, emerging looking like the surface of the moon with all its pockmarked indentations. We tried to re-create this in our regular kitchen in London (lining a baking sheet with lots of stones from the local garden center) and can confirm that this alternative does not work.

TAGHMEES, roughly translated as "dipping," refers to one of the most common methods of eating in the Arabic world. It's not just about dipping a piece of flatbread in hummus, though, it's much more about a way of life. It's about making bread into a scoop-shape and using it like a utensil to pick up food. It's bread as an accompaniment, bread as a utensil, bread as an extension of the hands.

TAHINI is the paste made from grinding sesame seeds. There are no other ingredients, so you'd be surprised how different one brand is from the next. We favor the creamy Lebanese, Israeli, and Palestinian brands (rather than the Greek and Cypriot ones, which we find to be a bit gummy). The Arabic brands we love—Al Arz, Al Taj, as just two examples—are creamy, nutty, and pourable, easily drizzled over a multitude of things. Roasted vegetables, fish, and meat all love tahini sauce (see page 87), and tahini as it is can just be spread on your toast or spooned over vanilla or chocolate ice cream.

TAMARIND brings its sharp, acidic, fruity, sweet-sour flavor to all sorts of soups and sauces. It first comes to a lot of Palestinians in the form of tamarind juice, sold ice-cold when the sun is out and hot. Pre-made tamarind paste is available in supermarkets, but these tend, on the whole, to be too acidic. For the best tamarind paste or water, start with a whole block of tamarind pulp and then soak and strain what you need from there.

ZA'ATAR is the name for both the wild herb (a variety of oregano) that grows throughout the region and the iconic Palestinian spice mix (which is a blend of dried za'atar, whole toasted sesame seeds, sumac, and salt). The leaves have a distinctive, savory aroma and their flavor is complex. There's a connection to oregano and marjoram but also to cumin, lemon, sage, and mint. It's lovely sprinkled over all sorts of things—eggs, leafy salads, grilled meat and fish—or served as it is with a little bowl of olive oil alongside, for bread to be dipped into.

ZAYTOUN, which means "olive" in Arabic, is a UK-based social enterprise that imports Palestinian olive oil, dates, almonds, freekeh, za'atar, and maftoul. The company began in 2004, when volunteers brought back products from their travels and started selling them through their local churches, Oxfam shops, village fairs, and so on. Although many of their sales are still made at a grass-roots level, you'll also see them in well-stocked produce markets and grocery stores. For more info see www.zaytoun.org.

A ZIBDIYEH is a heavy, unglazed clay bowl. It's a basic but often precious item in a lot of kitchens throughout Palestine, particularly Gaza. It's often accompanied by a lemonwood pestle and, like a mortar and pestle, is used for crushing garlic to a creamy pulp or for grinding dill (or other) seeds. The insides of the bowl are always rough, rather than smooth, to facilitate this grinding. As well as being used to mash and mix ingredients, it's also used for cooking some dishes, either on the stove top or in the oven, or for serving spicy dagga (see page 194).

A note on ingredients and cooking

Vegetable weights in parenthesis are net; that is, after peeling, chopping, etc. Our measurements are calculated on the basis that 1 tbsp is equal to 15ml and there are three 5ml tsp in 1 tbsp. Unless otherwise specified, olive oil is extra-virgin. Onions, garlic, and shallots are peeled, and garlic cloves are regular-size (rather than large). Chiles are used whole, or chopped, with their seeds left in. Salt is table salt, black pepper is freshly cracked, and parsley is flat-leaf. Eggs are large, yogurt is plain and full-fat, and tahini is from the Middle East. We use the Al Arz brand, but Al Taj and Al Nakhil are also good. Start with the best-quality produce you can, taste your food as you go, and, if ever in doubt, add a squeeze of lemon.

A note on plastic wrap

All efforts have been made to avoid single-use plastic (i.e., plastic wrap) in our recipes. Instead, we use parchment paper (which can be wiped clean and used again). In a couple of instances, plastic wrap is the only option we found to be properly effective. Biodegradable options are available.

Index

A

B

C

D

E

F

G

H

I

J

K

P

Q

R

T

V

W

Y

Z

Acknowledgments

Our biggest acknowledgment and thanks goes to Noor Murad. Noor was "loaned" to us by the Ottolenghi test kitchen for *Falastin* and is the secret behind so many of the kitchen's successes. Noor: thank you! For everything you created, tweaked, and fixed. "Team Falasteeeeen" could not have been, were it not for you.

Big thanks also to everyone else in the test kitchen, who tried, tasted, and tweaked our recipes: Yotam Ottolenghi, Gitai Fisher, Ixta Belfrage, and Verena Lochmuller. Claudine Boulstridge, as well—thank you for testing and tasting all our recipes—your feedback, as ever, is a crucial part of the process. Huge thank-yous also to Cornelia Staeubli and Noam Bar, for all your championing, support, help, and advice.

Thank you to Felicity Rubinstein, you were the first person to make us feel so excited about *Falastin* and all the possibilities it contained. Thank you for your unstinting support. Thank you, also, to Mark Hutchinson.

Huge thanks to team Ebury. Thank you to Louise McKeever, for setting us safely on our way, and then so many thank-yous to Lizzy Gray and Celia Palazzo, for taking over the reins and keeping us on such a good track. You guys are a great team! Sarah Bennie, Di Riley and team, you are everything two nervous authors could dream of. Thank you also to Joel Rickett for supporting us and for cooking Ottolenghi recipes at home on a seemingly nightly basis. Thank you also to Alice Latham and Rae Shirvington, for championing *Falastin* to overseas publishers, and to Annie Lee and Kate Parker, for their clever eyes. Thanks also to Aaron Wehner, Lorena Jones, Emma Rudolph, Kelly Booth, Doug Ogan, Jane Chinn, Mari Gill, Windy Dorresteyn, Kate Tyler and everyone at Ten Speed Press, as well as Kimberley Witherspoon, for support from across the seas. David Bond, thank you also for reminding us to enjoy the process.

For the design, photography, and look of the book, thanks to Harry Bingham, Caz Hildebrand, and Alex Merrett at Here Design. Jenny Zarins, we were so lucky to have you as our location and food photographer and travel companion—what a talented and totally gorgeous bean you are. And thank you for giving Tara a run for her money, appetite-wise. It was a dead heat, in the end! And Thomas Gonsard, thank you for the good vibes and two-week-long playlist. Wei Tang, thank you for working miracles on all the prop finding. For a task to find props for a book we didn't want to "prop," you really pulled it out of the bag.

Thank you also to Manal Ramadan White, Heather Masoud, and everyone at Zaytoun, for being so interested and supportive at every stage. You guys bring the best olive oil to the party. High-fives and full respect also to Gemma Bell, Katie Hagley, Jenny Baker, Veronica Pasteur, and everyone waving the Amos flag.

During our travels in Palestine, thanks to Vivien Sansour—team Zaki Zaki!—and Leila Sansour, your continued interest and support in what we are cooking up has been a joy. To Raya Manaa (and to Yasmin Khan for the introduction), for showing and driving us around. The way you take those speed bumps is inspiring. To Wisam, Esme, Holly, and all at the Walled Off Hotel in Bethlehem, thank you for generously putting us up. Thank you to everyone who shared their time, stories, and food with us on our travels: in particular to Islam Abu Aouda, Baseema Barahmeh, Alla Musa, Daher Zeidani, Mirna Bamieh, Suzanne Matar, Kamel Hashlamon, Fadi Kattan, Amal and Daoud Nassar, Nasser Abufarha, Salah Abu-Ali, Heba Al-Lahham, Nisrin Abuorf, and Ronit Vered. Your hospitality floored us, your steadfastness inspired us, your food delighted us.

In addition, Sami would like to say, Thank you to my parents, Hassan and Na'ama. To Jeremy for always being there for me and for eating all of my cooking. Gianluca Piermaria and his family for adopting us and for feeding us all the delicious Italian food. A big thank-you to Yotam, Noam, and Cornelia for letting us do this book. To Ramzi Khamis, I'm forever grateful and humble. I don't even know where to start or how to thank you for saving my life and for your love, care, and friendship, and of course Manal Khamis. Thanks to my *Falastin* journey partner, Tara, and the olives, preserved lemons, canned tuna, gallons of coffee, and all things Zaki. Thanks to my brothers and sisters and their families, Sawsan,

Kawthar, Olla, Adel, Adnan, Azam, Manal, Badria, Magdi, Amgad, Azza. Thanks to Alejandra Chavero, you are more than family to me. Big thank-you to the lovely Basia, for caring and all things spiritual. Special thank-you to Helen Goh, Maria Mok, Carmel Noy, Tali Levin, Dana Elemara, Danielle Postma, Dorit Mainzer, Eric Rodari. To the Kelly and Penny family, George, Maureen, Georgina and Louis, Bethany and Darren. Thanks so much to Karen Handler-Kermmerman, Adrien Von Ferscht, Lindy, and all the lovely ladies at Ceramica Blue, Eric Treuille from Books for Cooks. Naser Tawil, Israel Vatkin. Big thank-you also to my second family, all the amazing people working at Ottolenghi.

Tara would also like to thank the following. Suzanna and Richard Roxburgh, Alison and Alec Chrystal, and Sophie O'Leary, thank you for stepping in and scooping up the kids so often and keeping the show on the road. Justin and Lex, my big brothers, thank you for being such happy leftover takers, and, Lex, for eating so many more lemons than you might have liked to. An enormous thank-you to Vicki Howard, for reading all my words (and honing a fair few of them). Sarit Packer, thank you!—for calling me in for NOPI chats when I was clearly so ill-suited for the job and for making me realize that working in a professional kitchen was *not* my hottest idea. Yotam, thank you so much—for taking a chance on me back in the day and for always believing in me (even when I didn't). I have so much to thank you for. Sami, thank you for taking me on your journey with you back home, it's been a huge privilege. We got there! Thank you for eating my share of all the bread, and I promise never, ever to mention quinoa again. Thank you to my crew: Winnie, Ellie, Jessie (who first introduced me to Bethlehem, over 20 years ago), Nicky, Katherine, Neache, Sala, Carenza, Annie, and Ella; old friends, like bookends—extraordinary, bold, brilliant, women who I'd be lost without. Biggest hugs and high fives to Scarlett, Theo, and Casper—I'm sorry the house smells so often of charred eggplants!—and to Chris, as ever, sorry for springing the Palestine marathon on you when you thought you were just going for the culinary tour. Less running and more tequila shots from here on in.

Published in the United States by Ten Speed Press, an imprint of Random House, a division of Penguin Random House LLC, New York.
www.tenspeed.com

Originally published in Great Britain by Ebury Press, an imprint of Ebury Publishing, Penguin Random House Ltd., London.

Library of Congress Cataloging-in-Publication Data
is on file with the publisher.

Hardcover ISBN: 978-0-399-58173-1
eBook ISBN: 978-0-399-58174-8

Printed in China

Design by Here Design
Cover design by Kelly Booth
Prop styling by Wei Tang

10 9 8 7 6 5 4 3 2 1

First US Edition

e.guides

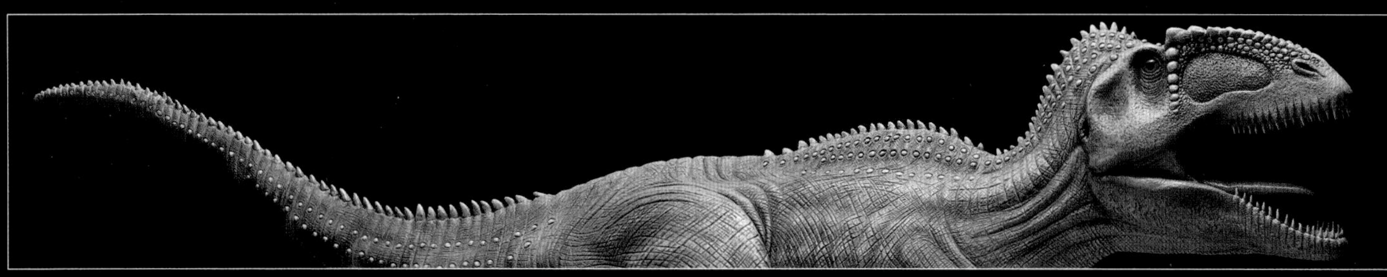

Dinosaur

LONDON, NEW YORK, MELBOURNE,
MUNICH and DELHI

Authors Dougal Dixon, John Malam

Senior Editor Margaret Hynes
Project Editors Fran Baines, Frank Ritter, Miranda Smith

Weblink Editors Clare Lister, Mariza O' Keeffe, Phil Hunt, John Bennett

Managing Editor Camilla Hallinan

Digital Development Manager Fergus Day
Production Erica Rosen
DTP Co-ordinator Toby Beedell
DTP Designers Gavin Brabant, Pete Quinlan

Category Publisher Sue Grabham

Consultant Professor Michael Benton

Senior Designers Neville Graham, Smiljka Surla, Owen Peyton Jones, Yumiko Tahata
Project Designers Janice English, Nick Harris, Rebecca Painter
Illustrators Mark Longworth, Peter Winfield
Cartography Robert Stokes

Managing Art Editor Sophia M Tampakopoulos Turner

Picture Researchers Veneta Bullen, Julia Harris-Voss, Alison Floyd
Picture Librarians Sarah Mills, Karl Strange, Kate Ledwith

Jacket Neal Cobourne

Art Director Simon Webb

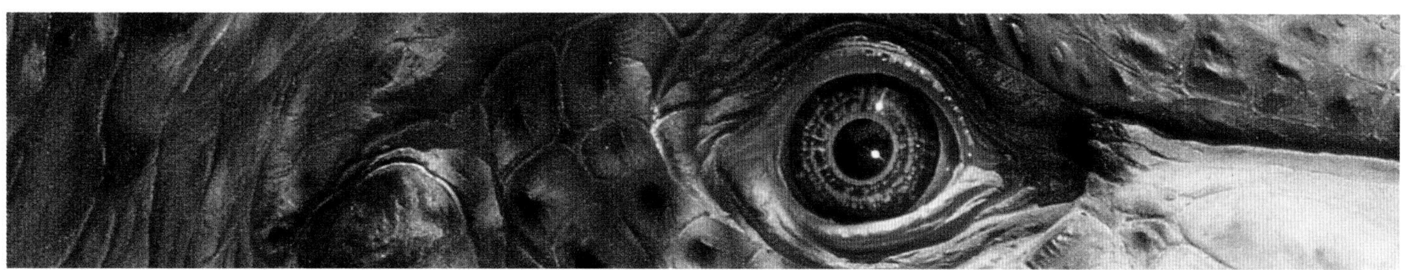

First American Edition, 2004

Published in the United States by DK Publishing, Inc.
375 Hudson Street, New York, New York 10014

04 05 06 07 08 09 10 9 8 7 6 5 4 3 2 1

Published in Great Britain by Dorling Kindersley Limited.

A Cataloging-in-Publication record for this book is available from the Library of Congress.

ISBN 0 7566 0761 2

Color reproduction by Colourscan, Singapore
Printed in China by Toppan Printing Co. (Shenzen) Ltd.

Discover more at
www.dk.com

e.guides

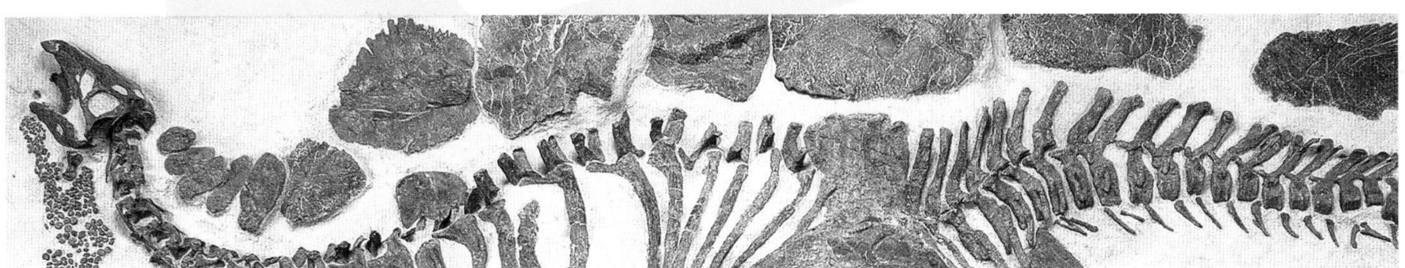

Dinosaur

Written by Dougal Dixon
and John Malam

Google™

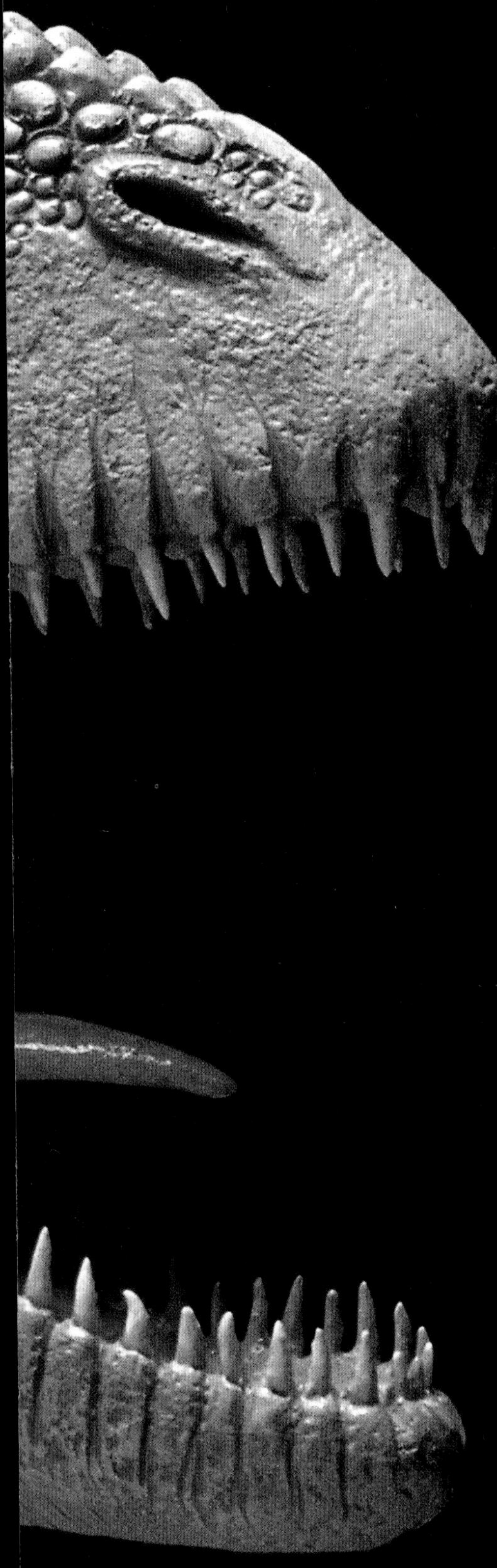

CONTENTS

How to use the Web site

e.guides Dinosaur has its own Web site, created by DK and Google™. When you look up a subject in the book, the article gives you key facts and displays a keyword that links you to extra information online. Just follow these easy steps.

http://www.dinosaur.dke-guides.com

1 Enter this Web site address...

2 Find the keyword in the book...

You can only use the keywords from the book to search on our Web site for the specially selected DK/Google links.

3 Enter the keyword...

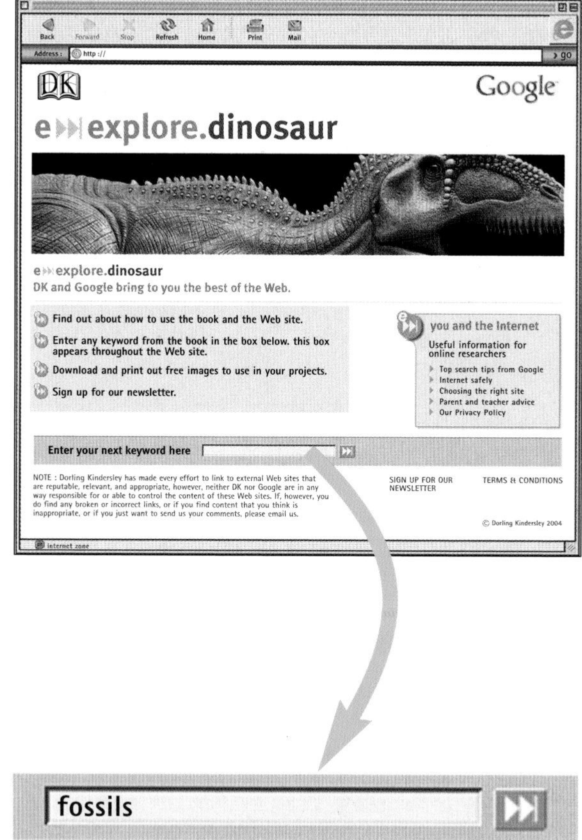

Be safe while you are online:

- Always get permission from an adult before connecting to the Internet.
- Never give out personal information about yourself.
- Never arrange to meet someone you have talked to online.
- If a site asks you to log in with your name or email address, ask permission from an adult first.
- Do not reply to emails from strangers—tell an adult.

Parents: Dorling Kindersley actively and regularly reviews and updates the links. However, content may change. Dorling Kindersley is not responsible for any site but its own. We recommend that children are supervised while online, that they do not use Chat Rooms, and that filtering software is used to block unsuitable material.

Click on your chosen link...

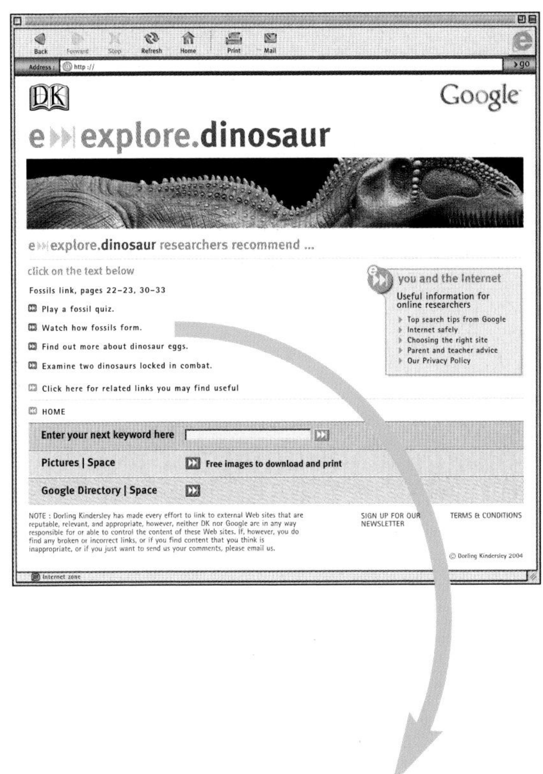

Watch how fossils form.

Links include animations, videos, sound buttons, virtual tours, interactive quizzes, databases, timelines, and real-time reports.

Download fantastic pictures...

Pictures | Dinosaurs

Triceratops skeleton

The pictures are free of charge, but can be used for personal, non-commercial use only.

Go back to the book for your next subject...

WHAT IS A DINOSAUR?

In the middle of the 1800s, the first fossil skeletons of some extraordinary creatures were unearthed. These skeletons are of the dinosaurs—prehistoric reptiles that have captured the imaginations of people ever since. Dinosaurs, which means "terrible lizards," ruled the world for more than 160 million years before they died out 65 million years ago. Everything we know about them has come from the examination of skeletons, or bits of skeletons, found by paleontologists, the dinosaur-hunters of the modern world, and by other scientists.

▼ GIGANOTOSAURUS
To find out more about the remains that are found, scientists reconstruct dinosaurs, sometimes from only a few fragments of fossilized bone or a skull. The fossils of this *Giganotosaurus* have told scientists a great deal about how this creature lived. The way that the hips and legs are put together shows that it was able to run after prey. The clawed feet and rows of teeth are evidence that once *Giganotosaurus* had caught the prey, the carnivore was equipped to tear it apart.

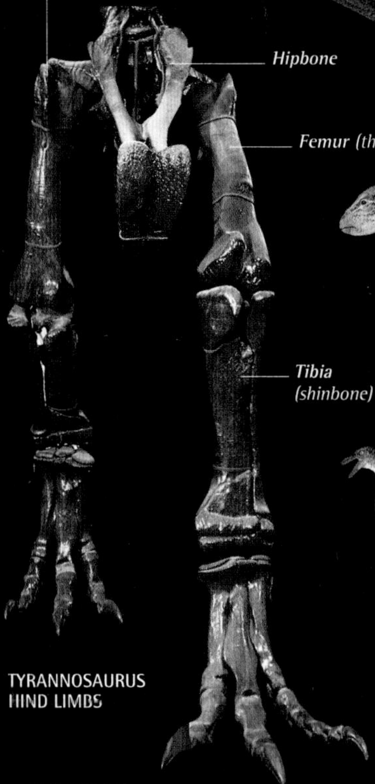

Hips and legs allowed dinosaur to move feet easily forward and backward

Head of femur fits into hip socket

Hipbone

Femur (thighbone)

Tibia (shinbone)

TYRANNOSAURUS HIND LIMBS

HYPSILOPHODON ORNITHISCHIAN ("BIRD-HIPPED")

GALLIMIMUS SAURISCHIAN ("LIZARD-HIPPED")

▲ LEG BONES
Dinosaurs were archosaurs—a group of reptiles that contained crocodiles, alligators, and flying pterosaurs. However, the legs of most reptiles stick out at the side and the body is slung beneath. Those of a dinosaur are more like those of a mammal. They are vertical, supporting the weight of the body above them. There is a ball-shaped plug at the head of the thighbone (femur) that protrudes sideways. This fits into a socket in the side of the hipbones. A shelf of bone above the socket prevents the leg from popping out.

▲ HIPBONES
Dinosaurs are divided into two separate groups based on the structure of their hipbones. The groups are called the "saurischians" and the "ornithischians." The saurischians had hipbones like a modern lizard—the three hipbones radiating away from the socket that held the leg, and the pubisbone pointing down and forward. The ornithischians had hipbones like a modern bird—the pubis sweeping back along the ischium, while a pair of extensions to the pubis reached forward.

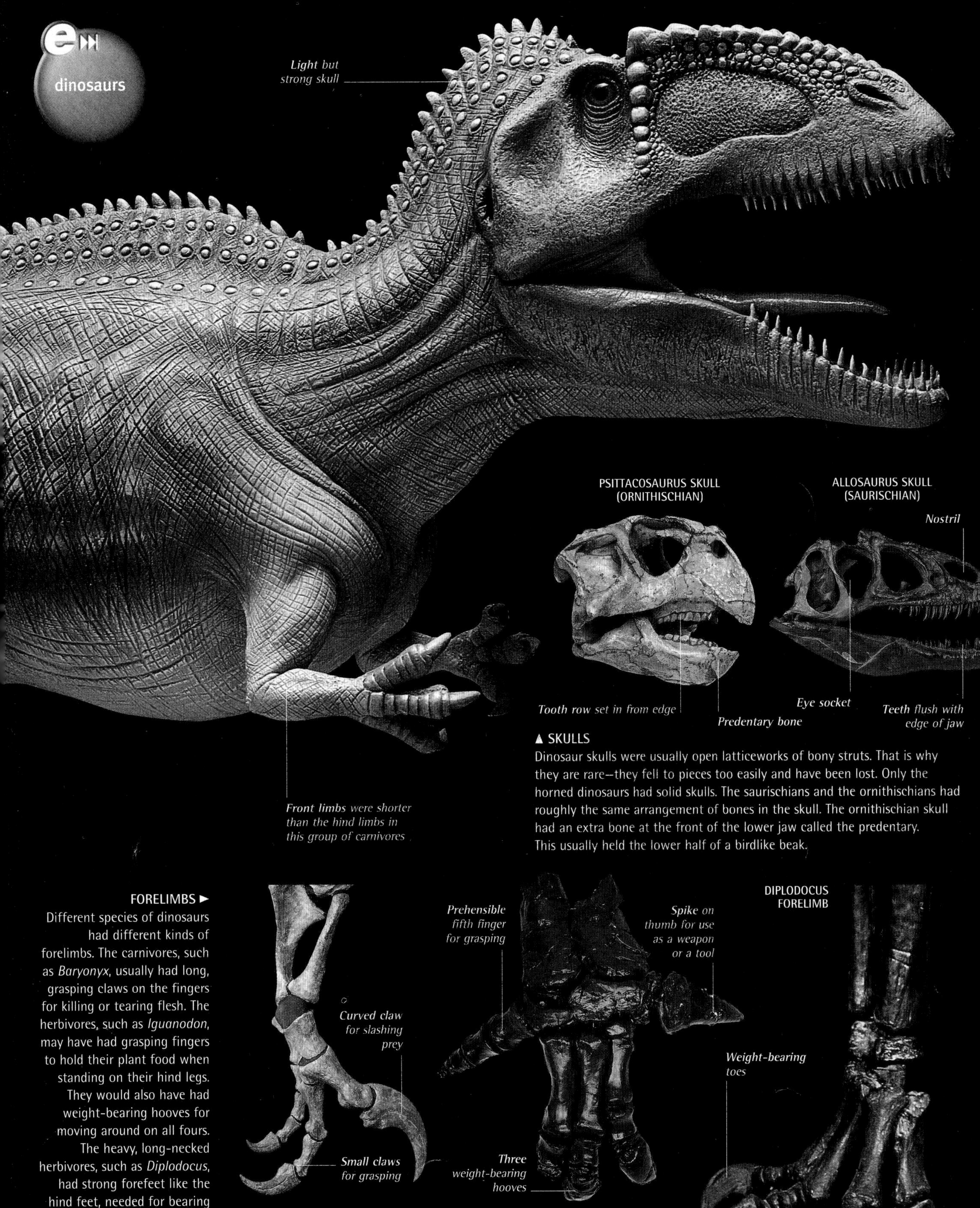

▲ SKULLS

Dinosaur skulls were usually open latticeworks of bony struts. That is why they are rare—they fell to pieces too easily and have been lost. Only the horned dinosaurs had solid skulls. The saurischians and the ornithischians had roughly the same arrangement of bones in the skull. The ornithischian skull had an extra bone at the front of the lower jaw called the predentary. This usually held the lower half of a birdlike beak.

FORELIMBS ►

Different species of dinosaurs had different kinds of forelimbs. The carnivores, such as *Baryonyx*, usually had long, grasping claws on the fingers for killing or tearing flesh. The herbivores, such as *Iguanodon*, may have had grasping fingers to hold their plant food when standing on their hind legs. They would also have had weight-bearing hooves for moving around on all fours. The heavy, long-necked herbivores, such as *Diplodocus*, had strong forefeet like the hind feet, needed for bearing the huge body weight.

BARYONYX CLAW

IGUANODON HAND

THE BIRD CONNECTION

There are dinosaurs flying in our skies today—despite more than a century of arguments, most scientists now believe that small meat-eating dinosaurs evolved into birds. The development of feathers turned dinosaurs that could run or climb into birds that could fly. The earliest true bird is *Archaeopteryx*, which lived during the late Jurassic in the area known today as southern Germany. A small hunting dinosaur called *Compsognathus* also lived in that area at that time. *Archaeopteryx* looked like a cross between a reptile and a bird, and it had strong legs and feathers that it would have used to fly. *Compsognathus* was birdlike, with long back legs and hollow bones.

SIMILARITIES BETWEEN COMPSOGNATHUS AND ARCHAEOPTERYX

1. Bony tail core
2. Ankle joint
3. Long legs
4. Short body
5. Enlarged breastbone
6. Teeth in long, slim jaws
7. Slim, flexible neck
8. Long, clawed fingers

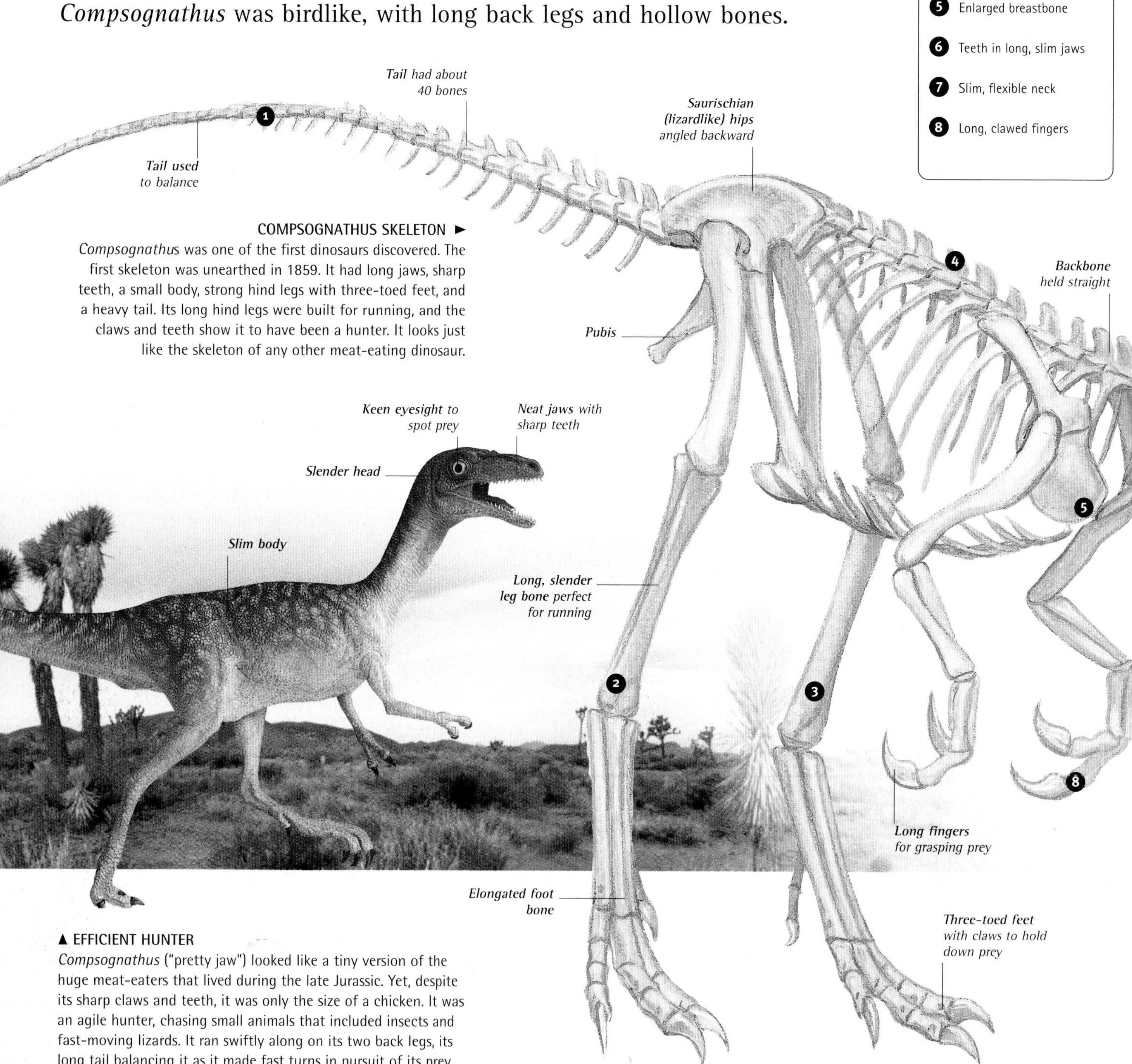

COMPSOGNATHUS SKELETON ►
Compsognathus was one of the first dinosaurs discovered. The first skeleton was unearthed in 1859. It had long jaws, sharp teeth, a small body, strong hind legs with three-toed feet, and a heavy tail. Its long hind legs were built for running, and the claws and teeth show it to have been a hunter. It looks just like the skeleton of any other meat-eating dinosaur.

▲ EFFICIENT HUNTER
Compsognathus ("pretty jaw") looked like a tiny version of the huge meat-eaters that lived during the late Jurassic. Yet, despite its sharp claws and teeth, it was only the size of a chicken. It was an agile hunter, chasing small animals that included insects and fast-moving lizards. It ran swiftly along on its two back legs, its long tail balancing it as it made fast turns in pursuit of its prey.

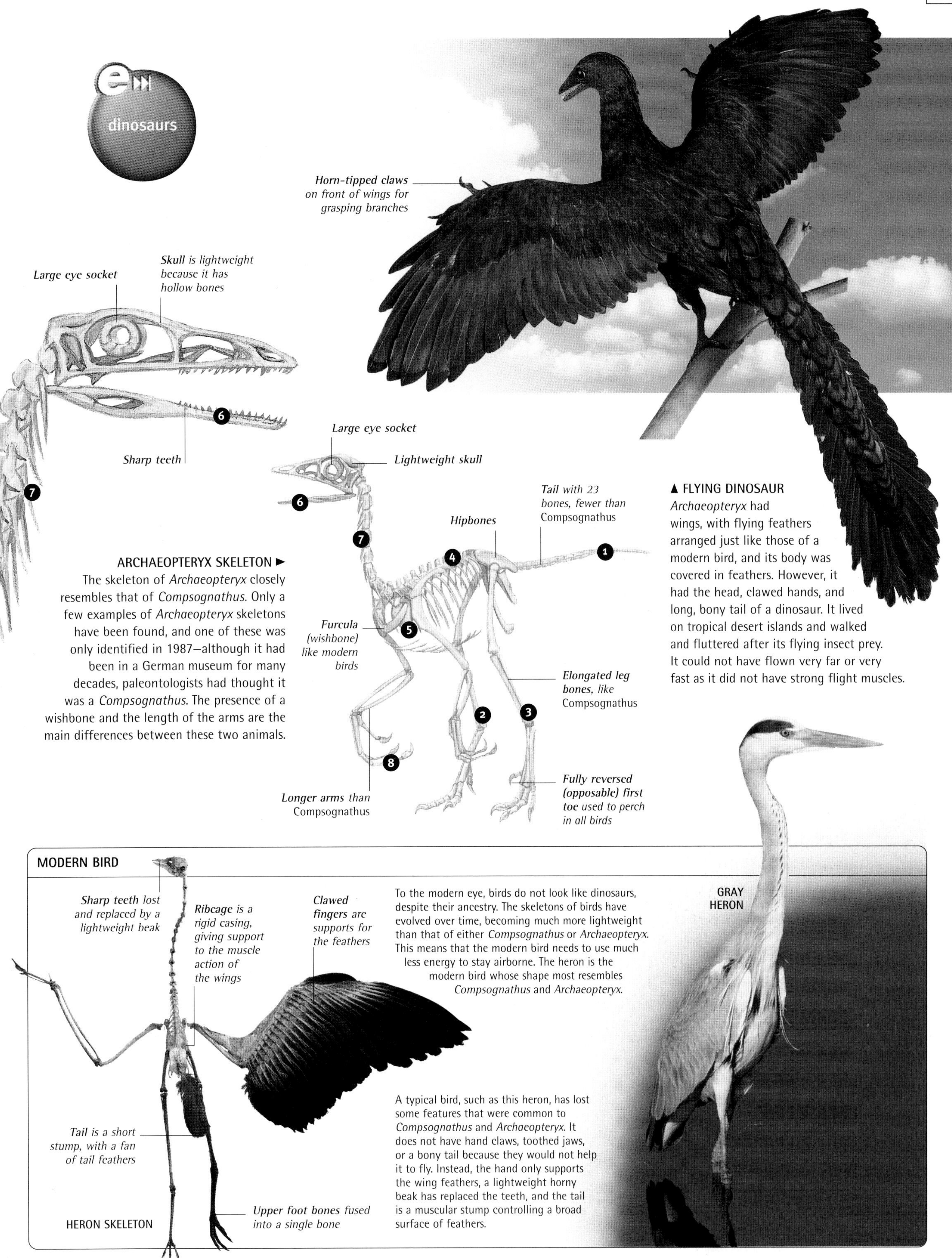

ARCHAEOPTERYX SKELETON ►
The skeleton of *Archaeopteryx* closely resembles that of *Compsognathus*. Only a few examples of *Archaeopteryx* skeletons have been found, and one of these was only identified in 1987—although it had been in a German museum for many decades, paleontologists had thought it was a *Compsognathus*. The presence of a wishbone and the length of the arms are the main differences between these two animals.

▲ FLYING DINOSAUR
Archaeopteryx had wings, with flying feathers arranged just like those of a modern bird, and its body was covered in feathers. However, it had the head, clawed hands, and long, bony tail of a dinosaur. It lived on tropical desert islands and walked and fluttered after its flying insect prey. It could not have flown very far or very fast as it did not have strong flight muscles.

MODERN BIRD

To the modern eye, birds do not look like dinosaurs, despite their ancestry. The skeletons of birds have evolved over time, becoming much more lightweight than that of either *Compsognathus* or *Archaeopteryx*. This means that the modern bird needs to use much less energy to stay airborne. The heron is the modern bird whose shape most resembles *Compsognathus* and *Archaeopteryx*.

A typical bird, such as this heron, has lost some features that were common to *Compsognathus* and *Archaeopteryx*. It does not have hand claws, toothed jaws, or a bony tail because they would not help it to fly. Instead, the hand only supports the wing feathers, a lightweight horny beak has replaced the teeth, and the tail is a muscular stump controlling a broad surface of feathers.

ERA OF THE DINOSAURS

Dinosaurs roamed the planet for about 165 million years, during a time in the Earth's history called the Mesozoic Era. It is difficult for us to imagine how long this was, until we compare it with ourselves: humans have lived on Earth for less than two million years. During the Mesozoic Era, the Earth's landmasses changed dramatically, new seas were formed, and plants and animals evolved.

PRECAMBRIAN			4,600–545 million years ago (mya)
PALAEOZOIC ERA ("ANCIENT LIFE")	CAMBRIAN PERIOD		545–490 mya
	ORDOVICIAN PERIOD		490–445 mya
	SILURIAN PERIOD		445–415 mya
	DEVONIAN PERIOD		415–355 mya
	CARBONIFEROUS PERIOD		355–290 mya
	PERMIAN PERIOD		290–250 mya
MESOZOIC ERA ("MIDDLE LIFE")	TRIASSIC PERIOD	DINOSAURS	250–200 mya
	JURASSIC PERIOD		200–145 mya
	CRETACEOUS PERIOD		145–65 mya
CENOZOIC ERA ("RECENT LIFE")	TERTIARY PERIOD		65–1.64 mya
	QUATERNARY PERIOD		1.64 mya–present day

▲ GEOLOGICAL TIMESCALE
Geologists divide Earth's long history into a series of time zones, from the origin of the planet, about 4.6 billion years ago, right up to the present day. The major divisions are called eras. These are subdivided into smaller time zones called periods. Within each period are smaller divisions called Ages (not shown in this diagram). Dinosaurs lived in the Mesozoic Era, which is divided into the Triassic, Jurassic, and Cretaceous Periods. Humans live in the Quaternary Period of the Cenozoic Era.

TRIASSIC PERIOD: 250–200 MILLION YEARS AGO

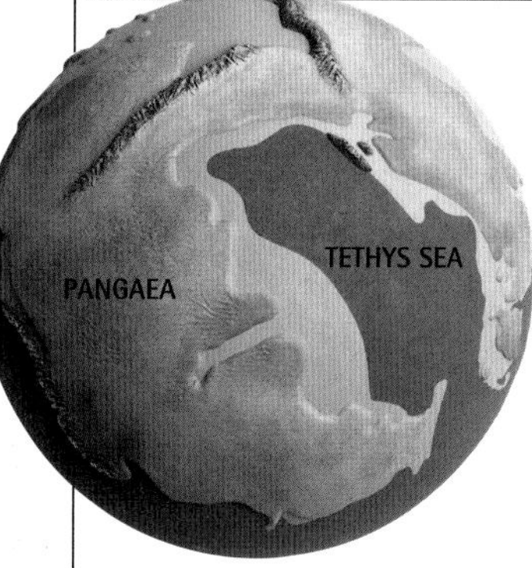

TRIASSIC PLANET
In the Triassic Period, all land was joined together as one great landmass. Scientists call this super-continent Pangaea, which means "All Earth."

FOSSILIZED *RHYNCHOSAURUS*

TRIASSIC ANIMALS
The first dinosaurs lived in the early Triassic. Other reptiles also lived in this period, such as plant-eating rhynchosaurs. Fish and turtles swam in the sea, pterosaurs flapped their leathery wings in the sky, and the first mammals appeared.

JURASSIC PERIOD: 200–145 MILLION YEARS AGO

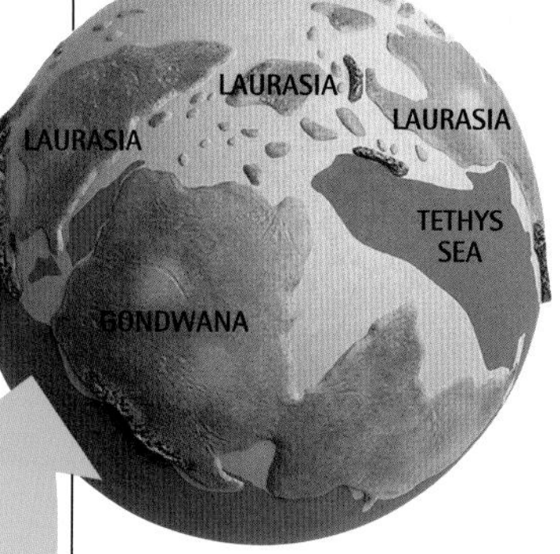

JURASSIC PLANET
Pangaea split into northern and southern landmasses in the Jurassic Period, divided by the ocean. In time, the two new continents moved apart.

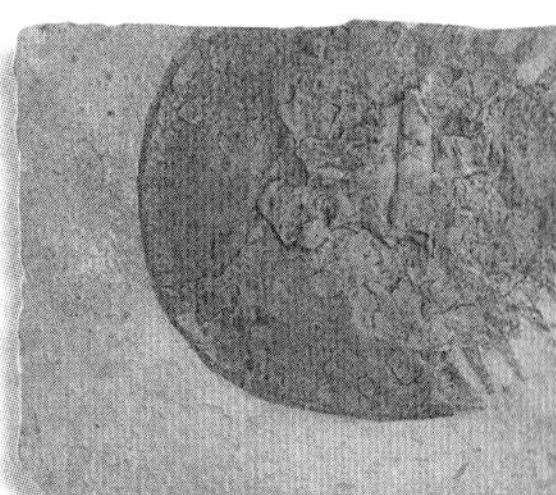

FOSSILIZED HORSESHOE CRAB

JURASSIC ANIMALS
Dinosaurs colonized the land, from huge plant-eating species to smaller meat-eating ones. Pterosaurs ruled the sky, the first birds appeared, and icthyosaurs and horseshoe crabs swam in the seas.

CRETACEOUS PERIOD: 145–65 MILLION YEARS AGO

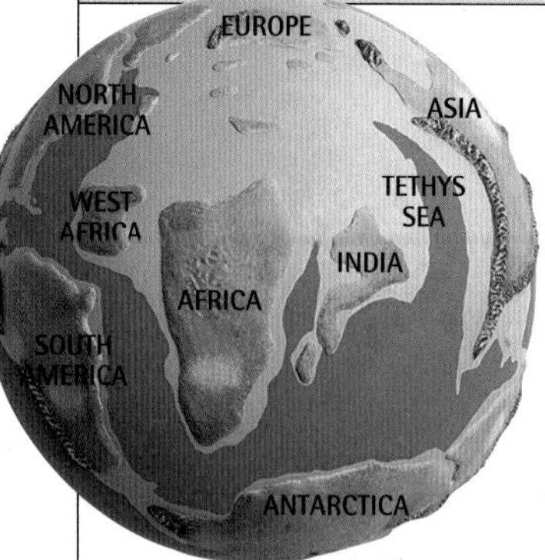

CRETACEOUS PLANET
During the Cretaceous Period, Laurasia and Gondwana broke up into several smaller parts, beginning the formation of the continents we have today.

FOSSILIZED DRAGONFLY

FERN

FOSSILIZED GINKGO

Fossilized leaf is similar to the modern version

TRIASSIC PLANTS

Ferns, ginkgoes, and palmlike cycadeoids and cycads grew near streams. Scattered forests of conifers grew on drier lands. There was no grass, and there were no flowering plants. Inland areas were covered in hot, barren deserts with little or no plant life.

JURASSIC PLANTS

Coniferous forests covered vast areas of land. Ginkgoes, monkey puzzle trees, cycads, tall tree ferns, and giant horsetails were common. Ferns and mosses grew on the ground, but there were still no flowering plants or grasses.

Perfect impression of a conifer leaf was preserved in this fossil

HORSETAIL

FOSSILIZED CONIFER SPRIG

MONKEY PUZZLE

CRETACEOUS ANIMALS

Fierce predatory dinosaurs hunted and scavenged for meat. Plant-eating dinosaurs grew body armor for protection. Crocodiles, turtles, and lizards flourished, and the first snakes appeared. Insects, birds, and pterosaurs flew in the sky, and small mammals ran on the ground.

Cones produced the earliest seeds

PINE WITH CONES

BETULITES LEAF IN IRONSTONE NODULE

CRETACEOUS PLANTS

Flowering plants appeared, which were the ancestors of today's herbs, flowers, and broad-leaved trees. They became the main type of plant-life. Oak, maple, walnut, magnolia, and beech trees grew alongside the still abundant conifers, cycads, and tree ferns. There was still no grass.

MAGNOLIA FLOWER

PASSION FLOWER

UP IN THE AIR

Soaring high above the land-living dinosaurs were the pterosaurs, which means "winged reptiles." The pterosaurs were relatives of dinosaurs, but they were not dinosaurs themselves. All had slim, hollow bones and wings made of skin that stretched between long fingerbones and the legs. Pterosaurs first appeared at the same time as the dinosaurs and lived alongside them until they too died out at the end of the Cretaceous Period. They were the supreme rulers of Earth's prehistoric skies, flapping their wings over land and sea.

Fur may have grown on their bodies

Beak was packed with many small teeth

PTERODACTYLUS ►

Pterodactylus was an agile flyer that probably fed on insects. Unlike other pterosaurs that had long tails, the tail of *Pterodactylus* was little more than a short, stubby point. Just 12 in (30 cm) long, it had a lightly built skeleton and thin, hollow bones. Perhaps these weight-saving features were designed to give *Pterodactylus* greater flight control, helping it to fly fast and giving it the ability to swoop and turn with ease.

Legs were short and probably had weak muscles

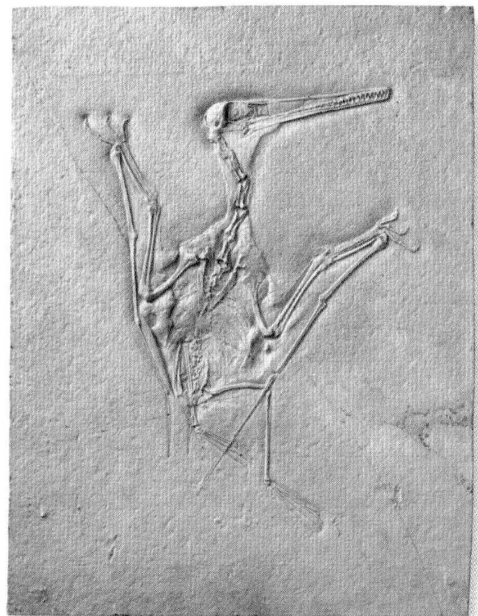

▲ FOSSILIZED PTERODACTYLUS FEATURES

This fossil skeleton embedded in limestone shows *Pterodactylus*'s delicate skull and fine bones. The pterosaur's four fingers can be seen clearly. Three fingers on each of its hands were short and hooklike, and it is possible they were used for defense. The fourth finger can be seen here running diagonally from the hand on the right to the leg on the right. *Pterodactylus*'s wings were attached to each of these extremely long fingers and its legs.

PTERODACTYLUS PROFILE

Pterodactylus belonged to the Pterodactyloid branch of the pterosaur family tree. These pterosaurs all had short tails.

Lived: 140 million years ago (Cretaceous)

Habitat: rivers, seas, lakes

Wingspan: up to 6 ft (1.8 m)

Length: up to 12 in (30 cm)

Diet: fish, insects

Fibers inside the skin wings made them stiff

FLAMBOYANT HEADS

Several species of pterosaur sported crests on their heads and beaks. They were made from hard bone or soft tissue. It is not yet known if the crests were grown by males or females, or by both sexes. Their function is also uncertain. As the shape, size, and possibly the color of crests differed between species, they may have helped pterosaurs recognize their own kind. They may also have been used in courtship displays or as stablilizers during flight.

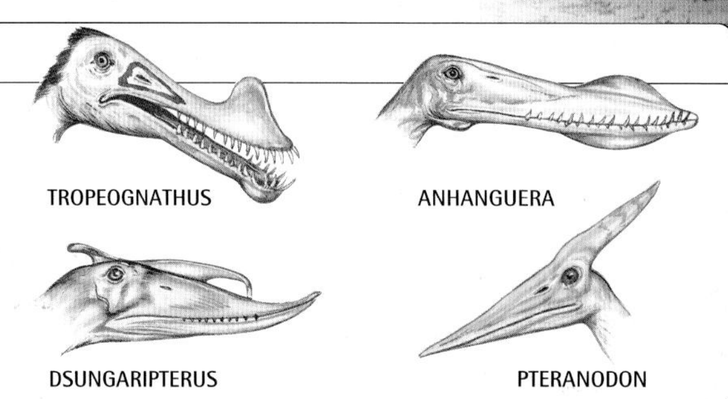

RHAMPHORHYNCHUS PROFILE
Rhamphorhynchus belonged to the Rhamphorhynchoid branch of the pterosaur family tree. These pterosaurs all had long tails.
Lived: 150 million years ago (Jurassic)
Habitat: rivers, seas, lakes
Wingspan: up to 6½ ft (2 m)
Length: up to 3⅓ ft (1 m)
Diet: fish, insects

▲ FOSSILIZED RHAMPHORHYNCHUS FEATURES

Found in Germany, this fossilized *Rhamphorynchus* is preserved in limestone. The preservation is so good that the ghostly outline of its wing membrane can be seen, as can the diamond-shaped skin membrane that grew along its tail. The fossil also reveals the presence of a pelicanlike throat pouch, which was possibly used to strain water out before swallowing its prey whole.

◄ RHAMPHORHYNCHUS

With its long tail trailing behind it as it flew, *Rhamphorynchus* was a formidable pterosaur. A fish-eating animal, it probably caught its prey by swooping low over the water and snapping it up with its beak. Its long front teeth pointed forward in its beak, in an arrangement called a "fish grab." They were designed to spear and hold on to fish. After catching a fish, *Rhamphorynchus* probably returned to the land where it ate its meal—head first, as many seabirds do with their prey today.

PELICAN—THE MODERN FISH GRABBER

Much can be learned about pterosaurs' lifestyles by studying today's animals that appear to share similar characteristics with them. Although pterosaurs were not birds, their fish-eating habit can be compared with that of modern pelicans. Many pterosaurs had long, narrow heads and throat pouches like modern pelicans. Perhaps, like pelicans, these pterosaurs were plunge-divers, grabbing fish by thrusting their beaks below the water's surface.

BELOW THE WAVES

While dinosaurs ruled the land, the ocean was the domain of many different families of marine reptiles, such as the nothosaurs, ichthyosaurs, pliosaurs, mosasaurs, and elasmosaurs. They were carnivores, preying on other sea creatures as well as each other. Although these reptiles spent their lives in water, they could not stay below the waves indefinitely. They breathed air, and had to swim to the surface to refill their lungs, before disappearing back into their underwater world.

marine reptiles

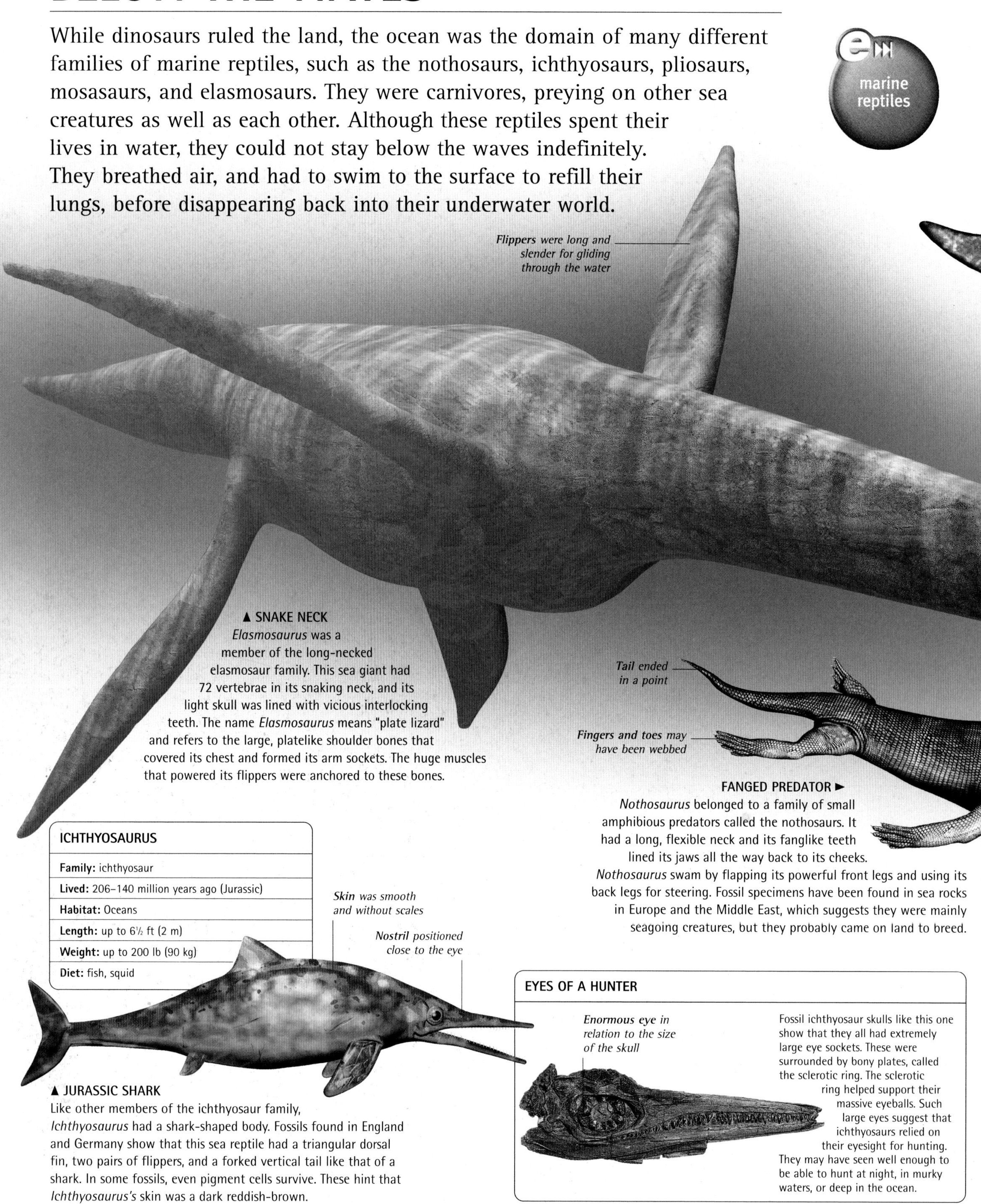

▲ SNAKE NECK
Elasmosaurus was a member of the long-necked elasmosaur family. This sea giant had 72 vertebrae in its snaking neck, and its light skull was lined with vicious interlocking teeth. The name *Elasmosaurus* means "plate lizard" and refers to the large, platelike shoulder bones that covered its chest and formed its arm sockets. The huge muscles that powered its flippers were anchored to these bones.

FANGED PREDATOR ►
Nothosaurus belonged to a family of small amphibious predators called the nothosaurs. It had a long, flexible neck and its fanglike teeth lined its jaws all the way back to its cheeks. *Nothosaurus* swam by flapping its powerful front legs and using its back legs for steering. Fossil specimens have been found in sea rocks in Europe and the Middle East, which suggests they were mainly seagoing creatures, but they probably came on land to breed.

ICHTHYOSAURUS
Family: ichthyosaur
Lived: 206–140 million years ago (Jurassic)
Habitat: Oceans
Length: up to 6½ ft (2 m)
Weight: up to 200 lb (90 kg)
Diet: fish, squid

▲ JURASSIC SHARK
Like other members of the ichthyosaur family, *Ichthyosaurus* had a shark-shaped body. Fossils found in England and Germany show that this sea reptile had a triangular dorsal fin, two pairs of flippers, and a forked vertical tail like that of a shark. In some fossils, even pigment cells survive. These hint that *Ichthyosaurus's* skin was a dark reddish-brown.

EYES OF A HUNTER

Fossil ichthyosaur skulls like this one show that they all had extremely large eye sockets. These were surrounded by bony plates, called the sclerotic ring. The sclerotic ring helped support their massive eyeballs. Such large eyes suggest that ichthyosaurs relied on their eyesight for hunting. They may have seen well enough to be able to hunt at night, in murky waters, or deep in the ocean.

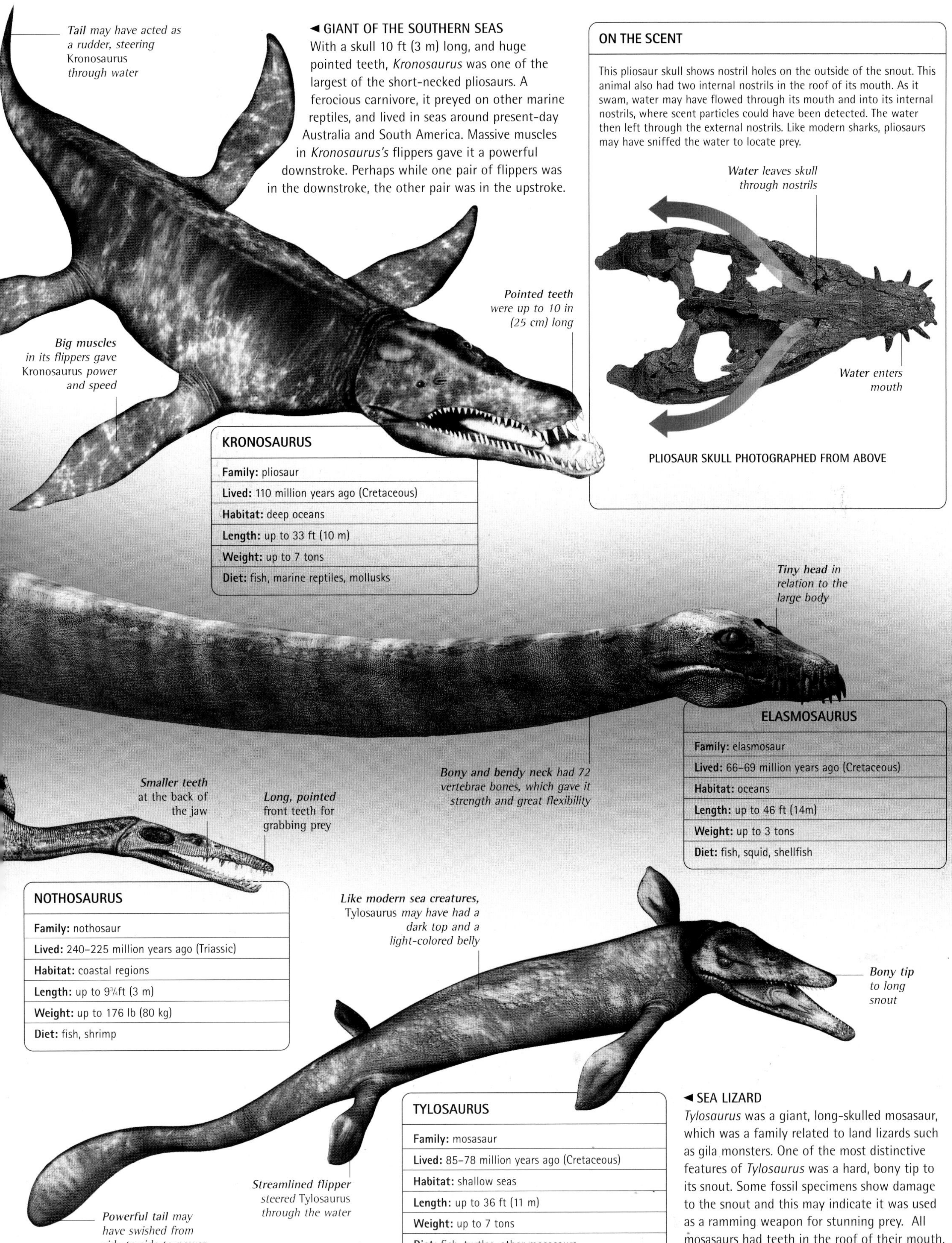

◄ GIANT OF THE SOUTHERN SEAS

With a skull 10 ft (3 m) long, and huge pointed teeth, *Kronosaurus* was one of the largest of the short-necked pliosaurs. A ferocious carnivore, it preyed on other marine reptiles, and lived in seas around present-day Australia and South America. Massive muscles in *Kronosaurus's* flippers gave it a powerful downstroke. Perhaps while one pair of flippers was in the downstroke, the other pair was in the upstroke.

ON THE SCENT

This pliosaur skull shows nostril holes on the outside of the snout. This animal also had two internal nostrils in the roof of its mouth. As it swam, water may have flowed through its mouth and into its internal nostrils, where scent particles could have been detected. The water then left through the external nostrils. Like modern sharks, pliosaurs may have sniffed the water to locate prey.

PLIOSAUR SKULL PHOTOGRAPHED FROM ABOVE

KRONOSAURUS
Family: pliosaur
Lived: 110 million years ago (Cretaceous)
Habitat: deep oceans
Length: up to 33 ft (10 m)
Weight: up to 7 tons
Diet: fish, marine reptiles, mollusks

ELASMOSAURUS
Family: elasmosaur
Lived: 66–69 million years ago (Cretaceous)
Habitat: oceans
Length: up to 46 ft (14m)
Weight: up to 3 tons
Diet: fish, squid, shellfish

NOTHOSAURUS
Family: nothosaur
Lived: 240–225 million years ago (Triassic)
Habitat: coastal regions
Length: up to 9¾ft (3 m)
Weight: up to 176 lb (80 kg)
Diet: fish, shrimp

TYLOSAURUS
Family: mosasaur
Lived: 85–78 million years ago (Cretaceous)
Habitat: shallow seas
Length: up to 36 ft (11 m)
Weight: up to 7 tons
Diet: fish, turtles, other mosasaurs

◄ SEA LIZARD

Tylosaurus was a giant, long-skulled mosasaur, which was a family related to land lizards such as gila monsters. One of the most distinctive features of *Tylosaurus* was a hard, bony tip to its snout. Some fossil specimens show damage to the snout and this may indicate it was used as a ramming weapon for stunning prey. All mosasaurs had teeth in the roof of their mouth, as well as those lining their jaws.

DINOSAUR HABITATS

Not all the dinosaurs lived at the same time. Nor did they all live in the same part of the world. During the 180 million years that dinosaurs walked the Earth, the breakup of the supercontinent Pangaea and the resulting major changes of climate produced many different habitats. Continental drift changed the world's climate because it altered the flow of ocean currents and controlled how much of the world was covered in ice. Different dinosaurs evolved to live in different environments. Those that had existed on the dry Triassic supercontinent were quite different from those that lived on the scattered landmasses of the Cretaceous.

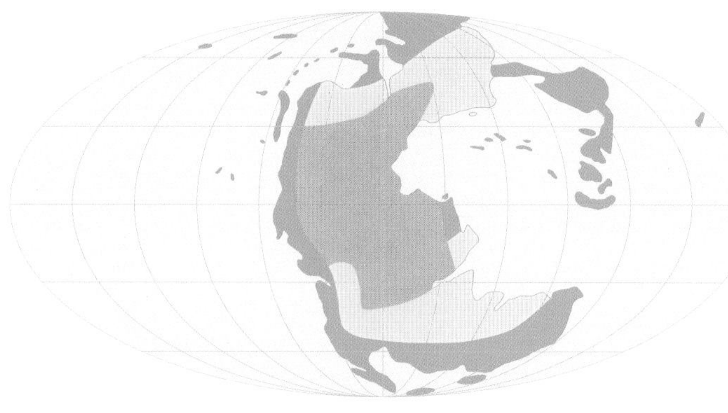

MAP KEY
- Desert
- Semidesert
- Temperate forest

▲ TRIASSIC HABITATS (250–200 MILLION YEARS AGO)
During the Triassic, all the landmasses of the world were joined together, forming the single supercontinent, Pangaea. Because the continent was so huge, most inland areas were a long way from the ocean and there were extensive deserts. Only around the edges of the continent was there enough moisture for any vegetation. This was the time of the first dinosaurs, and they lived everywhere.

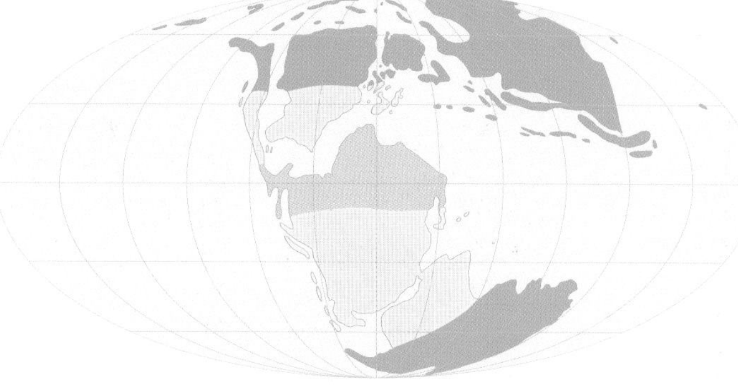

MAP KEY
- Desert and semidesert
- Temperate forest
- Tropical forest

▲ JURASSIC HABITATS (200–145 MYA)
By the Jurassic, Pangaea had begun to break up. Rift valleys produced long arms of ocean that reached into the depths of the continent, very much like today's Red Sea in Egypt. Shallow seas spread across the lowlands and reached into the former deserts, giving rise to damper climates in most areas. There was much more vegetation than during the Triassic, although the plants were the same types.

▲ RIVERSIDES
Plant and animal life was most common along the banks of rivers near the sea. The riverbanks were covered with ferns and the shallow water supported reed beds of horsetails. Early carnivorous dinosaurs such as *Herrerasaurus* hunted in these thickets.

▲ SCRUBLAND
The semidesert supported a scrubby growth of plants that could tolerate a lack of water. The landscape must have looked a bit like areas of southern Africa do today. The drought-resistant plants were browsed by early herbivores, such as the prosauropod *Plateosaurus*.

▲ RIPARIAN FOREST
As in the Triassic, the areas most covered by vegetation were by the riversides. Seasonal rainfall produced forests of tree ferns and ginkgoes, with an undergrowth of ferns and horsetails. These provided good feeding for herbivores such as *Stegosaurus*.

▲ DENSE CONIFEROUS FOREST
The forests were made up of primitive conifers such as monkey puzzles, cypresses, and podocarps (rare today), as well as relatives of the cycads. The tough needles on these evolved to guard against the intensive high browsing of sauropods such as *Mamenchisaurus*.

CORYTHOSAURUS

▲ MIXED FOREST
By the Cretaceous, flowering plants had begun to evolve. Dinosaurs with efficient chewing mechanisms, such as *Corythosaurus*, could both browse from trees and graze close to the ground. This led to the evolution of plants with seeds that could survive this treatment.

▲ CRETACEOUS HABITATS (145–65 MYA)
By the Cretaceous, the continents had broken apart, many of them beginning to look like the continents of today. The presence of so many different land areas meant that the climates were much more varied. The animal life was different on each continent as each group of animals evolved separately. So, for example, the dinosaurs of North America were different from those of South America.

SPINOSAURUS

▲ SWAMPLAND
Swamps and river deltas are ideal places for the preservation of fossils. Steamy swamps existed along the edges of the Cretaceous continents. Wet-loving trees such as swamp cypresses dominated these areas. They provided the perfect habitat for fish-eating dinosaurs such as *Spinosaurus*.

EDMONTONIA

▲ MOUNTAINS
Little is known about the vegetation of mountain habitats because most fossils come from lowland regions. But bones of armored dinosaurs, such as *Edmontonia*, that look as though they have been washed down from mountain areas, have been found.

GALLIMIMUS

▲ DESERT PLAINS
The deserts supported some specialized animals. Although there was little to eat, a large number of different species of dinosaur lived in Cretaceous desert sandstones. The open vistas would have been ideal for long-legged running dinosaurs such as *Gallimimus*.

THE END OF THE DINOSAURS

About 65 million years ago, at the end of the Cretaceous Period, the Earth was affected by major changes to its environment. Animal and plant life were plunged into danger. It may only have taken one of these changes to affect life on Earth, or perhaps it was a combination of several. Whichever is the case, one thing is certain: dinosaurs became extinct at this time. Many theories exist to explain how dinosaurs died out.

DEATH FROM SPACE? ►
Earth is continually bombarded by debris from space, from specks of dust to lumps of rock. Most burn up as they pass through Earth's atmosphere, but some are big enough to survive. Space rocks that land on the Earth's surface are called meteorites. Did a large meteorite slam into the Earth, causing massive disruption that led to the death of the dinosaurs?

IMPACT CRATER ►
In the 1990s, a meteorite crater 110 miles (180 km) across, on the seabed off the Yucatán Peninsula, Mexico, was dated to the late Cretaceous Period. The rock that made the Chicxulub crater was 6 miles (10 km) across. The impact may have made so much dust that the Sun's light was blotted out, leading to a mass extinction.

OTHER DINOSAUR EXTINCTION THEORIES

DEATH FROM VOLCANOES?
Toward the end of the Cretaceous Period, there were many volcanic eruptions in what is now central India. They were on a vast scale, blasting huge amounts of dust into Earth's atmosphere, where high winds [illegible] them around the planet. As with the meteorite impact theory, this theory also says that atmospheric dust blotted out sunlight, sending the world into many years of cold and dark. With no sunlight, plants could not grow. With no food, animals starved and died.

DEATH FROM GIANT WAVES?
If a giant meteorite had splashed into the ocean, it would have created a tsunami—a massive wave. Had it exploded on land, it would have made a shockwave big enough to trigger earthquakes and [illegible]ersea landslides that could have [illegible] megawaves. They would have raced at great [illegible] toward land all around the globe. Within a few hours, the waves might have pounded low-lying land, destroying habitats and disrupting Earth's plant and animal life.

DEATH FROM CLIMATE CHANGE?
As well as blasting dust into the atmosphere, volcanoes also create carbon dioxide—a poisonous gas that causes global warming. This extinction theory says [illegible] rising levels of carbon dioxide caused a [illegible] known as the "greenhouse [illegible]." Carbon dioxide prevented the Sun's heat from escaping back into space, so Earth's climate became hotter. Water evaporated. Plants withered and died. As animals lost their food sources, they died, too.

THE IMPACT THEORY: EXAMINING THE EVIDENCE

There is proof for the existence of the Chicxulub crater—but linking it to the death of the dinosaurs is harder to do. The first evidence for the crater came from boreholes that were made in the 1960s by a Mexican oil company, called Petrobas, which was exploring for oil in the Gulf of Mexico. Geologists noticed magnetic changes in the rocks they drilled into, and thought they had found volcanic rock. In the 1980s, Dr. Luis Alvarez claimed that a meteorite could have triggered the death of the dinosaurs, and the hunt began to find a crater. Then, in 1990, geologists re-examining the Petrobas borehole records realized they were looking at a buried meteorite crater. Attention soon focused on the Chicxulub crater because it was formed about 65 million years ago—the same time the dinosaurs died out.

SEEING THE CHICXULUB CRATER
The Chicxulub crater lies partly beneath the Gulf of Mexico and partly on land. In this gravity map, the white line is the coast of Mexico, above which is the sea. Even though half the crater is on the land, it is almost invisible to the eye as it is buried under layers of sediment. However, its circular outline becomes clear when changes in the region's magnetic field are plotted.

Close-up *of a mineral from space found in ancient clay on Earth*

Coin *shows the thickness of the iridium-rich clay layer*

LAYER THAT MARKS THE END OF THE DINOSAURS
The dark band in this photograph is clay containing iridium, a mineral found in meteorites. The iridium is thought to have got there after being blasted into the atmosphere following a meteorite impact. The band occurs worldwide, and was formed 65 million years ago—exactly the time when the dinosaurs died. It forms a boundary between rocks that have dinosaur fossils, and rocks that do not.

TURNING TO STONE

Most fossils are more than 10,000 years old, but many date back to the beginnings of life on Earth. Fossils are formed when animal or plant remains have been buried for millions of years. During this time, the remains change as minerals from the surrounding rock replace the minerals that make up the animal or plant. These changes happen so slowly that the remains keep their original shape. Most dinosaur skeletons are found in desert sandstones, after they have been buried by sandstorms, or in beds of rivers where river sand and mud have quickly covered them up.

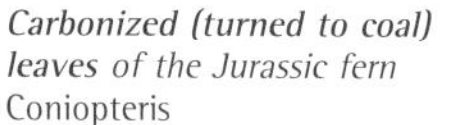

Carbonized (turned to coal) leaves of the Jurassic fern Coniopteris

1 DEATH IN A RIVER VALLEY
One day in the Late Triassic, a fleet-footed carnivore called *Coelophysis* lay down to die beside a river in Arizona. It may have been sick or old, or it may have been attacked by a larger carnivore—we will never know. But 220 million years later, its remains have been unearthed by paleontologists. An entire dinosaur skeleton can only survive as a fossil if it is buried immediately so that scavengers cannot tear it apart.

2 BURIED IN SEDIMENT
The *Coelophysis* became buried in river mud and sand. After it was covered over, the flesh and soft organs rotted away and were washed out by water seeping through the sediments. Even though this skeleton was buried quickly in a riverbed, the movements of the settling sand could have broken it up, pulling bone from bone and moving them around. The river current would have carried in more and more sediment, burying the skeleton deeper and deeper in the layers of sand and mud.

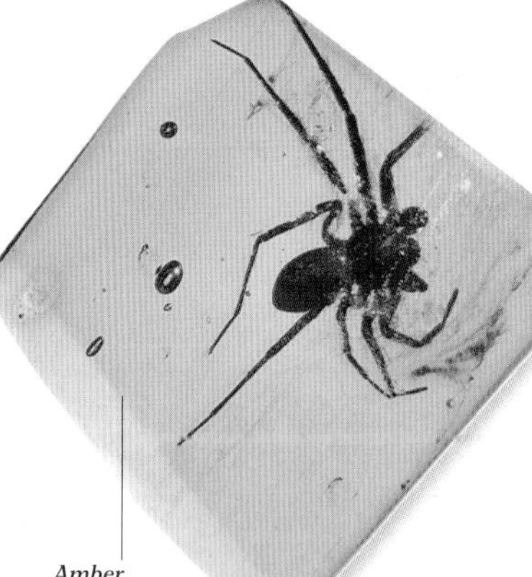

Amber

◄ PETRIFIED WOOD
A particularly detailed fossil is formed by a process called petrification. This happens when groundwater replaces bone or wood with a mineral such as silica. The cells of the bone or wood are gradually replaced, molecule by molecule, over millions of years. The resulting fossil, even though it may be made of silica, still has the cellular structure of the original, and allows scientists to examine its finest details.

▲ FOSSILIZED FERN
Some fossils contain some of the original organic material. Leaves compressed in beds of shale or mudstone often decay slowly. They are made up of the elements carbon, hydrogen, and oxygen. The hydrogen and oxygen are lost to the air, but the carbon may be left as a thin film on the rock. These films are usually in the shape of the leaf. Fossilized plant material like this, piled up into thick beds, forms coal seams.

JEWELED SPIDER ▲
Sometimes, although very rarely, a spider or some other small creature is preserved unaltered. This spider was trapped in the sticky resin seeping from the trunk of an ancient conifer. It was totally immersed, so no bacteria could reach it and it did not decay. The tree became buried and fossilized, and the resin changed into the mineral amber. The trapped creature is preserved complete.

Chamber of ammonite shell cast

FOSSIL CASTS ▲

Sometimes a fossil rots away completely as the surrounding rock turns to stone. This may leave a hole, called a mold, in the rock in the exact shape of the fossil. If this mold is later filled with minerals, it forms a lump in the shape of the original called a cast. A beautiful cast forms when the natural spaces in an organism, such as the chambers of this ammonite shell, are filled with minerals.

Mold of fossil of a 400-million-year-old starfish preserved in sandstone

PERFECT MOLDS ▲

When a fossil forms in a rock, it usually does so along the surface between two beds of the rock—the bedding plane. If the rock is split along this bedding plane, there may be part of the fossil on one piece of rock and part on the other. These two pieces of fossil are known as part and counterpart. Both are important to the paleontologist, as together, they will help reveal how the animal lived its life.

❸ MINERALIZATION

As layers of sediment piled up, the layers at the bottom became compressed. The sand grains were wedged together, and water seeping through them left behind minerals. These minerals cemented the whole mass into a solid sedimentary rock. The groundwater also affected the skeleton of the now long-dead dinosaur. It destroyed the substance of the original bones, replacing it with minerals, just like the surrounding rock.

SABER TOOTH ►

In more recent fossils, although the soft flesh and organs have disappeared, the hard parts of an animal—the shells, bones, or teeth—may have survived unchanged. Teeth are particularly hard as they are covered with enamel, and can survive even after the bones of the rest of the animal are lost. One survivor is this spectacular killing tooth of a saber-toothed cat from the Cenozoic Era.

❹ EXPOSED SKELETON

There the *Coelophysis* fossil may stay hidden forever, buried deep down where no one can see it. But the rocks of the area are lifted up into a mountain range, and wind, frost, and rain begin to wear away the solid mass. The beds of rock crumble and wash away. Eventually, what is left of the skeleton is exposed at the surface. At this point, if it is not excavated, it too will be eroded away by the weather.

EARLY DISCOVERIES

Dinosaur fossils have been emerging from the rocks for millions of years, and people have been collecting them long before they knew what creatures they belonged to. In ancient China, dinosaur bones were believed to be the bones of dead dragons. It was not until 1841 that scientists recognized that huge reptiles had existed in the remote past. An eminent scientist of the time, Sir Richard Owen, declared that this extinct group should be called Dinosauria.

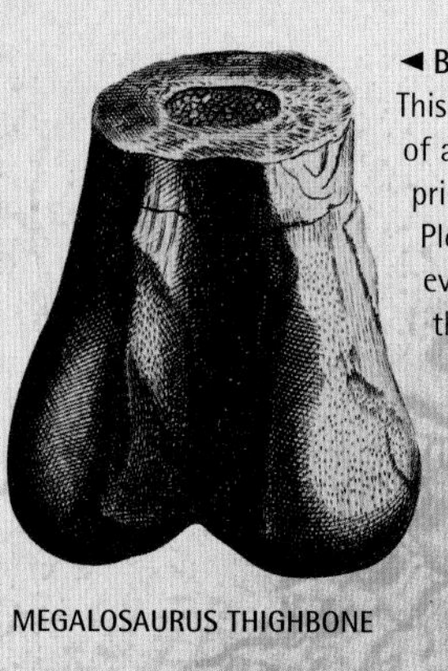

MEGALOSAURUS THIGHBONE

◄ BAFFLING BONE
This is the world's first picture of a dinosaur bone. It was printed in a book by Robert Plot in 1677. It baffled everyone at first—some people thought it belonged to a giant elephant. Scientists today know it was part of the thighbone of the giant dinosaur *Megalosaurus*.

▼ A NEW WORD IS BORN
This picture shows the anatomist and paleontologist Sir Richard Owen with an enormous extinct bird, called a boa. Owen was the first person to recognize dinosaurs as a distinct group, and he gave them their name in 1842. Combining the Greek words *deinos* ("terrible") and *sauros* ("lizard"), he created the word Dinosauria.

1822 Giant iguana

In 1822, Dr. Gideon Mantell and his wife, Mary Ann, found some large teeth and bones near a quarry in Lewes, England. Dr. Mantell concluded they belonged to a giant reptile, which he named *Iguanodon*.

GIDEON MANTELL

MARY ANN MANTELL

IGUANODON TOOTH

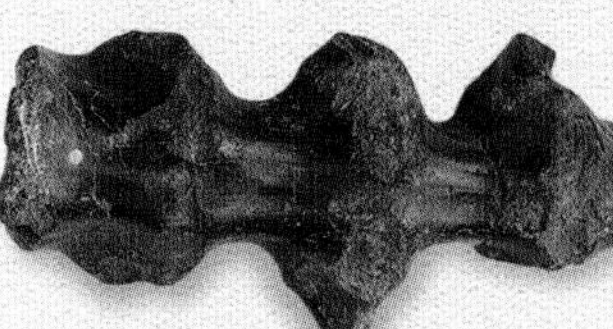

SECTION OF IGUANODON BACKBONE

MANTELL'S IGUANODON ►
Mantell's pen-and-ink sketch of *Iguanodon* shows how iguanalike he believed it to be. He based his ideas on the few bones that had been found, and on how living iguanas look. Mantell mistook *Iguanodon*'s thumb spike for a horn and placed it on its nose.

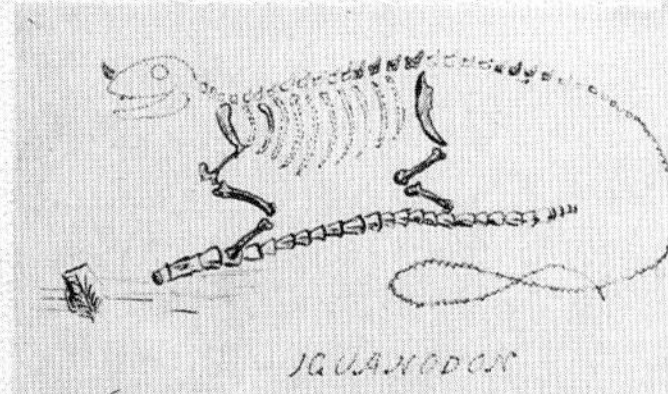

SKETCH OF IGUANODON

1824 First described

WILLIAM BUCKLAND

A specimen is recognized officially by scientists only when its description is published. The first person to describe and name a dinosaur was Dr. William Buckland. In 1824, he published a description of an animal he called *Megalosaurus*.

▲ MEGALOSAURUS JAW
Buckland's work on *Megalosaurus* was based on the study of a fossil jaw much like this one. It had been housed in a museum in Oxford, England, since 1818. The size and shape suggested that the jaw belonged to a giant reptile that was up to 40 ft (12 m) long. For this reason, Buckland gave the animal the name *Megalosaurus*, which means "big lizard."

fossil hunters

1853 First life-size models

In 1853, British sculptor Benjamin Waterhouse Hawkins teamed up with Richard Owen to build the first ever full-size dinosaur models. Using concrete, he created replicas of *Megalosaurus*, *Iguanodon*, and *Hylaeosaurus*.

▲ MONSTERS IN THE PARK
In 1854, Hawkins' dinosaurs were installed in Sydenham Park, London, where they can still be found. His *Iguanodon* was so huge that a dinner party was held inside its hollow body. Hawkins also built dinosaurs for Central Park, New York, but they were broken up and buried in 1871.

1878 First skeletons

In 1878, coal miners in Bernissart, Belgium, found a giant fossil skeleton. Over the next three years, excavators managed to recover the skeletons of 32 *Iguanodons* from the mine. They were the first complete skeletons ever found.

A BERNISSART IGUANODON

▲ MOUNTED IN BRUSSELS
The Bernissart fossils were transported to Brussels for assembly and study by Louis Dollo, a scientist from the Royal Natural History Museum in Belgium. With several skeletons for comparison, he proved that *Iguanodon* was two-legged, and the nose spike in Mantell's drawing was a thumb.

1860 First bird

In 1860, the impression of a feather was found in limestone in Bavaria, Germany. The next year, in the same area, the fossil of the earliest-known bird was found. It was named *Archaeopteryx*, which means "ancient feather."

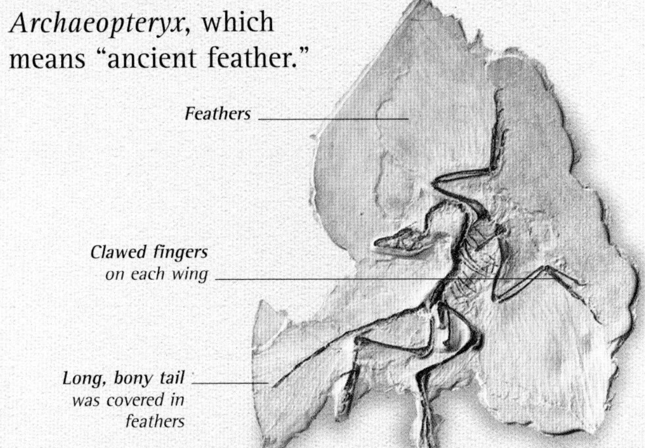

BAVARIAN BIRD ▲
The *Archaeopteryx* fossil was found in rocks that are 147 million years old. It shows this ancient bird was about the same size as a raven. It had a mixture of reptilian and birdlike features, such as teeth and clawed fingers, as well as feathers and a wishbone.

1880s The Bone Wars

In the 1880s, the fierce rivalry between fossil hunters Marsh and Cope drove them to find and identify nearly 130 new North American dinosaurs. At the time, this battle of egos was known as the Bone Wars.

CHARLES OTHNIEL MARSH

EDWARD DRINKER COPE

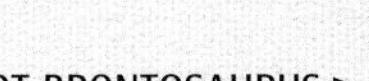

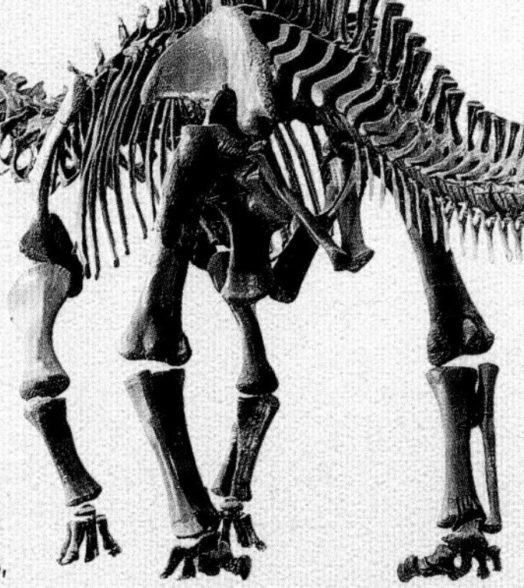

NOT BRONTOSAURUS ►
Marsh named a new dinosaur *Apatosaurus* in 1877. In 1879, he used *Brontosaurus* for yet another discovery, whose nearly complete skeleton was mounted in Yale's Peabody Museum. In 1903, it was found that the two dinosaurs were the same species, so it is no longer called *Brontosaurus*.

APATOSAURUS SKELETON

FOSSIL SITES

Dinosaurs lived all over the world, but their fossilized remains are not easy to find, or even, sometimes, to recognize. A desert surface free from vegetation, or the side of an eroding cliff, may expose fossils of dinosaurs buried in sediment millions of years ago. The remains may be incomplete, with many or most of the bones washed away by an ancient river. However, in nearly 200 years of painstaking exploration, paleontologists have located many exciting dinosaur sites.

1 UNITED STATES
In the Midwest and foothills of the Rocky Mountains are perhaps the most famous sites of all. In the Bone Wars of the 1880s, two US paleontologists, Edward Drinker Cope and Charles Othniel Marsh, competed to find bigger and better dinosaur remains for the museums they represented. The result was that over a period of only 20 years, an incredible 150 new types of dinosaur were discovered.

Excavating fossils in Utah

2 SOUTH AMERICA
Argentina and southern Brazil are the current hotbeds of paleontological activity. The work being done there is showing what dinosaur life was like in the Cretaceous on the great southern continent of Gondwana, which included today's Africa and India. The fossil remains found in South America include some of the oldest—*Eoraptor*—as well as the largest of all the dinosaurs—the titanosaurs.

DISTRIBUTION ►
A world map showing the distribution of dinosaur discoveries can give a misleading impression about the distribution of the dinosaurs themselves. Dinosaurs have not been excavated in all the places they lived in. There are many historical and political reasons for this—perhaps a team cannot reach an area because of war or because they are not welcome in a particular country. Also, the layout of the continents has changed since the Mesozoic Era—so we cannot tell exactly how many dinosaurs lived where.

fossil sites

3 ISLE OF WIGHT
The first dinosaur remains to be discovered and correctly identified were in various parts of England in the 1820s. The long tradition of discovery is continued today on the Isle of Wight, off the south coast. Early Cretaceous theropods such as *Megalosaurus* and huge sauropods such as *Diplodocus*—dinosaurs previously associated with North America—have recently been excavated there.

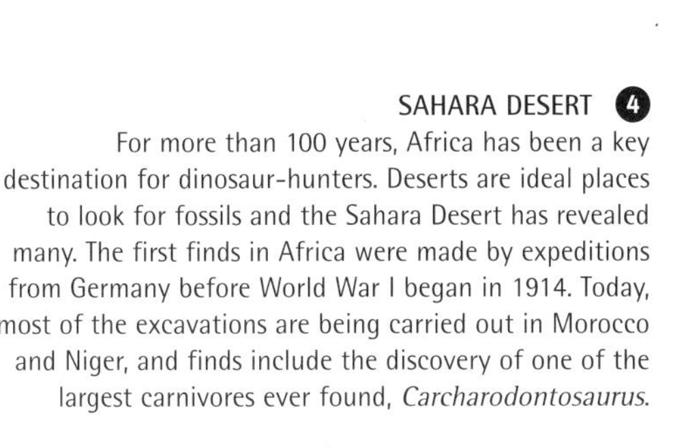

SAHARA DESERT 4

For more than 100 years, Africa has been a key destination for dinosaur-hunters. Deserts are ideal places to look for fossils and the Sahara Desert has revealed many. The first finds in Africa were made by expeditions from Germany before World War I began in 1914. Today, most of the excavations are being carried out in Morocco and Niger, and finds include the discovery of one of the largest carnivores ever found, *Carcharodontosaurus*.

Fossil of Ouranosaurus *found in Niger*

Parts of fossil skeleton *buried in desert sand*

KEY

- *Triassic sites*
- *Jurassic sites*
- *Cretaceous sites*

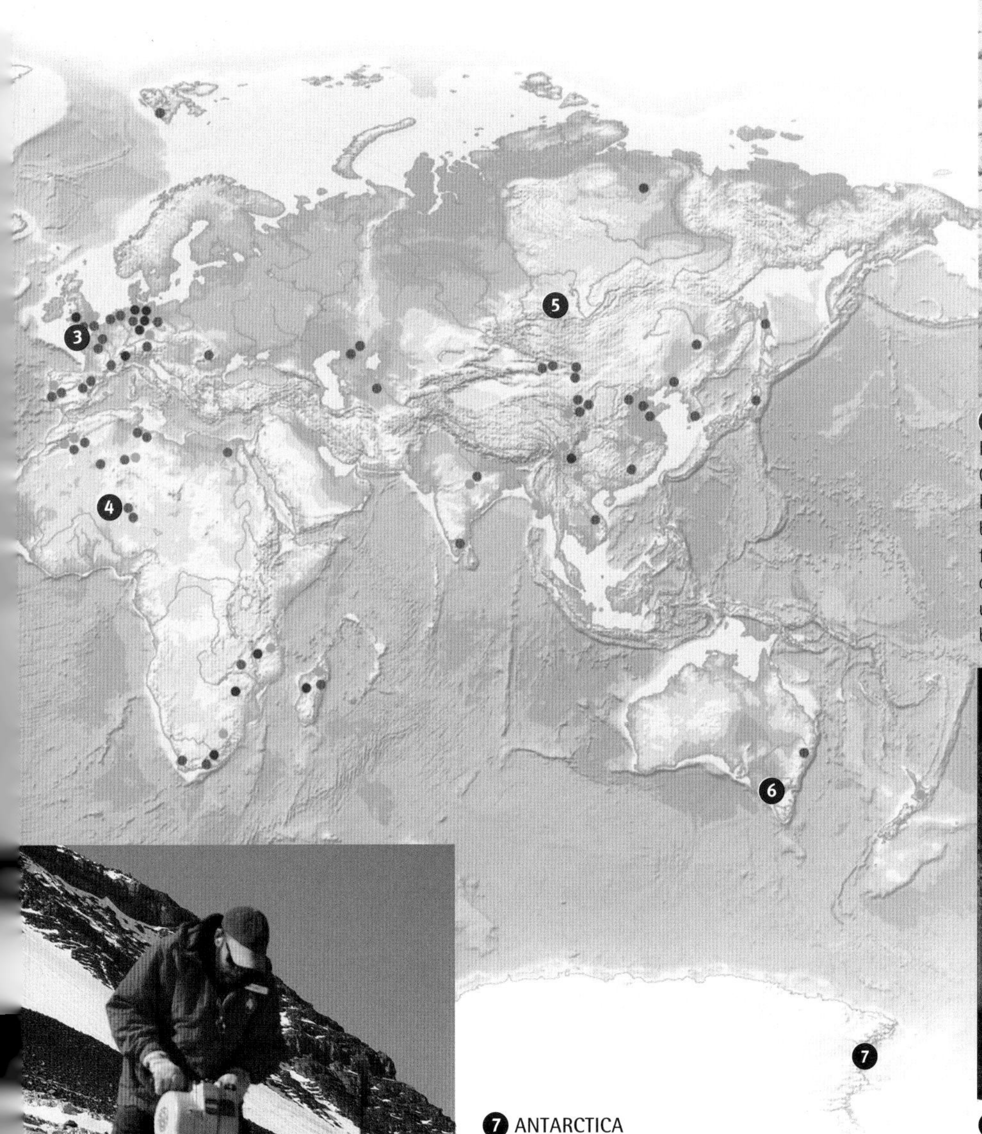

5 GOBI DESERT

In the 1920s, expeditions led by the American Roy Chapman Andrews found dinosaur remains in the Gobi Desert in Mongolia. The original discoveries were made by accident—the first expedition was actually looking for the remains of early humans. The most exciting discoveries were the first dinosaur nests and eggs to be unearthed. Fossils are still being discovered there, mostly by teams from China, the US, and Eastern Europe.

7 ANTARCTICA

It was thought that dinosaurs had lived on every continent except Antarctica. However, in 1986, the first fossil was exposed beneath the ice. In 1991, several carnivores, including the crested *Cryolophosaurus*, were found on Mount Kirkpatrick. There have been other finds since. In early Jurassic times, when these animals lived, Antarctica was part of the supercontinent Pangaea, and was much closer to the Equator.

6 AUSTRALIA

There have been several dinosaur discoveries in Australia, but the most important were made in the 1970s. The site, on the coast of Victoria, has since been named Dinosaur Cove. The finds there show that ornithopods were abundant in this area in the Cretaceous, when the land was within the Antarctic Circle. The remains of these dinosaurs show that they had adapted to long Antarctic winters of intense cold.

IN THE FIELD

In the past, dinosaur digs were very different from what they are today. Fragile fossils were broken by crude digging methods, and even more were shaken to pieces on their way to museums. Records were rarely kept of fossil sites. As a result, valuable specimens and information have been lost forever. Modern excavation involves studying both the skeleton and its surroundings. Like detectives, paleontologists examine the site for clues about the dinosaur's life. Then the fossils are carefully removed and prepared for transportation.

Leg bones are quite complete

Toebones have been scattered but are identifiable

excavation

1 PREPARING THE SITE
When a dinosaur skeleton is discovered, the first thing to do is remove the rock and soil above the layer in which the specimen lies. At this site, at Judith River in Montana, 20 ft (6 m) of material, known as overburden, was removed with bulldozers and explosives. The last 3 ft (1 m) of material was removed with hand tools, such as hammers and chisels, until only a thin layer was left over the skeleton.

2 EXPOSING THE FOSSIL
The rock that the fossil is embedded in is called the matrix. This is removed with great care, usually by hand, using fine chisels, brushes, and dental tools. Sometimes the fossilized bones are quite hard and the matrix is loose, crumbly, and easy to clear away. But often the fossil bones and rock have equal hardness, which makes the job more difficult.

3 MAPPING THE SITE
The next task is to record exactly where each specimen lies. To do this accurately, a grid of wire or strings is placed over the site to divide it into smaller areas. Everything is photographed, as well as drawn. The mapping covers not only the skeleton, but all the other fossils that lie in the same bed of rock. These might provide useful details about the behavior of the dinosaur, or how it died.

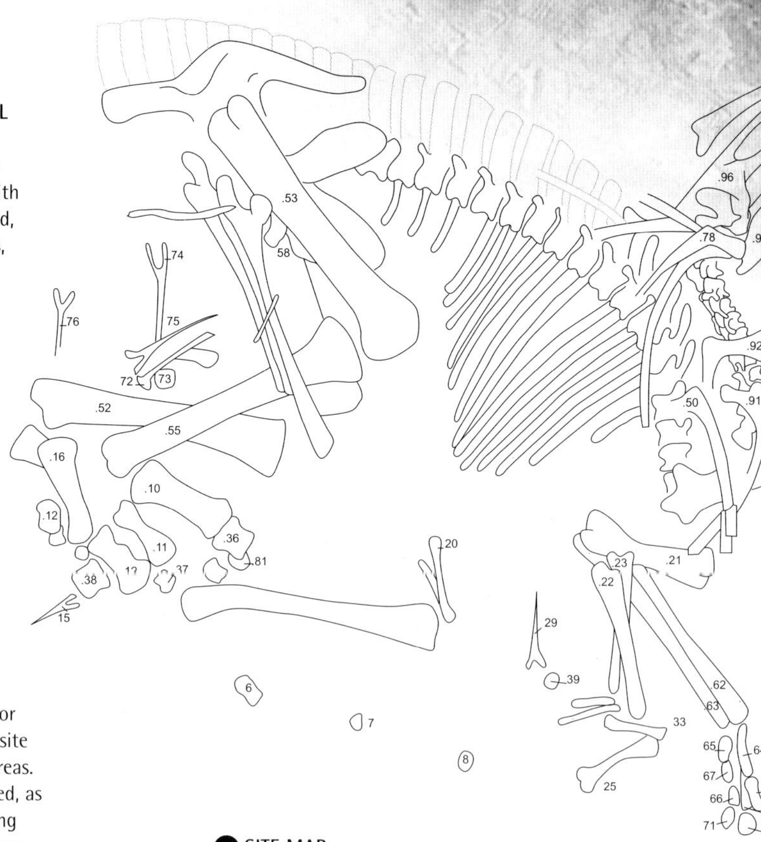

4 SITE MAP
A map of the site is drawn up showing the position of all the bones. Every piece is cataloged and numbered so it can be identified later when the skeleton is studied in the laboratory. Anything else of interest, such as other fossils or sedimentary structures, is also marked on the map.

Backbone appears to end abruptly—the tail is either missing, or is still to be uncovered

▼ EXPOSED FOSSIL

As the skeleton is exposed, paleontologists get a clearer picture of what the specimen is. They are able to identify the parts of the animal and can estimate how complete it is. These are the bones of a hadrosaur called *Brachylophosaurus*. It is lying on its side, with its skull twisted back over its spine. At this stage, it is important to work as quickly as possible, as newly exposed fossils are very vulnerable to the weather.

***Spinal column** (backbone) is still together*

***Skull** has broken up and the pieces are scattered*

***Front limbs** were less powerful than the back ones*

▲ LIFTOFF

Fossils must be extremely carefully packed so that they are not damaged on their way to the museum or laboratory. Sites are often in very remote areas and the trip can be long and bumpy. Fossils have been known to travel in jeeps, planes, boats, trucks, and even horse-drawn carts. On major excavations, helicopters are sometimes used to transport very delicate specimens.

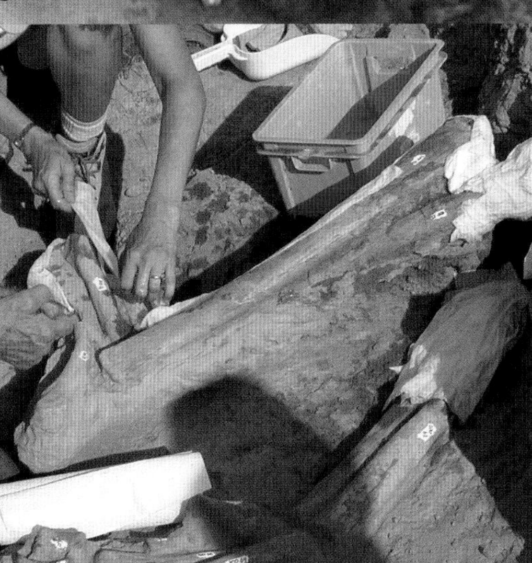

5 INNER DRESSING

Many fossils are very fragile and, before they can be removed and transported, they need to be carefully prepared. First, the fossil is sprayed or painted with a glue or resin that seeps into it and solidifies. This makes the fossil harder. Next, it is covered in a protective layer of paper or foil, and wrapped in bandages.

6 PLASTER FIELD JACKET

The top of the bone is then covered with runny plaster. When this has set hard, the underside of the fossil can be dug out. It is then turned over and covered in bandages and plaster, so that the whole thing is enclosed in a solid plaster jacket. The fossil is now ready to be packed in a crate and taken to a laboratory.

Fossil bones in plaster jackets can be very heavy—some blocks weigh several tons

BODY FOSSILS

Paleontologists can have a hard time finding and identifying dinosaur fossils because they are usually embedded in stone. Usually, only the hard parts of the animal have been fossilized, and even then, a complete skeleton is rare—isolated bones and teeth are more common. Now and again, however, particularly good fossils are unearthed: fossils of complete skeletons in their living position, fossil skin textures, or very occasionally, indications of soft anatomy. Rare though these finds are, there have been enough of them over the past two centuries to allow scientists to build up a good picture of how dinosaurs lived.

Tail chevrons (V-shaped bones) are still in place

Long whip-like tail

Bones of left leg are missing

Leg bones flexed in the living position

Right leg is missing its foot

Long finger bones for grasping plant food

▲ ALMOST COMPLETE SKELETON
This *Heterodontosaurus* is a paleontologist's dream! A nearly complete dinosaur skeleton, still articulated (with its joints in position), and in the pose of a living animal is an unusual find. It is possible to imagine this rabbit-sized plant-eater skipping along, head up and alert, tail swinging out behind. Unfortunately, a skeleton as well preserved as this is very rare. Usually, the bones are pulled apart and scattered by animals, bad weather, or flowing water. Most dinosaur fossils are fragments of bones or incomplete skeletons. The skull is so lightweight that it has nearly always collapsed into shards or is missing altogether.

MUMMIFIED DINOSAURS

Dinosaur "mummies" have been created after dead dinosaurs were washed into a river and lay in soft mud before they decayed. The soft mud takes the impression of the skin texture and this is preserved when the mud solidifies to stone. These skin impressions are immensely valuable because they give scientists an idea of what the outer covering of a dinosaur would have looked like. However, they can also be misleading. For decades, the shriveled skin of one hadrosaur's hand gave rise to the idea that the fingers were webbed and that the hadrosaurs were swimming animals. Dry heat has made the tendons of this *Edmontosaurus* carcass shrink. Found in Wyoming, the body gave scientists the first evidence that dinosaur skin was similar to that of today's reptiles.

Shriveled remains of weight-bearing pad, looking like webbed fingers

Impression of dried skin stretched tightly over rib cage

EDMONTOSAURUS CARCASS

Body is twisted because shrinking tendons have pulled on the bones

Head pulled right back

Neck folded back on shoulders

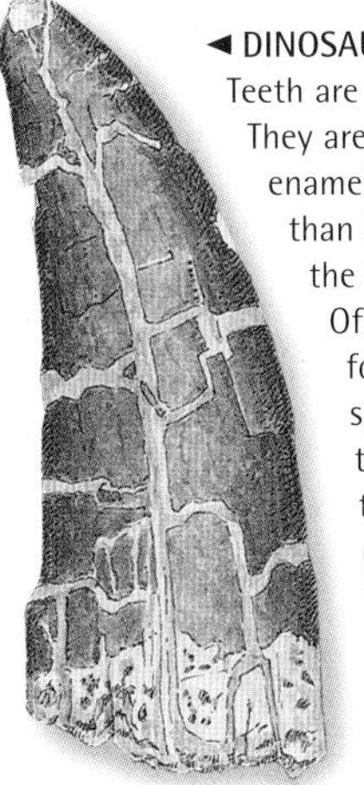

DAMAGED MEGALOSAURUS TOOTH

◄ DINOSAUR TOOTH

Teeth are particulary hard and last well. They are covered in a substance called enamel that makes them even harder than bone. Teeth may fossilize when the bone of the animal is lost. Often the teeth are all that is found of a dinosaur, and some species are known from their teeth alone. The carnivorous theropods shed their teeth and grew new ones throughout their lives, so theropod teeth, such as those of the dinosaur *Megalosaurus*, are common.

BRACHYLOPHOSAURUS SKULL

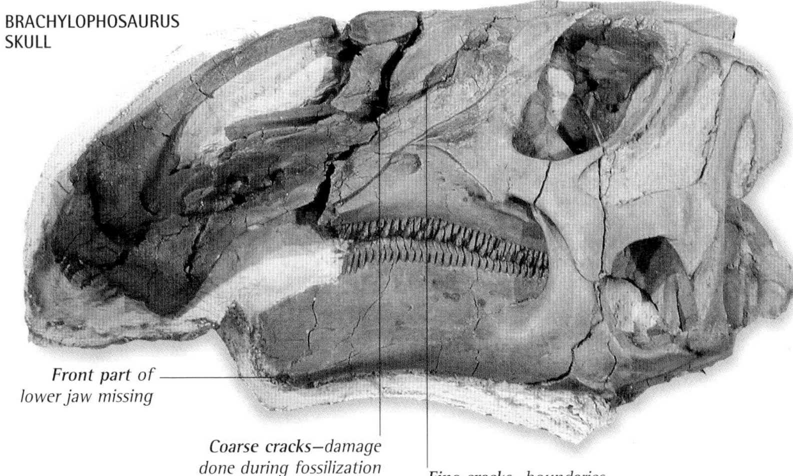

FRACTURED SKULL ▲

Skulls of dinosaurs are not often found by paleontologists. The skull is made up of many different sections all joined together, and soon after death, most skulls come apart. Each side of a skull has about a dozen individual bones and, not counting the teeth, each lower jaw has three—four in the ornithischians. This hadrosaur skull, even though it is broken and parts of it are missing, is still a valuable find and has helped the paleontologists understand the dinosaur better. Many dinosaur skeletons have been found that are almost complete but lack the skull—arguably the most important part of the animal's anatomy.

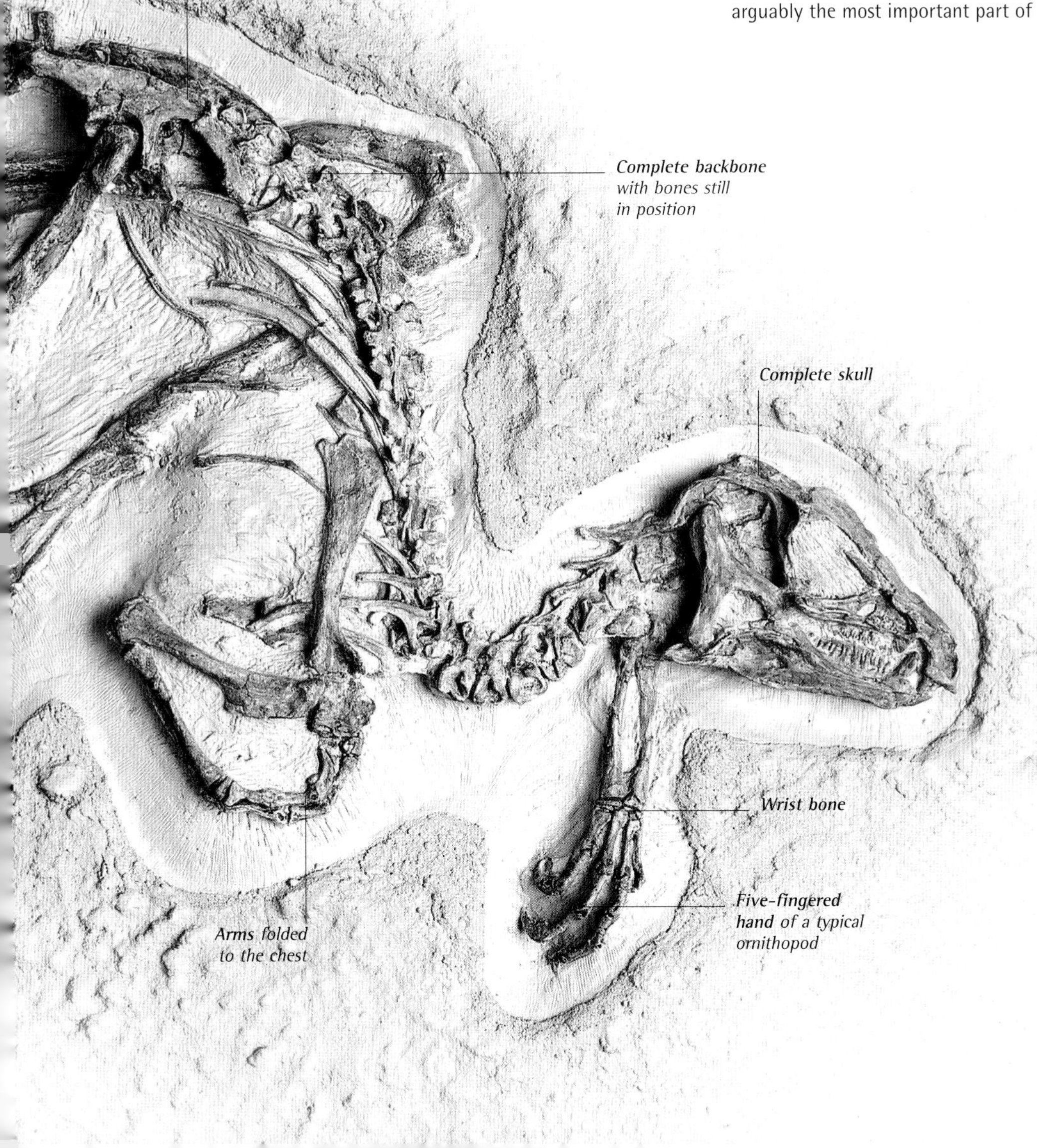

Bird-like hip bone

Complete backbone with bones still in position

Complete skull

Wrist bone

Five-fingered hand of a typical ornithopod

Arms folded to the chest

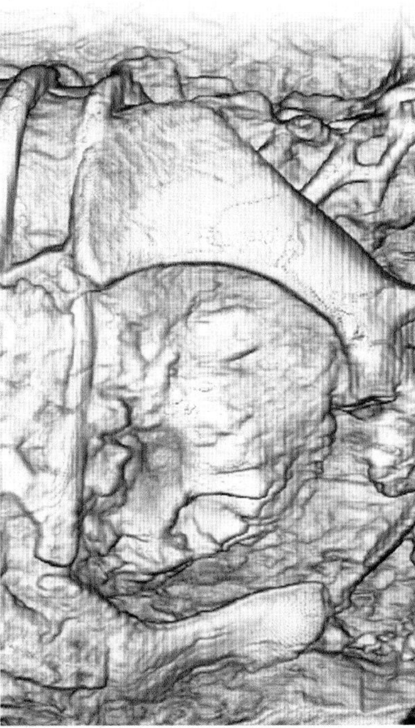

DINOSAUR HEART ▲

The rarest fossil find of all is that of an internal organ. The digestive system, lungs, heart, and all the other soft parts usually rot away quickly and leave nothing that can fossilize. Now and again, however, there is a lucky find. This fossil skeleton of the ornithopod *Thescelosaurus* was unearthed in the US in 1997. Just below the shoulder blade, which is the large bone running from top left down to center right, there is a round mineralized lump in the center of the picture. This may well be a fossilized dinosaur heart—the first ever to be found.

TRACE FOSSILS

Some of the most interesting fossils contain nothing of the dinosaur itself. They are simply the marks the animal left behind as it walked along and take the form of footprints, skin impressions, or even its droppings. Fossils like this are called trace fossils and can be very useful as they give scientists an insight into how the dinosaur lived. Nests and eggs also provide useful indications of a dinosaur's lifestyle. It is usually easier to identify a particular dinosaur from a nest or a fossilized egg than from a trace fossil.

SKIN PRINT ▲
Finding an impression of dinosaur skin is rare but very exciting for the paleontologist. A trace fossil of skin may happen when a dinosaur has laid or sat down in a muddy hollow. The mud, along with the impression, is later buried and turned to stone. More often, skin survives as a fossil when a dinosaur has been buried shortly after death, skin intact. The skin decays away, but the surrounding mud has already taken an impression.

Three-toed footprint in sandstone

◄ FOOTPRINTS
The most common type of trace fossils is footprints. Fossil tracks are sometimes more common than the animal's body fossils. A dinosaur will leave only one dead body, but possibly millions of footprints. They show how the animal walked, whether it lived alone or with others, and even whether or not it dragged its tail on the ground. However, it is always hard to match a footprint to a particular species.

COPROLITES ▲
Coprolites are the fossilized droppings of animals, identified by where they are found—for example, near a species' nest. These fossils can reveal a lot about the diet of the animal that formed them. Coprolites from a tyrannosaur may contain bits of hadrosaur bone. A hadrosaur's coprolites may contain undigested plant material, including identifiable spores and pollen. The shape of a coprolite can also tell us about the shape of a dinosaur's intestines.

THE MAKING OF A DINOSAUR TRACK

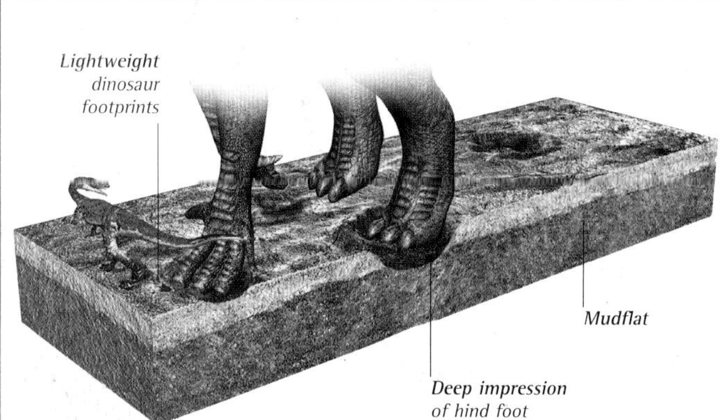

MAKING FOOTPRINTS
Fossil footprints can mislead scientists. In this scene, a four-footed dinosaur walks across a mudflat and a smaller dinosaur scampers by. The hind feet of the larger dinosaur are heavy enough to press through the top layer of wet mud into the firmer layer that lies underneath. The front feet of the larger dinosaur and those of the little dinosaur leave impressions only on the surface layer.

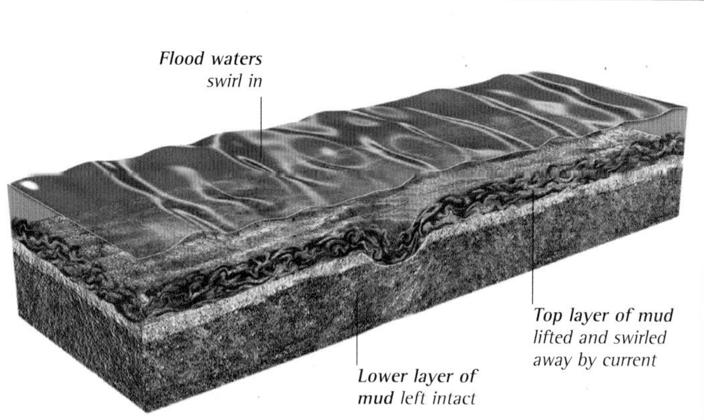

THE SURFACE IS FLOODED
Shortly after the footprints are made and the animals have moved on, the mudflat is flooded when the nearby river overflows its banks. The turbulent water current sweeps away the soft top layer of the mud, carrying with it and destroying the shallow prints of the larger dinosaur's front feet and those of the little two-footer. It does not touch the firmer layer of mud that lies underneath.

▲ DINOSAUR NEST
This fossilized nest was found in Montana in the 1980s. At first, scientists thought that it was the nest of a hypsilophodont called *Orodromeus*, because bones of *Orodromeus* were found scattered all around. It is now known that this is the nest of a carnivore called *Troodon*. It had probably been feeding its family on *Orodromeus* that it had caught. Each egg in a *Troodon* nest was embedded upright in mud to keep it warm, with only the top exposed to the air.

Reconstructed egg shell

Fossilized shell fragments

Impression of the left leg bones

EGG FOSSIL ►
It was clear what kind of dinosaur the nest belonged to when the eggs were cut open and examined. The fossilized bones inside were those of a baby *Troodon*. Many dinosaur eggs are fossilized in such detail that the microscopic structure of the egg shell can be seen. From this type of detail, it is possible to tell that dinosaur egg shells were hard, like those of a bird, rather than soft and leathery, like those of a lizard or crocodile.

MICROSCOPIC VIEW OF A DINOSAUR EGGSHELL

Head of baby tucked down between legs

Bones of left leg folded up against the chest

▲ INSIDE THE EGG
From the bones found fossilized inside the egg, it is possible to make a reconstruction of the baby *Troodon* as it got ready to hatch. Its head is tucked down between its legs. The head and eyes are large, as is usual with baby animals. There is also a horn on the nose that it would have used to break out from the inside through the tough shell. This horn would have been lost soon after the animal hatched.

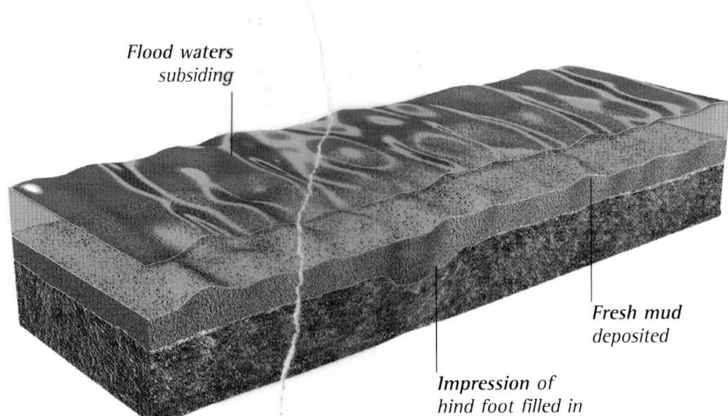

SEDIMENTATION CONTINUES
After the flood water subsides, the disturbed mud from the top layer settles once more in a different place. More mud is carried in by the waters flowing over the top, and this covers the whole area and fills in the impression left by the large dinosaur's hind feet. Later floods deposit more and more mud on top. Eventually, all these mud layers are compressed and, over time, become solidified into sedimentary rock.

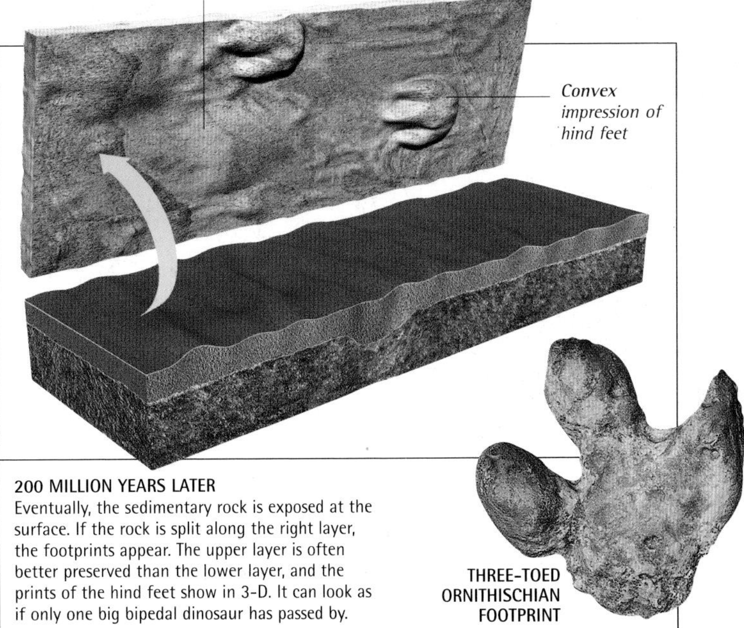

200 MILLION YEARS LATER
Eventually, the sedimentary rock is exposed at the surface. If the rock is split along the right layer, the footprints appear. The upper layer is often better preserved than the lower layer, and the prints of the hind feet show in 3-D. It can look as if only one big bipedal dinosaur has passed by.

THREE-TOED ORNITHISCHIAN FOOTPRINT

EXAMINING FOOTPRINTS

It has been said that the footprints of a dinosaur can tell us more about the dinosaur than its skeleton. This is because footprints are a record of the living, moving animal, while the skeleton is simply the remains of its dead body. The footprints of any animal can tell you a number of things about it, such as its size, and how it stood, ran, or walked. By comparing footprints with dinosaur skeletons, scientists are able to get a clearer picture of what dinosaurs were really like. A set of tracks can reveal more about dinosaur behavior, and can even give an idea of its speed. Some of the largest footprints are made by brontosaurs. These can be over 3 ft (1 m) long and 2 ft (0.7 m) across.

FOOTPRINT LENGTH

FOOTPRINT WIDTH

LEFT PRINT

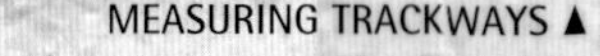

MEASURING TRACKWAYS ▲

When analyzing trackways, such as these *Iguanodon* footprints, many different measurements are taken. The length and width of the footprint, and the trackway width, can tell us about the dinosaur's size. The trackway width can also reveal the dinosaur's stance. Other measurements such as pace length (distance between successive footprints), stride length (distance between prints made by the same foot), and the angle between the prints of alternate feet (pace angulation), can tell us how the animal moved.

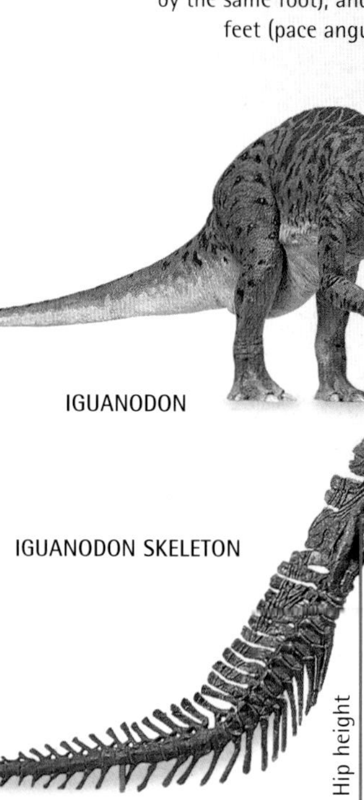

▲ INDICATORS OF BEHAVIOR

These tracks in Arizona were made by agile, meat-eating ceratosaurs called *Dilophosaurus,* which ran on two legs. A set of footprints like this can give an idea of how the animal that made them behaved. A single line of footprints suggests a loner, while several parallel trackways may mean the animal lived as part of a herd. Occasionally, we find trackways of large and small footprints together, from dinosaurs that lived in a family group. Trackways can also show carnivorous dinosaurs pursuing prey.

▲ CALCULATING DIMENSIONS

The size of a dinosaur can be figured out from its footprint. The key measurement is the height of the hip, which is usually estimated as about four times the length of the footprint. If there is a set of prints, it should be possible to tell whether the dinosaur walked on two legs or four, and to get a more accurate idea of the size and shape of the animal, and how it stood and moved. *Iguanodon* was 26–40 ft (8–12 m) long, and probably walked with its body held horizontally.

COMPARING THE STANCE OF ANIMALS

If dinosaurs were like most modern reptiles, you would expect them to stand with their limbs sticking out from the sides of the body, and elbows and knees bent at right angles. This is called the sprawling stance. Or you might imagine that they walked in a semisprawling stance, with elbows and knees slightly bent, like modern crocodiles. However, fossil footprints are too close together to have been produced by either stance. They show that dinosaurs walked upright, like modern mammals, with vertical legs directly below the body, and supporting its weight. This erect stance was crucial to the survival of the dinosaurs. It meant that many were swift and agile on land. Also, because they did not need to use energy supporting their bodies, they were able to be very active—looking for food, for example.

BAROSAURUS

Hip height = 4 x foot length

ERECT STANCE

COMMON IGUANA

SPRAWLING STANCE

DWARF CROCODILE

SEMISPRAWLING STANCE

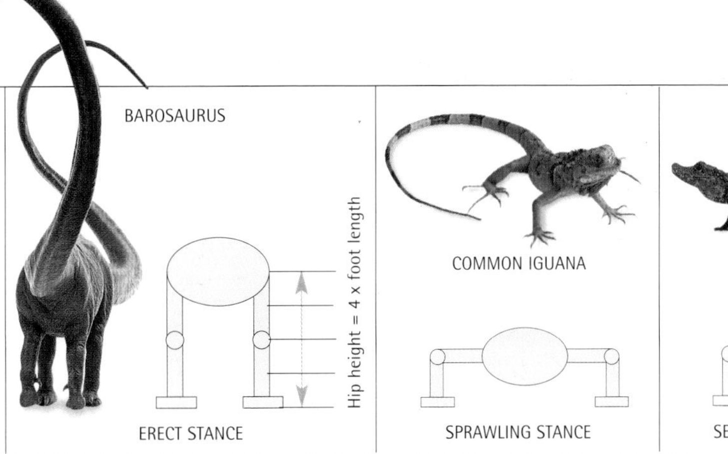

RUNNING AND WALKING SPEEDS

How fast were the dinosaurs? We cannot be sure. It is only possible to estimate the speeds achieved by dinosaurs. Figures have been produced using mathematical calculations based on trackway measurements, leg length, weight, and several other measurements. But there are unknown factors, such as the strength of the leg bones, and the uncertainty of whether or not the dinosaurs were warm blooded—these would affect the calculations and mean that the results cannot be reliable. A few estimated speeds are shown in this chart.

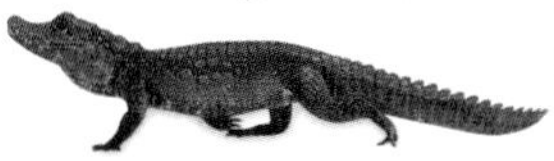

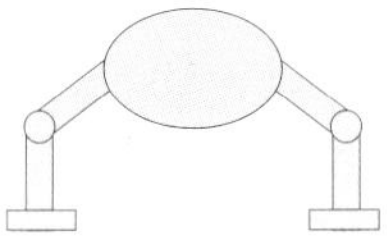

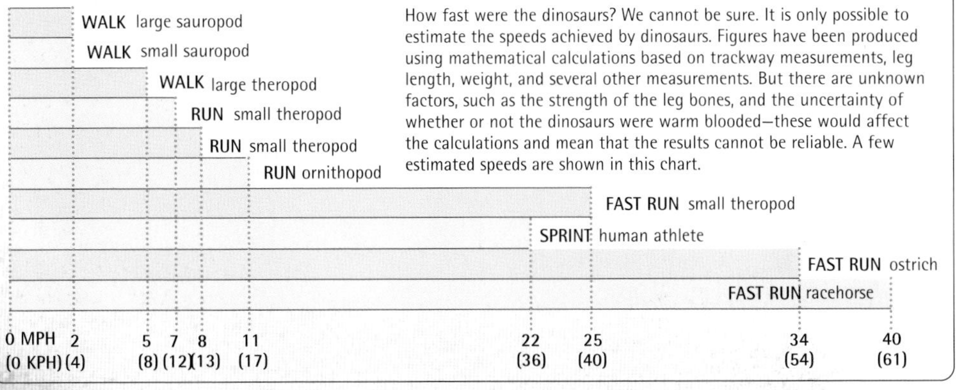

WALK large sauropod
WALK small sauropod
WALK large theropod
RUN small theropod
RUN small theropod
RUN ornithopod
FAST RUN small theropod
SPRINT human athlete
FAST RUN ostrich
FAST RUN racehorse
0 MPH (0 KPH)
2 (4)
5 (8)
7 (12)
8 (13)
11 (17)
22 (36)
25 (40)
34 (54)
40 (61)

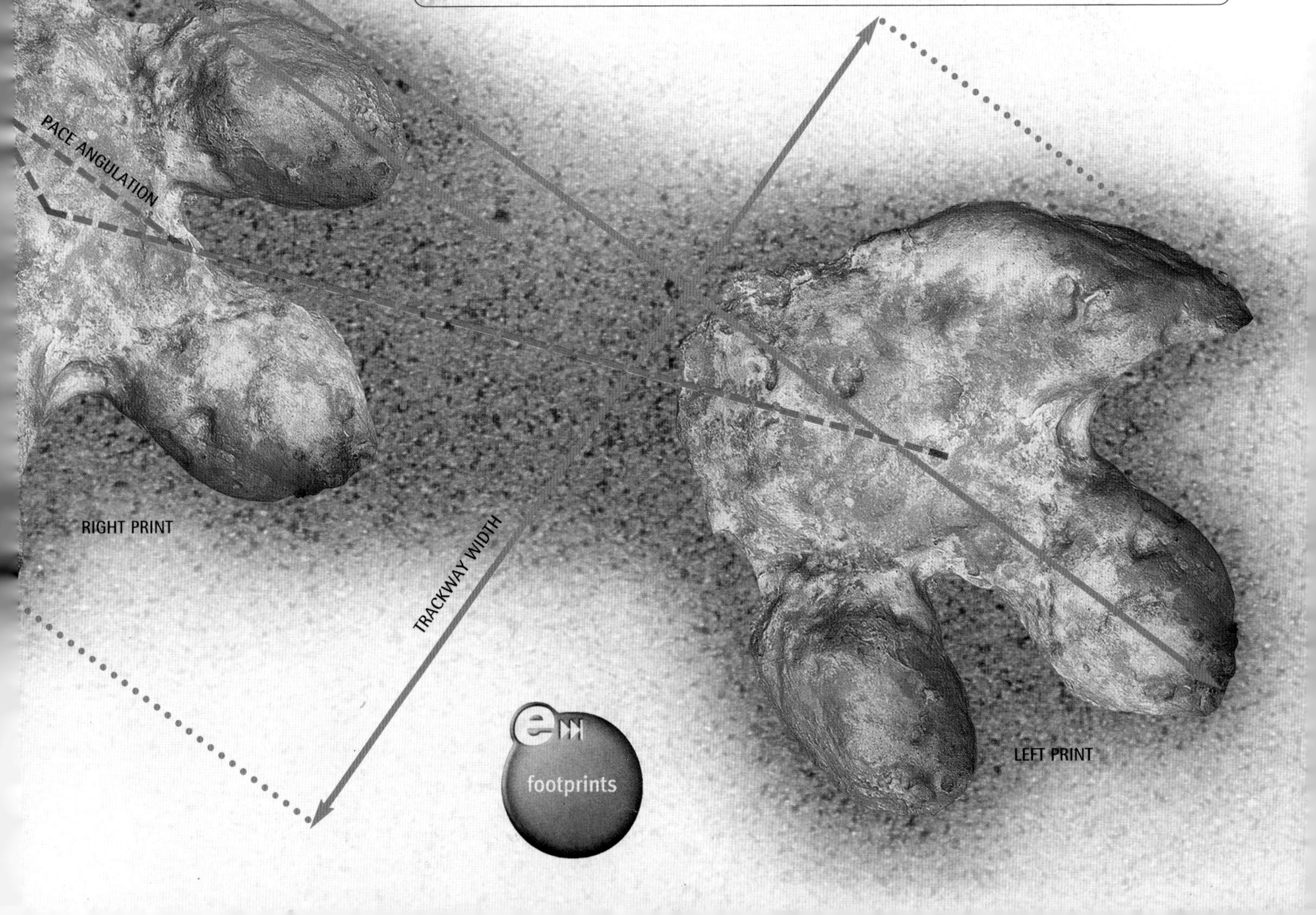

STRIDE LENGTH
PACE LENGTH
PACE ANGULATION
RIGHT PRINT
TRACKWAY WIDTH
footprints
LEFT PRINT

IN THE LAB

When a fossil arrives in a laboratory, it is usually embedded in a chunk of the rock it was found in. The first job for the specially trained technicians, called preparators, is to free the fossil from the rock and clean it up. Sometimes they can remove the rock from the fossil with chemicals. The fossil is left in a bath of acid for several months while the rock around the fossil, called the matrix, dissolves. Preparators also repair bones, strengthen any weak parts with glues and resins, and may make missing bones if the skeleton is to be reconstructed. Preparation is very time-consuming work. The *Tyrannosaurus* skeleton in the Field Museum in Chicago, for example, took 12 people a total of 25,000 hours to complete.

e preparation

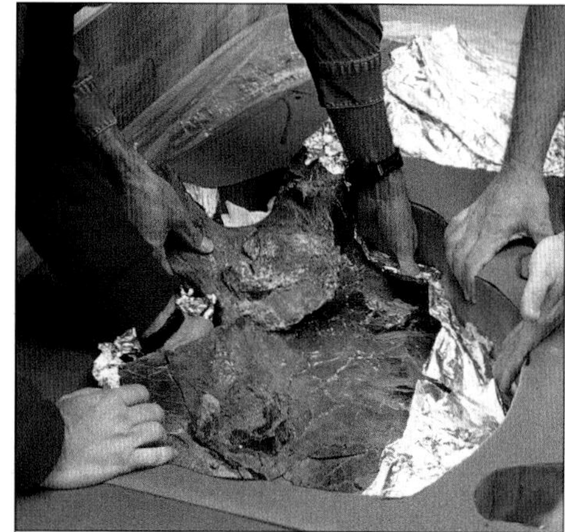

UNPACKING
Technicians at the Field Museum in Chicago open the carefully packed crates of bones from a *Tyrannosaurus* skeleton—here a hip bone. Although the sex of the dinosaur is not known, the team have named it Sue, after the woman who discovered it.

REMOVING THE FIELD JACKET
First the plaster jacket that protected the fossil during transportation is taken off. Here a preparator is using a cast-cutting saw to cut carefully through the jacket on some of Sue's backbones. Beneath the plaster is a layer of protective foil or paper, which is also removed.

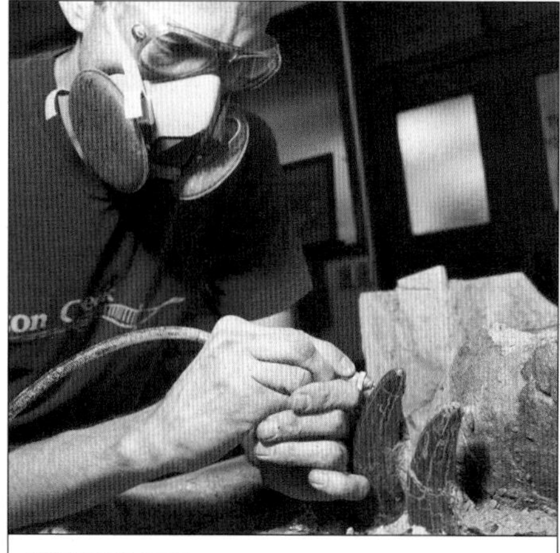

PNEUMATIC DRILL
A range of tools are used to clean up the fossil. Here a preparator uses a pneumatic drill to break up the main body of rock around the fossil. He wears a mask so that he does not breathe in any rock dust. At this stage, pieces of rock are removed in quite large pieces.

FINE CLEANING
Finer cleaning is done with a pen-shaped device, called a scribe, which crumbles the rock using high-frequency vibrations. This technician is working on one of Sue's 58 teeth, the largest of which were 1 ft (30 cm) long. Over 3,500 hours were spent working on Sue's skull.

AIR ABRASION
Another method of fine cleaning is to shoot baking soda at the specimen in powerful blasts of air. This is called air abrasion. Very detailed cleaning is sometimes carried out under a microscope with dental tools. Broken bones can now be repaired using special glues and adhesives.

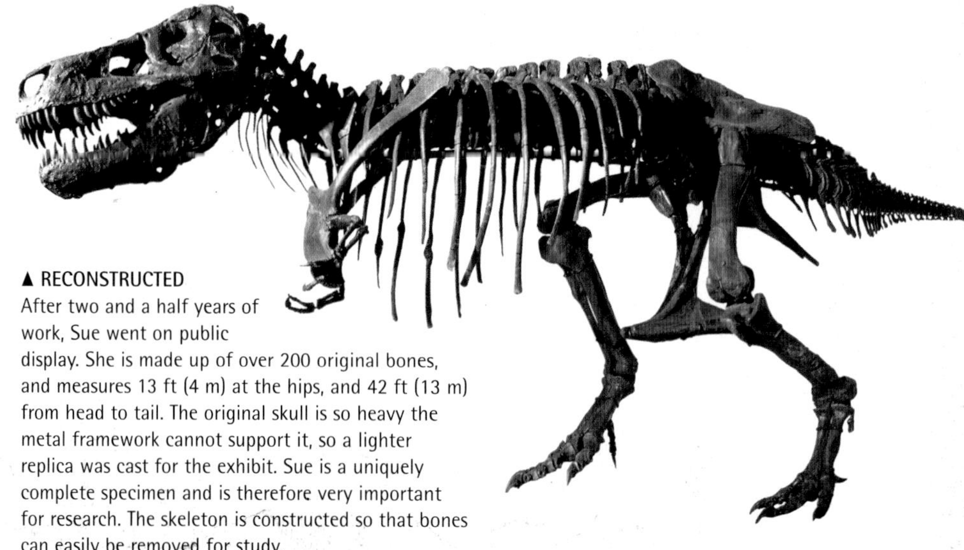

▲ RECONSTRUCTED
After two and a half years of work, Sue went on public display. She is made up of over 200 original bones, and measures 13 ft (4 m) at the hips, and 42 ft (13 m) from head to tail. The original skull is so heavy the metal framework cannot support it, so a lighter replica was cast for the exhibit. Sue is a uniquely complete specimen and is therefore very important for research. The skeleton is constructed so that bones can easily be removed for study.

COMPUTER RECONSTRUCTION

Today, computers are used in all aspects of dinosaur study. In the field, fossil sites can be mapped and plotted using electronic measuring devices. In the laboratory, techniques such as computer reconstruction enable paleontologists to create dinosaurs from fossils on screen, and study them as never before–inside and out.

DINOSAUR ON SCREEN ►
If doctors want to look inside the human body, they can do this by creating a Computerized Axial Tomography (CAT) scan. This involves taking X-rays of the patient from many angles, putting the results into a computer, and building up a 3-D image of the patient's insides. This technique can be used to look inside dinosaur fossils, too, and has produced images of the insides of dinosaur bones and inside dinosaur eggs, for example. Here a paleontologist compares a CAT scan of the brain of a *Tyrannosaurus*, taken from a fossil, with a drawing of another *Tyrannosaurus* brain.

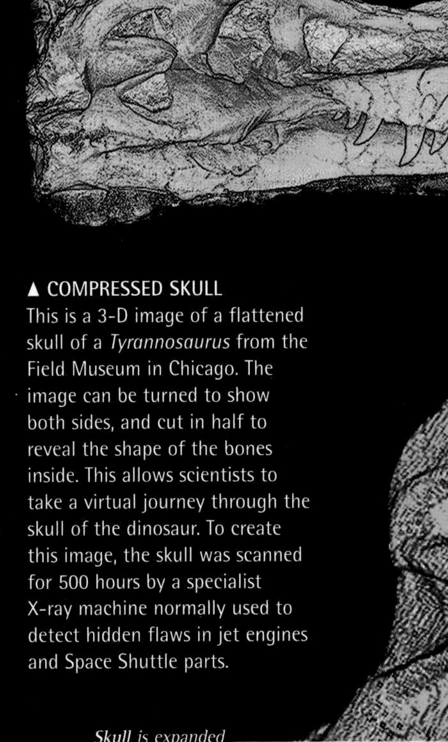

Crushed snout *and the top and bottom parts of the skull have smashed together*

▲ COMPRESSED SKULL
This is a 3-D image of a flattened skull of a *Tyrannosaurus* from the Field Museum in Chicago. The image can be turned to show both sides, and cut in half to reveal the shape of the bones inside. This allows scientists to take a virtual journey through the skull of the dinosaur. To create this image, the skull was scanned for 500 hours by a specialist X-ray machine normally used to detect hidden flaws in jet engines and Space Shuttle parts.

▼ REBUILT IN 3-D
When a fossil is found, it is usually crushed and distorted by the pressure of sediment and rock over millions of years. However, the image produced by a CAT scan can be manipulated to undo any damage to the specimen. In this image, the flattened skull of the *Tyrannosaurus* has been pulled out to show what it would have looked like before it was deformed, with bones shown in their proper proportions and positions. Although the brain of the *Tyrannosaurus* did not become fossilized, the braincase surrounding it was well preserved, giving scientists a good picture of the brain itself. It is likely that *Tyrannosaurus* had a good sense of smell, as half of its brain appears to be dedicated to interpreting smells.

Skull's shape *and size show that Sue's brain was 1 ft (30 cm) long*

Skull *is expanded vertically to show the original proportions of the skull*

Cheeks *are expanded horizontally to reverse the effects of crushing*

DATING FOSSILS

The Age of Dinosaurs was so many millions of years ago that it is very difficult to date exactly. Scientists use two kinds of dating techniques to figure out the age of rocks and fossils. The first method is called relative dating. This considers the positions of the different rocks in sequence (in relation to each other) and the different types of fossil that are found in them. The second method is called absolute dating and is done by analyzing the amount of radioactive decay in the minerals of the rocks.

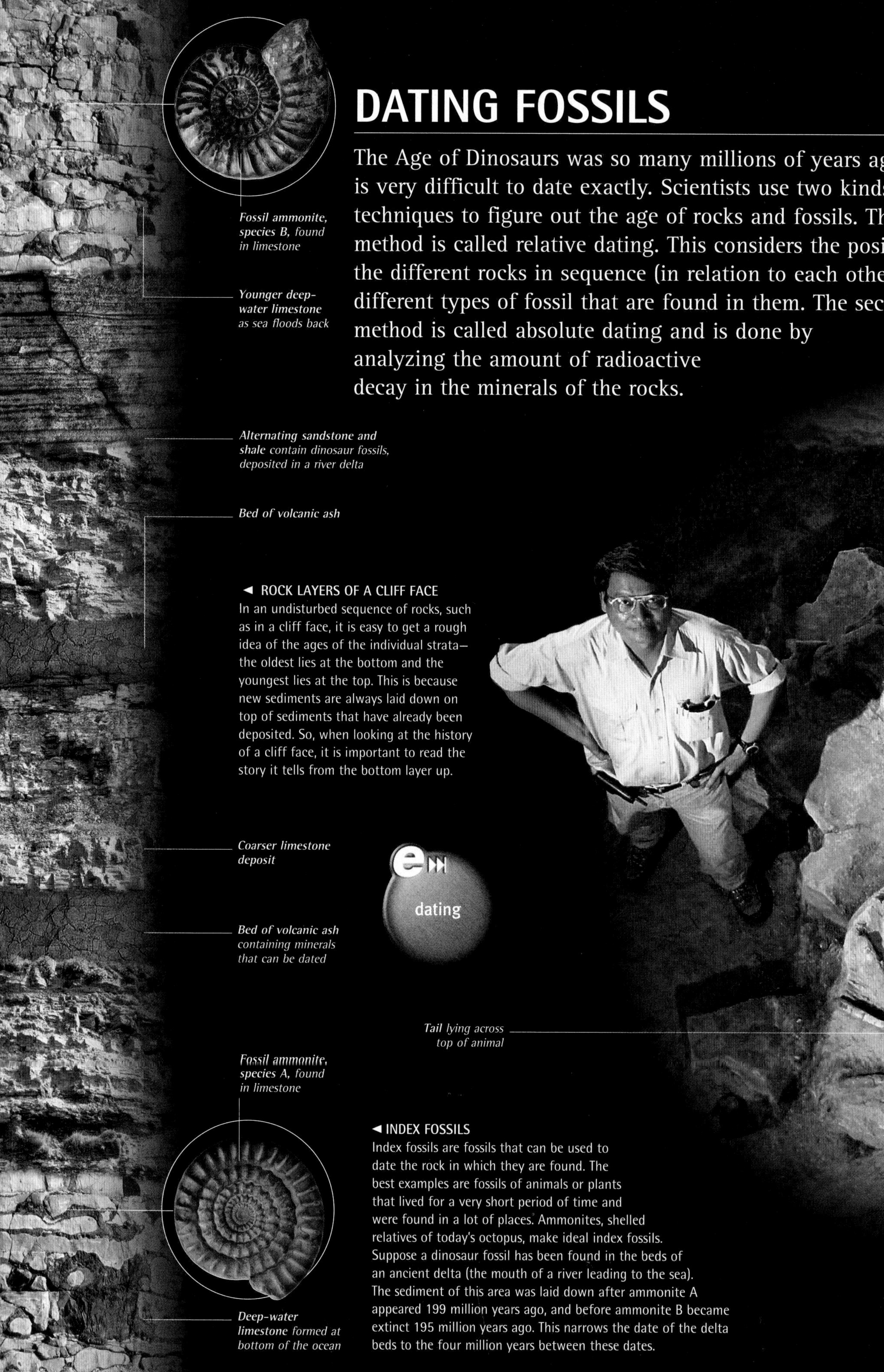

Fossil ammonite, species B, found in limestone

Younger deep-water limestone as sea floods back

Alternating sandstone and shale contain dinosaur fossils, deposited in a river delta

Bed of volcanic ash

◄ ROCK LAYERS OF A CLIFF FACE
In an undisturbed sequence of rocks, such as in a cliff face, it is easy to get a rough idea of the ages of the individual strata—the oldest lies at the bottom and the youngest lies at the top. This is because new sediments are always laid down on top of sediments that have already been deposited. So, when looking at the history of a cliff face, it is important to read the story it tells from the bottom layer up.

Coarser limestone deposit

Bed of volcanic ash containing minerals that can be dated

Tail lying across top of animal

Fossil ammonite, species A, found in limestone

Deep-water limestone formed at bottom of the ocean

◄ INDEX FOSSILS
Index fossils are fossils that can be used to date the rock in which they are found. The best examples are fossils of animals or plants that lived for a very short period of time and were found in a lot of places. Ammonites, shelled relatives of today's octopus, make ideal index fossils. Suppose a dinosaur fossil has been found in the beds of an ancient delta (the mouth of a river leading to the sea). The sediment of this area was laid down after ammonite A appeared 199 million years ago, and before ammonite B became extinct 195 million years ago. This narrows the date of the delta beds to the four million years between these dates.

Fossil of Phuwiangosaurus *found in layers of sandstone and shale*

Fossils in surrounding rock *are also gathered for analysis*

▼ DATING A DINOSAUR SKELETON

Scientists find out the age of a dinosaur fossil by dating not only the rocks in which it lies, but those below and above it. This *Phuwiangosaurus* was the first fossil dinosaur found in Thailand, and it is known that it lived in the Cretaceous because of other fossils found nearby. Sometimes, scientists already know the age of the fossil because fossils of the same species have been found elsewhere and it has been possible to establish accurately from those when the dinosaur lived. Geologists call this the principle of lateral continuity. A fossil will always be younger than fossils in the beds beneath it and this is called the principle of superposition.

RADIOMETRIC DATING

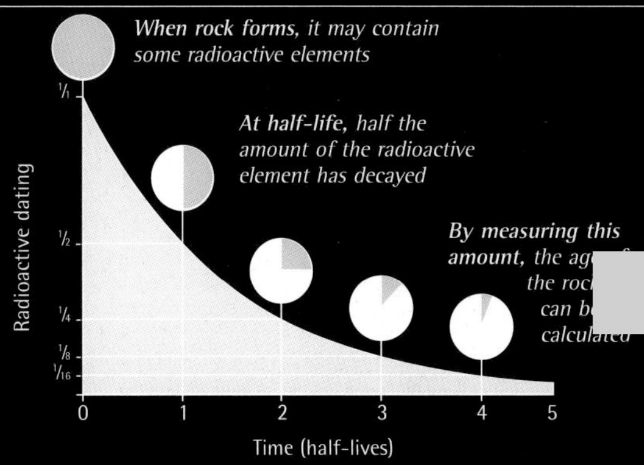

There are some radioactive elements in rock that decay by giving off energy and turning into different, more stable elements. This radioactive decay takes place at a constant rate for each radioactive element. Scientists know exactly how long it will take for half the quantity of the element to change, and this state is known as its half-life. After another half-life has passed, the element will have decayed to a quarter of its original amount. After another half-life has passed, it will have decayed to an eighth, and so on.

A good example of this is potassium-argon dating. The half-life of potassium-40 is 1,310 million years, after which half of its substance will have changed into stable argon-40.

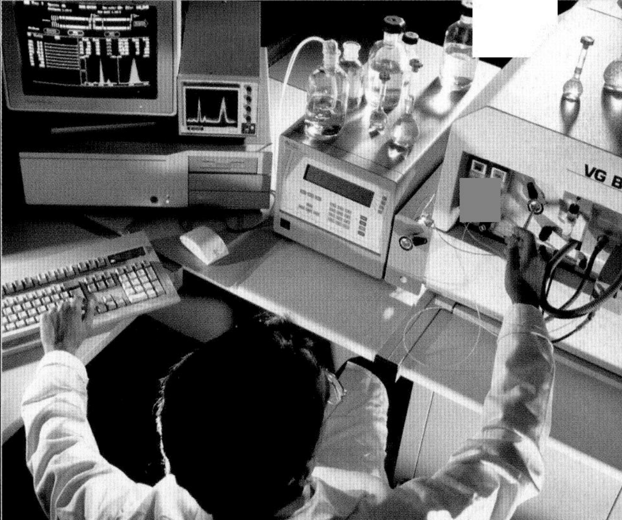

▲ ABSOLUTE DATING

By looking at the layers of volcanic ash in a sedimentary sequence, it is possible to work out the exact time of an ancient volcanic eruption. Scientists do this by using radiometric dating in a laboratory to [illegible] the minerals created by the eruption. The two beds of volcanic ash in the cliff face on the left are dated at 197 and 196 million years respectively. The dinosaur bed is above these, so it is younger. By combining this knowledge with what is known about the ammonites, it is possible to date the dinosaur fossil at 196 or 195 million years old.

Bones *are still articulated (in position), showing that the burial took place suddenly*

RECONSTRUCTING THE PAST

Reconstructing a dinosaur skeleton is a complex job as usually only a fraction of the skeleton is recovered. Paleontologists assume the missing pieces will resemble those of the animal's closest relatives, and use these as guides for making replacement parts. Most excavated fossils are too delicate to put back together, so technicians construct a lightweight replica of the skeleton, which is then erected in a lifelike pose. Rearing on its hind legs, the American Museum of Natural History's *Barosaurus* is the world's largest freestanding dinosaur exhibit.

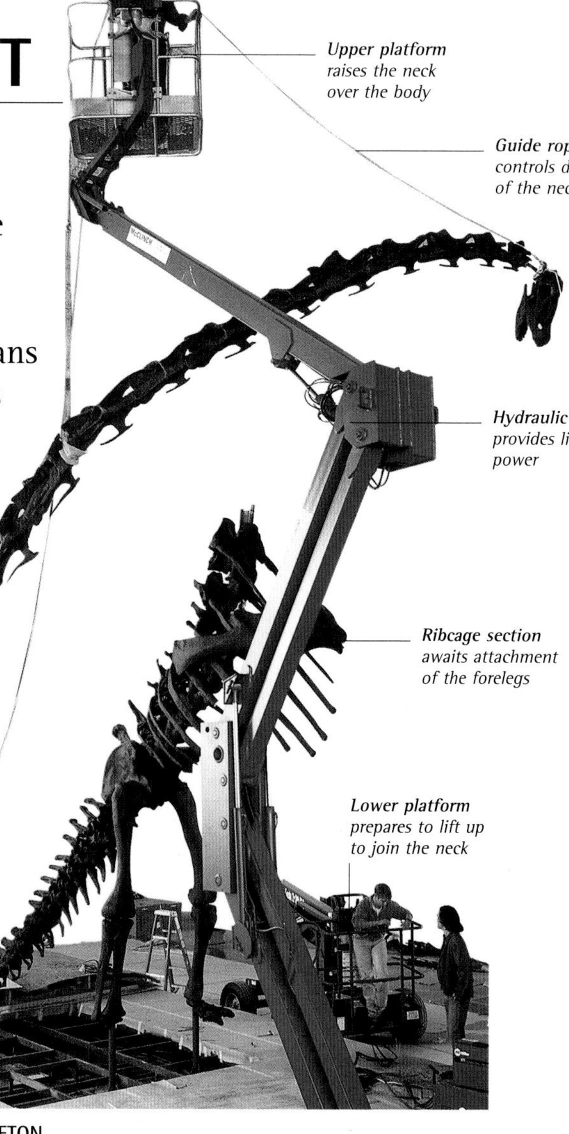

▲ ASSEMBLING THE SKELETON
With its head rearing more than 50 ft (15 m) into the air, the *Barosaurus* skeleton was mounted on a supporting metal frame. It took two hydraulic lifting platforms to assemble it safely. First, the tail sections were joined together in their upward-curving shape. Then the tail's metal frame was welded to the frame of the hind legs. The huge ribcage followed. The assembled head and neck section was then raised above the body.

CREATING THE BAROSAURUS REPLICA

MAKING THE MOLDS
The fossilized bones were labeled with their positions within the skeleton. Each fossil bone was then thickly painted with liquid rubber. After it had set into a flexible mold of each fossil, the rubber was peeled away. Cotton gauze and plastic were added to the outside of each mold to strengthen it.

PREPARING FOR CASTING
The molds of the long limb bones were made in two halves that fitted together exactly. The inside of each half was painted with a liquid plastic that would form the outer surface of the replica bone. The outsides of the molds were stiffened with a fiberglass layer, and the halves were fitted together.

MAKING THE CAST
The hollow molds with their inner linings of tough plastic were filled with another type of liquid plastic. This set in a rigid but honeycombed form, made lightweight by thousands of air bubbles. Without the strengthening of this solid foam-plastic core, the plastic inner linings might break.

REMOVING THE MOLD
Each mold was left until the foam-plastic casting inside had hardened. The mold with its tough outer jacket was then eased away to reveal the shape of the original fossil bone inside. The tough plastic outer surface of the cast was smoothed down and carefully painted to match the coloring of the fossil bone.

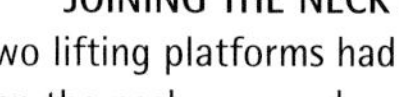

JOINING THE NECK ►
The teams operating the two lifting platforms had to work very closely when the neck was ready to be attached to the body. Suspended by strong ropes from the upper platform, the long neck section was inched downward, with men on the ground pulling on ropes to help control its movement. A worker on the lower platform guided the neck's connecting rod until it finally slotted into a tube in the body's frame.

Lifting platform supports lower assembly team

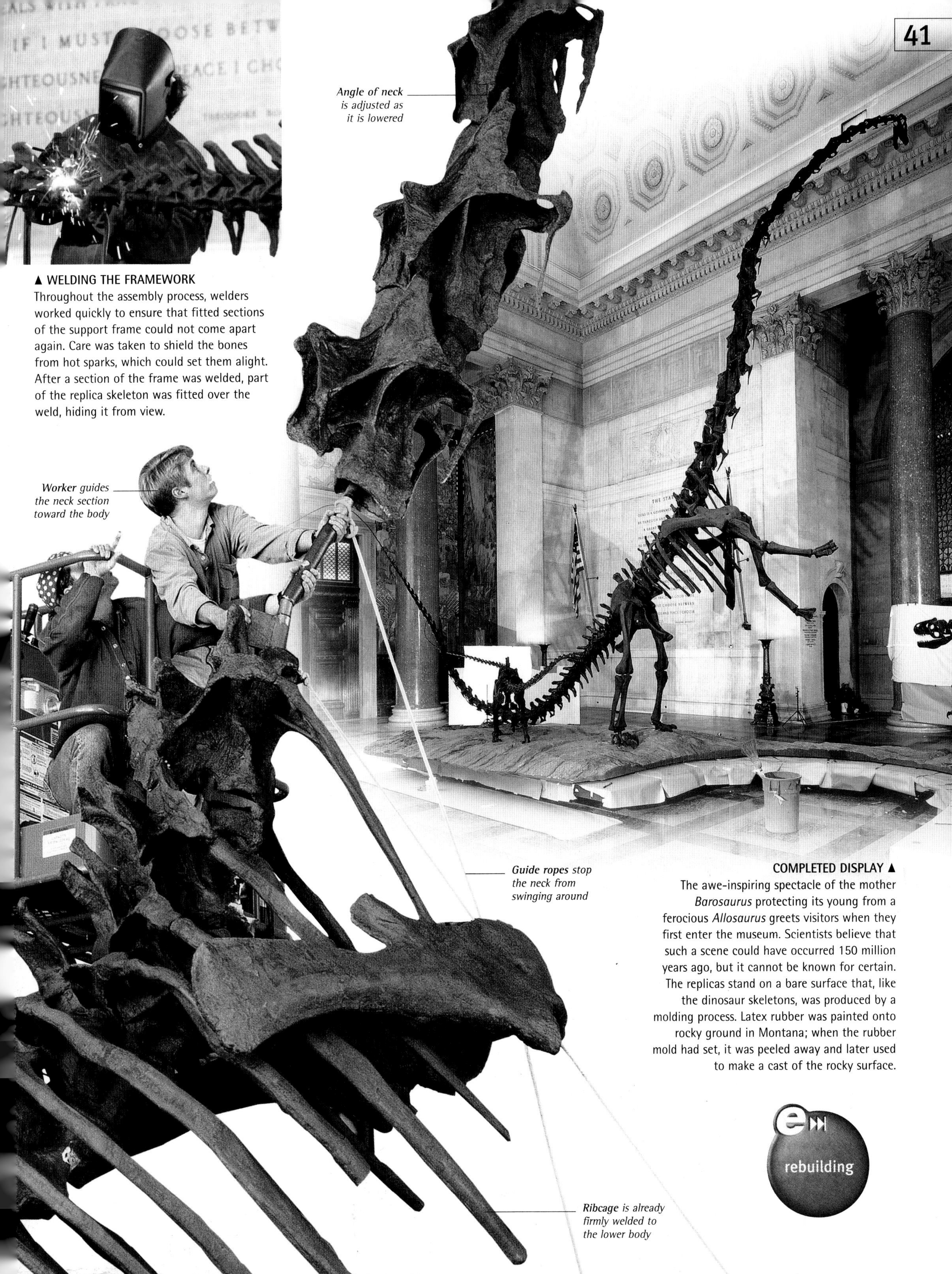

▲ WELDING THE FRAMEWORK
Throughout the assembly process, welders worked quickly to ensure that fitted sections of the support frame could not come apart again. Care was taken to shield the bones from hot sparks, which could set them alight. After a section of the frame was welded, part of the replica skeleton was fitted over the weld, hiding it from view.

COMPLETED DISPLAY ▲
The awe-inspiring spectacle of the mother *Barosaurus* protecting its young from a ferocious *Allosaurus* greets visitors when they first enter the museum. Scientists believe that such a scene could have occurred 150 million years ago, but it cannot be known for certain. The replicas stand on a bare surface that, like the dinosaur skeletons, was produced by a molding process. Latex rubber was painted onto rocky ground in Montana; when the rubber mold had set, it was peeled away and later used to make a cast of the rocky surface.

BIPEDAL CARNIVORES

The scientific name for meat-eating dinosaurs is theropods, which means "beast-footed." These fierce hunting carnivores were saurischian—they had hipbones arranged like those of a lizard. The pubisbone reached forward and down, the ischium bone reached down and back, and the ilium bone along the top held the leg muscles. Most of the carnivores were wholly bipedal, standing and running on their two back legs. Many, such as the efficient predators *Deinonychus* and *Suchomimus*, had long fingers and claws on their front legs, which they used to grip food or slash prey.

Muscular neck *holding up heavy head and jaws*

Backbone *held horizontally when running*

Small intestine

Saurischian *(lizardlike) hipbones*

Ilium

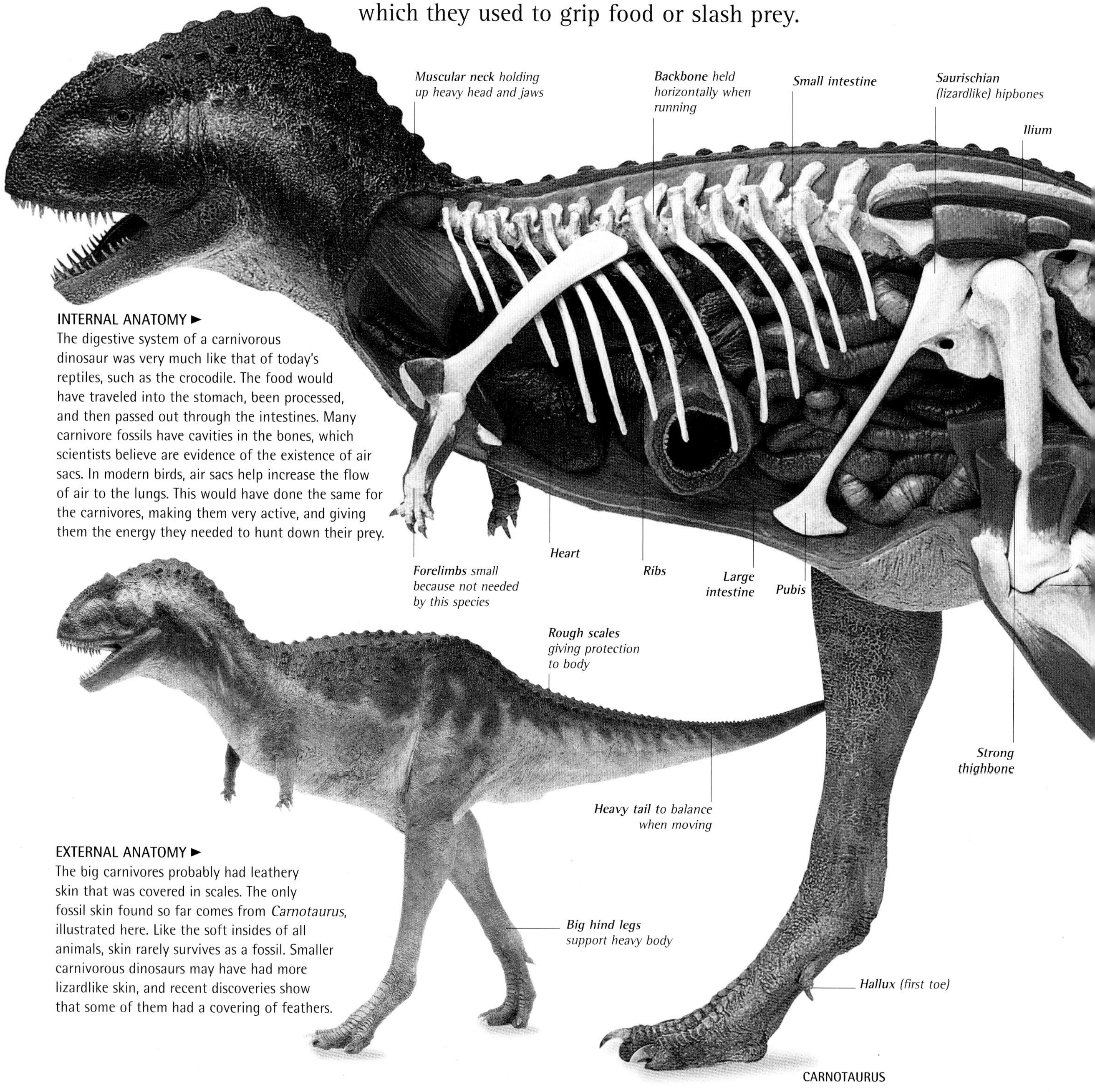

INTERNAL ANATOMY ►
The digestive system of a carnivorous dinosaur was very much like that of today's reptiles, such as the crocodile. The food would have traveled into the stomach, been processed, and then passed out through the intestines. Many carnivore fossils have cavities in the bones, which scientists believe are evidence of the existence of air sacs. In modern birds, air sacs help increase the flow of air to the lungs. This would have done the same for the carnivores, making them very active, and giving them the energy they needed to hunt down their prey.

Heart

Forelimbs *small because not needed by this species*

Ribs

Large intestine

Pubis

Rough scales *giving protection to body*

Strong thighbone

Heavy tail *to balance when moving*

EXTERNAL ANATOMY ►
The big carnivores probably had leathery skin that was covered in scales. The only fossil skin found so far comes from *Carnotaurus*, illustrated here. Like the soft insides of all animals, skin rarely survives as a fossil. Smaller carnivorous dinosaurs may have had more lizardlike skin, and recent discoveries show that some of them had a covering of feathers.

Big hind legs *support heavy body*

Hallux *(first toe)*

CARNOTAURUS

RARE SKULL ►

Most dinosaur skulls, including those of the carnivores, were made up of a lightweight framework of struts and plates. Soon after a dinosaur died, the skull would fall to pieces and be scattered. To find a complete skull like this *Tyrannosaurus* is quite rare. It reveals many things about the dinosaur. For example, its eyes were set in sockets that faced forward so that it could judge the distance to its prey accurately.

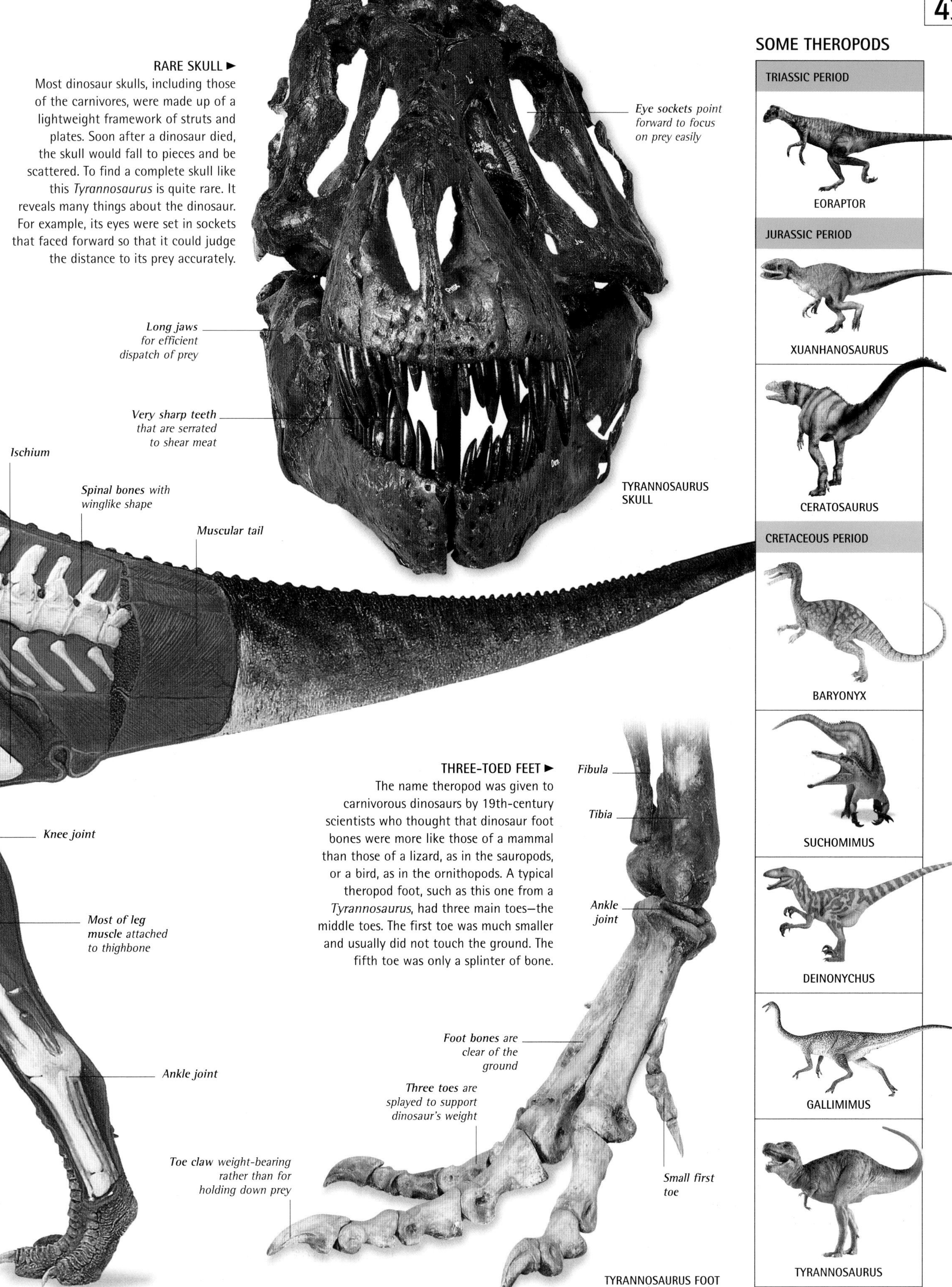

THREE-TOED FEET ►

The name theropod was given to carnivorous dinosaurs by 19th-century scientists who thought that dinosaur foot bones were more like those of a mammal than those of a lizard, as in the sauropods, or a bird, as in the ornithopods. A typical theropod foot, such as this one from a *Tyrannosaurus*, had three main toes—the middle toes. The first toe was much smaller and usually did not touch the ground. The fifth toe was only a splinter of bone.

SOME THEROPODS

TRIASSIC PERIOD

EORAPTOR

JURASSIC PERIOD

XUANHANOSAURUS

CERATOSAURUS

CRETACEOUS PERIOD

BARYONYX

SUCHOMIMUS

DEINONYCHUS

GALLIMIMUS

TYRANNOSAURUS

LONG-NECKED HERBIVORES

The biggest land animals to have lived on Earth were the sauropods, which means "lizard feet." These giants were the long-necked herbivorous (plant-eating) dinosaurs. They had small heads, long, flexible necks, bulky bodies, and long tails. They walked slowly on all fours and fed on conifers and other plants with tall stems. They existed for 130 million years, from the early Jurassic through to the late Cretaceous. Footprints show that they lived in herds or in family groups for protection against their cousins, the big carnivores.

▼ INTERNAL ANATOMY
An animal that eats plants rather than meat needs a complex digestive system to break down the food. Long-necked herbivores such as this *Brachiosaurus* could not chew, so they swallowed plant food whole and it was ground up in their stomachs. They also swallowed gastroliths ("stomach stones"), which churned with the plants in the stomach, breaking them into smaller, more easily digestible pieces.

EXTERNAL ANATOMY ►
The big digestive system of the long-necked herbivores had to be carried well forward of the lizardlike hips. This means that the animal could not have balanced on its hind legs only. Some of these dinosaurs, like this *Brachiosaurus*, had very long front legs, while others, such as *Apatosaurus*, did not. Their skin may have been elephant-like or possibly scaly. Some may also have had spines down their backs, for ornamentation and display.

BRACHIOSAURUS

BRACHIOSAURUS

PROSAUROPODS

The earliest long-necked herbivores were the prosauropods, which means "before lizard feet." Prosauropods evolved in the Late Triassic and died out in the Early Jurassic. They ranged from rabbit-sized lightweights that could scamper around on their hind legs, to lumbering elephant-sized animals that looked like the later sauropods. *Anchisaurus* was typical and about the size of a human being. It probably spent some of its time on its hind legs, but usually moved about on all fours. The earliest prosauropods were the ancestors of the sauropods.

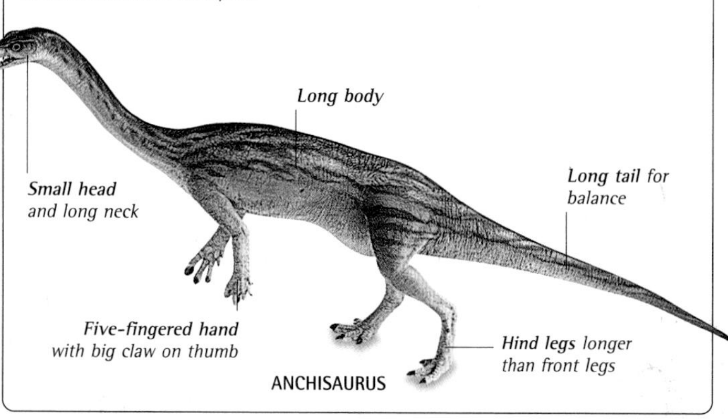

ANCHISAURUS

▼ TEETH FOR RAKING

Sauropods fed by raking and swallowing—they did not chew. And they would have had to keep eating all the time to feed their great bodies. The teeth of a *Diplodocus* were peglike and arranged like the teeth of a rake at the front of the jaw. The teeth of a *Camarasaurus* were more spoon-shaped and filled most of the jaw. Both were adapted for pulling food off trees.

Peglike teeth

DIPLODOCUS SKULL

CAMARASAURUS SKULL

▲ TEETH FOR COMBING

The wear on the narrow teeth of *Diplodocus* fossils reveals a lot about how the dinosaur fed itself and what it ate. The angle the skull was held at, the length of the neck, and the different types of wear on the teeth show that *Diplodocus* probably fed in two ways. It could reach up and eat from the tops of the trees for some of the time, but it could also reach around it on or near the ground for low-growing plants.

PILLARLIKE LEGS ►

Some sauropods weighed as much as 100 tons—about the same as a blue whale. Their legs had to be strong enough to support this weight. They walked on their tiptoes, but under the parts of the toes that were lifted from the ground there was a wedge of gristle. This spread out the weight and took the pressure off the toes themselves. Elephants have this kind of a foot for exactly the same reason.

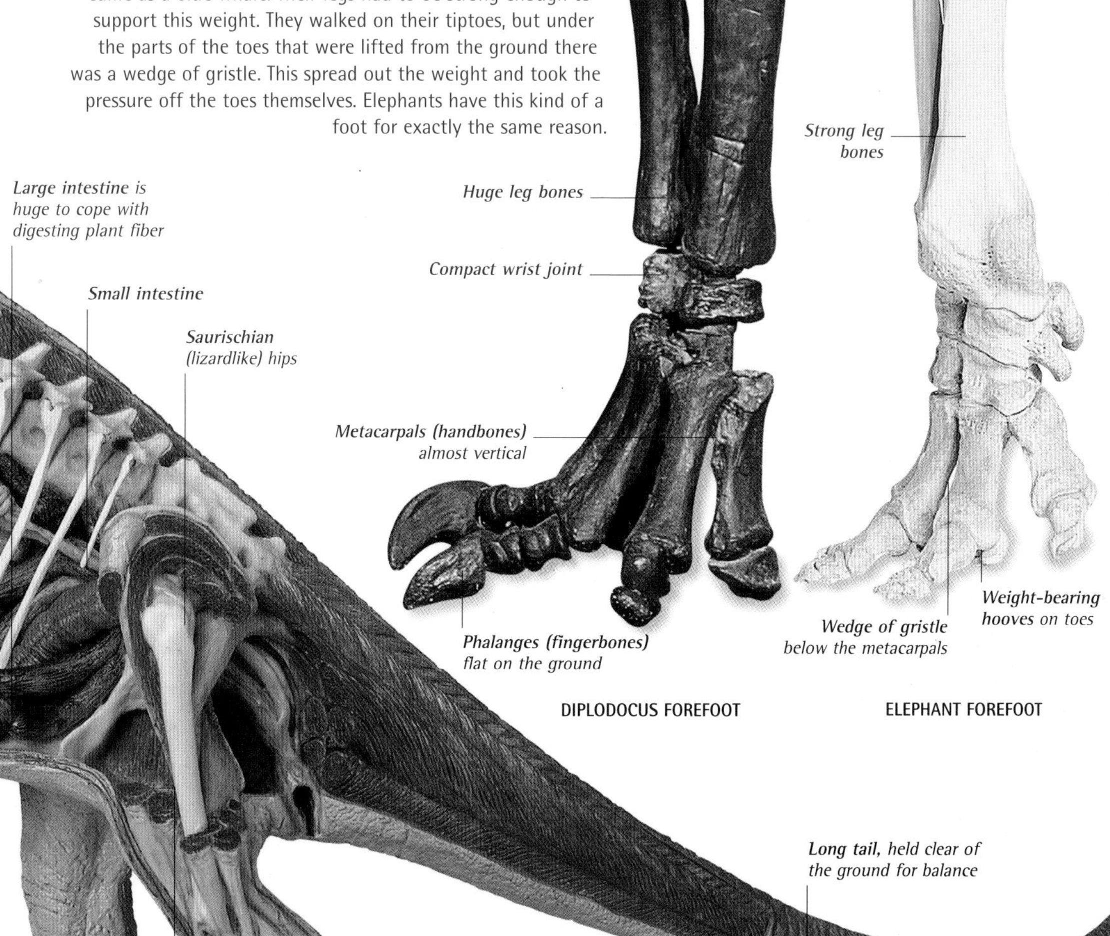

DIPLODOCUS FOREFOOT

ELEPHANT FOREFOOT

sauropods

SOME LONG-NECKED HERBIVORES

BIPEDAL HERBIVORES

As well as the giant plant-eaters, there were several other groups of smaller herbivores, including the ornithopods, which means "bird feet." These successful and widespread dinosaurs first appeared 200 million years ago in the Jurassic and were abundant in the Cretaceous. They had ornithischian (birdlike) hipbones and a big plant-eating gut carried well back. This allowed the animals to walk and run away from danger on their hind legs. Unlike the sauropods, their teeth and jaws were adapted for chewing plant material.

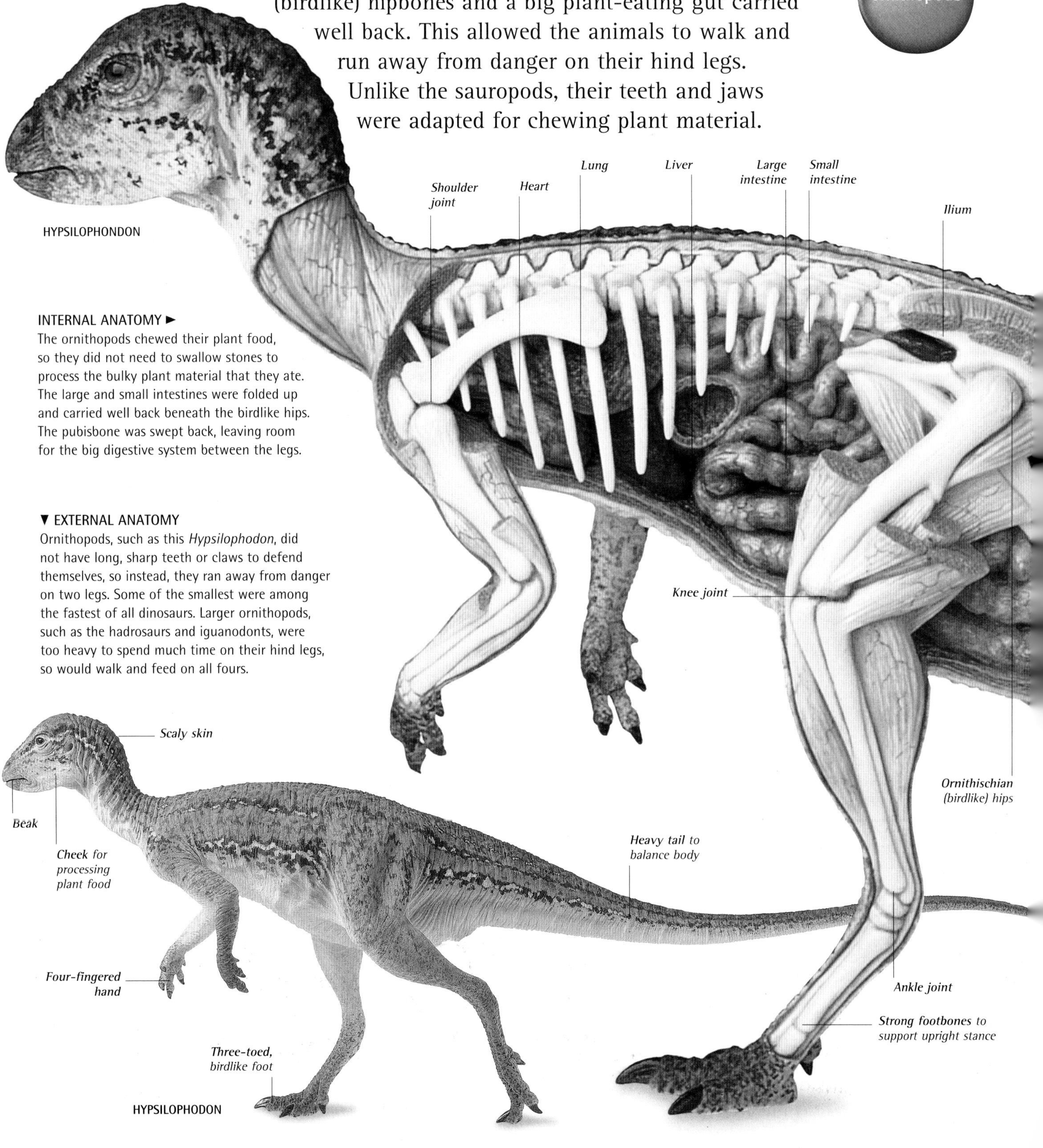

INTERNAL ANATOMY ►
The ornithopods chewed their plant food, so they did not need to swallow stones to process the bulky plant material that they ate. The large and small intestines were folded up and carried well back beneath the birdlike hips. The pubisbone was swept back, leaving room for the big digestive system between the legs.

▼ EXTERNAL ANATOMY
Ornithopods, such as this *Hypsilophodon*, did not have long, sharp teeth or claws to defend themselves, so instead, they ran away from danger on two legs. Some of the smallest were among the fastest of all dinosaurs. Larger ornithopods, such as the hadrosaurs and iguanodonts, were too heavy to spend much time on their hind legs, so would walk and feed on all fours.

BRACHYLOPHOSAURUS SKULL

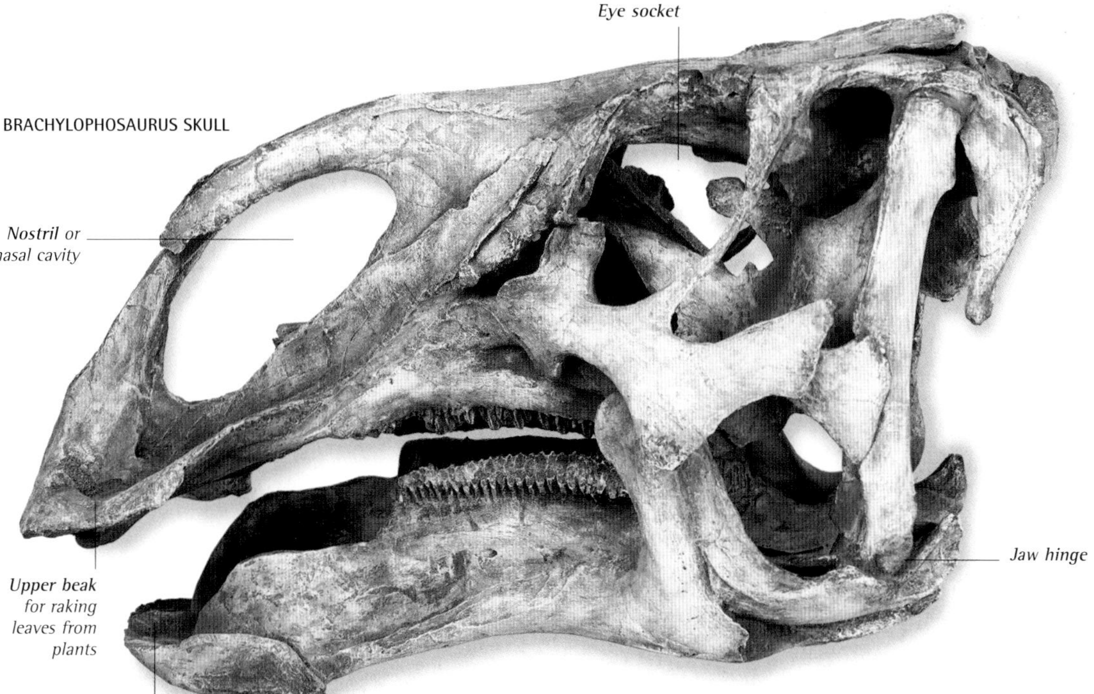

Eye socket

Nostril or nasal cavity

Jaw hinge

Upper beak for raking leaves from plants

Lower beak

▲ TOOTHLESS BEAK AND CHEEK TEETH
The skull of this *Brachylophosaurus* shows that this was an animal that could chew its food. The ornithopod would gather leafy plants with the birdlike toothless beak at the front of the mouth. The rows of teeth were set in from the side of the skull, suggesting that the back of the mouth was enclosed in prominent cheeks. The cheeks stored the plant food while it was being processed by the ridged cheek teeth. These would have ground the plant food to a pulp, ready for swallowing and digesting.

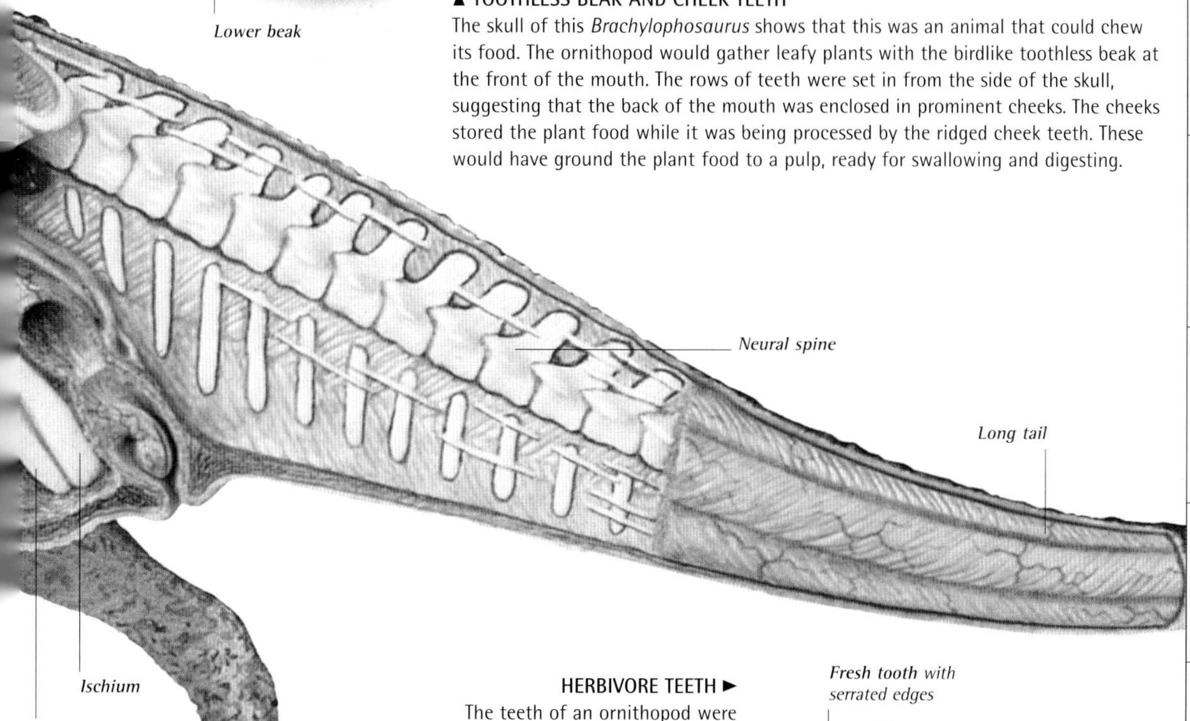

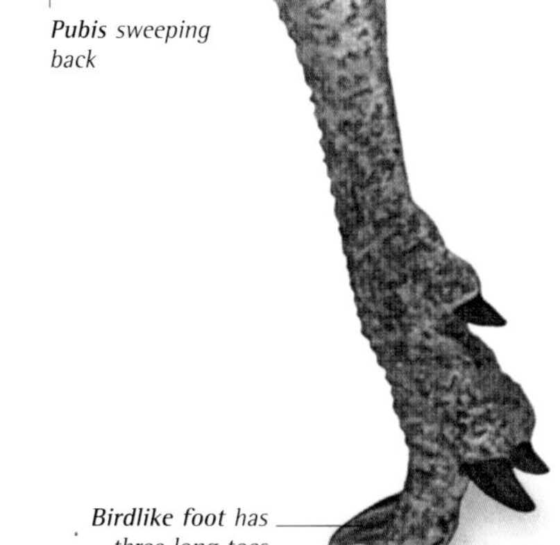

Neural spine

Long tail

Ischium

Pubis sweeping back

Birdlike foot has three long toes

HERBIVORE TEETH ►
The teeth of an ornithopod were tightly packed together and arranged in ranks, or batteries, at the back of the mouth. Often the teeth were coarsely serrated like a cheese grater, as can be seen from these *Iguanodon* fossilized teeth. The jaw was jointed in such a way that it allowed the surfaces of the teeth to grind past one another to pulp the plant food efficiently. The teeth wore out like the tooth on the right because of this constant grinding. They were replaced by new teeth that grew from underneath.

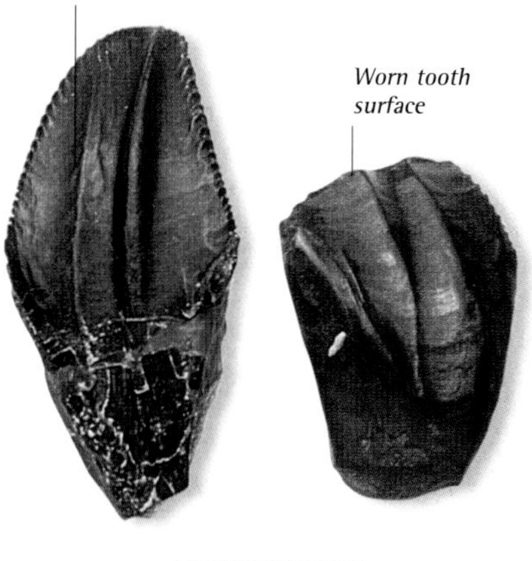

Fresh tooth with serrated edges

Worn tooth surface

IGUANODON TEETH

SOME BIPEDAL HERBIVORES

JURASSIC PERIOD

HETERODONTOSAURUS

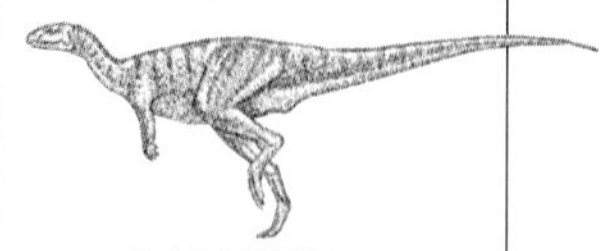

DRYOSAURUS

CAMPTOSAURUS

CRETACEOUS PERIOD

IGUANODON

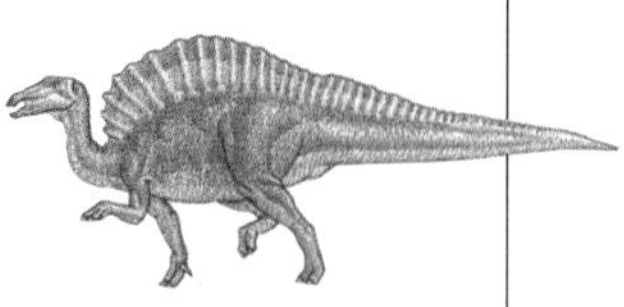

OURANOSAURUS

MAIASAURA

PARASAUROPHOLUS

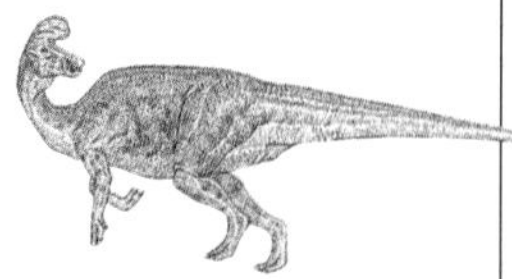

LAMBEOSAURUS

ORODROMEUS

THESCELOSAURUS

HORNED AND ARMORED

Three major groups of plant-eating dinosaurs were well equipped to defend themselves—some of the larger ones against the fiercest of the carnivores. The plated stegosaurs were largely a Jurassic group and were armed with plates and tail spines. The horned ceratopsians lived at the end of the Cretaceous and sported a heavy neck shield and an array of horns. The armored ankylosaurs were among the last of the dinosaurs to appear and had backs covered with armored shields and horny plates.

▼ EXTERNAL ANATOMY

The heavy horned, plated, or armored dinosaurs walked on four feet. Their hind legs were bigger than the front legs, suggesting that the dinosaurs evolved from earlier two-footed types, possibly resembling ornithopods. Like the ornithopods, they had mouths adapted for chewing, with teeth that could chop or grind. They also had beaks at the front of their mouths and cheeks at the sides. Most carried a mosaic of fine studded armor, or flat plates called scutes, on their bodies.

Scaly skin covered with flat plates called scutes

Armored body studded with spikes

Powerful legs to carry heavy body

Tail club could be wielded as a weapon

Toothless beak

Toes

Broad feet

EUOPLOCEPHALUS (AN ANKYLOSAUR)

INTERNAL ANATOMY ►

All the armored dinosaurs had ornithischian (birdlike) hips. The big plant-eating gut was carried well back like the ornithopods, but the armor usually made the animal too heavy to be bipedal. The weapons—horns, plates, tail clubs—were supported by strong muscles, which meant they could be put to good use when the animal needed to defend itself. Powerful leg muscles were needed to support the heavy body.

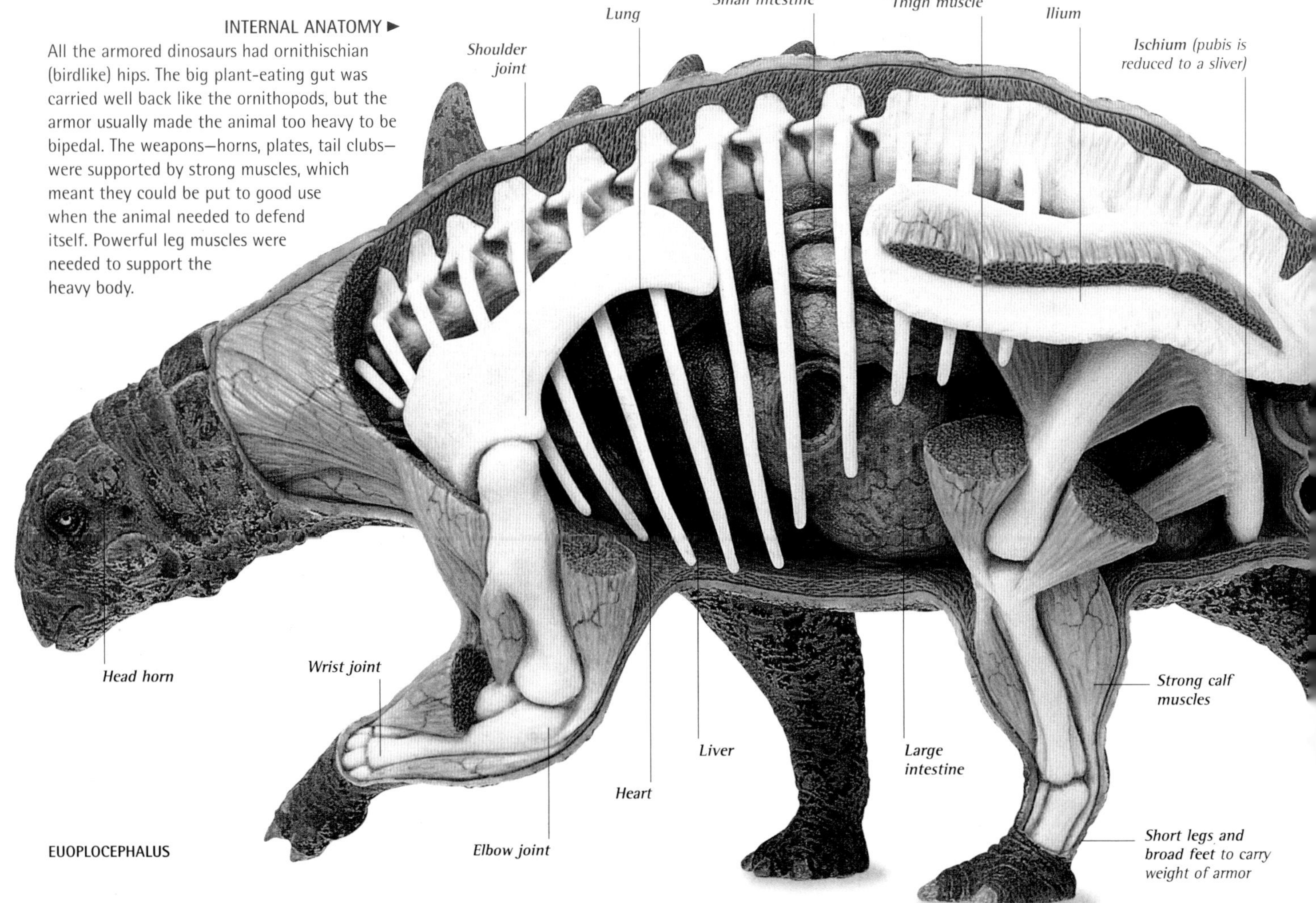

EUOPLOCEPHALUS

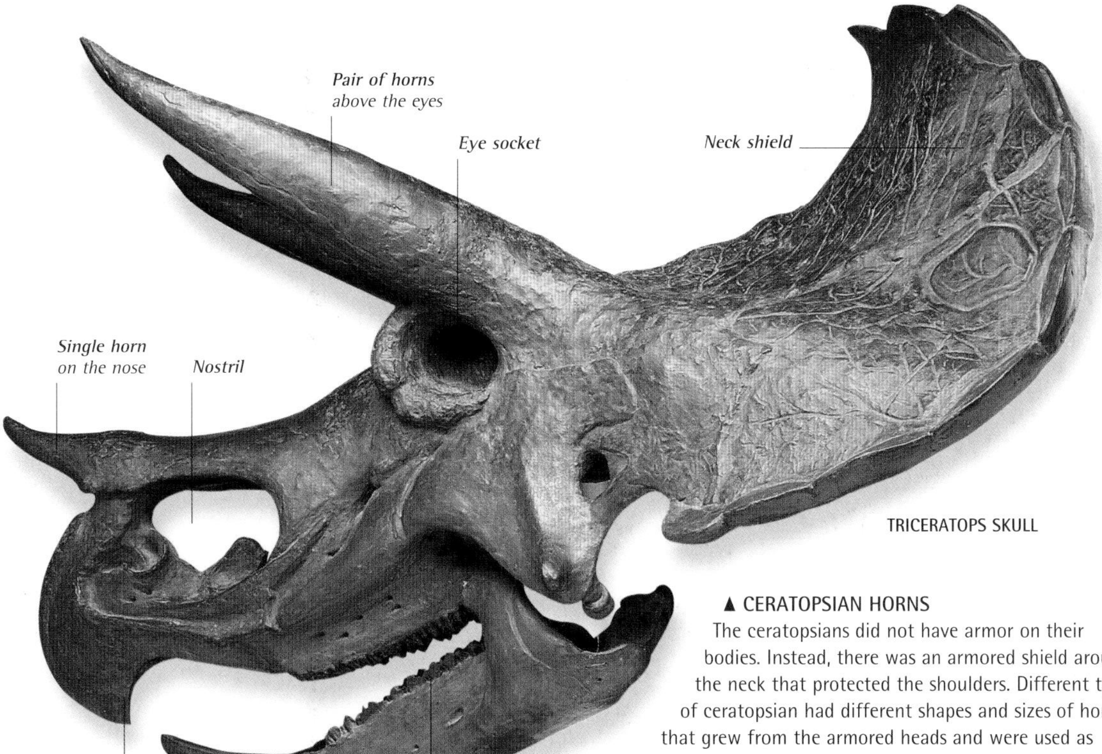

Pair of horns above the eyes

Eye socket

Neck shield

Single horn on the nose

Nostril

Beak for snipping leaves

Chopping teeth

TRICERATOPS SKULL

▲ CERATOPSIAN HORNS

The ceratopsians did not have armor on their bodies. Instead, there was an armored shield around the neck that protected the shoulders. Different types of ceratopsian had different shapes and sizes of horns that grew from the armored heads and were used as weapons or for display. Some had a single straight or curved horn on the nose. Others had horns above the eyes. Yet others had horns arranged around their necks.

ANKYLOSAUR SCUTES ►

The ankylosaurs had armor embedded in the skin of their heads, necks, backs, and tails. Their armor was a fine mosaic of studs and scutes. The scutes were platelike masses of bone covered in horn and usually had a keel (ridge) along the center. Some were armed with shoulder-mounted spikes. Others, such as *Euoplocephalus*, had a club on the end of their tail. Big ankylosaurs even had armored eyelids.

Keel

GASTONIA SCUTE

protection

◄ STEGOSAUR PLATES

Stegosaurs had a series of flat plates and spines that stuck up in a double line along their backs. The plates may have been covered in horn, with bladelike edges and corners, and used for defense. Or they may have been covered with skin and used as heat-exchangers. Turning the plates to face the sun would have warmed the blood in them and so warmed the stegosaur. Turning them into the wind would have cooled them.

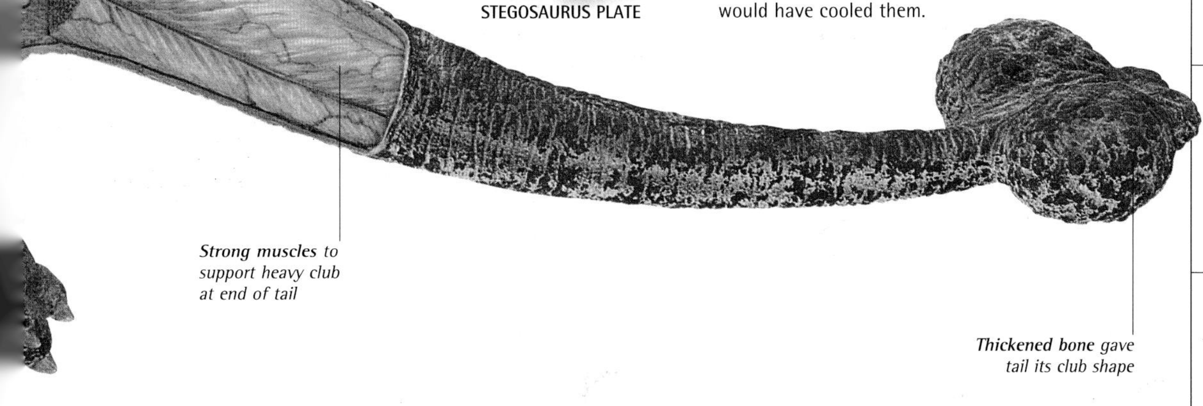

STEGOSAURUS PLATE

Strong muscles to support heavy club at end of tail

Thickened bone gave tail its club shape

SOME ARMORED DINOSAURS

JURASSIC PERIOD

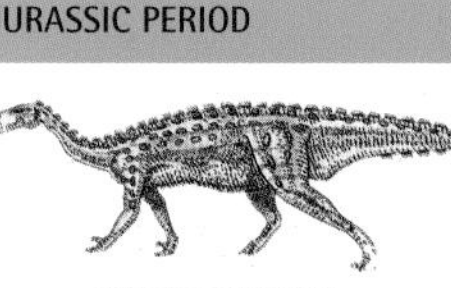

SCELIDOSAURUS

STEGOSAURUS

CRETACEOUS PERIOD

ACANTHOPHOLIS

PROTOCERATOPS

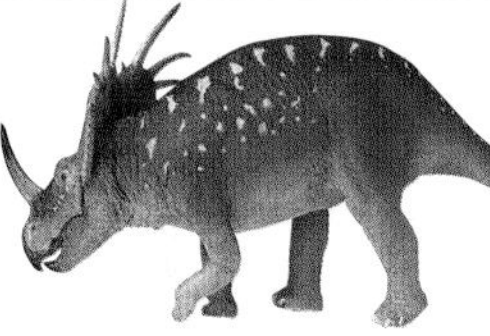

STYRACOSAURUS

PENTACERATOPS

ANKLYOSAURUS

TRICERATOPS

MOVING AROUND

No one has ever seen a dinosaur in action. However, the bones and the joints of fossilized skeletons can give us clues as to how the animals moved. Marks on the bones can show where the muscles were attached. The articulation of the bones (the way the bones move in relation to one another) shows how the limbs were flexed and how far they could reach. The size of the feet shows whether a dinosaur was a slow plodder (big, solid feet) or a fast runner (lightweight feet). Above all, scientists can find out more about dinosaurs by comparing what they know with the anatomy and lifestyle of modern animals.

▲ RUNNING STYLE OF AN OSTRICH
The modern equivalent of a running dinosaur would be one of today's flightless birds, such as an ostrich (above) or a rhea. Like a dinosaur, these keep their bodies horizontal and their heads high. The long legs, with their muscular thighs and their lightweight feet, are very similar to those of their theropod ancestors.

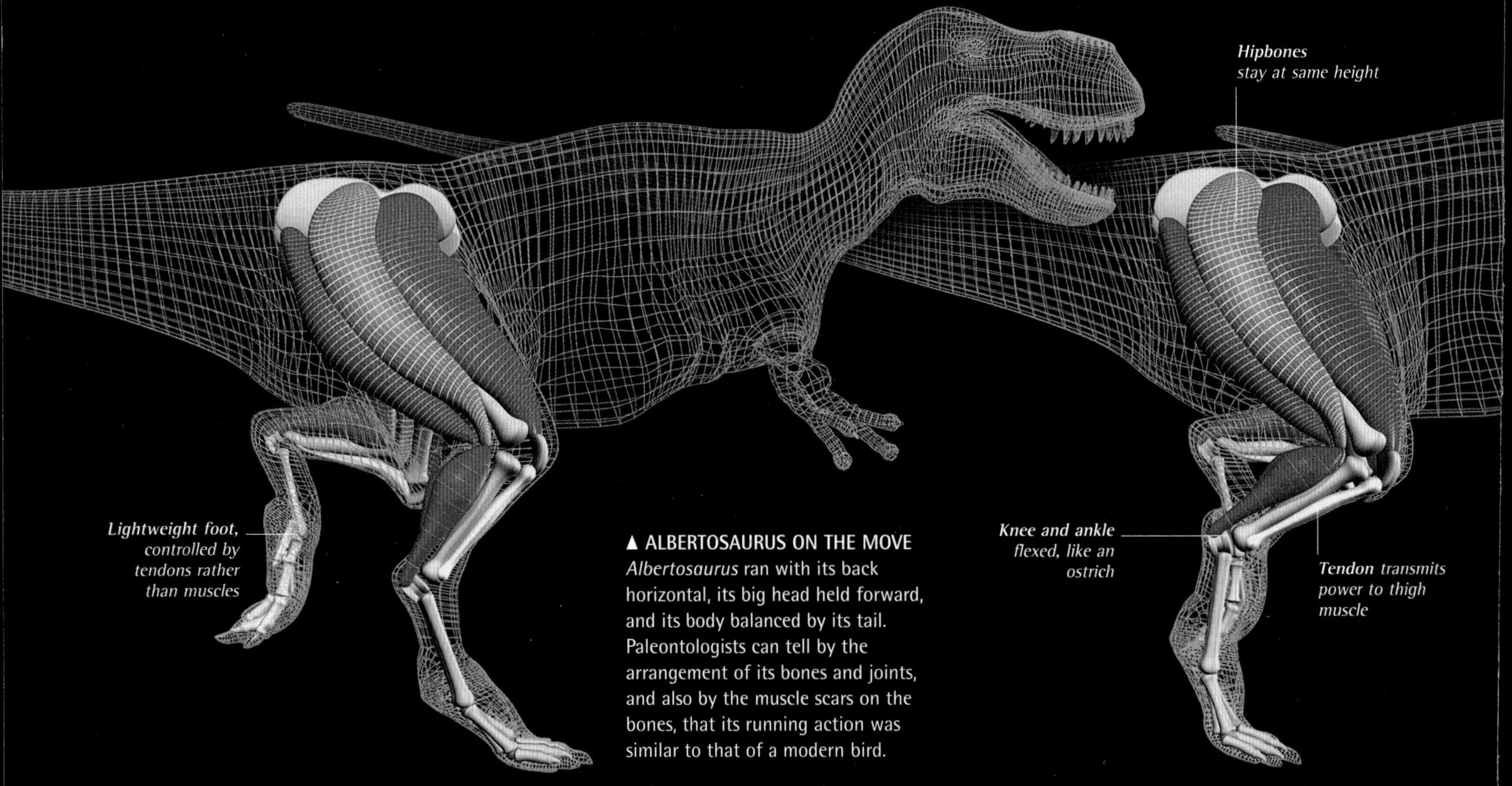

Hipbones stay at same height

Lightweight foot, controlled by tendons rather than muscles

Knee and ankle flexed, like an ostrich

Tendon transmits power to thigh muscle

▲ ALBERTOSAURUS ON THE MOVE
Albertosaurus ran with its back horizontal, its big head held forward, and its body balanced by its tail. Paleontologists can tell by the arrangement of its bones and joints, and also by the muscle scars on the bones, that its running action was similar to that of a modern bird.

HOW A TYRANNOSAURUS STOOD UP

LEVERING UP
The shape of the hipbones suggests that *Tyrannosaurus* would have rested flat on its belly. While it was in this position, the weight of the hips would have been carried by the broad "boot" at the end of the pubisbone. How, then, did the dinosaur manage to stand up? It is possible that it used its tiny arms to give itself some leverage.

LEANING FORWARD
As *Tyrannosaurus* rose to its feet by straightening its legs, it would have been in danger of toppling forward and sliding along the ground. The little arms, however, would have gripped the ground and prevented this from happening. If the head was thrown backward, this would have moved the center of gravity back toward the hip.

UPRIGHT STANCE
The normal stance of a *Tyrannosaurus* was with the body held horizontally, the head pushed forward, and the tail out at the back to provide balance. Like this, the dinosaur would have been a formidable fighting machine propelled by powerful legs, with its main weapons—its teeth—held well forward to attack or defend.

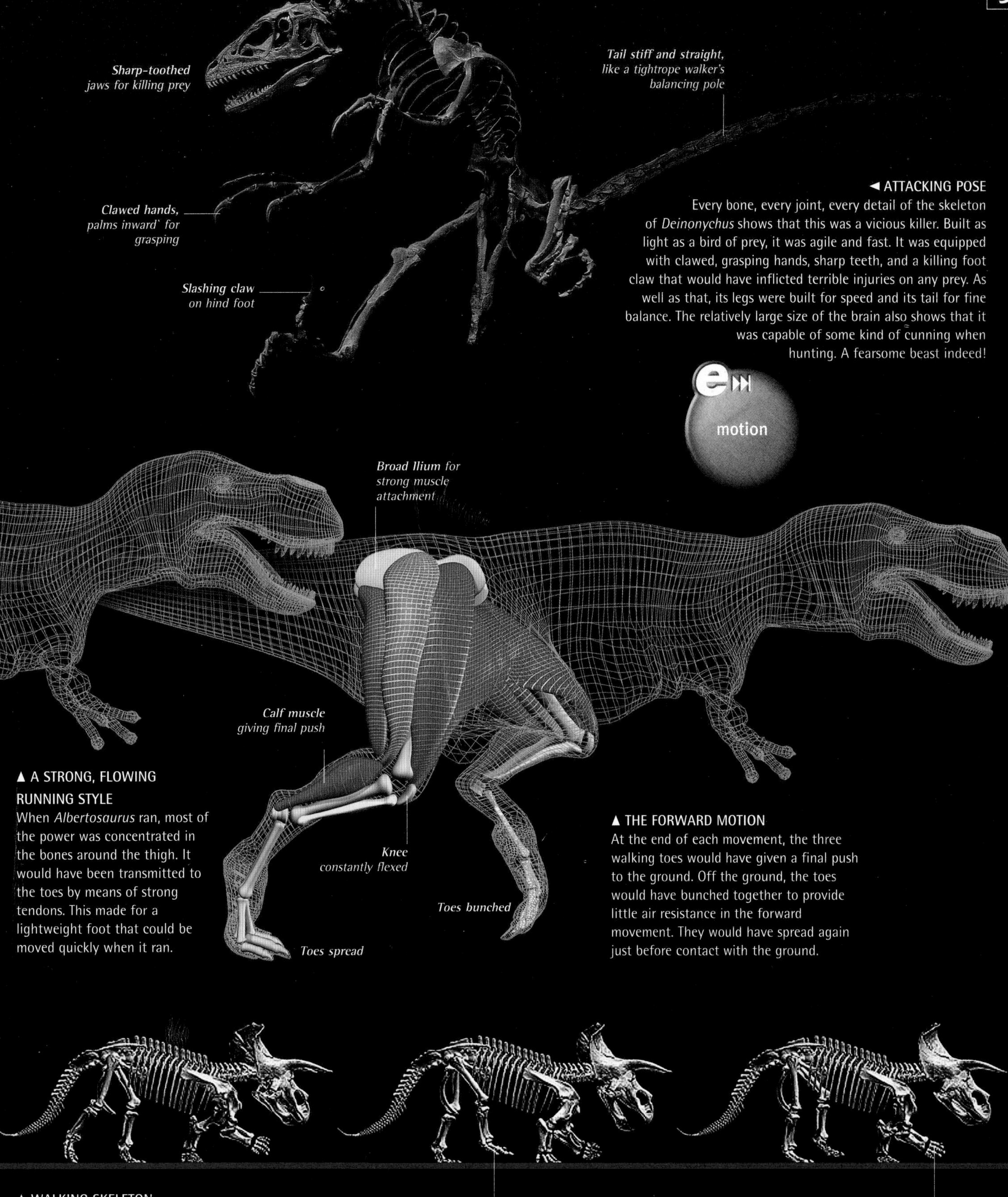

◄ ATTACKING POSE
Every bone, every joint, every detail of the skeleton of *Deinonychus* shows that this was a vicious killer. Built as light as a bird of prey, it was agile and fast. It was equipped with clawed, grasping hands, sharp teeth, and a killing foot claw that would have inflicted terrible injuries on any prey. As well as that, its legs were built for speed and its tail for fine balance. The relatively large size of the brain also shows that it was capable of some kind of cunning when hunting. A fearsome beast indeed!

▲ A STRONG, FLOWING RUNNING STYLE
When *Albertosaurus* ran, most of the power was concentrated in the bones around the thigh. It would have been transmitted to the toes by means of strong tendons. This made for a lightweight foot that could be moved quickly when it ran.

▲ THE FORWARD MOTION
At the end of each movement, the three walking toes would have given a final push to the ground. Off the ground, the toes would have bunched together to provide little air resistance in the forward movement. They would have spread again just before contact with the ground.

▲ WALKING SKELETON
In 2001, the Smithsonian Institution in Washington D.C. had to replace its famous mounted skeleton of a *Triceratops*. It had been standing for a century and was deteriorating. To help in the reconstruction, every bone was measured and a virtual skeleton constructed on a computer. Not only did this help in preparing casts of the bones, but it could be animated to show how a living *Triceratops* would have walked—how it swung its legs, how it carried its head, and how it balanced with its tail.

FEEDING

Throughout the dinosaur era, communities of dinosaurs were made up of plant-eaters (herbivores) and meat-eaters (carnivores). Different dinosaurs had different feeding habits. Giant herbivorous dinosaurs, such as the sauropods, munched high in the treetops. Smaller plant-eaters were well adapted for chomping on lower-level plants, or grazing on ground cover. Large predators, and medium-sized pack hunters, tended to eat the meat of other dinosaurs. Smaller meat-eaters ate animals such as lizards, and insects.

◄ TREETOP BROWSER
Not only was the 40-ton *Barosaurus* one of the heaviest sauropods of the Jurassic Period, it had one of the longest necks of any dinosaur. A fully-grown adult measured about 89 ft (27 m) from nose to tail. Its neck accounted for one-third of its length. Why such a long neck? It is thought that *Barosaurus* stretched up to leaves that were out of reach of shorter-necked plant-eaters.

▲ BALANCING ACT
Barosaurus had short front legs and longer back legs. This meant there was less weight at the front its body, so it may have been able to rock back on its hind legs, lifting its lightweight front legs off the ground to reach up to plants growing 49 ft (15 m) above the ground. It could have used its tail to support it in this stretching position. *Barosaurus* could not have remained upright for very long as its bones and muscles would have been under considerable strain.

▲ LOW BROWSER
Triceratops lived about 70 million years ago, at the end of the Cretaceous Period. It ate the new flowering plants that first appeared at this time, such as magnolia, oak, and laurel. *Triceratops* used its sharp beak to snip off leaves, twigs, and bark, and could reach food that grew up to 9 ft (3 m) from the ground. Only taller plants were safe from its giant appetite. It lived in herds, and grazed in forests and along the edges of rivers and swamps.

VEGETARIAN MOUTHS

DIFFERENT-TOOTHED MOUTH
Heterodontosaurus had three kinds of teeth. Incisors at the front of the top jaw were used for cutting. Tusklike teeth may have been used for defense. Chisel-like teeth were for shredding food plants.

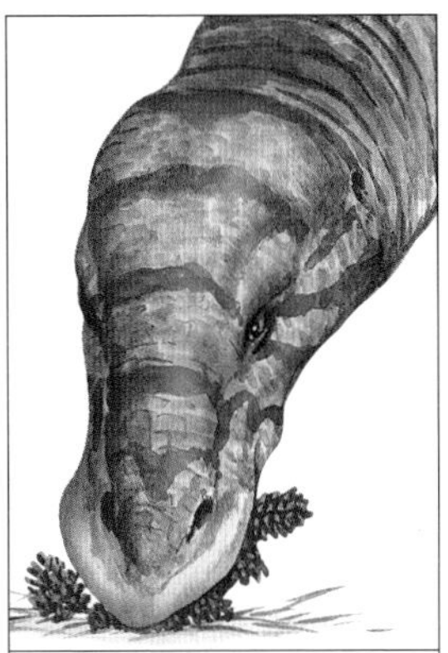

MIXED DIET
Edmontosaurus had a broad snout for gathering up big mouthfuls of different kinds of vegetation. It used its toothless beak for cropping, and its cheek teeth for cutting up and chewing food.

PICKY EATER
Hypsilophodon had high-ridged cheek teeth, which made it very efficient at chewing tough vegetation. Its narrow mouth helped this dinosaur to choose which plants to pick at.

CRETACEOUS FOOD CHAIN

Any animal community has food chains of predators and prey. Interlinked chains form a food web. This diagram shows who ate whom in Late Cretaceous western North America. Arrows point to the predator. The top predators were the tyrannosaurs, but all dinosaurs ultimately depended on plants.

FOOD CHAIN KEY
- *Insect food*
- *Lizard food*
- *Herbivores' food*
- *Ornithomimid food*
- *Dromaeosaur food*
- *Tyrannosaur food*

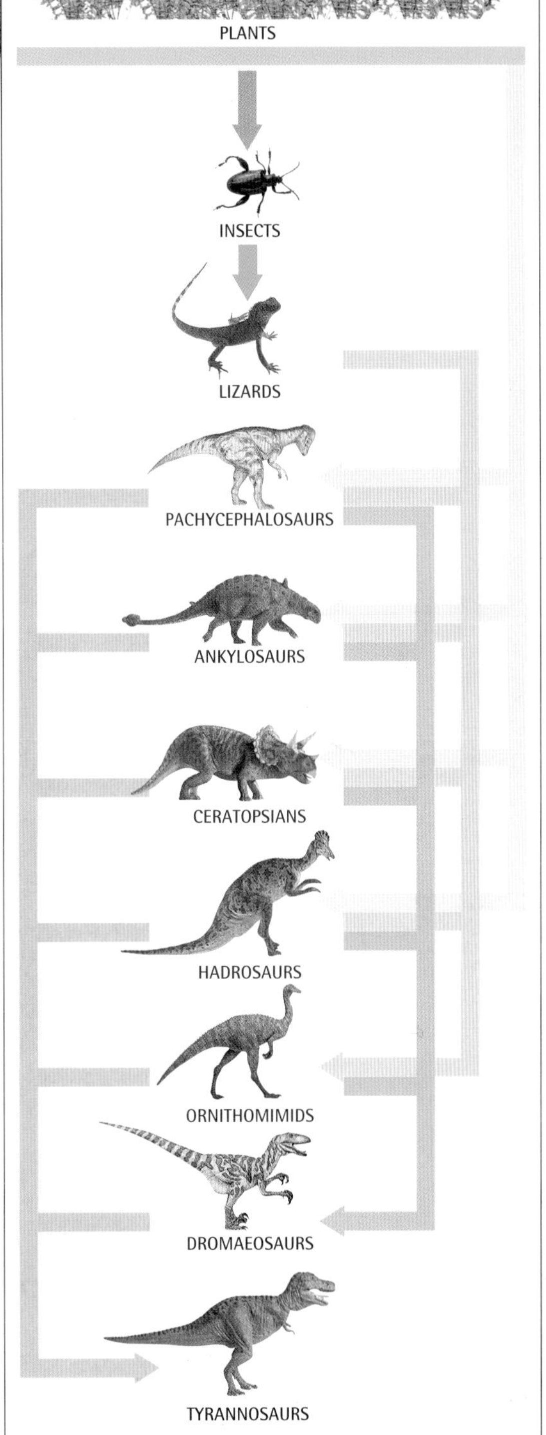

DIGESTIVE SYSTEMS

Carnivorous and herbivorous dinosaurs are quite easy to tell apart. As well as the different types of jaws and teeth, their body shapes were distinct from one another because of the different digestive systems they needed to absorb their food. Carnivores had much simpler digestive systems than herbivores, and their hipbones were arranged differently. These two characteristics meant that the carnivorous theropods were two-legged, the herbivorous sauropods were four-legged, and the herbivorous ornithopods could move around on either their hind legs or on all fours.

▲ CARNIVORE'S SERRATED TOOTH
The tooth of a carnivorous dinosaur such as *Tyrannosaurus* is shaped like a steak knife. It is narrow like a blade, for slicing through flesh. It is also pointed for making incisions in its prey. Its edges had dozens of little serrations, like a fine saw, to tear through tough meat and tendons. Carnivore teeth quickly wore out and were easily damaged, breaking off if the dinosaur chomped on bone. Inside a carnivore's jaw, other teeth were constantly growing and replacing those teeth that were lost.

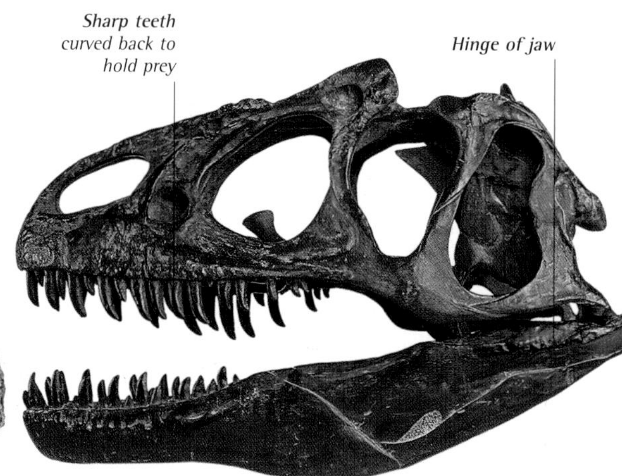

CARNIVORE'S JAWS FOR TEARING ▲
A carnivore's skull, like this one of an *Allosaurus*, was arranged so that it could work backward and forward. This movement allowed the rows of teeth to shear past each other, tearing the flesh of its prey between them. The teeth were curved back like barbs, so that anything held in its jaws would not stuggle out. The lightweight latticework of the skull and jaws meant that the sides of the mouth were able to move outward. This widened the mouth so that the carnivore could swallow huge mouthfuls.

◄ CARNIVORE'S STOMACH
There are very few fossils that actually show the insides of a dinosaur. However, the digestive system of a carnivore would have been quite simple and fairly small compared with the size of the animal. Meat does not have tough fibers, so it is easily digested, and a carnivorous dinosaur did not need the huge guts of a herbivore to process its food. Nearly all of the carnivore's digestive system would have been carried in front of the pubisbone of the lizardlike hips. This compact arrangement would have allowed the dinosaur to move swiftly when chasing its prey.

e feeding

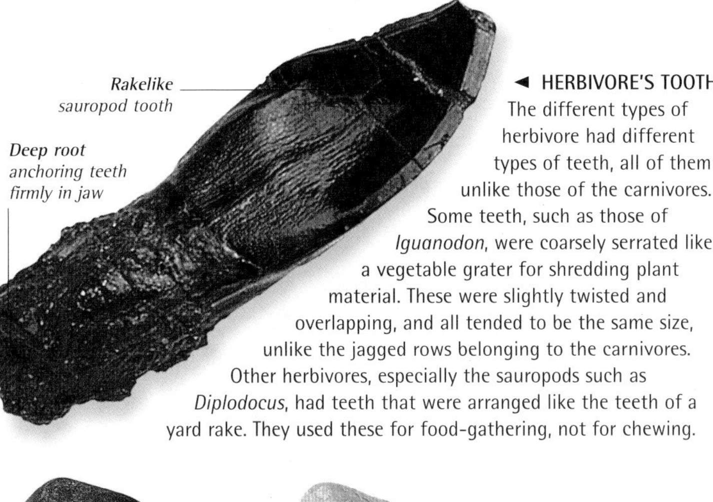

◄ HERBIVORE'S TOOTH
The different types of herbivore had different types of teeth, all of them unlike those of the carnivores. Some teeth, such as those of *Iguanodon*, were coarsely serrated like a vegetable grater for shredding plant material. These were slightly twisted and overlapping, and all tended to be the same size, unlike the jagged rows belonging to the carnivores. Other herbivores, especially the sauropods such as *Diplodocus*, had teeth that were arranged like the teeth of a yard rake. They used these for food-gathering, not for chewing.

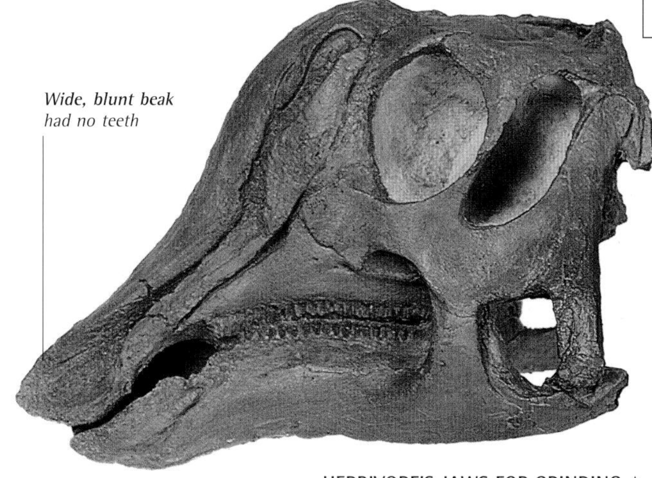

HERBIVORE'S JAWS FOR GRINDING ▲
This skull of a young *Lambeosaurus* shows the features of a typical ornithopod. The front of the mouth has a beak for snipping shoots and gathering plants. The position of the teeth right inside the mouth shows that there were cheek pouches at the side. The teeth were arranged in grinding rows, or batteries, that slid past each other, pulping the food while it was held in the cheeks. The angle of the jaw hinge helped the chewing muscles to work efficiently.

Surface worn smooth by grinding together

▲ STOMACH STONES
Sauropods spent all their time raking the leaves from trees and plants and swallowing them. They did not chew because their teeth were the wrong shape. So, to break down their food, the herbivores swallowed stones. These gathered in an area of the stomach called the gizzard, forming a grinding mill to mash up the plant material. Skeletons of sauropods are sometimes found with polished stones, or gastroliths. Today's plant-eating birds, such as chickens, swallow grit for the same reason.

IGUANODON

FEATURES OF A SAUROPOD'S STOMACH

The digestive system of a sauropod such as this *Brachiosaurus* was much bigger than that of the carnivores. It needed a large gut to break down the fibers in the plant material it ate. A sauropod would also have had a gizzard, where stomach stones ground up the food before it was passed into the stomach. All this weight had to be carried in front of the pubisbone, and that is why most sauropods could not support themselves for long on just their back legs.

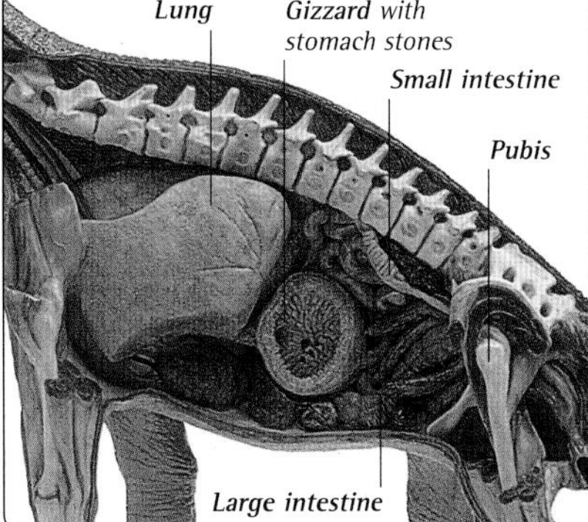

▲ ORNITHOPOD'S STOMACH
The digestive system of a two-footed ornithopod was much bigger than that of a carnivore—more like a sauropod's. However, unlike in a sauropod, it was carried well back in the body and the pubisbone was swept back out of the way. This meant the center of gravity of the animal was much closer to the hips and it could move around on its hind legs. It also lacked a gizzard. With its efficient chewing system, an ornithopod did not need stomach stones.

ATTACK

Flesh-eating dinosaurs had different methods of attack that varied with their size, agility, and victims. Large predators crept up on giant herbivores and killed them with a sudden charge. Smaller hunters chased game at speed. Predators struck mainly with their fangs and claws, but some, such as *Baryonyx*, might have seized fish in their crocodilelike jaws. It is also possible that certain dinosaurs poisoned their unfortunate victims with a toxic bite.

▲ SNATCH AND GRAB
Standing perfectly still, knee-high in water, *Baryonyx* might have snatched up unsuspecting fish in its narrow jaws, and pierced the scaly prey with its slender teeth. It may also have used its powerful forelimbs and curved thumb claws to hook fish from the water. We know this dinosaur ate fish because paleontologists found the scales of *Lepidotes*, a large fish, in its ribcage.

BARYONYX CLAW

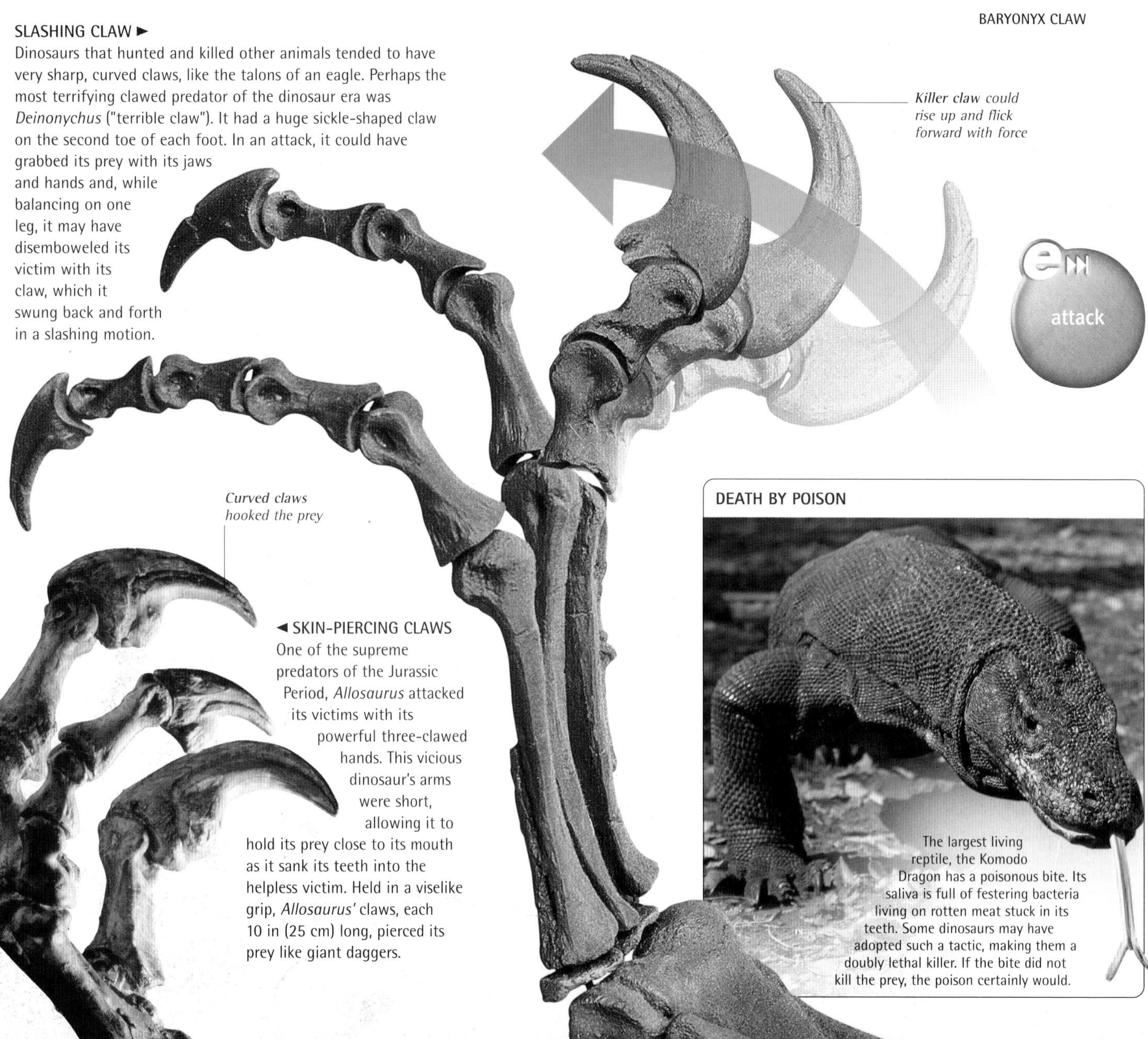

SLASHING CLAW ►
Dinosaurs that hunted and killed other animals tended to have very sharp, curved claws, like the talons of an eagle. Perhaps the most terrifying clawed predator of the dinosaur era was *Deinonychus* ("terrible claw"). It had a huge sickle-shaped claw on the second toe of each foot. In an attack, it could have grabbed its prey with its jaws and hands and, while balancing on one leg, it may have disemboweled its victim with its claw, which it swung back and forth in a slashing motion.

◄ SKIN-PIERCING CLAWS
One of the supreme predators of the Jurassic Period, *Allosaurus* attacked its victims with its powerful three-clawed hands. This vicious dinosaur's arms were short, allowing it to hold its prey close to its mouth as it sank its teeth into the helpless victim. Held in a viselike grip, *Allosaurus'* claws, each 10 in (25 cm) long, pierced its prey like giant daggers.

DEATH BY POISON

The largest living reptile, the Komodo Dragon has a poisonous bite. Its saliva is full of festering bacteria living on rotten meat stuck in its teeth. Some dinosaurs may have adopted such a tactic, making them a doubly lethal killer. If the bite did not kill the prey, the poison certainly would.

CHASING DOWN PREY ►

Compsognathus and other lightweight theropods had a slender build, with long necks and balancing tails. Such features would have made them fast sprinters. These predators would have used their speed and agility to pursue lizards, frogs, and other small creatures. When they caught up with them, they either grabbed them with their clawed hands, or thrust out their long necks and snapped up their victim with their narrow, sharp-toothed jaws.

Jaws agape and ready to snap shut on a victim

SUDDEN AMBUSH ►

Giganotosaurus was an immense carnivore. It probably hunted by ambush, hiding in trees until a slow-moving herbivore came by. With jaws gaping wide, *Giganotosaurus* could have run at its prey head on. Powerful muscles slammed its jaw shut, and its 7 in- (18 cm-) long teeth sliced deep into its victim's flesh. Like a tiger, it probably gorged itself, then went days before its next meal.

Bony tail was held stiff and straight as Gallimimus ran

Three clawed toes on each foot

▲ SPRINT FROM DANGER
Not all dinosaurs were huge and lumbering. Some were built for speed, which they used to beat a hasty retreat from attackers. *Gallimimus* had the physical features of a sprinter. With its long, thin back legs, *Gallimimus* could take large strides efficiently, and its light body was pefectly balanced by a slender tail. By measuring their legs and comparing their shape to those of modern animals, experts have estimated that *Gallimimus* reached speeds of 35 mph (56 kph). This is almost as fast as a racehorse, and certainly speedy enough to evade capture by a larger predator, such as *Tyrannosaurus*.

DEFENSE

The dinosaur world was not overrun by gangs of vicious killers. Most dinosaurs were peaceful creatures that never attacked anything. Even so, each group had different ways of protecting itself against attack. For speedy dinosaurs, being able to outrun a predator was their main means of self-defense. Large sauropods may have used their great bulk to intimidate their enemies. Some dinosaurs carried weapons to defend themselves, striking back with their tails, horns, or claws. Other dinosaurs were more passive and relied on camouflage or body armor for their protection.

e protection

◄ BLENDING IN
Well-preserved fossils of dinosaur skin are rare and do not show the color of the skin. We know that patterns and color help modern reptiles to hide from their enemies, so it seems certain dinosaurs would also have used color to blend in with their surroundings. If *Iguanodon* was green, it might have escaped detection by the flesh-eating predators that prowled its forest home.

CLUB TAIL ►

No living reptiles have defensive tails with attachments as spectacular as the clubs used by the ankylosaurs. The huge club at the end of *Euoplocephalus*'s tail was made out of several chunks of bone, all fused together into a single lump. Powerful tail muscles were used to swing the tail from side to side, delivering a bone-shattering blow to an attacker.

◄ WHIP TAIL

Heavy and lumbering sauropods, such as *Diplodocus*, could inflict stinging blows on attackers with their tapered, whiplike tails. Aside from their daunting size, this was their main form of defense. The ends of their tails were made up of narrow, cyclinder-shaped bones which were designed to lash out sharply. The mere sound of the tail cracking may have scared away a predator.

ARMORED JACKET ▼

With their protective studs, plates, and spikes, armored dinosaurs were like walking fortresses. When under attack, they may have crouched down to protect their soft bellies, presenting a completely armored shell. The armored dinosaurs evolved from small, lightweight species with just a few rows of studs on their back into huge beasts with full suits of armor.

WINNING A MATE

All animals must reproduce themselves if their species is to survive. Today's animals have developed their own special ways of attracting mates. They send out signals through displays of body color and distinctive call signs, and also by behaving differently at certain times of the year. By observing modern animals, it is possible to suggest how dinosaurs might have found their mates. Some species of dinosaurs developed highly distinctive features, such as head crests, bone skull domes, and extra-long face horns. Each of these features may have had its own uses in helping its owner to win a mate.

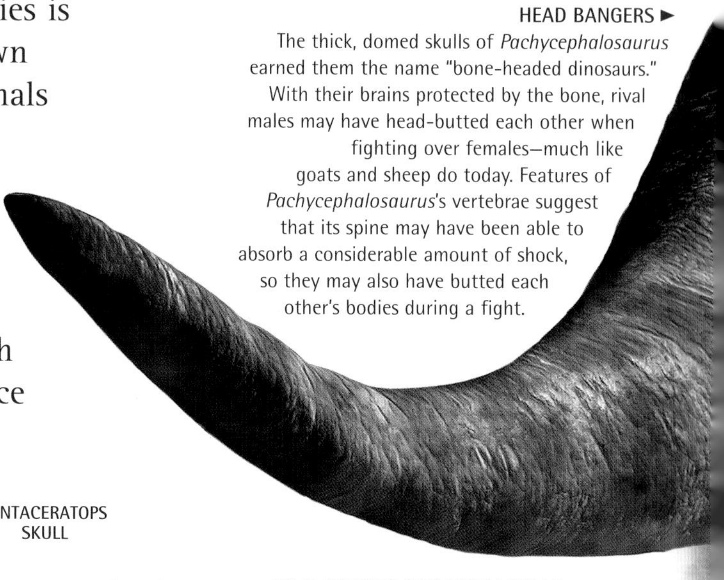

HEAD BANGERS ►
The thick, domed skulls of *Pachycephalosaurus* earned them the name "bone-headed dinosaurs." With their brains protected by the bone, rival males may have head-butted each other when fighting over females—much like goats and sheep do today. Features of *Pachycephalosaurus*'s vertebrae suggest that its spine may have been able to absorb a considerable amount of shock, so they may also have butted each other's bodies during a fight.

PENTACERATOPS SKULL

Brow horns grew above its eyes

◄ FIVE-HORNED FACE WITH FRILLS
Pentaceratops means "five-horned face," but despite it name, this dinosaur really had three horns. It had a pair of long, curved ones on its forehead and a short horn on its snout. The other two "horns" that seemed to grow from the sides of its face were actually extended cheekbones. *Pentaceratops*'s fantastic frill was nearly 3 ft (1 m) wide. Huge, empty, skin-covered gaps in the bone meant the frill was lightweight.

▼ BATTLING MALES
In a Late Cretaceous woodland clearing in North America, about 70 million years ago, a pair of adult *Pentaceratops* face up to each other in a contest for a mate. Their neck frills are covered in richly pattered skin, perhaps designed to impress females. The bone frills also act like shields, deflecting stabs from incoming horns and protecting the animals' soft bodies. At the end of the battle, the winner celebrates by snorting triumphantly and pawing at the ground.

Opponent shoves rival to gain ground

Hard head could withstand very heavy knocks

mating

BIGGEST BONE-HEAD ►

Pachycephalosaurus had the largest skull of all the bone-headed dinosaurs. Its head was 2 ft 7 in (80 cm) long and the dome was made of solid bone 10 in (25 cm) thick. There were bony nodules at the back, and on its snout were several short, bony spikes. These would have scratched and scraped an opponent in a head-to-head tussle.

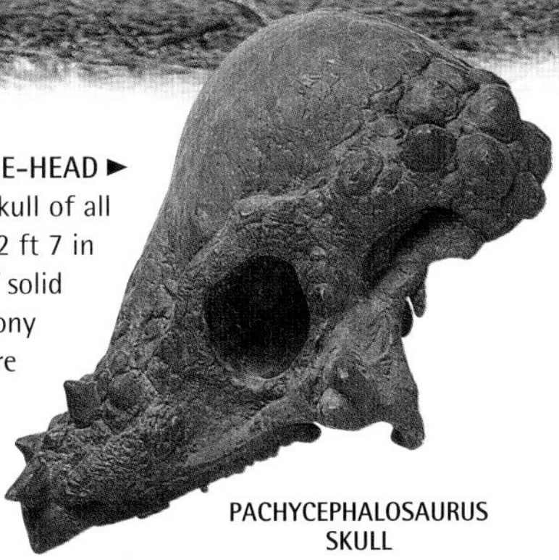

PACHYCEPHALOSAURUS SKULL

HEAD CREST FOR COURTING

Corythosaurus was a member of the hadrosaur, or duckbill, family of dinosaurs. On top of its head was a semicircular, helmet-shaped bony crest. Males appear to have grown larger crests than females. This suggests they may have been used in courtship rituals when males competed for the attention of females. The crests may have been colored, possibly changing color in the mating season. Inside the crests were passages, through which *Corythosaurus* could snort and blow to make distinctive sounds. These sounds could have been mating calls which attracted the females.

Skin on crest may have had an eye-catching pattern

CORYTHOSAURUS

◄ RUTTING STAGS

Ideas of how the horned dinosaurs used their frills and horns come partially from the rutting behavior of modern stags (male deer). In the fall, the rutting season takes place, when adult stags compete for hinds (females). Stags roar at each other, then clash heads and lock antlers in an attempt to shove each other backward. The one who gains the most ground gets to mate with the hinds.

BODY TEMPERATURE

Scientists cannot agree whether dinosaurs were cold-blooded or warm-blooded. Cold-blooded animals, such as reptiles, become hot or cold, depending on the temperature of their environment. Warm-blooded animals, such as birds, have a regulation system that keeps the body temperature constant. A warm-blooded animal needs to eat ten times as much food as a cold-blooded animal, just to fuel this system. It seems likely that giant herbivores, such as sauropods, could not have eaten enough to support such a system, and were cold-blooded. The carnivorous, active theropods, however, may have been warm-blooded.

When too cold a lizard warms up by basking in the heat of the sun

When too hot a lizard hides in the shade

▲ TEMPERATURE CONTROL
A lizard shows the behavior typical of a cold-blooded animal. It has no internal mechanism to regulate its body temperature. When the environment turns cold, the lizard becomes cold and inactive. When the environment heats up, the lizard warms up too, and becomes active. It is capable of great bursts of speed, but it has to spend much of its time either basking in the sun or hiding in the shade.

SOLAR PANELS ▼
Stegosaurus was one of the plated dinosaurs, with a series of bony plates up along its back. When it was discovered in the 1870s, scientists assumed the plates were covered in horn and used for defense. Then, a century later, tracks of blood vessels were found in fossils of the plates. This gave rise to the idea that the plates may actually have been covered in skin, not horn, and used for temperature regulation instead of defense.

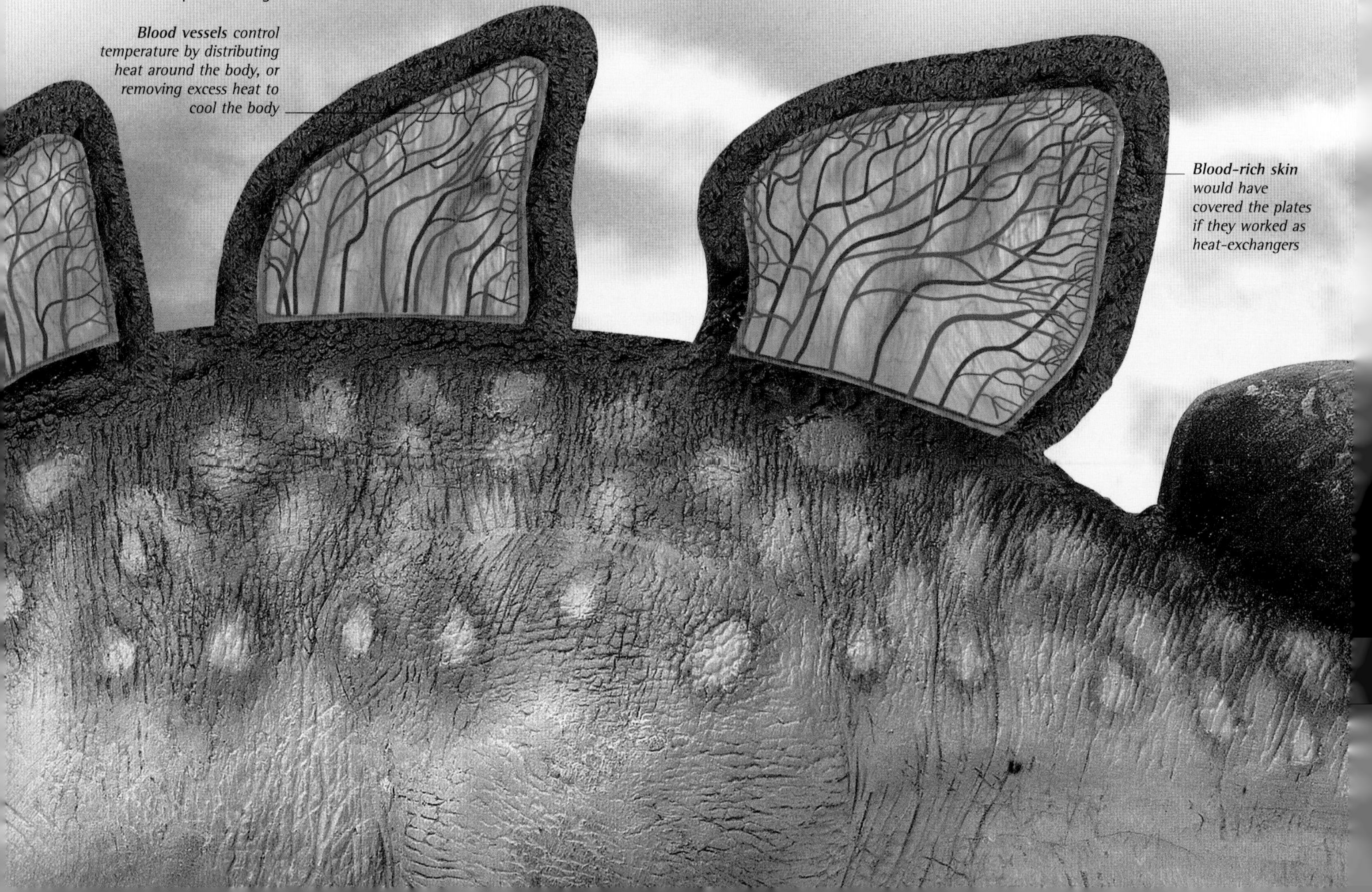

Blood vessels control temperature by distributing heat around the body, or removing excess heat to cool the body

Blood-rich skin would have covered the plates if they worked as heat-exchangers

FUZZY RAPTOR

The fine detail of the feathers is preserved in volcanic dust

Soft, downy feathers on the body would have been used for insulation

ENLARGED VIEW OF FEATHER-COVERED BODY

Each hand had 3 long, narrow fingers with sharp claws

Tail feathers would have been used for display

COMPLETE SKELETON OF A FUZZY RAPTOR

For decades, scientists have argued over whether dinosaurs were warm-blooded or cold-blooded. Proof was hard to find, one way or another. Then, at the turn of this century, the beautifully preserved fossil of a chicken-sized theropod was found in China. The detailed fossil showed that the animal was covered in fine feathers. Only warm-blooded animals would need an insulating covering such as this. For many scientists, the discovery was the evidence they had been looking for. It showed that the small theropods, at least, were warm-blooded and had an active lifestyle. As yet, this feathered dromaeosaur has not been given a scientific name, and is only referred to as the "fuzzy raptor." The discovery of this fossil also seems to support the theory that birds evolved from meat-eating dinosaurs.

HEAT REGULATION ►

If the plates of *Stegosaurus* were used for temperature regulation, they might have worked a little like solar panels. If the animal was feeling cold, it could turn so that the broad sides of its plates, with their large surface area, faced the sun to absorb its heat. If it wanted to cool down, the animal would turn its plates away from the sun. It might also turn to find a position in the wind so moving air would circulate around the plates and cool them.

Plates may also have served to attract mates, or to help animals of the same species to recognize each other

Circulation of air around the plates would carry excess heat away

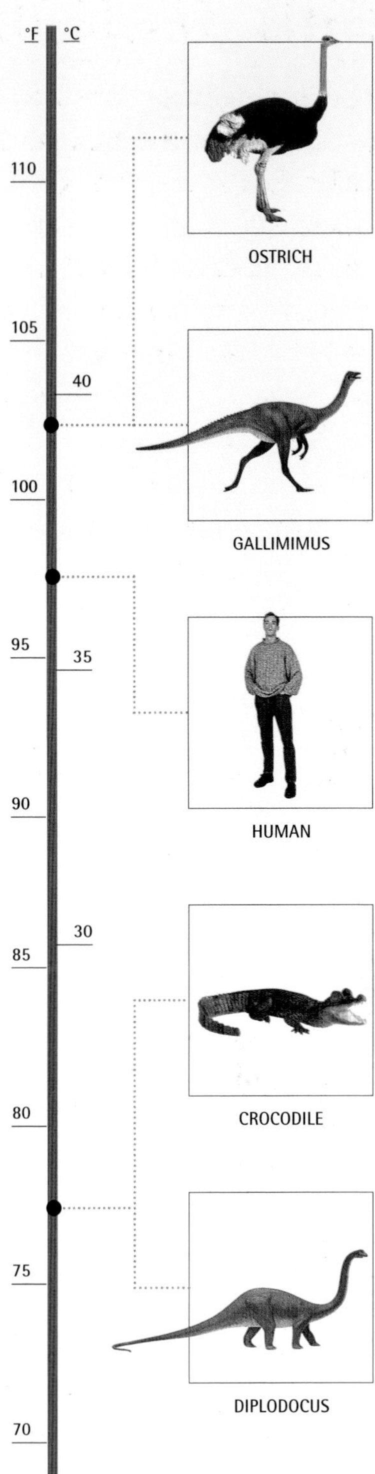

▲ IDEAL BODY TEMPERATURE

Different animals function best at different body temperatures. Active, warm-blooded animals tend to have higher ideal body temperatures than slow, cold-blooded types. The ideal body temperature varies between animal types, with warm-blooded and cold-blooded animals at either end of a gradual scale. It may be that dinosaurs ranged along a similar scale, with big plant-eaters like sauropod's functioning a bit like cold-blooded reptiles, and active theropods at the higher end of the scale, with birds. Other dinosaurs may have ranged between these two extremes.

BRAINS AND INTELLIGENCE

How intelligent were dinosaurs? It is difficult to know how smart dinosaurs were because their brains rarely survive as fossils. Casts taken from the inside of fossil skulls show that some dinosaurs had large brains, while others had small ones. A big brain does not necessarily mean higher intelligence. Scientists look at the size of the brain in relation to the animal's total body weight. They also take into account the animal's behavior. A dinosaur's intelligence was suited to its lifestyle and the tasks it needed to perform.

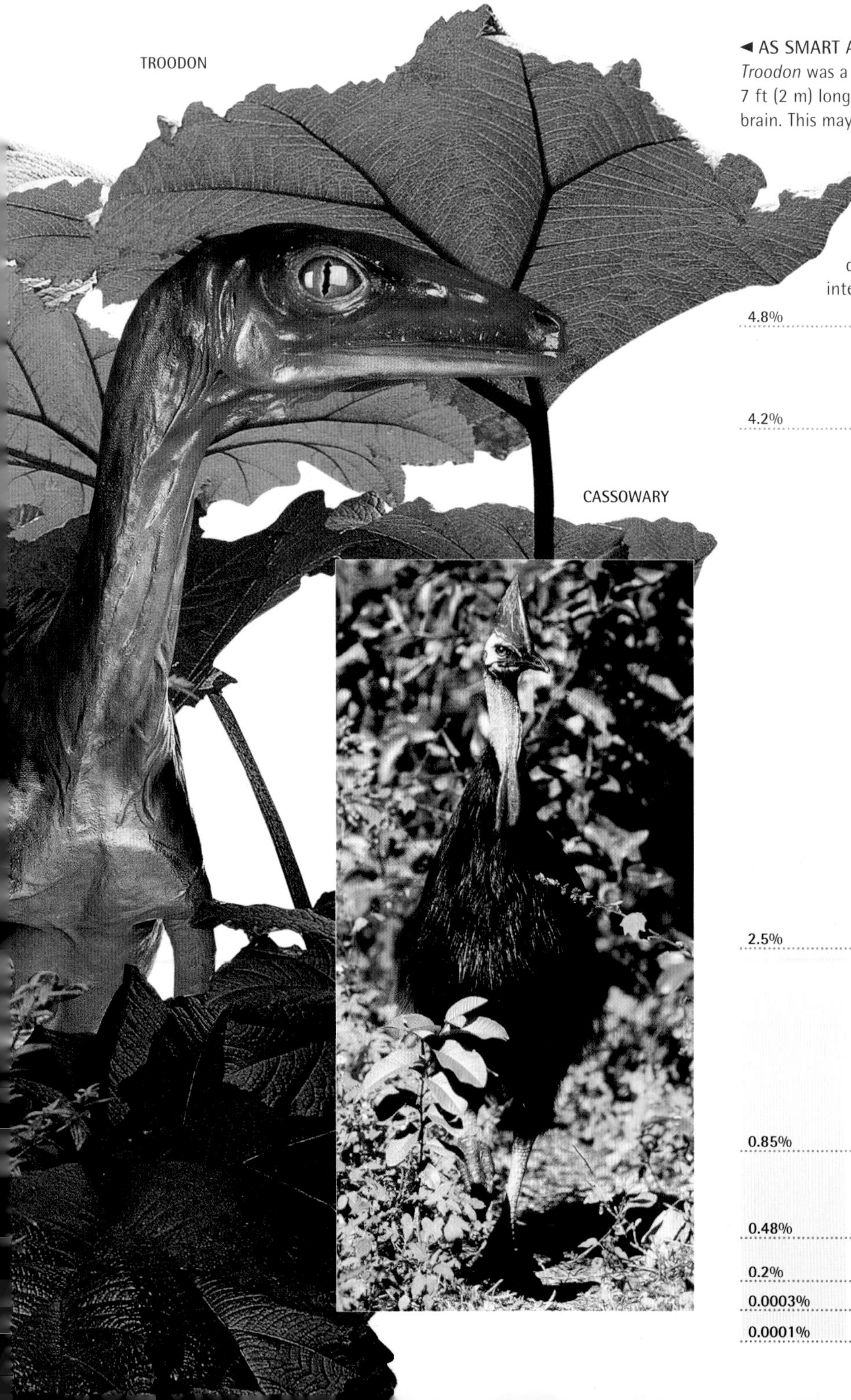

TROODON

CASSOWARY

◄ AS SMART AS A CASSOWARY?
Troodon was a keen-eyed hunter. It grew to 7 ft (2 m) long, and for its size, it had a large brain. This may have given it the mental capacity and sophistication to trap its prey. The cassowary has a similar build and brain size to *Troodon*, so it is possible that the speedy dinosaur had the same level of intelligence as the modern bird.

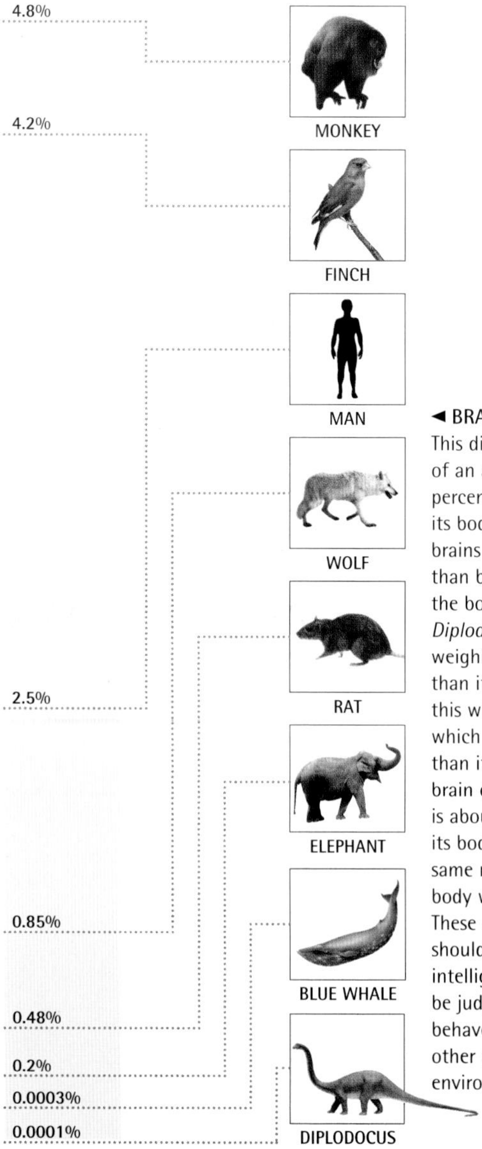

Brain to body weight	Animal
4.8%	MONKEY
4.2%	FINCH
2.5%	MAN
0.85%	WOLF
0.48%	RAT
0.2%	ELEPHANT
0.0003%	BLUE WHALE
0.0001%	DIPLODOCUS

◄ BRAIN TO BODY WEIGHT
This diagram shows the weight of an animal's brain as a percentage of the weight of its body. Dinosaurs had smaller brains relative to their size than birds or mammals. At the bottom of the chart, *Diplodocus* had a brain weighing 100,000 times less than its body weight. Compare this with a small bird's brain, which is only 12 times lighter than its overall weight. The brain of an adult human is about 40 times lighter than its body. This is about the same ratio as the brain to body weight of a mouse. These comparisons alone should not be used to indicate intelligence, which must also be judged on how animals behave in comparison with other animals in their environment.

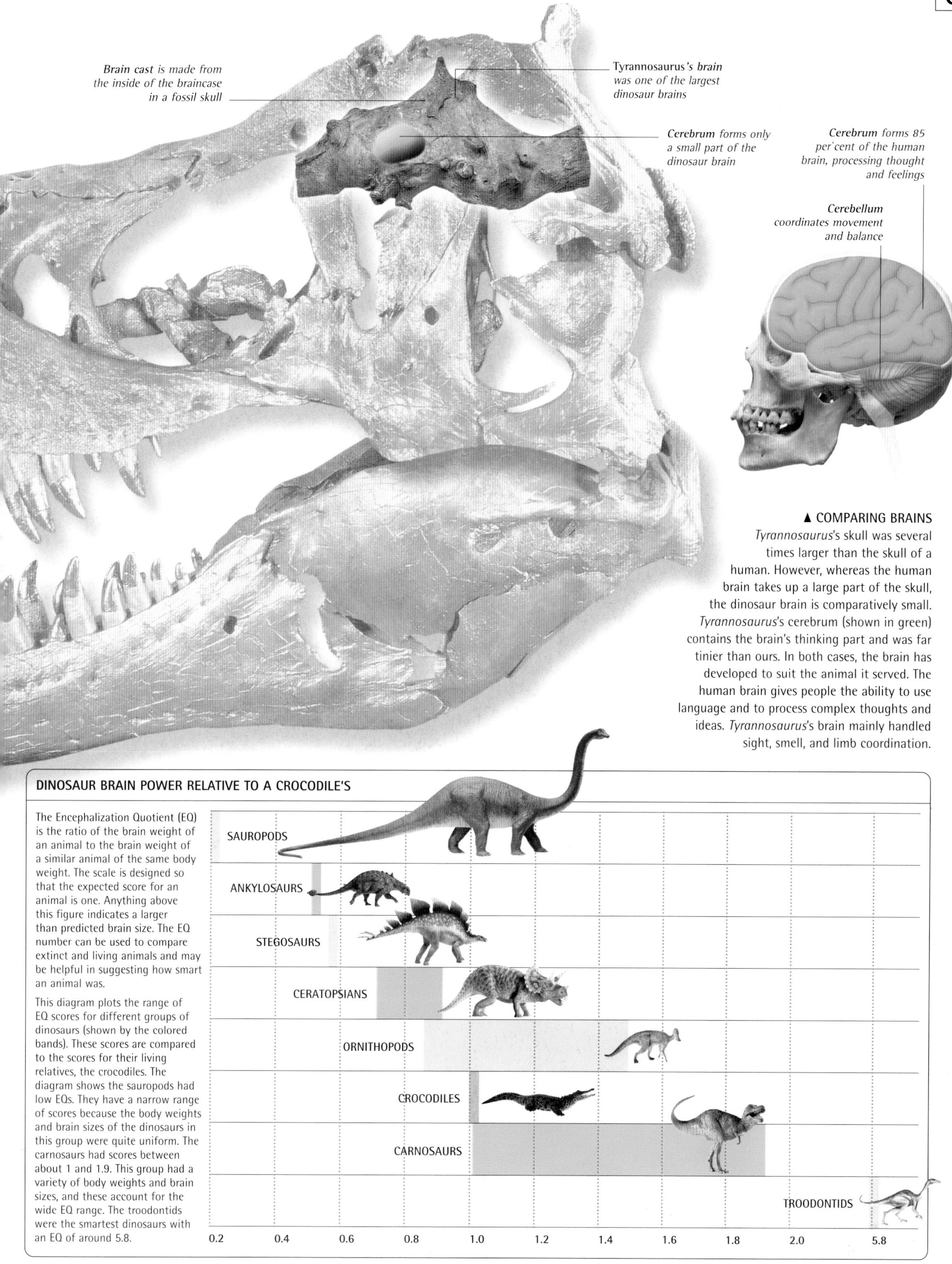

▲ COMPARING BRAINS

Tyrannosaurus's skull was several times larger than the skull of a human. However, whereas the human brain takes up a large part of the skull, the dinosaur brain is comparatively small. *Tyrannosaurus*'s cerebrum (shown in green) contains the brain's thinking part and was far tinier than ours. In both cases, the brain has developed to suit the animal it served. The human brain gives people the ability to use language and to process complex thoughts and ideas. *Tyrannosaurus*'s brain mainly handled sight, smell, and limb coordination.

DINOSAUR BRAIN POWER RELATIVE TO A CROCODILE'S

The Encephalization Quotient (EQ) is the ratio of the brain weight of an animal to the brain weight of a similar animal of the same body weight. The scale is designed so that the expected score for an animal is one. Anything above this figure indicates a larger than predicted brain size. The EQ number can be used to compare extinct and living animals and may be helpful in suggesting how smart an animal was.

This diagram plots the range of EQ scores for different groups of dinosaurs (shown by the colored bands). These scores are compared to the scores for their living relatives, the crocodiles. The diagram shows the sauropods had low EQs. They have a narrow range of scores because the body weights and brain sizes of the dinosaurs in this group were quite uniform. The carnosaurs had scores between about 1 and 1.9. This group had a variety of body weights and brain sizes, and these account for the wide EQ range. The troodontids were the smartest dinosaurs with an EQ of around 5.8.

SENSES

Perhaps the most difficult part of dinosaurs' makeup to study is their senses. Were they slow and stupid, or were they alert and intelligent? Delicate organs such as brains and nerves do not fossilize well, and the bones associated with the sense organs are difficult to interpret. For example, it is impossible to find out about a dinosaur's senses of taste or smell—structures in the nasal cavities may be to do with either smelling or breathing. However, it is possible to make educated guesses about how a dinosaur sensory system would have worked.

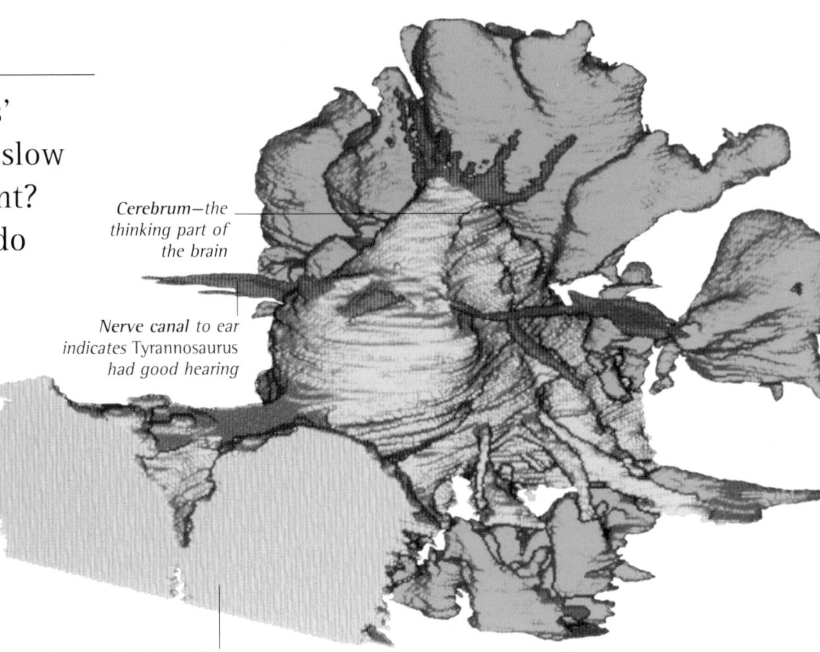

▲ 3-D MODEL OF A TYRANNOSAURUS BRAIN

Brains do not fossilize, but the bones that surround them do. Sometimes it is possible to tell the shape of a dinosaur's brain by looking at the gap left between the bones. If a skull has escaped from being crushed, electronic scanning can produce a three-dimensional image of the shape of the brain. Scientists can tell from this what parts of the brain were well developed, and so which senses were the most essential to the dinosaur.

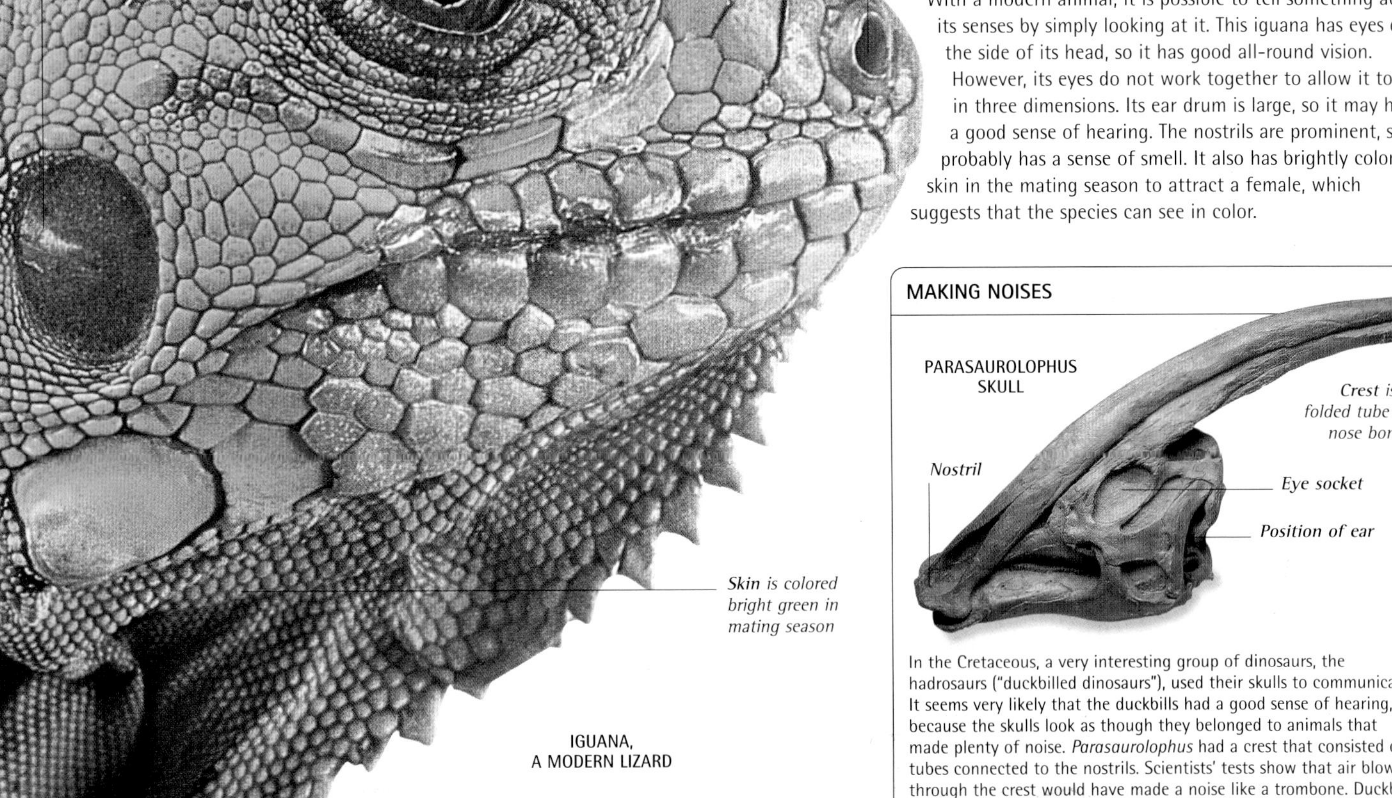

IGUANA,
A MODERN LIZARD

◄ ANIMAL SENSES

With a modern animal, it is possible to tell something about its senses by simply looking at it. This iguana has eyes on the side of its head, so it has good all-round vision. However, its eyes do not work together to allow it to see in three dimensions. Its ear drum is large, so it may have a good sense of hearing. The nostrils are prominent, so it probably has a sense of smell. It also has brightly colored skin in the mating season to attract a female, which suggests that the species can see in color.

MAKING NOISES

PARASAUROLOPHUS SKULL

Crest is a folded tube of nose bones

Nostril

Eye socket

Position of ear

In the Cretaceous, a very interesting group of dinosaurs, the hadrosaurs ("duckbilled dinosaurs"), used their skulls to communicate. It seems very likely that the duckbills had a good sense of hearing, because the skulls look as though they belonged to animals that made plenty of noise. *Parasaurolophus* had a crest that consisted of tubes connected to the nostrils. Scientists' tests show that air blown through the crest would have made a noise like a trombone. Duckbills with no crests may have had a flap of skin over their broad beaks that was inflated to make a noise, like the throat-pouch of a bullfrog.

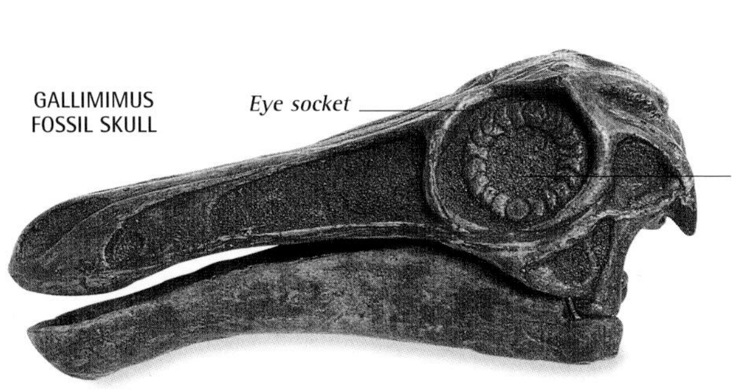

▲ EYE SOCKETS
Some dinosaurs, particularly those with big eyes like *Gallimimus*, had a ring of tiny bones inside the eye. This is called the sclerotic ring. Many modern birds have this. It helps to support the eye and also helps it to focus or pinpoint something it is looking at. Sea reptiles of the Mesozoic had heavy sclerotic rings to protect their eyes from the pressure of the water. Dinosaurs that had a sclerotic ring probably had very sharp eyesight.

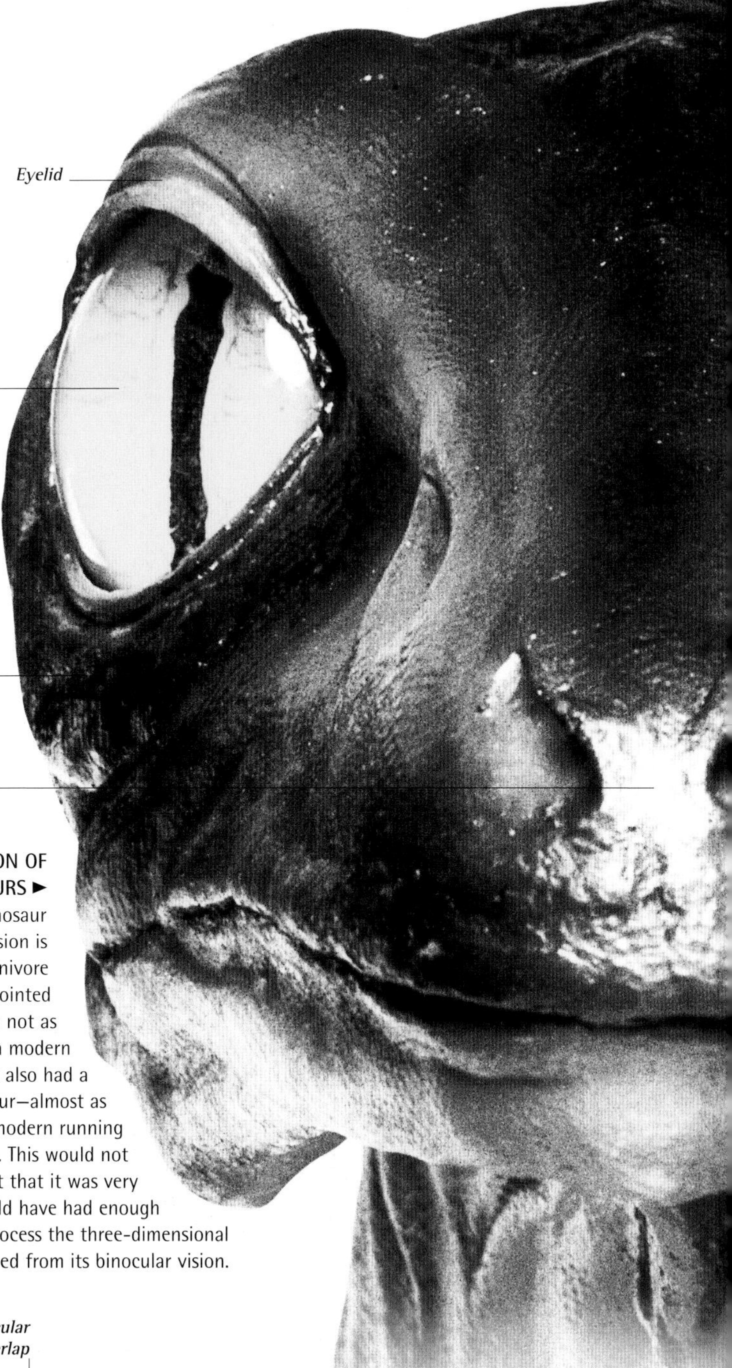

Eyelid

Eye facing forward

Deep eye socket

Narrow snout

BINOCULAR VISION OF THE DINOSAURS ►
The most famous dinosaur with binocular vision is the turkey-sized carnivore *Troodon*. Its eyes pointed forward, although not as much as those of a modern cat or bird of prey. It also had a big brain for a dinosaur—almost as big as the brain of a modern running bird such as an emu. This would not necessarily have meant that it was very intelligent, but it would have had enough brain power to process the three-dimensional images that it received from its binocular vision.

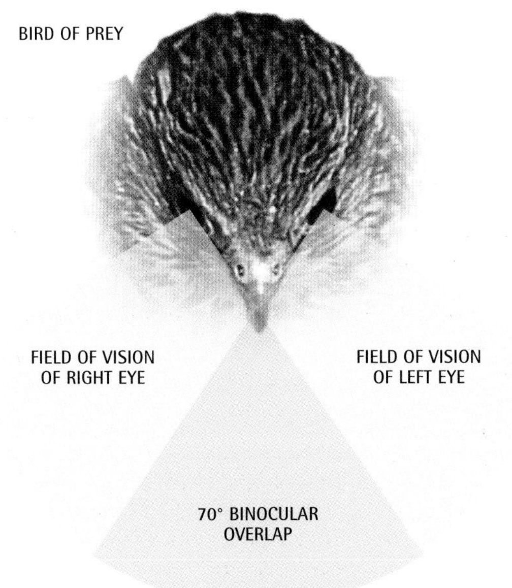

▲ BINOCULAR VISION OF MODERN ANIMALS
Hunting animals like birds of prey and people can see in three dimensions. Look at an object with only one eye, then the other. The object's position will appear to change slightly. A person's brain, and that of a bird of prey, can compare the binocular (two-eyed) images and use them to figure out how far away the object is—useful if the object is moving prey. Several of the hunting dinosaurs may have had this ability.

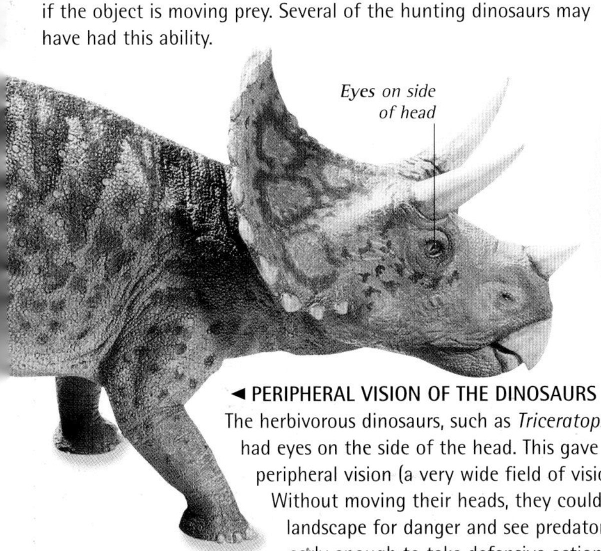

◄ PERIPHERAL VISION OF THE DINOSAURS
The herbivorous dinosaurs, such as *Triceratops*, had eyes on the side of the head. This gave them peripheral vision (a very wide field of vision). Without moving their heads, they could scan the landscape for danger and see predators coming early enough to take defensive action.

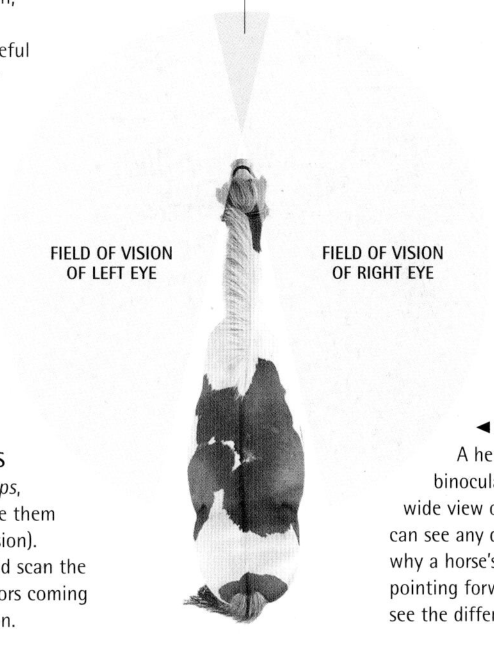

Little binocular overlap

FIELD OF VISION OF LEFT EYE

FIELD OF VISION OF RIGHT EYE

◄ PERIPHERAL VISION OF MODERN ANIMALS
A herbivore such as a horse does not need binocular vision. It finds it more useful to have a wide view of everything around it—mainly so that it can see any danger coming while it is eating. That is why a horse's eyes are on the side the head and not pointing forward. It does not see in color, but it can see the difference between light and shade.

GROWING UP

Some of the most exciting fossil finds over the last fifty years have been those that have something to do with young dinosaurs—their nests, eggs, or skeletons. When skeletons are found as part of a herd or as a nesting group, it is much easier to tell the young from the adults. The size of a dinosaur's head, eyes, and feet can give clues. The bone itself, if well-enough preserved, sometimes has textures and structures that show different growth rates.

▼ COMPLETE BABY

For a time, the prosauropod *Mussaurus* ("mouse lizard") was thought to be the smallest dinosaur known. Then scientists realized that the skeletons that had been found were all of young hatchlings. The skeletons found were only 9 ins (18 cm) long and could have fit in a person's hand. The adults would in fact have been about 10 ft (3 m). Some of the bones of the hatchlings had not developed fully, and like most young animals, the skull, eye sockets, and feet were big for the size of the animal.

Big head with large eye sockets

Large feet in proportion to rest of body

LIFESIZE SKELETON OF A MUSSAURUS HATCHLING

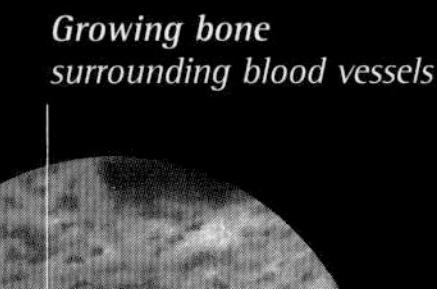

Growing bone surrounding blood vessels

Blood vessels (vascular canals)

SECTION OF BABY THEROPOD BONE

SECTION OF ADULT THEROPOD BONE

▲ DEVELOPING BONE TISSUE

Some dinosaur bones are so well preserved that it is possible to see their structure through a microscope. Like modern animals, the bones of dinosaurs consisted of living tissue, with blood vessels passing through and a space for bone marrow at the center. Sometimes, when families of dinosaurs are unearthed, it is possible to look at different ages of the same species. Examinations of bones like these has shown that the bones of theropod dinosaurs grew throughout their lives, unlike mammal bones which reach a particular age and then stop growing.

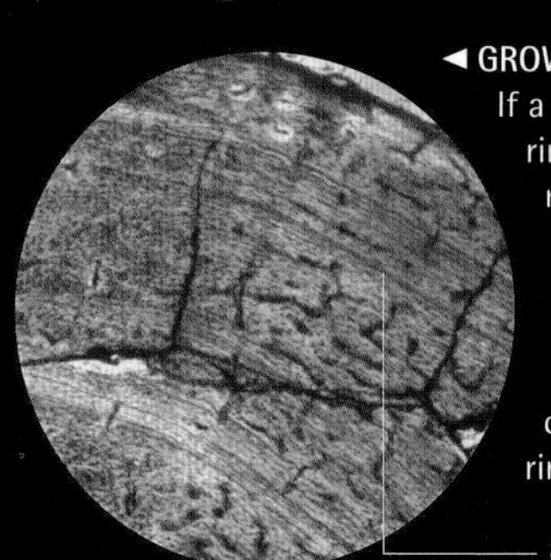

Lines showing a yearly growth

SECTION OF A TYRANNOSAURUS BONE

◄ GROWTH RINGS

If a tree is cut down, an examination of the trunk will show rings in the wood from the core of the tree to the bark. Each new ring represents a year of growth of the living tree. The rings are known as growth rings. Sometimes this effect can be seen in dinosaur bones as well. However, it is not possible to simply count the rings to tell what age the dinosaur was when it died. Often the structure of the older bone will have changed during the lifetime of the animal, and the growth rings that were formed earlier will have disappeared.

STAGES OF GROWTH

Herds of the horned dinosaur *Protoceratops* roamed the Cretaceous plains of Asia like flocks of sheep. Hundreds of fossils of these dinosaurs have been found buried in desert sandstones. They were probably overwhelmed and suffocated in the sandstorms of the period. The remains are at all stages of growth, showing that they moved around in herds or in family groups. The fossils provide very good evidence of how this species developed as they grew older. For example, the skulls and jaws developed at different rates between the time that the *Protoceratops* hatched and the time it reached full adulthood.

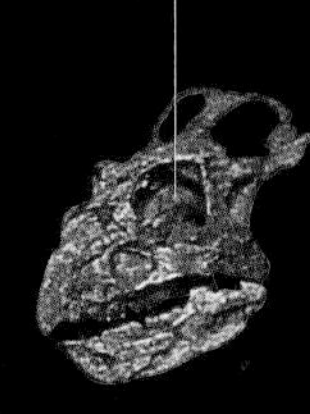

Eye socket in skull of a newly hatched Protoceratops

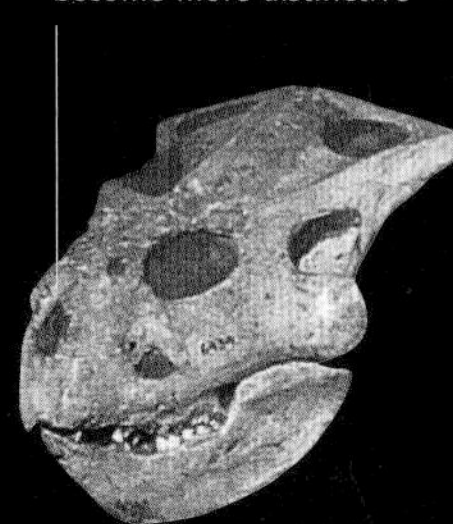

As animal grows, features such as beak become more distinctive

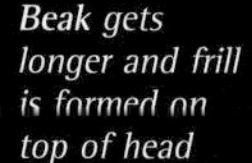

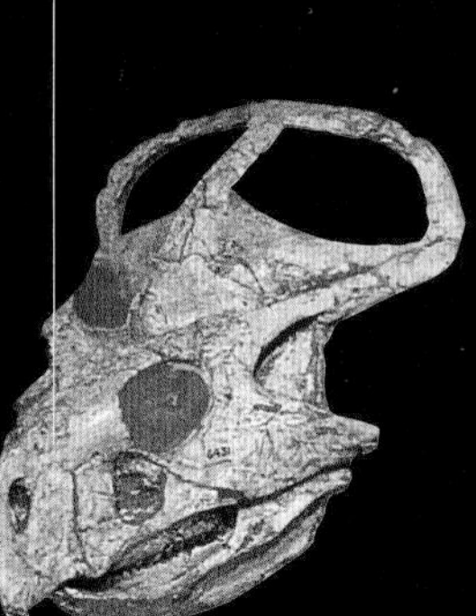

Beak gets longer and frill is formed on top of head

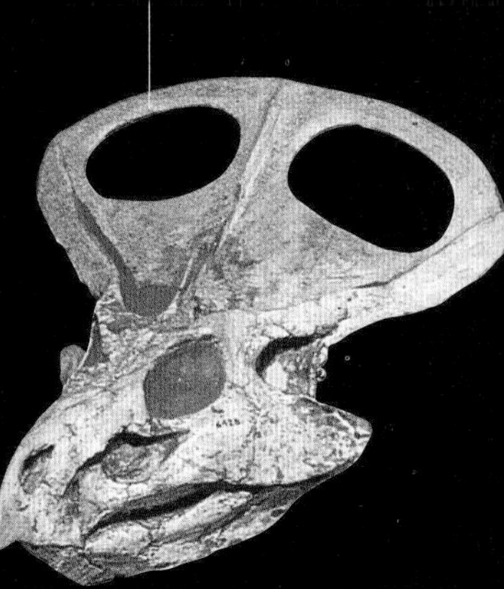

Bone of frill develops as the animal grows

▼ PARENTAL CARE

Dinosaurs like this herbivorous dinosaur, *Leaellynasaura*, probably nested together in large groups. After the eggs hatched, the adults would have cared for the hatchlings until they were big enough to fend for themselves. We know the rates at which ornithopods like these grew from the bones found at nesting sites. The hatchlings grew very quickly for a few months. Then, for six years or so, the juveniles would still be growing fast. By the time they reached adulthood, the growth rate would have slowed down or stopped completely. This growth rate is very like that of modern birds.

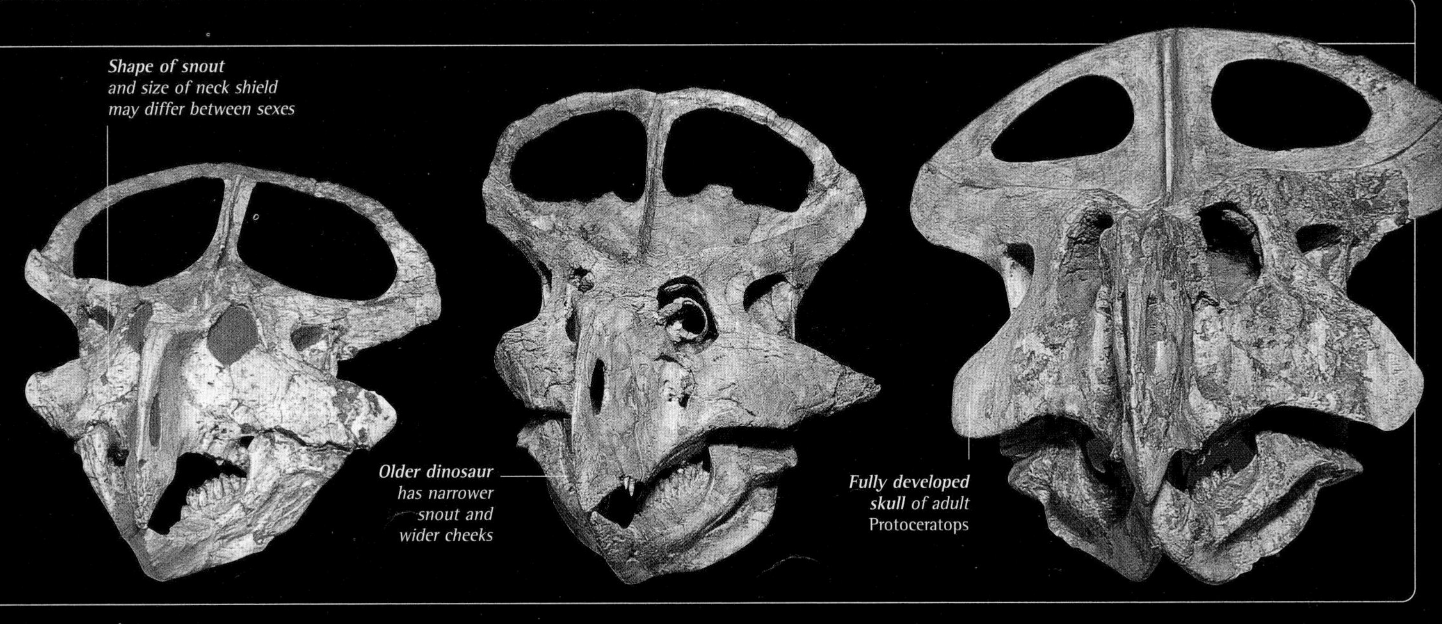

Shape of snout *and size of neck shield may differ between sexes*

Older dinosaur *has narrower snout and wider cheeks*

Fully developed skull *of adult* Protoceratops

DEATH AND DISEASE

Few dinosaurs reached old age. These creatures were constantly at risk from the environment and from other animals. Many dinosaur species are known only from fossils of juveniles that died before they could become adults. Some dinosaurs died in fights, some starved, some became diseased, and some died from injury. What is known about dinosaur illnesses is very limited. Only if a disease affected the bone is there any direct fossilized proof of what kind of illness it could have been. The study of such events is called paleopathology.

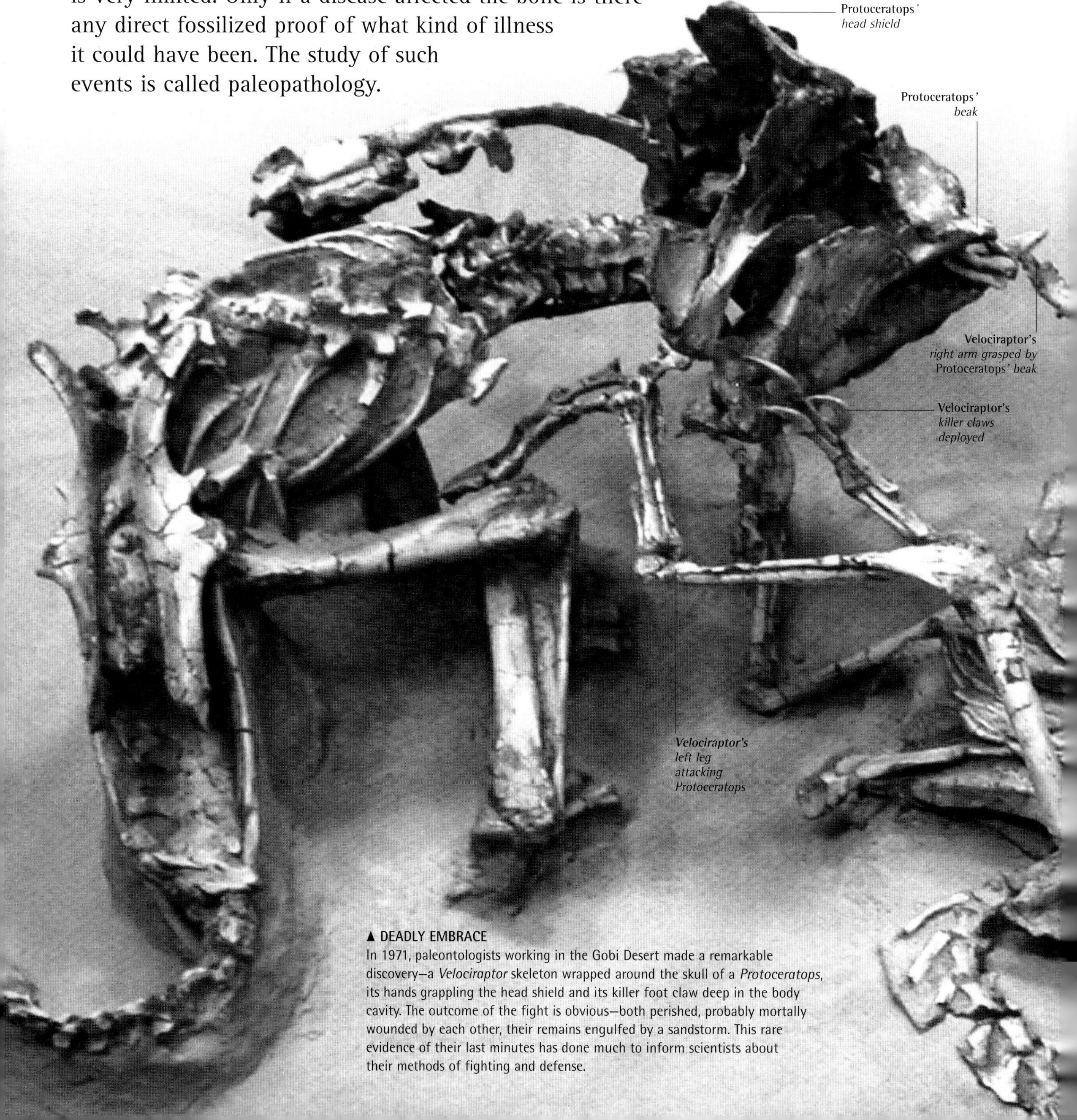

death

▲ **DEADLY EMBRACE**
In 1971, paleontologists working in the Gobi Desert made a remarkable discovery—a *Velociraptor* skeleton wrapped around the skull of a *Protoceratops*, its hands grappling the head shield and its killer foot claw deep in the body cavity. The outcome of the fight is obvious—both perished, probably mortally wounded by each other, their remains engulfed by a sandstorm. This rare evidence of their last minutes has done much to inform scientists about their methods of fighting and defense.

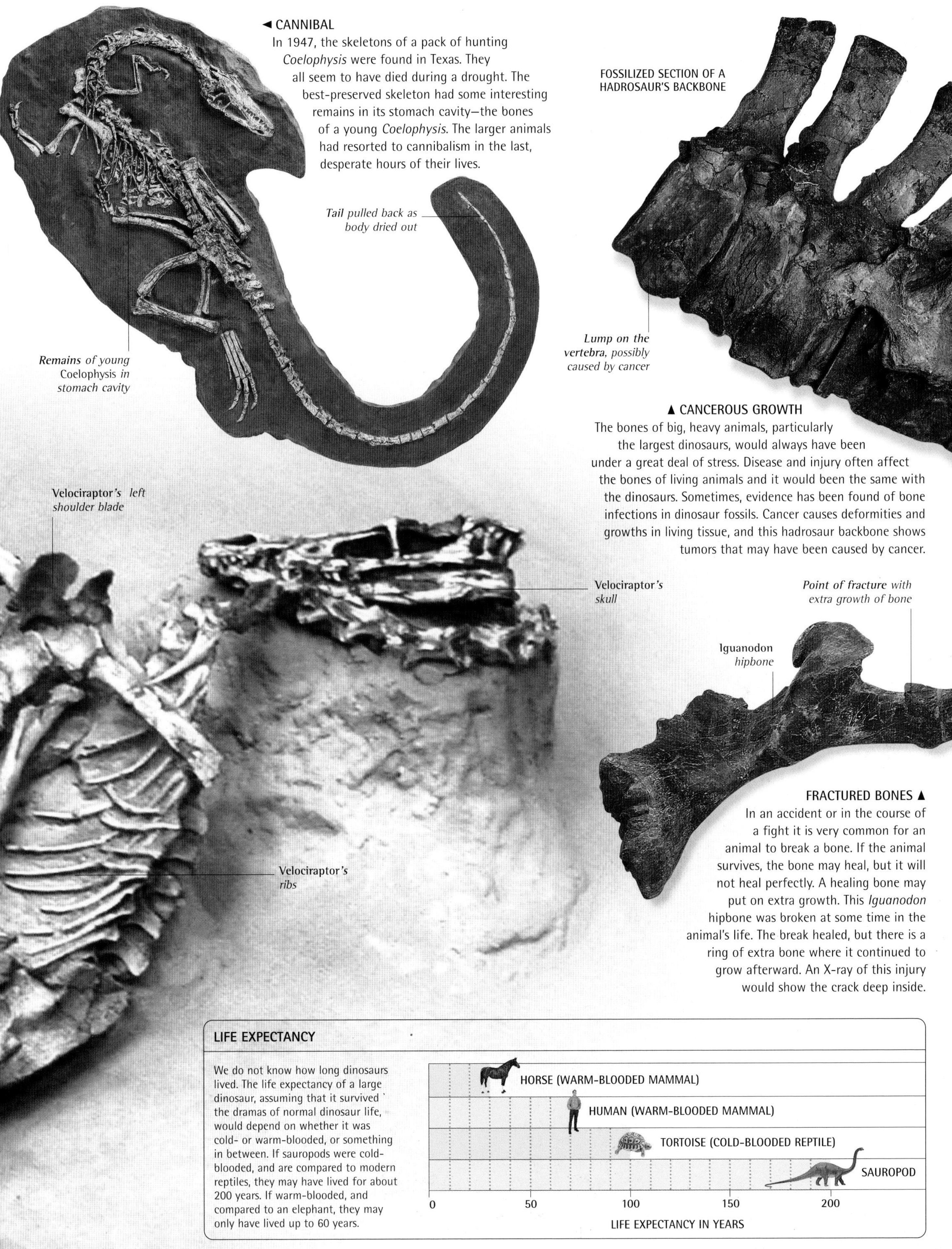

◄ CANNIBAL

In 1947, the skeletons of a pack of hunting *Coelophysis* were found in Texas. They all seem to have died during a drought. The best-preserved skeleton had some interesting remains in its stomach cavity—the bones of a young *Coelophysis*. The larger animals had resorted to cannibalism in the last, desperate hours of their lives.

▲ CANCEROUS GROWTH

The bones of big, heavy animals, particularly the largest dinosaurs, would always have been under a great deal of stress. Disease and injury often affect the bones of living animals and it would been the same with the dinosaurs. Sometimes, evidence has been found of bone infections in dinosaur fossils. Cancer causes deformities and growths in living tissue, and this hadrosaur backbone shows tumors that may have been caused by cancer.

FRACTURED BONES ▲

In an accident or in the course of a fight it is very common for an animal to break a bone. If the animal survives, the bone may heal, but it will not heal perfectly. A healing bone may put on extra growth. This *Iguanodon* hipbone was broken at some time in the animal's life. The break healed, but there is a ring of extra bone where it continued to grow afterward. An X-ray of this injury would show the crack deep inside.

LIFE EXPECTANCY

We do not know how long dinosaurs lived. The life expectancy of a large dinosaur, assuming that it survived the dramas of normal dinosaur life, would depend on whether it was cold- or warm-blooded, or something in between. If sauropods were cold-blooded, and are compared to modern reptiles, they may have lived for about 200 years. If warm-blooded, and compared to an elephant, they may only have lived up to 60 years.

PACK HUNTERS

Just as modern meat-eating animals such as lions combine forces to pull down animals larger than themselves, many flesh-eating theropods hunted in packs. Roaming in gangs, heavily muscled, and armed with vicious claws and powerful jaws lined with sharp teeth, they were intelligent enough to band together before going into the attack. Like some sophisticated hunters today, dinosaurs may have developed tactics to outsmart their prey, such as luring them into traps or surrounding them before the attack.

▲ FAMILY FEASTING

Lions are sociable animals that live together in prides of a dozen or more, including several lionesses and their cubs. They hunt together and later feast on the spoils as a group. Packs of small, carnivorous dinosaurs may have shared larger prey in this way. There was no need for them to defend the kill from the attentions of scavengers as it was quickly devoured. They were then free to move on to their next victim.

Deep wounds are inflicted by sharp teeth and claws

Attacking Allosaurus *slashes at the prey's flank from a safe position*

ATTACK ON A CAMARASAURUS ▼

A lone, plant-eating *Camarasaurus*, separated from the safety of its herd, had neither the killer instincts nor the sharp weaponry to ward off an attack by two hunting *Allosaurus*. The predators were powerful and agile, able to leap high onto the back of their prey and inflict deep wounds to its head, neck, and spine with their teeth and claws. They continued to slash at the dinosaur until it succumbed from either loss of blood or exhaustion.

TRAPPED IN A QUAGMIRE ▲
Deep, waterlogged mud could become a death trap for victims and flesh-eating predators alike. Cries from a trapped dinosaur, in this case a *Stegosaurus*, would attract the attention of heavyweight predators such as the *Allosaurus*, which would in turn sink and be engulfed by the mud. Numerous other predators would try for the easy meat and drown. The Cleveland-Lloyd Dinosaur Quarry in Utah was once the site of just such a predator trap. Since scientists first found fossils there in 1927, more than 10,000 dinosaur bones have been unearthed, most of them from predators.

e hunting

Scavenging pterosaurs circle overhead and wait for leftovers

Teeth of prey are better suited to foraging than to fighting predators

Allosaurus *draws the prey's attention while its teammate inflicts the damage*

TACTICS OF MODERN HUNTERS

Hungry lions work together as a team to secure food for their pride, including the young and old. Hunting in open grassland, they silently encircle their prey, making it impossible to escape in any direction.

1 Female lions creep toward the prey through the long grass, taking care not to arouse suspicion.
2 Males quietly take up positions to the rear of the prey.
3 The prey animals graze in the open, unaware of the threat.
4 Abandoning stealth, some of the males charge straight for the prey.
5 Other members of the pride follow ready to head off any veering prey.
6 The prey animals flee toward the trap.
7 Keeping still, the females choose an animal to attack, then burst out and bring it down.

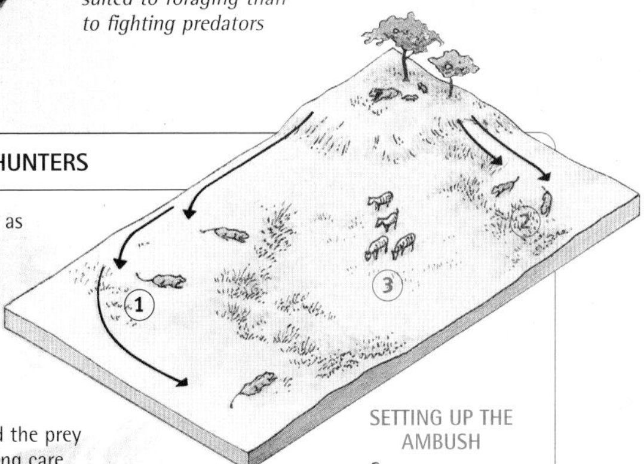

SETTING UP THE AMBUSH

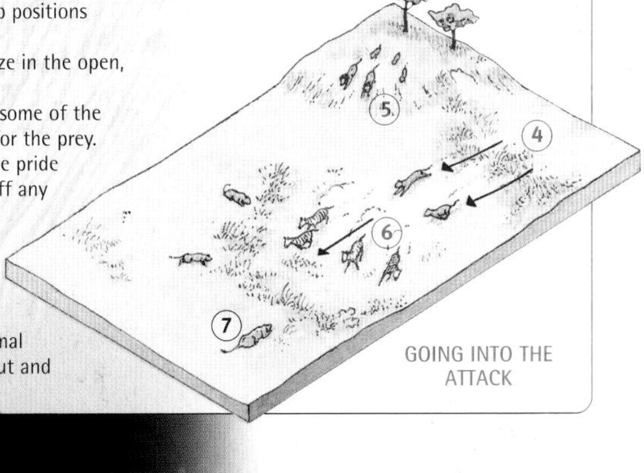

GOING INTO THE ATTACK

HUNTER OR SCAVENGER?

Tyrannosaurus was the biggest, fiercest, most formidable hunting animal that ever lived. Or was it? Although it looks like a terrifying predator, and its teeth, jaws, and eyesight seem to confirm that it was, other features such as the muscles and bones suggest that it was a slow mover, unable to run fast after prey. Perhaps *Tyrannosaurus* used different techniques when it needed to find its food. It may have hunted by running in short spurts and catching slow-moving prey. It may have scavenged on dead animals caught by other, speedier theropods, simply scaring them away as they tried to eat.

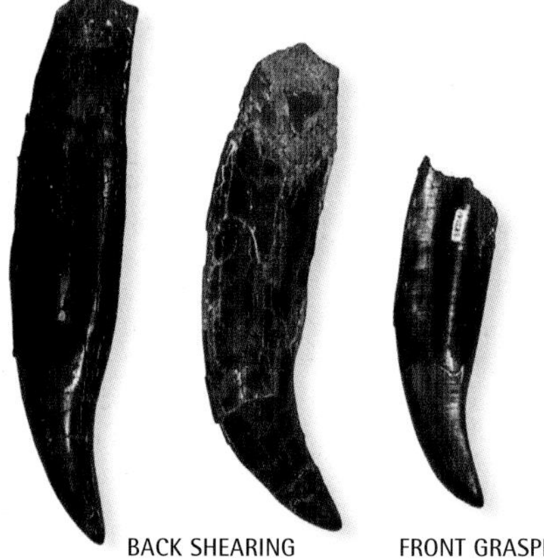

▲ TEETH
The sharp teeth of a *Tyrannosaurus* suggest that it was a hunter. Those at the front are short, thick, and ideal for clamping into struggling prey and stopping it from escaping. The long teeth at the side were more bladelike, serrated on both edges, and curved backward. This made them perfect for slicing off meat that was already dead. All would have been replaced as they broke off or wore out.

CARNIVORE ►
This dinosaur was made for meat-eating—just like the other theropods. Its long jaws housed rows of sharp teeth. Its long hind legs were strong. Its body was relatively small, and was balanced by a heavy tail. But it is difficult to tell if the meat *Tyrannosaurus* ate came from prey that it hunted for itself, or from already dead animals that it found. Its fearsome teeth look like those of a killer, but its sheer size suggests that it was too big and clumsy for hunting.

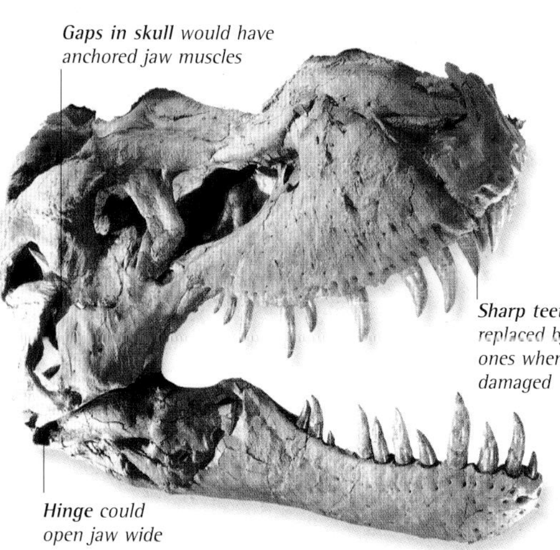

▲ AWESOME JAWS
The muscles that powered the jaws of *Tyrannosaurus* were immense. They would have been strong enough to grip a big animal, tear it limb from limb, and crush the bones. Scientists have found *Tyrannosaurus* tooth marks in the broken bones of horned dinosaurs. The volume of the mouth shows that it could have swallowed up to 500 lb (227 kg) of flesh at a single gulp. Such jaws could have been used by either a hunter or a scavenger.

◄ STEREOSCOPIC EYESIGHT
Tyrannosaurus had eyesight that could have been that of a hunter. The eyes were angled forward, so the field of view overlapped at the front. This would have given the dinosaur stereoscopic vision—it could have judged distances and seen things in three dimensions as we do. This is a vital ability that a hunting animal needed for targeting its prey. But the overlap is not nearly as marked as that of a modern hunter such as a cat.

AVAILABILITY OF FOOD FOR SCAVENGING

In nature, a dead animal is a rich source of food. The flesh, internal organs, and even the marrow of the bones are all highly nutritious. Whenever a source of food exists, something will evolve to exploit it. In modern times, dead animals are not left for long—they are soon eaten by scavenging animals. It must have been the same in the Age of Dinosaurs. Living creatures, including *Tyrannosaurus* and other dinosaurs, would have scavenged the corpses of dead dinosaurs.

◄ LEG MUSCLES
The evidence provided by the legs of a *Tyrannosaurus* have not helped scientists decide whether this animal was a hunter or not. Its leg bones were huge, and possibly too massive for it to be a fast runner. The amount of muscle also seems to suggest that it was a slow mover because there was simply not enough muscle to allow it to run fast. All this would argue against it being an active hunter. However, the way the bones are jointed suggests that they were designed to be moved quickly. So the evidence found so far is contradictory.

▲ MODERN HUNTERS AND SCAVENGERS
Although we think of hyenas (seen here on the right) as scavenging animals, they do not always eat animals that are already dead. Hyenas sometimes hunt in packs and bring down swift prey. Likewise, we think of lions (left) as being the ultimate hunting machines. However, lions often scavenge, eating prey that has been killed by another animal. The line between hunting and scavenging is not always clear. Perhaps, back in the Cretaceous, *Tyrannosaurus* adopted both techniques, hunting when necessary, and scavenging corpses when it found them.

TYRANNOSAURUS PROFILE

Fast or slow? Predator or scavenger? Either way, *Tyrannosaurus* was one of the biggest carnivores ever to have stalked the Earth.

Height: 22 ft (6.5 m)

Length: 42 ft (12.8 m)

Weight: Up to 7 tons

Leg length: 8 ft (2.5 m)

Stride length: 2–15 ft (3.7–4.6 m)

Estimated top speed: 5–45 mph (8–72 kph)

Young Pachyrhinosaurus is surrounded by adults

HERDING DINOSAURS

Traveling as a herd provides safety in numbers because it is difficult for a hungry predator to pick out just one animal for slaughter. Group members can also warn each other if there are flesh-eaters on the prowl. It is possible that, for these reasons, some plant-eating dinosaurs formed herds. We know that certain dinosaurs traveled in groups because large clusters of their fossil bones and footprints have been found together. These dinosaurs may also have trudged vast distances together to find good grazing land and breeding sites. These journeys are called migrations. Today, many animals follow a herding life for much the same reasons as their ancient ancestors.

Footprints show the direction of travel

◀ PRESERVED IN STONE
Found on the Colorado Plateau in the western US, these fossilized footprints consist of tracks made by a number of *Apatosaurus*. Multiple dinosaur tracks provide evidence that some dinosaurs traveled together in herds. Scientists analyzing such trackways have also found that, in some cases, smaller, juvenile footprints overprint those made by the adults. From this we know the older, stronger dinosaurs led the herds, while the young ones either followed at the rear or marched along in the middle, protected at the front and back by the adults.

Larger footprints belong to the adults

Smaller footprints belong to the young

▲ BOUND FOR THE ARCTIC
In Late Cretaceous times, herds of *Pachyrhinosaurus* migrated north from what is now Alberta, Canada, to the Arctic. Feeding on large-leafed plants, they remained there until driven south again by the bitterly cold winter. We know they made these epic treks because fossils of this lumbering herbivore have been discovered in Alberta and 2,200 miles (3,500 km) away in northern Alaska.

◄ HAZARDOUS JOURNEYS
Long journeys can prove hazardous for migrating animals because predators lurk at every turn. Traveling in search of fresh grass, wildebeest migrate distances of up to 1,800 miles (2,900 km) through Tanzania and Kenya. They often risk attack by crocodiles as they cross rivers. It is likely migrating dinosaurs would have faced similar dangers, possibly also falling victim to crocodilians.

DINOSAUR HIGHWAY

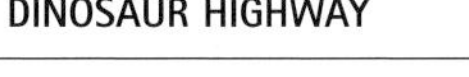

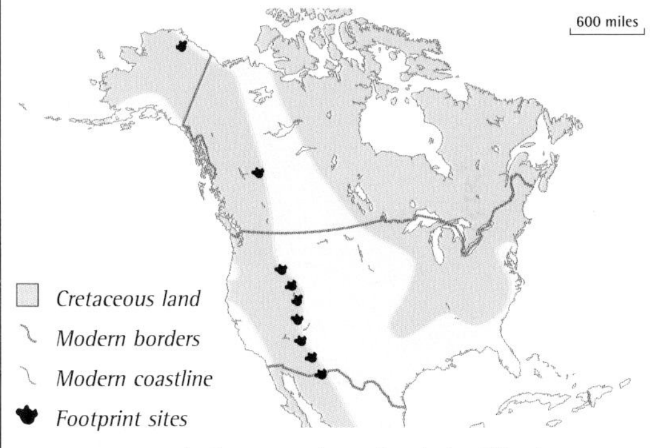

In Cretaceous times, the whole of North America was divided by a vast sea, called the Western Interior Seaway (shown in blue). The present-day fossil footprint sites on this map show a migration route to northern Alaska along the western edge of the seaway, in the shadow of the Rocky Mountains. These *Iguanodon* footprints were made in the wet, coastal sediments. They eventually hardened to rock, preserving in stone the evidence for migratory behavior in some North American dinosaurs.

▲ DEFENSIVE CIRCLE
Dinosaur herds may have used group defense tactics to protect themselves from predators. *Triceratops* could have formed a circle and faced an attacker with their three fearsome horns and bony frills. Any predator rash enough to approach may have been driven off by a charging adult. At full tilt, *Triceratops* may have been able to run at a speed of 15 mph (25 kph). This could have deterred even *Tyrannosaurus*.

Adult musk oxen face outward toward threats

▲ CHILD REARING
Like *Triceratops*, this group of musk oxen keep their young within a close, protective circle. The threat of predators is not the only reason for this behavior. Older members of the herd are on hand to lead by example and teach the young how to survive and grow into adulthood. It is quite likely that some of the adults in a herd of dinosaurs also took responsibility for the rearing and education of their young.

NESTING COLONIES

Ever since dinosaurs were identified as reptiles, scientists have assumed that they laid eggs, in the same way that most modern reptiles lay eggs. This was confirmed when the first dinosaur eggs and nests were found in the Gobi Desert, Mongolia, in the 1920s. Since then, many more finds have been made—most importantly, the discovery of a nesting colony of *Maiasaura* in Montana. Many nesting sites show evidence of birdlike behavior that adds weight to the theory of some scientists that birds evolved from feathered dinosaurs.

▼ FAMILY LIFE
In the 1970s, at a place named Egg Mountain in Montana, a whole colony of fossilized hadrosaur nests was found. They belonged to a dinosaur called *Maiasaura*. The nests had been made of mud, and were about 3 ft (1 m) high with a bowl-like depression in the top. It is thought that migrating herds of *Maiasaura* returned to this mass breeding ground year after year to lay their eggs and raise their young.

Young Maiasaura *grew to around 10 ft (3 m) in one year*

◀ HATCHING OUT
There were many different fossils at the Montana site. Egg shells in the nest showed where the eggs had hatched. The bones of hatchlings revealed that some of the babies did not survive the first few days. The bones of older youngsters showed that the young remained at the nesting site for a long time before becoming independent. It seems the parents looked after them in the same way as birds care for their young, feeding and caring for them until they are ready to leave.

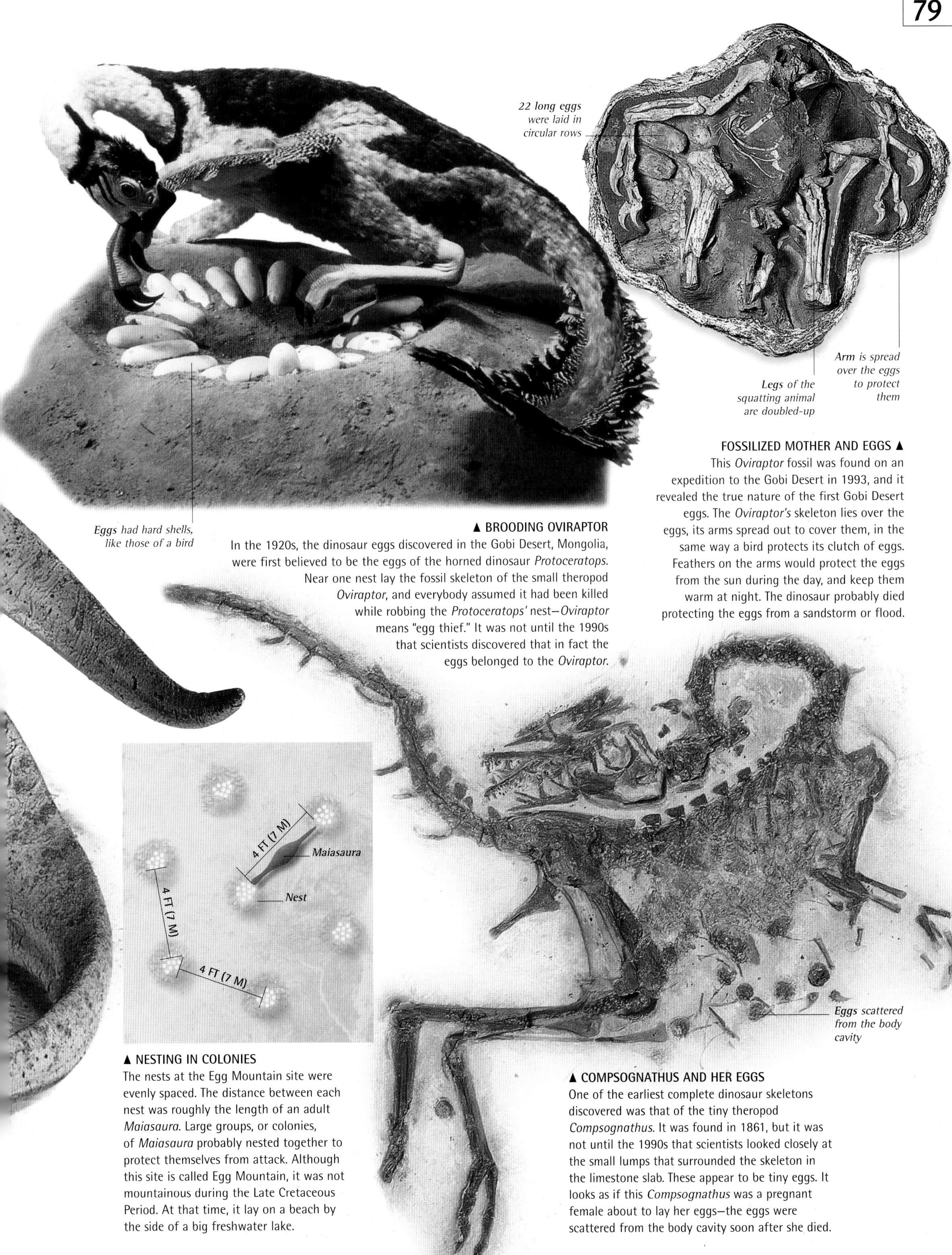

▲ BROODING OVIRAPTOR
In the 1920s, the dinosaur eggs discovered in the Gobi Desert, Mongolia, were first believed to be the eggs of the horned dinosaur *Protoceratops*. Near one nest lay the fossil skeleton of the small theropod *Oviraptor*, and everybody assumed it had been killed while robbing the *Protoceratops'* nest—*Oviraptor* means "egg thief." It was not until the 1990s that scientists discovered that in fact the eggs belonged to the *Oviraptor*.

FOSSILIZED MOTHER AND EGGS ▲
This *Oviraptor* fossil was found on an expedition to the Gobi Desert in 1993, and it revealed the true nature of the first Gobi Desert eggs. The *Oviraptor's* skeleton lies over the eggs, its arms spread out to cover them, in the same way a bird protects its clutch of eggs. Feathers on the arms would protect the eggs from the sun during the day, and keep them warm at night. The dinosaur probably died protecting the eggs from a sandstorm or flood.

▲ NESTING IN COLONIES
The nests at the Egg Mountain site were evenly spaced. The distance between each nest was roughly the length of an adult *Maiasaura*. Large groups, or colonies, of *Maiasaura* probably nested together to protect themselves from attack. Although this site is called Egg Mountain, it was not mountainous during the Late Cretaceous Period. At that time, it lay on a beach by the side of a big freshwater lake.

▲ COMPSOGNATHUS AND HER EGGS
One of the earliest complete dinosaur skeletons discovered was that of the tiny theropod *Compsognathus*. It was found in 1861, but it was not until the 1990s that scientists looked closely at the small lumps that surrounded the skeleton in the limestone slab. These appear to be tiny eggs. It looks as if this *Compsognathus* was a pregnant female about to lay her eggs—the eggs were scattered from the body cavity soon after she died.

CHANGING FACES

No one has ever seen a living dinosaur, so scientists rely on fossil remains to provide clues to how these ancient reptiles looked and behaved when they were alive. Scrappy evidence in the past meant the early dinosaur experts had certain beliefs about dinosaurs we now know to be incorrect. New discoveries are being made all the time, and each one expands what we know about dinosaurs—sometimes confirming, and sometimes overturning, the accepted thinking about a particular species. Examples of the changing faces of certain dinosaurs are shown on these pages.

▼ FIERCE, BUT FLUFFY
One of the most significant leaps in how we think dinosaurs looked has happened since the mid-1990s. Before then it was thought that, because dinosaurs were reptiles, they all had scaly skin. Many scientists no longer believe this to be the case for all dinosaurs, based on fossils found in China. The evidence suggests that some small predators, such as *Velociraptor*, had bodies clothed in feathers and down. These coverings are usually associated with birds, so the finds provide evidence supporting the theory that dinosaurs and birds are related.

VELOCIRAPTOR WITHOUT FUR AND FEATHERS

◄ DOWN FROM THE TREES
The first *Hypsilophodon* fossils were discovered in 1849, on the Isle of Wight, England. At the time, it was believed this small, agile, plant-eating dinosaur had lived in trees, where it used its long tail for balancing on branches, and its sharp claws for clinging on. This theory has now been proved completely wrong. Today, scientists believe *Hypsilophodon* was actually a ground-living dinosaur, which held its stiff tail off the ground, using it as a stabilizer as it moved. It probably used its clawed hands to pull at the plants it ate.

Tail held off the ground

***Featherless legs** lessen air-resistance and help Velociraptor run faster*

Hands are too feeble to cling on to branches

HYPSILOPHODON ON THE GROUND

CORYTHOSAURUS IN A SWAMP

◄ OUT OF THE SWAMP

Ideas about *Corythosaurus*'s lifestyle have altered over recent years. These changing views are based on theories about the function of its head crest. As it was hollow, the crest was once thought to be an underwater breathing tube used like a snorkel. This led scientists to believe *Corythosaurus* lived in water. It is now thought that *Corythosaurus* was a land animal, and that its crest was either for display, or a sound chamber through which it made noises.

CORYTHOSAURUS ON DRY LAND

VELOCIRAPTOR WITH FEATHERS

IGUANODON OVER TIME

1850s IGUANODON
In 1853, British sculptor Benjamin Waterhouse Hawkins created a concrete model of an *Iguanodon*. Guided by Sir Richard Owen, the sculptor showed the dinosaur as a heavily built quadruped with a horn on the tip of its nose.

Snout horn

1880s IGUANODON
Fossil skeletons found at Bernissart, Belgium revised the view of this dinosaur radically. *Iguanodon* no longer had a nose horn, and it was depicted in a strictly bipedal, kangaroolike posture, but with its tail dragging on the ground.

Tail on ground

PRESENT-DAY IGUANODON
It is now believed *Iguanodon* held its heavy tail off the ground, using it to counter-balance the weight of its body. It might not have been strictly bipedal as once imagined. Recent studies show it could move on either two or four legs.

Tail off ground

DINOSAURS ON DISPLAY

Dinosaur displays in museums can take many forms. Original fossils are shown in glass cases, often presented in the rock in which they are embedded. Complete dinosaur skeletons can be mounted to give a more three-dimensional impression of the animal, and to show its scale and structure. A mounted skeleton is called a reconstruction. There are also displays that show what a dinosaur was like when alive, such as a painting, or a model of a dinosaur set in the environment it would have lived in. This is called a restoration.

Long, stiff tail helped the dinosaur to balance while running and leaping

Mounting framework lies inside the replica bones and is invisible

Birdlike feet with terrifying hooked claws for tearing prey apart

Skeleton is so light it can be attached to the floor at only one point

THE DIFFERENT FUNCTIONS OF A MUSEUM

FOSSIL STORE
The majority of dinosaur fossils are never put on display. They are kept in the storerooms of museums and universities where they are available for scientists. Sometimes this is because they are too valuable or fragile to be displayed in public. Often, it is because they do not look impressive. Only the most spectacular exhibits are put on show. Fossils may also be too heavy or fragile to mount, so some exhibits are made up of copies cast from the original bones.

LAB ON VIEW
In some modern museums the preparation laboratories have a viewing gallery so that the public can see the technicians and paleontologists at work. This helps to show that the study of dinosaurs is going on all the time, and demonstrates the enormous amount of work involved in paleontology. Sometimes, too, the public is able to meet paleontologists and ask them questions.

TRADITIONAL DISPLAY
A mounted skeleton with the original fossilized bones, assembled on a sturdy steel framework, has been the traditional way to display dinosaur fossils in museums. They still give a dramatic impression of the scale and structure of these incredible animals. In the past, fossils were covered in a dark, tarry varnish to preserve them, but this is not done today since it hides many of the details.

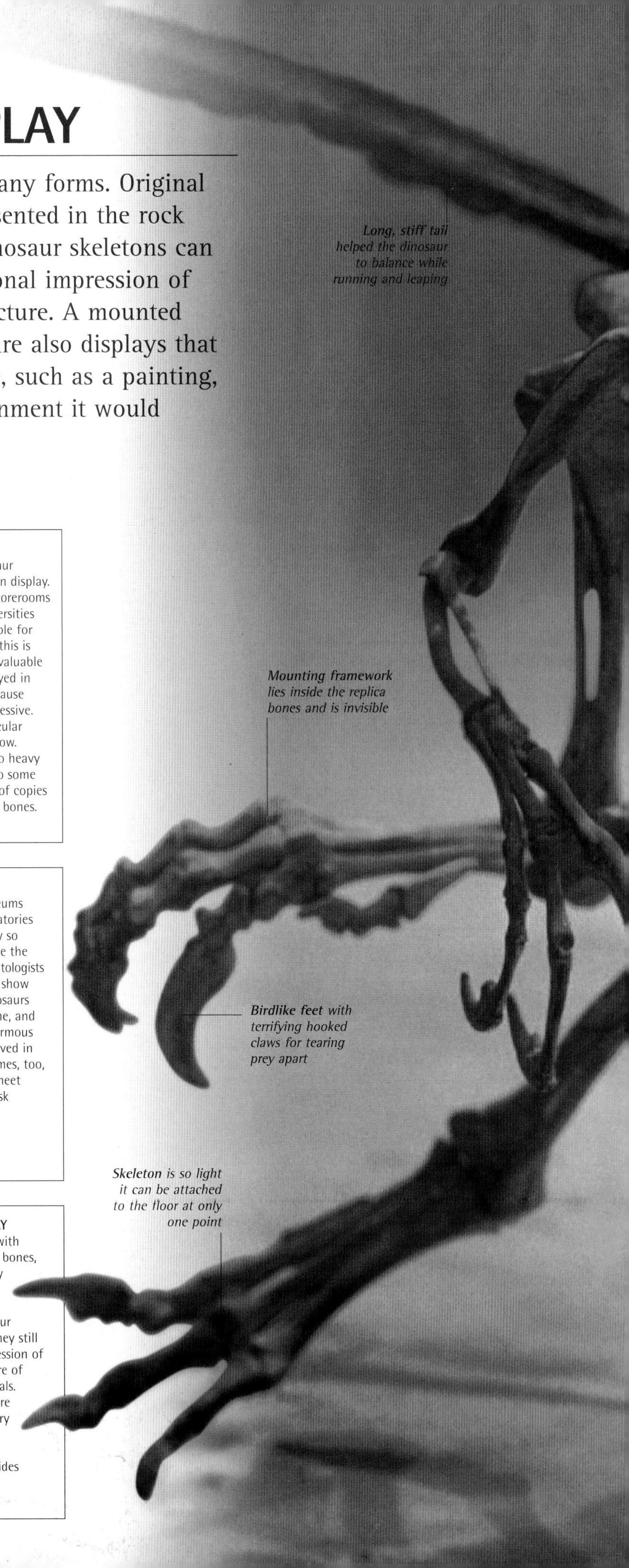

Curved spine, as the dinosaur twists and turns, suggests speed and mobility

Lightweight skull *needs little support*

Jaws *lined with the large, sharp teeth of a hunter*

Long, thin front limbs *with lethal grasping claws*

museums

▲ RECONSTRUCTION
This sickle-clawed dromaeosaur skeleton has been mounted to show the dinosaur in action, rather than in the more traditional standing pose. Dromaeosaur means "running lizard," and it was an aggressive hunter. This is dramatically conveyed by the positions of the legs and the gaping jaws. A mount like this uses replicas of the original bones, made in a sturdy but lightweight material, which are much easier to handle and mount.

◄ RESTORATION
Some museums have full-scale models that are able to move as if they were alive. The flesh of this *Allosaurus* hides a whole array of animatronics—robotic mechanisms that make the arms move, the jaws open and close, the eyes blink, and the rib cage expand and contract, as if the animal were breathing. Such models are often equipped with sound devices to make them even more realistic. Some even smell—to convey the foul breath of a carnivorous dinosaur with pieces of rotten meat trapped in its teeth.

EVOLUTION

When young animals grow up, they may be similar to their parents but they are never identical. If one animal is able to move faster than another of the same species, it can probably catch more prey and be better fed. It is more likely to be healthy and to attract a mate. Its ability to move fast will probably be passed down to its young, and to their young. Over many generations, the species will evolve (change) to become superb hunters. This process, known as natural selection, was first described by Charles Darwin in the 1800s and explains the way that life on Earth has evolved from the earliest times.

Date	Era	Period	Name	Events	Examples
4,600-545 MYA			PRECAMBRIAN	*Origin of life and evolution of Vendian organisms*	Mawsonites, Collenia
545-490 MYA	PALAEOZOIC ERA		CAMBRIAN	*Single-celled and multicellular life appear in the seas*	Olenellus
490-445 MYA	PALAEOZOIC ERA		ORDOVICIAN	*Nautiloids and jawed vertebrates swim in the seas*	Orthoceras, Crytoceras
445-415 MYA	PALAEOZOIC ERA		SILURIAN	*Plants and arachnids grow on land*	Baragwanathia, Pseudocrinites
415-355 MYA	PALAEOZOIC ERA		DEVONIAN	*Vertebrates develop four limbs and digits*	Pteraspis
355-290 MYA	PALAEOZOIC ERA		CARBONIFEROUS	*Reptiles and flying insects populate the land*	Sandalodus
290-250 MYA	PALAEOZOIC ERA		PERMIAN	*Sail-back synapsids roam the Earth*	Edaphosaurus, Diplocaulus
250-200 MYA	MESOZOIC ERA		TRIASSIC	*First dinosaurs, mammals, turtles, and frogs appear*	Lystrosaurus
200-145 MYA	MESOZOIC ERA		JURASSIC	*Pterosaurs fly in the air, dinosaurs rule the land*	Proceratosaurus, Pterodactylus
145-65 MYA	MESOZOIC ERA		CRETACEOUS	*Dinosaurs die out, first modern mammals take over*	Triceratops
65-53 MYA	CENOZOIC ERA	TERTIARY PERIOD	PALAEOCENE EPOCH	*Owls, shrews, and hedgehogs make an appearance*	Taeniolabis, Phenacodus
53-33.7 MYA	CENOZOIC ERA	TERTIARY PERIOD	EOCENE EPOCH	*Horses, elephants, dogs, and cats establish themselves*	Palaeochiropteryx, Hyracotherium
33.7-23.5 MYA	CENOZOIC ERA	TERTIARY PERIOD	OLIGOCENE EPOCH	*First monkeys, deer, and rhinoceroses arrive on the scene*	Phiomia
23.5-5.3 MYA	CENOZOIC ERA	TERTIARY PERIOD	MIOCENE EPOCH	*First apes, mice, and many new mammals appear*	Samotherium
5.31-1.64 MYA	CENOZOIC ERA	TERTIARY PERIOD	PLIOCENE EPOCH	*Cattle and sheep are common; whales diversify*	Bison, Balaena
1.64-0.01 MYA	CENOZOIC ERA	QUATERNARY PERIOD	PLEISTOCENE EPOCH	*First modern humans appear*	Gigantopithecus
0.01 MYA - PRESENT	CENOZOIC ERA	QUATERNARY PERIOD	HOLOCENE EPOCH	*Extinctions are caused by human activity*	Homo sapiens

CLASSIFICATION

Scientists have developed various systems of classification to describe living things. The one used here is a cladogram, which is a diagram that shows the relationship between different species of animal. Each branch of the cladogram is a clade, which includes an ancestral species and its descendants, showing how a particular group of dinosaurs evolved. Each clade of dinosaurs shared certain characteristics—they may have looked alike, moved in a similar way, or had the same habits or lifestyles.

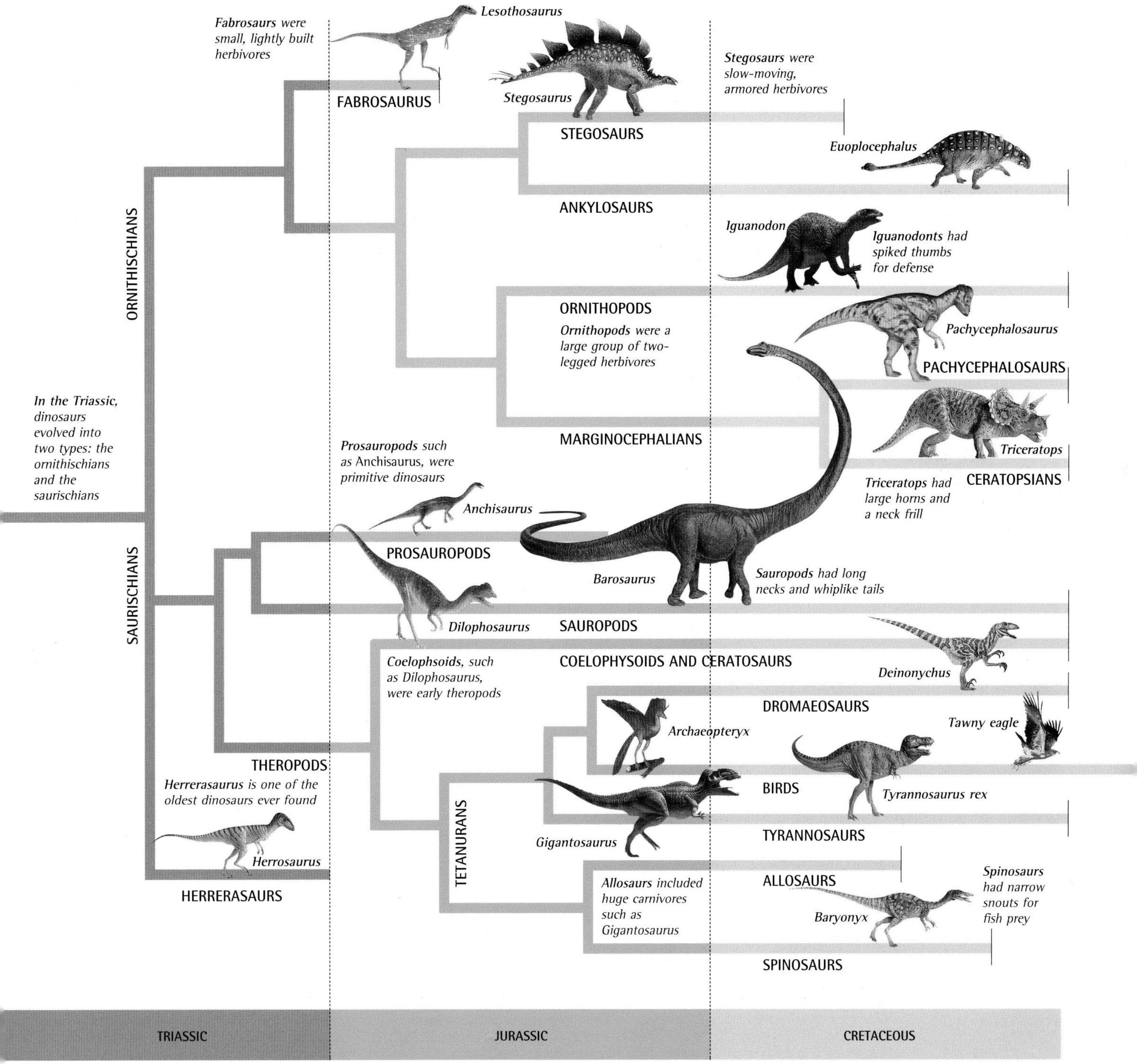

In the Triassic, dinosaurs evolved into two types: the ornithischians and the saurischians

ORNITHISCHIANS

Fabrosaurs were small, lightly built herbivores

Lesothosaurus

FABROSAURUS

Stegosaurus

Stegosaurs were slow-moving, armored herbivores

STEGOSAURS

Euoplocephalus

ANKYLOSAURS

Iguanodon

Iguanodonts had spiked thumbs for defense

ORNITHOPODS

Ornithopods were a large group of two-legged herbivores

Pachycephalosaurus

PACHYCEPHALOSAURS

MARGINOCEPHALIANS

Triceratops

Triceratops had large horns and a neck frill

CERATOPSIANS

SAURISCHIANS

Prosauropods such as Anchisaurus, were primitive dinosaurs

Anchisaurus

PROSAUROPODS

Barosaurus

Sauropods had long necks and whiplike tails

SAUROPODS

Dilophosaurus

Coelophsoids, such as Dilophosaurus, were early theropods

COELOPHYSOIDS AND CERATOSAURS

Deinonychus

DROMAEOSAURS

Archaeopteryx

Tawny eagle

BIRDS

Tyrannosaurus rex

TYRANNOSAURS

THEROPODS

Herrerasaurus is one of the oldest dinosaurs ever found

Herrosaurus

HERRERASAURS

TETANURANS

Gigantosaurus

Allosaurs included huge carnivores such as Gigantosaurus

ALLOSAURS

Baryonyx

Spinosaurs had narrow snouts for fish prey

SPINOSAURS

TRIASSIC | JURASSIC | CRETACEOUS

PROFILES

Dinosaur fossils have been found all over the world, and more are being found all the time. Each time a new fossil is examined by a paleontologist or other scientist, more information is gleaned about how and where the animal lived. The dinosaur profiles on these pages summarize what is known today about the dinosaurs that appear in this book.

ACANTHOPHOLIS "SPINY SCALES"

Pronunciation: a-KAN-tho-FOLE-is
Maximum length: 13 ft (4 m)
Time: Early Cretaceous
Diet: plants
Habitat: rivers, woodland
Fossil finds: South America (Bolivia), Europe (England)

ALBERTOSAURUS "LIZARD FROM ALBERTA"

Pronunciation: al-BERT-oh-SAW-rus
Maximum length: 26 ft (8 m)
Time: Late Cretaceous
Diet: hunted and scavenged meat
Habitat: open woodland
Fossil finds: North America (US, Canada)

ALLOSAURUS "DIFFERENT LIZARD"

Pronunciation: AL-oh-SAW-rus
Maximum length: 39 ft (12 m)
Time: Late Jurassic
Diet: meat
Habitat: open countryside
Fossil finds: North America (western US), Australia

ANCHISAURUS "NEAR LIZARD"

Pronunciation: AN-ki-SAW-rus
Maximum length: 8 ft (2.5 m)
Time: Early Jurassic
Diet: plants
Habitat: dry savanna
Fossil finds: North America (Connecticut, Massachusetts)

ANHANGUERA "OLD DEVIL"

Pronunciation: AN-han-GER-a
Wingspan: 15 ft (4.5 m)
Time: Early Cretaceous
Diet: fish
Habitat: coastal regions
Fossil finds: South America (Brazil)

ANKYLOSAURUS "FUSED LIZARD"

Pronunciation: an-KY-low-SAW-rus
Maximum length: 34 ft (10.5 m)
Time: Late Cretaceous
Diet: plants
Habitat: forests
Fossil finds: North America (Montana; Alberta, Canada), South America (Bolivia)

APATOSAURUS "DECEPTIVE LIZARD"

Pronunciation: a-PAT-oh-SAW-rus
Maximum length: 69 ft (21 m)
Time: Late Jurassic
Diet: plants
Habitat: flood plain
Fossil finds: North America (Oklahoma, Utah, Wyoming)

ARCHAEOPTERYX "ANCIENT WING"

Pronunciation: ar-kee-OP-ter-ix
Wingspan: 1 ft 6 in (0.5 m)
Time: Late Jurassic
Diet: small animals
Habitat: tropical desert islands
Fossil finds: western Europe

BARAPASAURUS "BIG LEG"

Pronunciation: ba-RA-pa-SAW-rus
Maximum length: 59 ft (18 m)
Time: Early Jurassic
Diet: plants
Habitat: low-lying flood plain
Fossil finds: Asia (India)

BAROSAURUS "HEAVY LIZARD"

Pronunciation: BAR-o-SAW-rus
Maximum length: 89 ft (27 m)
Time: Late Jurassic
Diet: plants
Habitat: flood plain
Fossil finds: North America (western US), Africa (Tanzania)

BARYONYX "HEAVY CLAW"

Pronunciation: BAR-ee-ON-ix
Maximum length: 31 ft (9.5 m)
Time: Early Cretaceous
Diet: fish
Habitat: rivers, woodlands
Fossil finds: Europe (England)

BRACHIOSAURUS "ARMED LIZARD"

Pronunciation: BRACK-ee-oh-SAW-rus
Maximum length: 82 ft (25 m)
Time: Middle to Late Jurassic
Diet: plants
Habitat: open woodland
Fossil finds: Africa (Tanzania), Europe (Portugal), North America

BRACHYLOPHOSAURUS "SHORT-CRESTED LIZARD"

Pronunciation: brack-ee-LOAF-oh-SAW-rus
Maximum length: 23 ft (7 m)
Time: Late Cretaceous
Diet: plants
Habitat: swamps
Fossil finds: North America (Alberta, Canada)

CAMARASAURUS "CHAMBERED LIZARD"

Pronunciation: kam-AR-a-SAW-rus
Maximum length: 59 ft (18 m)
Time: Late Jurassic
Diet: plants
Habitat: flood plain
Fossil finds: North America (Colorado, New Mexico, Utah, Wyoming), Europe (Portugal)

CAMPTOSAURUS "FLEXIBLE LIZARD"

Pronunciation: KAMP-toe-SAW-rus
Maximum length: 23 ft (7 m)
Time: Late Jurassic to Early Cretaceous
Diet: low-lying plants
Habitat: wooded lowlands
Fossil finds: North America (Utah), Europe

CARCHARODONTOSAURUS "SHARK-TOOTHED LIZARD"

Pronunciation: kar-KAR-oh-DONT-oh-SAW-rus
Maximum length: 40 ft (13.5 m)
Time: Early Cretaceous
Diet: hunted and scavenged meat
Habitat: wooded river valleys
Fossil finds: North Africa (Egypt, Morocco, Tunisia, Algeria, Libya, Niger)

CARNOTAURUS "FLESH-EATING"

Pronunciation: KAR-noh-TOR-us
Maximum length: 25 ft (7.5 m)
Time: Middle to Late Cretaceous
Diet: meat
Habitat: arid plains
Fossil finds: South America (Argentina)

CERATOSAURUS "HORNED LIZARD"

Pronunciation: SER-a-toe-SAW-rus
Maximum length: 20 ft (6 m)
Time: Late Jurassic
Diet: hunted and scavenged meat
Habitat: open countryside
Fossil finds: North America (Colorado, Utah), Africa (Tanzania)

COELOPHYSIS "HOLLOW FORM"

Pronunciation: SEEL-oh-FY-sis
Maximum length: 9 ft (2.8 m)
Time: Late Triassic
Diet: reptiles, fish, other dinosaurs
Habitat: dry savanna
Fossil finds: North America (Arizona, Utah, New Mexico)

COMPSOGNATHUS "PRETTY JAW"

Pronunciation: KOMP-sow-NAY-thus
Maximum length: 4 ft 6 in (1.4 m)
Time: Late Jurassic
Diet: insects, lizards, other small animals
Habitat: desert islands
Fossil finds: Europe (Germany, France)

CORYTHOSAURUS "HELMET LIZARD"

Pronunciation: ko-RITH-oh-SAW-rus
Maximum length: 33 ft (10 m)
Time: Late Cretaceous
Diet: low-lying plants
Habitat: forests
Fossil finds: North America (Montana; Alberta, Canada)

CRYOLOPHOSAURUS "FROZEN-CRESTED LIZARD"

Pronunciation: KRIE-ol-lof-oh-SAW-rus
Maximum length: 20 ft (6 m)
Time: Early Jurassic
Diet: hunted prosauropods and other plant-eating dinosaurs
Habitat: moist riverside
Fossil finds: Antarctica

DEINONYCHUS "TERRIBLE CLAW"

Pronunciation: DIE-no-NIKE-us
Maximum length: 10 ft (3 m)
Time: Early Cretaceous
Diet: meat
Habitat: open woodland
Fossil finds: North America (Montana, Utah, Wyoming)

DIPLODOCUS "DOUBLE-BEAMED"

Pronunciation: dip-LOD-oh-kus
Maximum length: 89 ft (27 m)
Time: Late Jurassic
Diet: plants
Habitat: flood plain
Fossil finds: North America (Colorado, Montana, Utah, Wyoming)

DILOPHOSAURUS "TWO-RIDGE LIZARD"

Pronunciation: DYE-lo-fuh-SAW-rus
Maximum length: 20 ft (6 m)
Time: Late Jurassic
Diet: meat
Habitat: scrub and open woodland
Fossil finds: North America (Arizona), China

DROMAEOSAURUS "RUNNING LIZARD"

Pronunciation: DROME-ee-oh-SAW-rus
Maximum length: 6 ft (1.8 m)
Time: Late Cretaceous
Diet: meat, including other dinosaurs
Habitat: open woodland
Fossil finds: North America (Montana; Alberta, Canada)

DRYOSAURUS "OAK TREE LIZARD"

Pronunciation: DRY-oh-SAW-rus
Maximum length: 10 ft (3 m)
Time: Late Jurassic
Diet: low-growing plants
Habitat: forest
Fossil finds: Africa (Tanzania), North America (Colorado, Wyoming)

DSUNGARIPTERUS "JUNGGAR BASIN WING"

Pronunciation: JUNG-gah-RIP-te-rus
Wingspan: 10 ft (3 m)
Time: Early Cretaceous
Diet: fish, mollusks, seashore animals
Habitat: coastal shores
Fossil finds: Asia (China)

EDMONTONIA "FROM EDMONTON"

Pronunciation: ed-MONT-oh-NIA
Maximum length: 23 ft (7 m)
Time: Late Cretaceous
Diet: low-growing plants
Habitat: open woodland
Fossil finds: North America (Alberta in Canada, Alaska, Montana in US)

EDMONTOSAURUS "EDMONTON LIZARD"

Pronunciation: ed-MONT-oh-SAW-rus
Maximum length: 43 ft (13 m)
Time: Late Cretaceous
Diet: low-lying plants
Habitat: swamps
Fossil finds: North America (Wyoming, Montana, and New Jersey, US; Alberta, Canada)

ELASMOSAURUS "THIN-PLATED LIZARD"

Pronunciation: ee-LAZ-mo-SAW-rus
Maximum length: 46 ft (14 m)
Time: Late Cretaceous
Diet: fish, swimming mollusks
Habitat: shallow seas
Fossil finds: North America (Wyoming, Kansas), Asia (Japan)

EORAPTOR "DAWN RAPTOR"

Pronunciation: ee-oh-RAP-tor
Maximum length: 3 ft (1 m)
Time: Late Triassic
Diet: hunted and scavenged meat
Habitat: river valleys
Fossil finds: South America (Argentina)

EUOPLOCEPHALUS "WELL-ARMORED LIZARD"

Pronunciation you-op-luh-SEF-uh-lus
Maximum length: 23 ft (7 m)
Time: Late Cretaceous
Diet: low-lying plants
Habitat: open woodland
Fossil finds: North America (Montana; Alberta, Canada)

GALLIMIMUS "ROOSTER MIMIC"

Pronunciation GAL-ih-MIME-us
Maximum length: 20 ft (6 m)
Time: Late Cretaceous
Diet: insects, lizards, eggs, plants
Habitat: river valleys
Fossil finds: Asia (Mongolia)

GASTONIA "FOR GASTON"

Pronunciation gas-TONE-ia
Maximum length: 16 ft (5 m)
Time: Early Cretaceous
Diet: low-lying plants
Habitat: open woodland
Fossil finds: North America (Utah)

GIGANTOSAURUS "GIANT SOUTHERN LIZARD"

Pronunciation gi-GANT-oh-SAW-rus
Maximum length: 43 ft (13 m)
Time: Late Cretaceous
Diet: meat
Habitat: flood plain
Fossil finds: South America (Argentina)

HADROSAURUS "BULKY LIZARD"

Pronunciation: HAD-roe-SAW-rus
Maximum length: 33 ft (10 m)
Time: Late Cretaceous
Diet: plants
Habitat: wooded lowlands
Fossil finds: North America (New Jersey, Montana, and New Mexico, US; Alberta, Canada)

HERRERASAURUS "HERRERA'S LIZARD"

Pronunciation: her-rare-uh-SAW-rus
Maximum length: 13 ft (4 m)
Time: Late Triassic
Diet: meat
Habitat: river valleys
Fossil finds: South America (Argentina)

HETERODONTOSAURUS "DIFFERENT-TOOTHED LIZARD"

Pronunciation: HET-er-oh-DONT-oh-SAW-rus
Maximum length: 4 ft (1.3 m)
Time: Late Triassic to Early Jurassic
Diet: plants
Habitat: dry lowlands
Fossil finds: Africa (South Africa)

HYLAEOSAURUS "WOODLAND LIZARD"

Pronunciation: HY-lee-oh-SAW-rus
Maximum length: 13 ft (4 m)
Time: Early Cretaceous
Diet: plants
Habitat: open woodland
Fossil finds: South America (Bolivia), England

HYPSILOPHODON "HIGH-CRESTED TOOTH"

Pronunciation: hip-see-LOAF-oh-don
Maximum length: 6 ft (2.3 m)
Time: Early Cretaceous
Diet: low-growing plants
Habitat: woodlands
Fossil finds: Europe (UK, Spain, Portugal), North America (South Dakota, USA)

ICHTHYOSAURUS "FISH LIZARD"

Pronunciation: ICK-thee-oh-SAW-rus
Maximum length: 10 ft (3 m)
Time: Early Jurassic to Early Cretaceous
Diet: fish, squid
Habitat: open ocean
Fossil finds: North America (Alberta, Canada), Greenland, Europe (England, Germany), South America

IGUANODON "IGUANA TOOTH"

Pronunciation: ig-WA-no-don
Maximum length: 40 ft (12 m)
Time: Early Cretaceous
Diet: leaves, branches, fronds, ferns
Habitat: woodlands
Fossil finds: Europe, North Africa, Asia (Mongolia), North America

KRONOSAURUS "KRONO'S LIZARD"

Pronunciation: kro-no-SAW-rus
Maximum length: 30 ft (9 m)
Time: Early Cretaceous
Diet: marine reptiles, fish, mollusks
Habitat: open ocean
Fossil finds: Australia (Queensland), South America (Columbia)

LAMBEOSAURUS "LAMBE'S LIZARD"

Pronunciation: LAM-bee-oh-SAW-rus
Maximum length: 49 ft (15 m)
Time: Late Cretaceous
Diet: pine needles, leaves, twigs
Habitat: forests
Fossil finds: North America (Montana; Alberta, Canada), Mexico (Baja California)

LEAELLYNASAURA "LEAELLYN'S LIZARD"

Pronunciation: lee-al-in-ah-SAW-ra
Maximum length: 10 ft (3 m)
Time: Middle Cretaceous
Diet: plants
Habitat: cold, icy regions
Fossil finds: Australia (Victoria)

LESOTHOSAURUS "LESOTHO LIZARD"

Pronunciation: leh-SOTH-uh-SAW-rus
Maximum length: 3 ft (1 m)
Time: Early Jurassic
Diet: low-lying plants
Habitat: semideserts
Fossil finds: South America (Venezuela), southern Africa (Lesotho)

MAIASAURA "GOOD MOTHER LIZARD"

Pronunciation: MY-a-SAW-ra
Maximum length: 30 ft (9 m)
Time: Late Cretaceous
Diet: plants
Habitat: wooded riverbanks
Fossil finds: North America

MAMENCHISAURUS "MAMEXI LIZARD"

Pronunciation: ma-MENCH-ih-SAW-rus
Maximum length: 82 ft (25 m)
Time: Late Jurassic
Diet: plants
Habitat: flood plain
Fossil finds: Asia (China)

MEGALOSAURUS "GREAT LIZARD"

Pronunciation: MEG-a-low-SAW-rus
Maximum length: 30 ft (9 m)
Time: Middle Jurassic
Diet: meat
Habitat: coastal woodland
Fossil finds: Europe (UK, France), Africa (Morocco)

MUSSAURUS "MOUSE LIZARD"

Pronunciation: muss-AW-rus
Maximum length: 10 ft (3 m)
Time: Late Triassic
Diet: plants
Habitat: dry desert
Fossil finds: South America (Argentina)

NOTHOSAURUS "SOUTHERN LIZARD"

Pronunciation: noth-uh-saw-rus
Maximum length: 10 ft (3 m)
Time: Triassic
Diet: fish
Habitat: shallow tropical seas
Fossil finds: Europe (Germany, Italy, The Netherlands, Switzerland), North Africa, Asia (Russia, China, Israel)

ORODROMEUS "MOUNTAIN RUNNER"

Pronunciation: OR-ro-DRO-me-us
Maximum length: 8 ft (2.5 m)
Time: Late Cretaceous
Diet: plants
Habitat: open woodland
Fossil finds: North America (Montana)

OURANOSAURUS "BRAVE LIZARD"

Pronunciation: oo-RAN-oh-SAW-rus
Maximum length: 23 ft (7 m)
Time: Early Cretaceous
Diet: plants
Habitat: flood plains
Fossil finds: Africa (Niger)

OVIRAPTOR "EGG ROBBER"

Pronunciation: OVE-ih-RAP-tor
Maximum length: 8 ft (2.5 m)
Time: Late Cretaceous
Diet: meat, eggs
Habitat: semidesert
Fossil finds: central Asia (Mongolia)

PACHYCEPHALOSAURUS "THICK-HEADED LIZARD"

Pronunciation: PAK-ee-KEF-al-oh-SAW-rus
Maximum length: 15 ft (4.6 m)
Time: Late Cretaceous
Diet: leaves, fruit, small animals
Habitat: forests
Fossil finds: North America (US; Alberta, Canada), Europe (UK), Asia (Mongolia), Africa (Madagascar)

PACHYRHINOSAURUS "THICK-NOSED LIZARD"

Pronunciation: PAK-ee-RINE-oh-SAW-rus
Maximum length: 23 ft (7 m)
Time: Late Cretaceous
Diet: cycads and other plants
Habitat: forests
Fossil finds: North America (Alberta, Canada, and Alaska, US)

PARASAUROPHOLUS "BESIDE SAUROPHOLUS"

Pronunciation: par-a-SAWR-oh-LOAF-us
Maximum length: 40 ft (12 m)
Time: Late Cretaceous
Diet: pine needles, leaves, twigs
Habitat: swamps
Fossil finds: North America (New Mexico and Utah, US; Alberta, Canada)

PENTACERATOPS "FIVE-HORNED FACE"

Pronunciation: PEN-ta-SER-a-tops
Maximum length: 26 ft (8 m)
Time: Late Cretaceous
Diet: cycads, palms, and other plants
Habitat: swamps, forests
Fossil finds: North America (New Mexico)

PHUWIANGOSAURUS "PHU WIANG LIZARD"

Pronunciation: poo-WYAHNG-O-SAW-rus
Maximum length: 102 ft (30 m)
Time: Early Cretaceous
Diet: plants
Habitat: tropical woodland
Fossil finds: Asia (Thailand)

PLATEOSAURUS "FLAT LIZARD"

Pronunciation: PLAT-ee-oh-SAW-rus
Maximum length: 26 ft (8 m)
Time: Late Triassic
Diet: conifers, cycads, and other plants
Habitat: dry desert

PROTOCERATOPS "FIRST-HORNED FACE"

Pronunciation: pro-toe-SER-a-tops
Maximum length: 8 ft (2.5 m)
Time: Late Cretaceous
Diet: plants
Habitat: desertlike scrubland
Fossil finds: Asia (Mongolia, China)

PSITTACOSAURUS "PARROT LIZARD"

Pronunciation: si-TAK-oh-SAW-rus
Maximum length: 8 ft (2.5 m)
Time: Early Cretaceous
Diet: plants, small animals
Habitat: desertlike scrubland
Fossil finds: Asia (Mongolia, China, Thailand)

PTERANODON "WINGED AND TOOTHLESS"

Pronunciation: ter-AN-uh-don
Wingspan: 30 ft (9 m)
Time: Late Cretaceous
Diet: fish, mollusks, shore animals
Habitat: shallow intercontinental seas
Fossil finds: North America (South Dakota, Kansas, Oregon in USA), Europe (England), Asia (Japan)

PTERODACTYLUS "WINGED FINGER"

Pronunciation: TER-uh-DAK-ti-lus
Wingspan: 3 ft (1 m)
Time: Late Jurassic
Diet: fish, insects
Habitat: coastal plains and cliffs
Fossil finds: Europe (England, France, Germany), Africa (Tanzania)

RHAMPHORHYNCHUS "BEAK SNOUT"

Pronunciation: RAM-for-RINE-cus
Wingspan: 4 in (1.75 cm)
Time: Late Jurassic
Diet: fish
Habitat: coastal plains and cliffs
Fossil finds: Europe (Germany, England), Africa (Tanzania)

SALTASAURUS "SALTA PROVINCE LIZARD"

Pronunciation: SALT-a-SAW-rus
Maximum length: 40 ft (12 m)
Time: Late Cretaceous
Diet: plants
Habitat: lowlands
Fossil finds: South America (Argentina, Uruguay)

SCELIDOSAURUS "LIMB LIZARD"

Pronunciation: skel-IDE-oh-SAW-rus
Maximum length: 13 ft (4 m)
Time: Early Jurassic
Diet: plants
Habitat: river valleys
Fossil finds: Europe, North America (Arizona, USA)

SEISMOSAURUS "QUAKE LIZARD"

Pronunciation: SIZE-mo-SAW-rus
Maximum length: 171 ft (52 m)
Time: Late Jurassic
Diet: conifers and other plants
Habitat: flood plain

SPINOSAURUS "SPINY LIZARD"

Pronunciation: SPINE-O-SAW-rus
Maximum length: 49 ft (15 m)
Time: Middle Cretaceous
Diet: fish, other dinosaurs, may have scavenged
Habitat: wooded river valleys
Fossil finds: Africa (Egypt, Morocco)

STEGOSAURUS "ROOF LIZARD"

Pronunciation: STEG-O-SAW-rus
Maximum length: 30 ft (9 m)
Time: Late Jurassic
Diet: low-lying plants
Habitat: open woodland
Fossil finds: North America (Utah, Wyoming, Colorado), Europe (UK), Asia (India, China), Africa

STYRACOSAURUS "SPIKED LIZARD"

Pronunciation: sty-RAK-oh-SAW-rus
Maximum length: 16 ft (5 m)
Time: Late Cretaceous
Diet: ferns, cycads, and other plants
Habitat: open woodland
Fossil finds: North America (Arizona and Montana, US; Alberta, Canada)

SUCHOMIMUS "CROCODILE MIMIC"

Pronunciation: SOOK-O-MIEM-US
Maximum length: 36 ft (11 m)
Time: Early Cretaceous
Diet: fish, meat
Habitat: flood plain
Fossil finds: Africa (Niger)

THESCELOSAURUS "WONDERFUL LIZARD"

Pronunciation: THES-kel-o-SAW-rus
Maximum length: 4 m (13 ft)
Time: Late Cretaceous
Diet: plants
Habitat: wooded lowlands
Fossil finds: North America (Montana, South Dakota, and Wyoming, US; Alberta and Saskatchewan, Canada)

TITANOSAURUS "TITAN LIZARD"

Pronunciation: tie-TAN-oh-SAW-rus
Maximum length: 66 ft (20 m)
Time: Late Cretaceous
Diet: plants
Habitat: open plains
Fossil finds: South America (Argentina), Europe (France), Asia (India), Africa (Madagascar)

TRICERATOPS "HORRIBLE THREE-HORNED FACE"

Pronunciation: try-SER-a-tops
Maximum length: 30 ft (9 m)
Time: Late Cretaceous
Diet: low-lying plants
Habitat: forests
Fossil finds: western North America

TROODON "WOUNDING TOOTH"

Pronunciation: TROE-o-don
Maximum length: 11 ft (3.5 m)
Time: Late Cretaceous
Diet: meat
Habitat: open woodland
Fossil finds: North America (Montana and Wyoming, US; Alberta, Canada)

TROPEOGNATHUS "KEEL JAW"

Pronunciation: TRO-peog-NA-thus
Wingspan: 20 ft (6 m)
Time: Early Cretaceous
Diet: fish, squid
Habitat: open ocean
Fossil finds: South America (Brazil)

TYLOSAURUS "SWOLLEN LIZARD"

Pronunciation: TIE-lo-SAW-rus
Wingspan: 26 ft (8 m)
Time: Late Cretaceous
Diet: fish, squid, turtles
Habitat: open ocean
Fossil finds: North America (Manitoba, Northwest Territories, Kansas, Colorado, Alabama, Mississippi), Europe (Belgium)

TYRANNOSAURUS "TYRANT LIZARD"

Pronunciation: tie-RAN-oh-SAW-rus
Maximum length: 39 ft (12 m)
Time: Late Cretaceous
Diet: hunted and scavenged meat
Habitat: forests
Fossil finds: western North America, Asia (Mongolia)

VELOCIRAPTOR "SPEEDY THIEF"

Pronunciation: vel-O-si-RAP-tor
Maximum length: 6 ft (2 m)
Time: Late Cretaceous
Diet: meat, including other dinosaurs
Habitat: dry desert
Fossil finds: Asia (Mongolia, China)

VULCANODON "VULCAN TOOTH"

Pronunciation: vul-KAN-oh-don
Maximum length: 21 ft (6.5 m)
Time: Early Jurassic
Diet: plants
Habitat: dry savannah
Fossil finds: Africa (Zimbabwe)

XUANHANOSAURUS "XUANHAN COUNTY LIZARD"

Pronunciation: zwan-HAN-O-SAW-rus
Maximum length: 20 ft (6 m)
Time: Middle Jurassic
Diet: meat
Habitat: wet lowland areas
Fossil finds: Asia (China)

BIOGRAPHIES

Paleontology is the science of extinct forms of life. In order to find out about extinct animals and plants, a paleontologist has to be a naturalist, geologist, historian, archaeologist, zoologist, biologist—or a combination of some or all of these. On these pages, you will find the biographies of some of the palseontologists and other scientists who have contributed to our extensive knowledge of the extraordinary world of the dinosaurs.

GEORGES LOUIS LECLERC, COMTE DE BUFFON *1707–1788*

This French naturalist and author popularized natural history. His treatise *Histoire Naturelle* (*Natural History*) has appeared in several editions and has been translated into many languages. He was able to express complex ideas in a clear form, and his enthusiasm for the Jardin du Roi while he was keeper was so great that he made the gardens the center of botanical research in France.

GEORGES CUVIER *1769–1832*

The founder of comparative anatomy, French naturalist Baron Georges Cuvier led the way in the reconstruction of vertebrate animals. He systematically classified mollusks, fish, and fossil mammals and reptiles. He wrote on the structure of living and fossil animals, and believed that the development of life on Earth was greatly affected by occasional catastrophes. With Alexandre Brongniart, he explored the geology of the Paris Basin.

ALEXANDRE BRONGNIART *1770–1847*

A French mineralogist, geologist, and chemist, Brongniart was the first to develop a systematic study of trilobites and a system for the classification of reptiles. Working with Georges Cuvier, he pioneered stratigraphy, the examination of rock layers to reveal past environments and life forms. In 1822, Brongniart and Cuvier mapped the Tertiary strata of the Paris Basin and collected local fossils.

WILLIAM BUCKLAND *1784–1856*

This English clergyman and geologist dedicated himself to a systematic examination of the geology of Great Britain. In 1819, he discovered the first *Megalosaurus*, although he did not recognize it as a dinosaur. He wrote extensively about his finds and his treatise *Geology and Mineralogy* (1836) went through three editions. In 1845, he was appointed Dean of Westminster Abbey.

GIDEON MANTELL *1790–1852*

A very successful doctor on the south coast of England, Mantell was also an amateur fossil hunter, one of the first in the world. His wife, Mary Ann Mantell, is thought to have found the first *Iguanodon* tooth in 1822, but it took many years for Mantell to establish its identity. He also discovered the first brachiosaur, *Pelorosaurus*, and *Hylaeosaurus*, an early ankylosaur.

MARY ANNING *1799–1847*

A pioneering fossil collector, Anning's father sold fossil specimens in Lyme Regis on the south coast of England. It was there that she discovered the first *Ichthyosaurus* in 1811, and went on to discover the first plesiosaur in 1821 and the first pterodactyl in 1828.

RICHARD OWEN *1804–1892*

Trained as a doctor, Owen went on to become an expert in comparative anatomy. He worked for the British Museum and founded the Natural History Museum in London. A pioneer in vertebrate paleontology, he conducted extensive research on extinct reptiles, mammals, and birds. He coined the word "dinosaur" in 1842, and was responsible for the first full-scale dinosaur reconstructions, which were displayed in Crystal Palace Gardens in London.

DOUGLAS AGASSIZ *1807–1873*

In 1826, Agassiz, a Swiss-American naturalist, was chosen to classify a large collection of fish that had been captured in the Amazon River region of Brazil, South America. He then researched in detail the extinct fish of Europe. By 1844, he was established as a pioneer in the study of extinct life, and had named nearly 1,000 fossil fish.

CHARLES DARWIN *1809–1882*

English naturalist Charles Darwin's ideas are now the cornerstone of paleontological research worldwide. In 1831, he traveled to the Galapagos Islands aboard the HMS *Beagle*, as a naturalist for a surveying expedition. His observations on the relationship between living animals, newly extinct animals, and fossil finds led him to develop a theory of evolution, a theory that was very controversial at the time. He believed that species evolve by a process of natural selection. His theories were published in 1859, in *On the Origin of Species by Natural Selection*, and *The Descent of Man* followed in 1871.

CHARLES OTHNIEL MARSH *1831–1899*

After studying geology and paleontology in Germany, this American paleontologist was appointed professor of paleontology at Yale University in 1860. He persuaded his uncle, George Peabody, to establish the Peabody Museum of Natural History at Yale, and organized scientific expeditions to the western states of the US. He and his great rival, Edward Drinker Cope, dominated fossil-hunting in the late 1880s. He named about 500 species of fossil animals. His finds include *Pterodactylus*, *Apatosaurus*, *Allosaurus*, and early horses.

ERNST HAECKEL *1834–1919*

Biologist Ernst Haeckel was the first prominent German to support Darwin's theories of evolution. He also drew up a genealogical tree, laying out the relationship between the various orders of animals. He coined the word "phylum" for the major group to which all related classes of organisms belong. He traced the descent of humans from single-celled organisms through chimpanzees and so-called *Pithecanthropus erectus*, which he saw as the link between apes and human beings.

WILLIAM PARKER FOULKE *d.1865*

This US scientist and dinosaur artist found the first US hadrosaur skeleton. The bones were found by workmen in New Jersey in 1838. Foulke heard of the discovery in 1858 and recognized its importance. Joseph Leidy named the dinosaur after him, as *Hadrosaurus foulkii*.

EDWARD DRINKER COPE *1840–1897*

After teaching comparative zoology and botany in Pennsylvania from 1864 to 1867, Cope spent 22 years exploring the area between Texas and Wyoming, where he discovered several extinct species of fish, reptiles, and mammals. He worked for the US Geological Survey as a paleontologist, studying the evolutionary history of the horse and of mammal teeth. He published more than 1,200 books and papers, and was the author of Cope's Law, which stated that over time species tend to become larger. He is also remembered for his famous rivalry with Charles Othniel Marsh. His finds include *Camarasaurus* and *Ceolophysis*.

LOUIS DOLLO *1857–1931*

This Belgian civil engineer and paleontologist was responsible for the first reconstruction of *Iguanodon*. In 1878, he worked alongside Louis De Pauw to study the *Iguanodon* skeletons found in a coalmine at the village of Bernissart in Belgium. He identified the thumb spike, which had originally been thought to be a horn. Dollo's law states that organisms can evolve specializations, but that these are later lost. For example, horses cannot re-evolve the side toes that they have lost.

EUGENE DUBOIS *1858–1940*

A Dutch anatomist and geologist, Dubois was interested in human evolution, and in 1887, traveled to the East Indies to look for ancient human remains. In 1891, he discovered the remains of Java Man, the first known fossils of the early human *Homo erectus*. He found a one-million-year-old jaw fragment, skullcap, and thighbone of a hominid that had distinctive brow ridges and a flat, receding forehead. He named it *Pithecanthropus* ("apeman") *erectus*.

EBERHARD FRAAS *1862–1915*

In 1900, when German naturalist Fraas was traveling through Tanzania (then called Tanganyika) he visited Tendaguru Hills and helped to excavate more than 250 tons of dinosaur bones. He also found *Efraasia*, a primitive plant-eating dinosaur named after him, in what is now Germany, and named *Procompsognathus* in 1915. With Charles Andrews he suggested that creodonts (primitive carnivores) were the ancestors of whales.

ERNST STROMER VON REICHENBACH *1870–1952*

German paleontologist Stromer discovered the first dinosaurs in Egypt between 1911 and 1914, in the Bahariya Oasis, southwest of Cairo. The original specimens of the spinosaurids that he found were destroyed in the Bayerische Staatssammnung Museum when Madrid was bombed in 1944. He later identified the giant meat-eater.

BARNUM BROWN *1873–1963*

This US paleontologist was one of the greatest dinosaur hunters of the 20th century. His finds include *Ankylosaurus*, *Anchiceratops*, *Corythosaurus*, *Saurolophus*, and the first *Tyrannosaurus* ever discovered. From 1910 to 1915, Brown recovered a spectacular variety of complete dinosaur skeletons from the Red Deer River in Alberta, Canada. In the 1930s, he excavated a wealth of Jurassic fossils at Howe Ranch, Wyoming. As assistant curator, Brown also acquired fossils from all over the world for the American Museum of Natural History. He worked not only throughout the United States, but in Canada, India, South America, and Ethiopia.

WILLIAM BEEBE *1877–1962*

US biologist, explorer, author, and inventor. An enthusiastic fossil collector from childhood, Beebe was an explorer and naturalist who became curator of ornithology at New York Zoological Gardens in 1899. In 1915, he described a hypothetical ancestor to *Archaeopteryx*, which he called *Tetrapteryx*. He also proposed that the ornithomimosaur (bird mimic) dinosaurs, such as *Deinocheirus*, ate insects.

ROY CHAPMAN ANDREWS *1884–1960*

US naturalist Andrews graduated in 1906 and then went to Alaska and Japan on expeditions for the American Museum of Natural History (AMNH). Between 1922 and 1925, he led four expeditions to the Gobi Desert in Outer Mongolia, where he pioneered the use of a new vehicle, the car, backed up by camel trains, to explore remote regions. His teams discovered the first-known fossilized dinosaur nests and hatchlings as well as the world's first *Velociraptor* skeleton. He became the director of the AMNH in 1934. His other finds include *Protoceratops*, *Oviraptor*, and *Saurornithoides*.

LOUIS LEAKEY *1903–1972*
MARY LEAKEY *1913–1996*

Husband and wife team Louis and Mary proved with their fossil finds that human evolution was centered on Africa. These British anthropologists also proved that the human species was older than had been thought. They were working in the Olduvai Gorge, Tanzania, in 1959, when Mary discovered a 1.7-million-year-old fossil hominid. Between 1960 and 1973, the Leakeys discovered remains of *Homo habilis*, which Louis theorized was a direct ancestor of modern humans. After their deaths, their son Richard Leakey (b.1944) continued their work. Finds include *Proconsul*, *Australopithecus boisei*, and *Homo habilis*.

MARTIN GLAESSNER *1906–1989*

Glaessner was an Australian geologist who produced the first detailed descriptions of the Precambian Ediacaran fossils from the Flinders Range mountains of southern Australia. In 1961, he recognized that the Ediacaran fossils were the oldest-known multicelled organisms.

LUIS ALVAREZ *1911–1988*
WALTER ALVAREZ *b.1940*

This US father (geologist) and son (physicist) team publicized the discovery of a worldwide layer of clay rich in the rare element iridium. This element was present in rocks from the K-T boundary, the border between the Cretaceous and Tertiary periods. They argued that the iridium was deposited when a meteorite hit the Earth. They speculated that this event may have been the reason the dinosaurs became extinct.

ELSO BARGHOORN *b.1915*

In 1956, this US paleontologist discovered two-billion-year-old Precambrian gunflint fossils in Ontario. These are some of the best-preserved microfossils in the world and Barghoorn found them in silica-rich flint rocks. In 1968, he showed how fossils of biomolecules such as amino acids can be preserved in rocks.

ZOFIA KIELAN-JAWOROWSKA *b.1925*

A Polish paleontologist, Kielan-Jaworowska was the first woman to organize and lead fossil-hunting expeditions to the Gobi Desert, which took place from 1963 to 1971. In Mongolia, she discovered sauropods, tarbosaurs, duckbilled dinosaurs, ostrich mimics, and rare mammals from the Cretaceous and early Tertiary. Her book, *Hunting for Dinosaurs* (1969), has done much to popularize paleontology worldwide, but particularly in Mongolia. Her finds include a *Protoceratops* fighting a juvenile *Velociraptor*.

JOSÉ F. BONAPARTE *b.1928*

This Argentinian paleontologist has found and named many South American dinosaurs, including *Mussaurus* and *Saltasaurus*. In 1993, with Rodolfo Coria, he named *Argentinosaurus*.

RODOLFO CORIA *(unknown)*

Coria, an Argentinian paleontologist, worked with José F. Bonaparte in Argentina, naming *Argentinosaurus*. He then went on to identify a giant predator, *Gigantosaurus*, whose remains were spotted in 1994 in the foothills of the Andes by an amateur fossil-hunter.

RINCHEN BARSBOLD *b.1935*

As Director of the Institute of Geology at the Mongolian Academy of Sciences, this Mongolian paleontologist discovered many new dinosaurs. *Barsboldia*, a 30 ft- (10 m-) long duck-billed dinosaur that lived in Mongolia in the Late Cretaceous, was named after him in 1981. His other finds include *Conchoraptor*, *Anserimimus*, and *Gallimimus*.

DONG ZHI-MING *b.1937*

Dong, a Chinese paleontologist, studied under the father of Chinese paleontology, Yang Zhongdian. A prolific dinosaur fossil-hunter, Dong has led expeditions to the Gobi Desert and China's Yunnan province. His finds include *Yangchuanosaurus*, *Chungkingosaurus*, and *Archaoeceratops*.

PETER GALTON *b.1942*

English paleontologist Galton successfully demonstrated that hadrosaurs such as *Maiasaura* and *Hadrosaurus* did not drag their tails, but used them to act as a counterbalance to their heads. In the 1970s, he suggested that birds and dinosaurs should be grouped together as the Dinosauria. His other finds include *Lesothosaurus* and *Aliwalia*.

ROBERT T. BAKKER *b.1945*

This charismatic American paleontologist and film consultant has promoted a number of controversial and revolutionary theories, including that dinosaurs are the hot-blooded relatives of birds, rather than cold-blooded giant lizards. His reconstructions of dinosaurs show them standing upright, not dragging their tails. He has organized digs in many countries, including South Africa, Mongolia, Zimbabwe, Canada, and the states of Colorado, Utah, and Montana. He has found the only complete *Apatosaurus* skull and a baby allosaur tooth in an *Apatosaurus* bone. As part of his mission to popularize dinosaurs, Bakker acted as consultant on Steven Spielberg's film *Jurassic Park*. His other finds include a baby *Tyrannosaurus*, and a *Stegosaurus*.

JENNIFER CLACK *b.1947*

Clack examined Devonian fossils and showed that legs that evolved for navigating in water later became adapted for walking on land. This English paleontologist's finding revolutionized theories about tetrapods, the first vertebrate animals that had legs. She also discovered *Acanthostega* and *Eucritta*.

SUE HENDRICKSON *b.1949*

In South Dakota in 1990, American marine archaeologist and fossil-hunter Hendrickson found the largest and most complete *Tyrannosaurus* to date. The fossil is now displayed at the Chicago Field Museum and is known as "Sue."

PHILIP J. CURRIE B.1949

A Canadian paleontologist, Currie is a curator at the Royal Tyrrell Museum of Paleontology, Drumheller in Canada, and a major research scientist. He has written a number of dinosaur books including *Newest and Coolest Dinosaurs* (1998). He specializes in Permian fossil reptiles including diapsid reptiles from Africa and Madagascar, and early kinds of synapsids from Europe and the US. Finds include *Caudipteryx*.

DEREK BRIGGS *b.1950*

Known for his work on the Middle Cambrian Burgess Shale, English paleontologist Briggs described a number of arthropods found there. The Burgess Shale is a 530-million-year-old mudstone deposit in British Columbia. He has discovered, with others, several Burgess Shale sites, showing that the animals found there were common inhabitants of the Cumbrian seas.

ERIC BUFFETAUT *b.1950*

This French geologist worked on developing a complete picture of dinosaur evolution in Thailand. He discovered the oldest known sauropod dinosaur, *Isanosaurus attavipachi* from the Upper Triassic, and numerous dinosaur fossil footprints. In Europe, he found a giant pterosaur with a wingspan of 19.5 ft (9 m). He also found the first late Cretaceous birds in France.

PAUL SERENO *b.1957*

Sereno, an American paleontologist, has discovered dinosaurs on five continents. He named the oldest-known dinosaur, *Eoraptor*, and found the first complete skull of *Herrerasaurus* in the foothills of the Andes in Argentina. His team also found *Afrovenator* and the gigantic skull of *Carcharodontosaurus* in the Sahara. He has also been on expeditions to the Gobi Desert and India. He has rearranged the dinosaur family tree, reorganizing the ornithischians and naming the clade Cerapoda.

LUIS CHIAPPE *b.1962*

Argentinian vertebrate paleontologist, and curator of vertebrate paleontology at the Los Angeles County Museum, Chiappe is one of the world's leading authorities on ancient birds, and on the relationship between birds and dinosaurs. In 1998, in the Rio Colorado region of Patagonia, Chiappe's team unearthed thousands of *Titanosaurus* eggshells and the first dinosaur embryos to be found in the southern hemisphere. They also found the first identified eggs belonging to sauropods.

GLOSSARY

Adaptation the response of a living organism to changes in its environment.

Age a unit of geological time, which is characterized by some feature (like an Ice Age).

Amber a yellowish, fossilized tree resin that sometimes contains trapped matter.

Ammonite an early marine creature. It was protected by a spiral-coiled shell, which contained many air-filled chambers.

Amphibians animals that live in the water during their early life (breathing through gills), but usually live on land as adults (and breathe with lungs), for example frogs and salamanders.

Bipeds animals that walk on two legs are bipeds. Many carnivorous dinosaurs were bipedal, including *T. rex.*

Body fossils fossilized body parts, such as bones, teeth, claws, skin, and embryos.

Carnivores carnivores are animals that eat meat. They usually have sharp teeth and powerful jaws. All the theropods were carnivores, and some were hunters, while others scavenged.

Cold-blooded animals that rely upon the temperature and their behavior (like sunning themselves) to regulate their body temperature are cold-blooded.

Coprolite ("dung stone") fossilized faeces. Coprolites record the diet and habitat of prehistoric animals.

Cretaceous Period the last Period in the Mesozoic Era, from 145 to 65 million years ago. Flowering plants flourished and dinosaurs were at their height during the Cretaceous Period. There was a mass extinction at the end of the Cretaceous, marking the end of the dinosaurs and many other species of animals and plants.

Cycads primitive seed plants that dominated the Jurassic landscape. They have palmlike leaves and produce large cones.

Dinosaurs ("terrible lizard") extinct land reptiles that walked with an erect stance during the Mesozoic Era. Their hip structure caused their legs to stick out from under their bodies, and not sprawl out from the side like other reptiles.

Encephalization Quotient (EQ) the ratio of the brain weight of the animal to the brain weight of a similar animal of the same body weight.

Evolution a process in which the gene pool of a population gradually (over millions of years) changes in response to environmental pressures, natural selection, and genetic mutations. All forms of life came into being by this process.

Extinction the process in which groups of organisms (species) die out. Species go extinct when they are unable to adapt to changes in the environment or compete effectively with other organisms.

Fossils mineralized impressions or casts of ancient plants and animals (or their traces, like footprints).

Gastroliths stones that some animals swallow and use to help grind up tough plant matter in their digestive system are called gastroliths. They are also called gizzard rocks.

Ginkgo a primitive, seed-bearing tree that was common during the Mesozoic Era. A deciduous tree, it has fan-shaped leaves.

Gondwana the southern continent formed after Pangaea broke up during the Jurassic Period. It included what are now the continents South America, Africa, India, Australia, and Antarctica.

Herbivores animals that eat plants. Most dinosaurs were herbivores.

Horsetail a primitive, spore-bearing plant with that was common during the Mesozoic Era. Its side branches are arranged in rings along the hollow stem. Horsetails date from the Devonian period 408-360 million years ago, but are still around today and are invasive weeds.

Index fossils index fossils are commonly found fossils that existed during a limited time span. They help in dating other fossils.

Iridium this is a heavy metal element that is rare on the Earth's surface, but abundant on meteors and in the Earth's core.

Jurassic Period the second Period of the Mesozoic Era, from 200 to 145 million years ago. Birds and flowering plants evolved, and many dinosaurs flourished during the Jurassic Period.

K-T Boundary boundary between the Cretaceous and Tertiary Periods, about 65 million years ago. This was a time of the huge mass extinction of the dinosaurs.

Laurasia this was the northern supercontinent formed after Pangaea broke up during the Jurassic Period. Laurasia included what are now North America, Europe, Asia, Greenland, and Iceland.

Mammals these are hairy, warm-blooded animals that nourish their young with milk. Mammals evolved during the Triassic Period. People are mammals.

Mesozoic Era this is was a major geological time span, from 250 to 65 million years ago. It is informally known as the Age of the Dinosaurs. The Mesozoic is subdivided into the Triassic, Jurassic, and Cretaceous Periods.

Ornithischians ("bird-hipped") dinosaurs that had a hip structure similar to that of birds. The two lower bones on each side lie parallel and point backward. They were also herbivores.

Ornithopods mainly bipedal ornithischian dinosaurs that developed special teeth to grind up tough plant food.

Paleonotologist a scientist who studies the forms of life that existed in former geological periods, mainly by studying fossils.

Pangaea a supercontinent consisting of all of Earth's landmasses. It existed during the Permian Period through the Jurassic Period. It began breaking up during the Jurassic, forming the continents Gondwana and Laurasia.

Prosauropods plant-eating saurischians with long necks and thumb claws.

Quadruped animals that walk on four legs are quadrupeds. Most of the horned, armored, and plated dinosaurs were quadrupeds.

Reptile a group of animals that have scales, breathe air, and usually lay eggs.

Saurischians ("lizard-hipped") the ancestors of birds, these dinosaurs had a hip structure similar to that of lizards—the two lower bones on each side point in opposite directions.

Sauropods large, quadrupedal plant-eating saurischians. They had long necks and tails.

Scavenger animals that eat dead animals that they did not kill themselves. Hyenas are modern-day scavengers.

Stratigraphy a method of dating fossils by observing how deeply a fossil is buried. Generally, deeper rocks and fossils are older than those found above them.

Theropods a group of saurischian dinosaurs that includes all the carnivores. Almost all the theropods were bipedal.

Trackways a series of footprints left behind as an animal walks over soft ground. They can indicate the animal's speed, weight, and herding behavior.

Triassic Period the first Period in the Mesozoic Era, from 250 to 200 million years ago. Dinosaurs and mammals evolved during the Triassic Period.

INDEX

A page number in **bold** refers to the main entry for that subject.

ACKNOWLEDGMENTS

Dorling Kindersley would like to thank Selina Wood for editorial assistance; Alyson Lacewing for proof-reading; Ann Barrett for the index; Jenny Siklós for Americanization; and Tony Cutting for DTP support.

Picture Credits
The publisher would like to thank the following for their kind permission to reproduce their photographs:

Abbreviations key:
t-top, b-bottom, r-right, l-left, c-center, a-above, f-far

1 DK Images: Jonathan Hateley. **7** DK Images: Royal Tyrrell Museum, Canada br. **8-9** DK Images: Jonathan Hateley. **9** DK Images: Natural History Museum cr; State Museum of Nature cr. **10** Corbis: Macduff Everton bl. **11** Corbis: Paul Funston; Gallo Images br. The Natural History Museum, London: tr. **12** DK Images: Natural History Museum tr. **13** DK Images: Natural History Museum c, bc. **13** N.H.P.A.: Joe Blossom cr. **15** Corbis: Galen Rowell br; Scott T. Smith t. Natural History Museum Basel: tr, bl. **16-17** DK Images: Bedrock Studios bc; Frank Denota c. **17** DK Images: Bedrock Studios tl, b; Natural History Museum tr. **18** Corbis: Charles Mamzy cfl; Gordon Whitten cl. DK Images: Bedrock Studios bcl; Jon Hughes br; Peter Winfield tl, tr. Science Photo Library: Ron Watts cfr. **19** Corbis: cb; Brenda Tharp bcr; Darrell Gulin tr; tl. DK Images: Jon Hughes bl, bc; Peter Winfield cr; Royal Tyrell Museum, Canada bc. **20** Corbis: David Pu'u cb. Katz/FSP: Eisermann/Life cr. The Natural History Museum, London: cra. Science Photo Library: Soames Summerhays bl **20-21** Kobal Collection: Dreamworks/ Paramount c. **21** Science Photo Library: Catherine Pouedras/Eurelios cbr; Geological Survey, Canada cr; Prof Walter Alvarez br. **24** The Natural History Museum, London: cl, crb. Science Photo Library: cr; George Barnard bc. **24-25** Institut Royal des Sciences Naturalles de Belgique: background. **25** American Museum Of Natural History: br. DK Images: Senekenberg Nature Museum bl. Mary Evans Picture Library: cl. Institut Royal des Sciences Naturalles de Belgique: tr, cra, cr. **26** Corbis: David Muench tl; James L. Amos ca; Philippe Eranian bl; Reuters/Carlos Barria cb. **27** Corbis: Bettmann ca; Dutheil Didier tr. Science Photo Library: Peter Menzel cb, br. Knight Rider / Tribune Media Services: William Hammer bl. **28** Judith River Dinosaur Institute: Judith River Dinosaur Institute c, crb, b, t. **28-29** Judith River Dinosaur Institute: Judith River Dinosaur Institute **29** Homer Montgomery, National Park Services, US Department of the Interior: Homer Montgomery, National Park Services, US Department of the Interior r. Judith River Dinosaur Institute: Judith River Dinosaur Institute c, bl. **31** Judith River Dinosaur Institute: Judith River Dinosaur Institute tr. Science Photo Library: Paul Fisher/North Carolina Museum of Natural Sciences/SPL br. **32** DK Images: Dinosaur State Park cl. The Natural History Museum, London: cl. **33** Museum of the Rockies: tl, car. Science Photo Library: Nieves Lopez/Eurelios cbl. **34** Corbis: Tom Bean l. 36 The Field Museum: The Field Museum tl, tr, bl, br. **36-37** The Field Museum: The Field Museum **37** The Field Museum: The Field Museum t; The Field Museum, courtesy Chris Brochu c, b. **38-39** Corbis: David Muench b; Kevin Schafer t; Tom Bean c. **39** Earth Sciences, University of Cambridge: Dr. James Hobro/Cambridge Earth Sciences, courtesy of Dr. James Miller cl. Science Photo Library: Geoff Tompkinson br. **43** DK Images: Royal Tyrrell Museum, Canada br. **45** DK Images: Natural History Museum tl; Senekenberg Nature Museum cr. **50-51** Science Photo Library: Smithsonian Museum t. **53** DK Images: Graham High and Centaur Studios tl. **55** The Natural History Museum, London: cl. **56** Corbis: Michael S. Yamashita bl. DK Images: Peabody Museum of Natural History Yale University bc; Photo: Colin Keates cr. N.H.P.A.: Jonathan & Angela Scott br. Oxford Scientific Films: Highlights For Children tr. **57** Corbis: George H. H. Huey tr. DK Images: Jon Hughes t. Science Photo Library: Simon Fraser ca, b. **58** Corbis: Frank Trapper bl. **58-59** Natural Visions: Richard Coombers background. **61** Oxford Scientific Films: Matthias Brieter bl. **63** Corbis: Craig Aurness background. The Natural History Museum, London: br. Jean Paul Ferrero bc. **64** DK Images: Jerry Young crb. N.H.P.A.: Martin Wendler bl. **64-65** Ardea.com: Francois Gohier; **65** DK Images: Philip Dowell cra. **66** The Field Museum: tr. **68** Prof. Anusuya Chinsamy-Turan: tl, tc, c. **70-71** Nakasato Museum: Sato Kazuhisa/Nakasato Museum, Japan. **73** FLPA: tr. **74** The Field Museum: The Field Museum, Chicago tl, bl. **74-75** Corbis: Charles Mauzy. **75** Corbis: Jonathan Blair t; Yann Arthus-Bertrand b. **76** Ardea.com: Francois Gohier bl. **76-77** Corbis: Theo Allofs t background. Oxford Scientific Films: Mark Deeble & Victoria Stone c. **77** Corbis: Brian A. Vikander br. Science Photo Library: Larry Miller c. Getty Images: Roine Magnusson bl. **78** DK Images: Gary Kevin t; Ray Moller bl. **79** American Museum Of Natural History: tr, tl. DK Images: Peter Winfield bl; Senekenberg Nature Museum: Andy Crawford br. **81** Corbis: t. **82** Corbis: Bill Varie bl. Science Photo Library: Philippe Plailly/Eurelios cl, clb. Smithsonian Institution: cla; National Museum of Natural History/Chip Clark tl. **82-83** Corbis: Paul A. Souders 83 Corbis: Jonathan Blair b.

Jacket images
Front: Corbis: Dutheil Didier (cr), Richard T. Nowitz (cfl); Science Photo Library: Roger Harris (cl). **Spine:** Science Photo Library: David Parker. **Back:** Corbis: Ferdaus Shamim (cfl); Science Photo Library: Chris Butler (cr), John Foster (cfr).